DEMOCRACY AND FAKE NEWS

This book explores the challenges that disinformation, fake news, and post-truth politics pose to democracy from a multidisciplinary perspective. The authors analyse and interpret how the use of technology and social media as well as the emergence of new political narratives has been progressively changing the information landscape, undermining some of the pillars of democracy.

The volume sheds light on some topical questions connected to fake news, thereby contributing to a fuller understanding of its impact on democracy. In the Introduction, the editors offer some orientating definitions of post-truth politics, building a theoretical framework where various different aspects of fake news can be understood. The book is then divided into three parts: Part I helps to contextualise the phenomena investigated, offering definitions and discussing key concepts as well as aspects linked to the manipulation of information systems, especially considering its reverberation on democracy. Part II considers the phenomena of disinformation, fake news, and post-truth politics in the context of Russia, which emerges as a laboratory where the phases of creation and diffusion of fake news can be broken down and analysed; consequently, Part II also reflects on the ways to counteract disinformation and fake news. Part III moves from case studies in Western and Central Europe to reflect on the methodological difficulty of investigating disinformation, as well as tackling the very delicate question of detection, combat, and prevention of fake news.

This book will be of great interest to students and scholars of political science, law, political philosophy, journalism, media studies, and computer science, since it provides a multidisciplinary approach to the analysis of post-truth politics.

Serena Giusti is Head of the Programme on Eastern Europe, Russia and Eurasia at Sant'Anna School of Advanced Studies in Pisa, Italy, and Senior Associate Research Fellow at the Institute for International Studies (ISPI) in Milan, Italy. She also sits on the Advisory board of Women in International Security (WIIS), Italy.

Elisa Piras is Postdoctoral Fellow in Political Philosophy at Dirpolis Institute at Sant'Anna School for Advanced Studies in Pisa, Italy. Her research focuses on contemporary political liberalism and its international implications for global justice and for democratic foreign policy.

Politics, Media and Political Communication

Titles in this series include:

Communication in Global Jihad
Jonathan Matusitz

Democracy and Fake News
Information Manipulation and Post-Truth Politics
Edited by Serena Giusti and Elisa Piras

For more information about this series, please visit: https://www.routledge.com/
Politics-Media-and-Political-Communication/book-series/POLMED

DEMOCRACY AND FAKE NEWS

Information Manipulation and
Post-Truth Politics

Edited by
Serena Giusti and Elisa Piras

Routledge
Taylor & Francis Group
LONDON AND NEW YORK

First published 2021
by Routledge
2 Park Square, Milton Park, Abingdon, Oxon OX14 4RN

and by Routledge
52 Vanderbilt Avenue, New York, NY 10017

Routledge is an imprint of the Taylor & Francis Group, an informa business

British Library Cataloguing-in-Publication Data
A catalogue record for this book is available from the British Library

Library of Congress Cataloging-in-Publication Data
Names: Giusti, Serena, editor. | Piras, Elisa, editor.
Title: Democracy and fake news : information manipulation and post-truth
    politics / edited by Serena Giusti and Elisa Piras.
Description: Abingdon, Oxon ; New York, NY : Routledge, 2021. | Series:
    Politics, media and political communication | Includes bibliographical
    references and index.
Identifiers: LCCN 2020031087 (print) | LCCN 2020031088 (ebook) |
    ISBN 9780367479558 (hardback) | ISBN 9780367479541 (paperback) |
    ISBN 9781003037385 (ebook)
Subjects: LCSH: Information society—Political aspects. | Fake
    news—Political aspects. | Mass media and public opinion. | Information
    society—Political aspects—Russia (Federation) | Fake news—Political
    aspects—Russia (Federation) | Information society—Political
    aspects—Europe. | Mass media and public opinion—Russia (Federation) |
    Fake news—Political aspects—Europe. | Mass media and public
    opinion—Europe.
Classification: LCC HM851 .D458 2021 (print) | LCC HM851 (ebook) |
    DDC 302.23—dc23
LC record available at https://lccn.loc.gov/2020031087
LC ebook record available at https://lccn.loc.gov/2020031088

ISBN: 978-0-367-47955-8 (hbk)
ISBN: 978-0-367-47954-1 (pbk)
ISBN: 978-1-003-03738-5 (ebk)

Typeset in Bembo
by Apex CoVantage, LLC

CONTENTS

List of figures   *viii*
List of tables   *ix*
Notes on contributors   *x*
Preface   *xiii*

Introduction: In search of paradigms: Disinformation,
fake news, and post-truth politics   1
Serena Giusti and Elisa Piras

PART I
Post-truth politics and the challenges to democracy   **17**

1   Reading Arendt to rethink truth, science, and politics
    in the era of fake news   19
    Federica Merenda

2   Inequality in the public sphere: Epistemic injustice,
    discrimination, and violence   30
    Elisa Piras

3   Incorporating intersectionality into AI ethics   40
    Liza Ireni-Saban and Maya Sherman

4   How post-truth politics transformed and shaped the outcome
    of the 2016 Brexit referendum   53
    Jennifer Cassidy

5 Information and democracy: Fake news as an
   emotional weapon   64
   Matthew Loveless

6 Searching for a unicorn: Fake news and electoral behaviour   77
   Luigi Curini and Eugenio Pizzimenti

7 Once upon Covid-19: A tale of misleading information
   going viral   92
   Alice Hazelton

PART II
From disinformation to post-truth Politics:
Evidences from Russia   **105**

8 Lie to live: The production of a faked reality as an
   existential function of Putin's regime   107
   Anna Zafesova

9 Playing the Russian disinformation game: Information
   operations from Soviet tactics to Putin's sharp power   119
   Francesco Bechis

10 Myths and realities of Putinism in post-truth politics   132
   Mara Morini

11 Responding to alleged Russian interference by focussing on
   the vulnerabilities that make it possible   143
   Giorgio Comai

PART III
Dilemmas of contrasting disinformation and fake news   **155**

12 Information spreading and the role of automated accounts
   on Twitter: Two case studies   157
   Guido Caldarelli, Rocco De Nicola, Marinella
   Petrocchi, and Fabio Saracco

13 Radical-right political activism on the web and the
   challenge for European democracy: A perspective from
   Eastern and Central Europe   173
   Manuela Caiani and Pál Susánszky

14 When a credible source turns 'fake': The Relotius affair
and the German system for combating fake news   188
Mihail Stojanoski

15 "But verifying facts is what we do!": Fact-checking and
journalistic professional autonomy   199
Urban Larssen

16 The EU Code of Practice on Disinformation and the risk of
the privatisation of censorship   214
Matteo Monti

Index   *226*

FIGURES

0.1	Post-truth politics	10
5.1	Is fake news a problem?	71
6.1	The analytical framework	79
11.1	Articles mentioning 'Russian interference' or 'Russian meddling' in a month in *The Guardian*	144
12.1	The communities of verified users in the migration flows dataset	160
12.2	The communities of verified users in the Covid-19 dataset	161
12.3	Interactions between verified and unverified users for the migration flows dataset	162
12.4	Interactions between verified and unverified users for the Covid-19 dataset	162
12.5	Mediterranean flows	164
12.6	Covid-19	164
12.7	The relative overlap matrix among the list of bots following the top 20 hubs	166
12.8	Subgraph of the largest group of users sharing bots	167
12.9	Statistics of the largest bot squad	168
12.10	The retweeting activity of genuine and automated accounts	169
13.1	The political functions of radical-right websites in Central Eastern Europe	178

TABLES

10.1 Summary of cyber incidents involving Russia 2001–11   138

13.1 Textual and visual online radical-right propaganda, by country   178

13.2 Radical-right propaganda through the web in
Western vs. Eastern Europe   181

14.1 Number of reports of fake news and removal rate   193

NOTES ON CONTRIBUTORS

Francesco Bechis is a journalist at Formiche.net and Junior Fellow at De Gasperi Foundation, Rome, Italy. He writes about foreign policy and intelligence, in particular on relations between the EU, Russia and China.

Manuela Caiani is Associate Professor in the Faculty of Political and Social Sciences at the Scuola Normale Superiore, Florence, Italy. Her research interests focus on left-wing and right-wing populism, extreme right political parties and movements, social movements and Europeanization, and qualitative methods of social research.

Guido Caldarelli is a theoretical physicist. He is an expert on scale-invariant phenomena and works on models of complex networks with specific applications to financial systems. He is president of the Complex Systems Society and Fellows of the APS.

Jennifer Cassidy is Departmental Lecturer in Global Governance and Diplomacy at the University of Oxford, UK, where she lectures on Diplomacy and International Law, Digital Diplomacy, and Gender and Diplomacy.

Giorgio Comai is researcher and data analyst at OBC Transeuropa (OBCT/CCI) based in Trento, Italy. His research has focused on de facto states as well as on different approaches for the bulk extraction and analysis of textual contents form the web.

Luigi Curini is Professor of Political Science in the Department of Social and Political Sciences at the Università degli Studi in Milan, Italy. He is also visiting Professor at Waseda University of Tokyo, Japan. His research spans a range of topics concerning party competition, public opinion, quantitative methods and text analytics.

Rocco De Nicola is Full Professor at IMT School for Advanced Studies in Lucca, Italy and a computer scientist expert of system modelling and analysis. He is author of many publications in journals and books. He is a member of the Academia Europaea and "Commander of the Order of Merit of the Italian Republic".

Serena Giusti is Head of the Programme on Eastern Europe, Russia and Eurasia at Sant'Anna School of Advanced Studies in Pisa, Italy, and Senior Associate Research Fellow at the Institute for International Studies (ISPI) in Milan, Italy. She also sits on the advisory board of Women in International Security (WIIS), Italy.

Alice Hazelton is responsible for science at the World Economic Forum, including programming for its Annual Meetings in Davos, Switzerland, and regional summits around the world. Her interests include science communication and public engagement.

Liza Ireni-Saban is the Deputy Dean and a Senior Lecturer at the Lauder School of Government, Diplomacy and Strategy at the Interdisciplinary Center (IDC) Herzliya, Israel. Her research fields include political philosophy, public administration, ethics in the public administration, disaster management and public policy.

Urban Larssen is a media anthropologist with a PhD from Stockholm University. He is a former reporter with local and regional newspapers in Sweden, and a lecturer in the Department of Journalism at Södertörn University, Sweden. His research interests include journalism and integration, fact-checking, and cross-border collaborative journalism.

Matthew Loveless is Associate Professor in the Department of Social and Political Sciences at the University of Bologna, Italy, and Co-Director of the Center for Research and Social Progress. He has worked on several topics related to how individuals make sense of politics in Europe, focusing on public opinion, media use and perceptions.

Federica Merenda is a PhD candidate in Human Rights and Global Politics at the Sant'Anna School of Advanced Studies in Pisa, Italy, with a thesis in political philosophy. Her research deals with issues at the crossroads between political theory and international legal studies, particularly related to Arendt's work.

Matteo Monti is Postdoctoral Fellow in Comparative Constitutional Law, Department of Law, University of Pisa, Italy. His research interests cover both comparative and Italian constitutional law, especially fundamental rights (freedom of expression, and information and non-discrimination), asymmetrical federalism, and the problem of secession in national and international law.

Mara Morini is Assistant Professor in the Department of Political Science at the University of Genoa, Italy. Her fields of research are party organizations, democratizations and Russian politics. She is co-chair of the Standing Group on "Russia and Post-Soviet Space" of the Italian Political Science Association.

Marinella Petrocchi is Senior Researcher at the Institute of Informatics and Telematics of the Italian National Research Council. Her research focuses on detection techniques able to unveil fake accounts and low reputable information sources.

Elisa Piras is Postdoctoral Fellow in Political Philosophy at Dirpolis Institute at Sant'Anna School for Advanced Studies in Pisa, Italy. Her research focuses on contemporary political liberalism and its international implications for global justice and for democratic foreign policy.

Eugenio Pizzimenti is Associate Professor of Political Science at the Department of Political Sciences, University of Pisa, Italy, where he also chairs the Observatory on Politics and Institutions. His research interests focus on party politics and organization theory, with special attention to the transnational dimension.

Fabio Saracco is Assistant Professor at the IMT School of Advanced Studies Lucca, Italy. He works on complex network theory and on its applications to economic and financial systems, online social networks, and biological systems.

Maya Sherman has worked in numerous hi-tech companies and government organizations in the fields of cybersecurity, darknet and intelligence analysis. Her spheres of interest are data ethics, AI warfare and cyber influence.

Mihail Stojanoski is the Assistant Manager of the European Roma Rights Centre in Brussels, Belgium. As a former lawyer at the European Court of Human Rights in Strasbourg, France, he researches and publishes in the field of human rights and in particular, freedom of expression. He is a PhD candidate at the University of Strasbourg, working on the research topic: "Redefining freedom of expression by regulating fake news".

Pál Susánszky is a Research Fellow at the Centre for Social Sciences at the Hungarian Academy of Sciences Centre of Excellence and a member of the ELTE University of Budapest FIKP Research Group, Hungary. His main research interests are social movement mobilization, civil society in the CEE and political inequality.

Anna Zafesova is a journalist and analyst specialized in Russian politics. She has been the Moscow correspondent for the Italian newspaper *La Stampa*, covering the post-Soviet transition. She continues to follow Russian current affairs for *La Stampa*, *Il Foglio*, *Centro Einaudi* and other media and think-tanks, in Italy and abroad.

PREFACE

What is the cost of lies? It's not that we'll mistake them for the truth. The real danger is that if we hear enough lies, then we no longer recognize the truth at all. What can we do then? What else is left but to abandon even the hope of truth and content ourselves instead with stories?

The words of Valery Legasov, as pronounced in the HBO *Chernobyl* miniseries of 2019, perfectly reflect the disorientation produced by misinformation and by an intense flow of fake news that affects politics as well as everyone else's everyday lives. While there is a more or less conscious acknowledgement that we are living in an epoch of post-truth politics, where everything can be true and false at the same time, the academic debate on the mechanisms and effects of this politics is still in its nascent phase, mainly because any comprehensive analysis on the phenomenon would require a solid expertise in different areas such as media studies, security studies, public opinion analysis, contemporary history, political communication, semiotics, ethics, informatics, and AI.

This edited volume tackles this research gap by offering a multidisciplinary perspective with the purpose of touching upon (at least some of) the challenges that the manipulation of information poses to democracy. The idea of this book emerged during the international conference "Information at a time of fake news, disinformation and post-truth politics" organised by the research group Res/East of the Sant' Anna School of Advanced Studies, Pisa. The conference, which happened in Pisa on the 6 and 7 of May of 2019, took place thanks to the funding of the Jean Monnet Activities Programme, "EU-Russia, Connecting People and Ideas: Revolution, Post-Soviet Space, Information". The presentations and debates focussed on the topic of manipulation of information from an interdisciplinary perspective, with special attention to the post-Soviet space.

The book has delved deeper into some of the more salient aspects related to the manipulation of information that emerged during the conference. Other contributions were later included, in order to further explore some aspects of the phenomenon and to cover issues which were not considered in the first place but emerged as relevant during the conference and the framing of the book.

We would like to thank all the scholars and students who took part in the Jean Monnet Activities Programme – among them, special thanks goes to Luigi Cino, for his valuable support in organising the scientific events carried out in Pisa. Our gratitude goes to the contributors to this volume, whose expertise, responsiveness, and swift delivery of work made the project possible. We feel indebted to the three anonymous reviewers who provided constructive feedback on the proposal and helped authors and editors to improve the quality of this book. Finally, we would like to thank Emily Ross and Hannah Rich from Routledge for having encouraged and supported this plan from the very beginning.

We gratefully acknowledge the financial support of the European Commission for the realisation of this project.

**With the support of the
Erasmus+ Programme
of the European Union**

Serena Giusti and Elisa Piras
Florence, June 2020

INTRODUCTION

In search of paradigms: Disinformation, fake news, and post-truth politics

Serena Giusti and Elisa Piras

This book aims to contribute to the debate on how the manipulation of information, under different guises, can deteriorate the status of democracy. The title conveys the ambition and scope of our volume, which seeks to examine and problematise the diffusion of practices of information manipulation thanks to the opportunities provided by the newest technological tools used for communication and information purposes. Although manipulating information can serve different goals, the authors who contributed to this volume focussed on its political implications and especially on the consequences that the diffusion of manipulated information can have on the quality of democracy.

In his 1922 essay *Public Opinion*, after a thorough investigation of the nexus between information and democratic decision-making, Walter Lippmann claimed that the quality of news revealed the strengths and weaknesses of a democratic society. Disguising the truth and manipulating information were means used by a few economic and/or political actors willing to substitute their particular interests to the public interest in order to obtain some advantages (Lippmann 1997: 364–365). Lippmann's pioneering intuition proves especially inspiring for current researches on the troubling relationship between information and democratic politics, not only in mature democracies, but also in those countries experiencing lengthy and stormy transitions from authoritarian rule. Moreover, the last century has provided abundant evidence of the strategic importance of the production and spread of information for the conduct of international affairs, facilitating or complicating cooperation among governments. Very recently, the global health emergency caused by the diffusion of Covid-19 has dramatically shown the importance as well as the difficulty of grounding policy-making on objective (i.e. unbiased) and reliable (i.e. verifiable, scientifically valid) information.

As we will show in our Introduction, the manipulation of information has a long history; however, the speed and extensiveness of the phenomenon has considerably increased during the last two decades, thanks to the massive and continuous consumption of news that smartphones allow to large numbers of citizens of developed and developing countries. Social media platforms, which are a particularly fertile breeding ground for amplifying any message, proved to be particularly effective means for detecting, targeting, and mobilising high numbers of individuals who would form their opinions on any piece of news which might serve to confirm and reinforce their preconceived ideas. The consequence is the viral diffusion of a plethora of mystified information products. Some of them – namely news propaganda, conspiracy theories, opinion pieces, pseudo-satire, etc. – are already part of the historical heritage of information manipulation, while others – such as hate speech, fake news, and deepfakes – constitute relatively new phenomena whose relationship to democratic practices and values is still unclear.

Each chapter of this book contributes to shed light on a specific aspect of the information-democracy nexus, from its author(s)' situated point of view. The first part of the Introduction will briefly present and discuss the main concepts that will ground the analyses and reflections presented in the chapters – namely disinformation, fake news, and post-truth politics – outlining the main attempts at contrasting the different phenomena included under the umbrella term of information manipulation. In the last part, the Introduction provides the readers with an analytical compass and a chapters' breakdown, the aim of which is to guide the readers throughout the book.

Disinformation

Until recently, the term most commonly used in political discourse to identify issues concerning the manipulation of information was disinformation, from the Russian word *dezinformatsiya*, deriving from the title of a KGB black propaganda department responsible for producing false information with the intention of deceiving public opinion. Disinformation is a relatively recent practice in comparison to 'propaganda', which originated in the 1600s and generally connotes the selective use of information aimed at producing some desired political effects (NED 2017). Propaganda seeks to manipulate or influence the opinion of groups to support a particular cause or belief; it often promotes the benefits and virtues of one idea or group, while simultaneously distorting the truth or suppressing the counter-argument (as it happened, for instance, in Nazi Germany).

While disinformation is to be intended as the product of the construction of a purposeful untruth, misinformation indicates an incomplete, vague, misleading, or ambiguous piece of information. Disinformation "can be composed of mostly true facts, stripped of context or blended with falsehoods to support the intended message, and is always part of a larger plan or agenda" (NED 2017). Disinformation, a term which had been neglected for a while by IR (International Relations) and security studies, has recently known a revival, especially within the European Union (EU) (la Cour 2020; Chesney and Citron 2019; Lanoszka 2019). Drawing on the 'Action Plan against Disinformation' issued in 2018,[1] several actions and programmes – including significant research funding – have been launched to detect and contrast disinformation on a variety of politically sensitive issues, such as Brexit, migration management, food safety, and health emergency management. For instance, the latest report published by the European External Action Service (EEAS) on disinformation activities related to the Covid-19 pandemic reveals many troubling facts, such as the significant number of coordinated disinformation campaigns by the Russian and Chinese governments to spread false health information in and around Europe, and conspiracy theories and claims that only authoritarian political systems – not democracies – are best suited to deal with the current crisis (European Commission 2020). The EU High Representative for Foreign Affairs and Security Policy Josep Borrell has thus made clear that "intentional and coordinated disinformation campaigns should be treated as a hybrid threat to European and global security" (Borrell 2020).

Fake news

In the preceding section, misinformation has been defined as an incomplete, vague, misleading, or ambiguous piece of information. Accordingly, fake news could be understood as an advanced and technological version of misinformation, since with this term we mean pieces of intentionally manipulated information which appear on the Internet and in social media especially. At first, the diffusion of fake news was connected to political life at its most sensitive moments, such as elections and international crises; afterwards, the use of fake news rapidly expanded to concern every aspect of politics and life. The term 'fake news' was, for instance, used by both candidates to the US presidency in the 2016 elections. On 8 December 2016, Democratic candidate Hillary Clinton made a speech in which she referred to "the epidemic of malicious fake news and false propaganda that flooded social media over the past year," and stressed that "It's now clear that so-called fake news can have real-world consequences" (Wendling 2018). President Donald Trump, the Republican candidate, even gave out 'Fake News Awards' to reporters who had made mistakes or unfortunate predictions – "with a special nod to all reporting on the ongoing and very real investigations into collusion between the Trump campaign and Russia" (ibid.).

Whereas the construction of a false, alternative, or altered reality and its diffusion through media and/or word of mouth – which depends on the contested nature of knowledge – is not a new phenomenon in politics, what is new is the massive worldwide use of digital communication systems and the extremely extensive reach of social media (see Corner 2017; Fuller 2018), which can spread news at a whirling pace, turning any message potentially 'viral'. Social media platforms and instant messaging apps have proven to be extraordinary amplifiers for fake news and have therefore acquired a strategic political role far beyond their initial function as platforms for recreation and socialisation. They are, indeed, powerful political weapons. The combination of fake news and social media is particularly fit for producing subliminal effects that can reach the deepest and most emotional strata of people's minds, with higher chances of persistence and persuasion compared to disinformation spread through other means.

Fake news can circulate in either a discrete or continuous way. In the first case, its appearance is inconsistent, even sporadic, while in the second, it may create a cluster or snowball effect. It can be diffused through many channels at the same time or in sequence, with different dosages of information manipulation. This bombardment of manipulated information generates a sort of 'nebulous phenomenon', capturing a potentially vast audience that can be a target to various waves of fake news attacks. When a flow of fake news reaches its target concomitantly, there is only a short time in which the recipients can stop to elaborate and discern the nature of the information they have been flooded with. This means that recipients, besides awareness, might also lack time and attention to rightly detect what has been transmitted.

The disruptive force of fake news has been widely recognised and already historicised. It is quite telling that two anti-Brexit fake banknotes claiming to be from the "Bank of Brexit lies" and declaring themselves to be "for the privileged few" have been deemed of such historical value they have been added to the collection of the British Museum (BM).[2] Tom Hockenhull, the museum's curator of modern money, said the notes belonged to its collection because "we capture history. By displaying fake banknotes, the British Museum recognises the relevance of the fake as testimony and protagonist of current politics" (Addley 2019). The BM's decision follows its previous acquisition of a Banksy artwork that depicts an equally fake banknote, designed in 2004 and displaying an image of Princess Diana. If even museums have transformed the falsification of reality and the diffusion of fake news into something to be exhibited, this means that the phenomenon is ubiquitous, powerful, and routinised.

In politics, fake news is already so widespread to be acknowledged (although not publicly recommended) among the available tools for the politicians willing to obtain consensus and to seek power within the domestic, as well as the international, political arena. The deployment of fake news may help the rise of a certain faction/party or leader, while causing the decay or the defeat of its political adversaries/enemies. Those who manipulate information and diffuse it might remain unknown, and the absence of a single responsible person or group of people renders the faking activity less biased and condemnable; moreover, it discourages possible reactions because of the lack of a clear target. The difficulty to neatly identify responsibility in such instances therefore makes the use of fake news an extremely powerful instrument of political influence and meddling.

In their public statements, politicians in power generally tend to condemn fake news and the unfair and illicit gain in terms of consensus that it produces. However, the fact that people are so accustomed to fake news seems to allow both authoritarian and democratic leaders to deploy it quite often (Farhall et al. 2019;

Egelhofer and Lecheler 2019) in order to pursue their political goals: *inter alia*, to delegitimise troublesome journalists and media, to discredit political opponents or leaders of foreign states – as in the case of the Covid-19 crisis which will be mentioned later in this introduction – or even to contribute to the justification of especially grave decisions, such as the one taken by the US and the UK to invade Iraq on the basis of the alleged presence of weapons of mass destruction (later revealed to be unproven).

Post-truth politics

In order to portray the complex contemporary relationship in which reality, false-hood, and power interact and mix in the world of media and social networks, many scholars, commentators, and politicians employ the expression 'post-truth politics' (Hannan 2018; McIntyre 2018; Corner 2017; Hopkin and Rosamond 2017; Rose 2017). This expression indicates a political phase in which people are inclined to accept arguments based on their consonance to their own emotions and beliefs rather than based on facts, and consequently important political deci-sions such as a vote in political elections or in a referendum are more related to emotional or 'ideological' impulses and superficial impressions rather than to the rational selection based on policy evaluations and economic considerations. The weakening of the relevance of rational reasoning opens up to the easy installation of counterfeit information. In this perspective, a lie is not necessarily something that is opposed to truth; it is rather a derivate of a distorted version of it, so that the boundaries between truth and lies are blurred.

As Bufacchi (2020) explains, "While a lie subverts a specific truth, post-truth tries to subvert truth itself" and the "prefix 'post' in post-truth refers to the claim that a specified idea has become redundant and therefore can safely be discarded. Post-truth is the belief that truth is no longer essential, that truth has become obso-lete." Fake news does not necessarily negate facts or what can be defined as truth, but rather suggests misleading interpretations or invents facts that do not exist but are nonetheless plausible or close to what the public could expect. Fake news can be anticipated by the spread of some information/soft fakes (closer to misinforma-tion) in order to prepare the terrain for the fake news to be credible and able to produce long-lasting effects; a sort of "political astroturfing" (Keller et al. 2020).

As we have underlined, the rise of post-truth politics has been propitiated by the sheer ease of creating and diffusing fake news. Besides technological facilities, systemic changes that may have favoured post-truth politics have also occurred. The disappearance of well-established comprehensive and coherent worldviews or ideologies concomitant to the end of the Cold War has brought a period of fluidity and diffusion of power that has bolstered the emergence of new actors, both formal and informal. World politics has become more and more hectic and unpredict-able. At the same time, flows of refugees, global movements, virtual groups, and networks have all contributed to moulding a de-territorialised form of citizenship, while states have progressively lost control over money flows, investments, information, security, and even warfare, which is becoming more and more hybrid.

During the last part of the 20th century, the progressive erosion of sovereignty seemed to be a prelude to the end of the traditional state, opening to a neo-medieval phase in politics marked by fragmentation of power, with many different legacies (Bull 1977). Instead, the 2008 financial and economic crisis, which caused the deterioration of the standard of living, therefore accentuating a sense of precariousness, has allowed a reinforcement of states, which have mostly intervened in the economy to remedy the negative effects of the crisis. States have, however, became the cradle of divisive politics: populist discourses and policies, the delegitimisation of competence, hate and resentment politics, the demonisation/enemisation of political adversaries, the personalisation and spectacularisation of politics, and processes of securitisation have now become common traits in both democratic and autocratic regimes (Polyakova and Meserole 2019). In order to master all these techniques of divisive politics, access to information as well as multi-media communication skills are crucial. Thus, we suspect that if the political conflict raises, we may see an intensification of the recurrence to the practice of fake news as a political weapon. In principle, easy access to data and information can contribute to vitalising the public sphere and encouraging citizens' participation in public decision-making, introducing new voices to the public debate and mobilising new actors willing to find alternative paths for political participation (see, for instance, the early stage of the so-called Arab Springs), but it can also be exploited to toxify the political and social sphere. Citizens would then become partisan of one side against another, or rather abandon any kind of civil and political engagement.

We are also witnessing an increasing use of information manipulation and spread of fake news by external actors in order to interfere, especially in the occasion of important political elections or referenda, in third countries' politics, emptying the concept of borders and eroding the principle of state sovereignty as a result. This is not simply about invalidating what should be a free and fair electoral competition but also the independency and security of states with serious implications for inter-state relations. When fake news is diffused by one country against another one, especially if the diffuser and amplifier is a high-ranking politician – such as President Trump, the Brazilian President Jair Bolsonaro, or the foreign Minister of China, Wang Yi – then the perceived distance between truth and untruth dramatically contracts, with serious risks of tensions and conflicts among the countries involved.[3]

There is also another sensitive point to consider: in some countries (e.g. India, Nigeria, Brazil), fake news has circulated prevalently through WhatsApp, the most popular messaging app in Africa, Latin America, and many Asian countries (with 1.6 billion active users monthly, in 180 countries), which is mainly used to share information with family and friends (Chinchilla 2019). Unlike other platforms such as Facebook, whose content can be monitored, encrypted peer-to-peer messaging platforms, for example WhatsApp, Messenger, Telegram, and Signal, escape any kind of formal control. While it is important to protect users' privacy, this easily enables criminal activity and the cynical spread of falsehoods and mass manipulation (ibid.).

We need also to pay attention to crises, because they produce both information voids and high demand of information. This combination further stimulates the construction of fake news and its dissemination, as the experience of Covid-19 pandemic demonstrates. World Health Organization (WHO) officials themselves introduced, for instance, the term 'infodemic' to describe the flood of information circulating online about the virus. People might find it difficult to discern which information sources are trustworthy, especially when scientists are also providing different explanations and solutions. Moreover, while on complex specialistic issues such as pandemics the production of precise and detailed information can be expensive and time-consuming, fake news can cheaply and quickly fill the gap and satisfy the public's demand for information, at least for a wide target. Therefore, the Covid-19 pandemic has, in a way, reinforced the idea that there is no certitude, even when scientists are charged with tackling a sanitary emergency.

The delicate link between science itself and politics has blatantly surfaced; although the former is still considered as a reliable source of information, its trustworthiness is questioned by a variety of truthers and conspiracists. Presumably, accurate scientific information can be the ground for taking tough but legitimate political decisions that restrict citizens' freedom. But to what extent can science declare a state of emergency and justify the adoption of extraordinary measures? Furthermore, on the basis of the same scientific studies, different governments have adopted different measures for the containment of the virus. Such a diversity might be the outcome of different political decisions, despite the common ground on which they are based, but also of a manipulation of scientific information for political purposes. The latter approach clearly poses threats to democracy.

Another challenge linked to the diffusion of fake news is that of 'social justice': while almost anyone with access to technologies and social media can forge fake news (although her/his social status and know-how can affect the reach and impact of the fake news' spread), the activity of recognising and interpreting fake news requires knowledge, expertise, and the capacity to use technological instruments. Therefore, there is a clear imbalance between the accession and detection phase, producing a situation of inequality. The risk here is that a weaker and less prepared part of the public might easily fall in the hands of professional fakers: a serious threat for any democracy. The advent of technology and social media has weakened traditional media gatekeepers, changed incentives for content providers, and promoted the rise of unprofessional and/or unscrupulous outlets capable of drawing large audiences at a low cost. The modification of the rhythms and language of information experts (Carlson 2018; Waisbord 2018) has accelerated the production of information, which impinges on people's emotional sphere, and people do tend to rely on debunked falsehoods when these portray their own view (Nyhan and Reifler 2010; Lewandowsky et al. 2012). So, even after fakes are denounced as such, they have already produced effects at a subconscious level that tend to persist, despite their possible disproval.

Finally, we have to be careful about the use of fakes as a scapegoat for events which are actually determined by other factors. To put it more simply: is it realistic to assert that President Trump was elected thanks to the Russians (through hacking and leaking operations targeted at the Democratic Party, personal attacks on Democratic candidate Hillary Clinton, cyberattacks on voter databases),[4] or is it plausible to claim that the Russians have helped the pro-Leave faction prevail in the Brexit referendum (anti-immigrant and pro-Brexit messages spread, narratives presumably spread by Russian bots and accounts)?[5] Even if these actions were to be proved, the question is to what extent this kind of external interference can be deemed responsible for phenomena caused by a multitude of other factors. In other words, while not underestimating the political impact of the use of the technological tools available, we should avoid falling into the trap of oversimplified explanations of complex political events. To assess the impact of information manipulation, therefore, we need a perspective that can account for the complexity of politics. It is also very difficult to establish a correlation between the surge of fake news and the consequent change of the recipients' political behaviour. The possible impact of fake news on actual electoral outcomes remains a highly contested issue, while it seems clear that electoral behaviour still depends primarily on socio-economic factors or people's positioning within social systems. In one of the first academic studies about the consumption of fake news, researchers at Princeton, Dartmouth and the University of Exeter estimated that about 25% of Americans visited a fake news website in a six-week period around the time of the 2016 US election; nevertheless, the researchers also found that the visits were highly concentrated – 10% of readers made 60% of the visits. Crucially, the researchers concluded that "fake news does not crowd out hard news consumption" (Guess, Nyhan and Reifler 2018). Further research in this field would be very valuable indeed.

Contrasting fake news

The debate on how to react to the omnipresence of fake news is lively, and solutions are very diversified. They range from legislating news media, to tweaking algorithms and moderating content, to adopting 'softer' approaches such as fact-checking, debunking, and investing in media literacy education (Fioriglio 2019; Friesem 2019; Graves 2018; Council of the European Union 2016; Select Committee on Communications 2019). Automated verification of rumours using machine learning algorithms (Vosoughi, Mohsenvand and Roy 2017) and real-time fact-checks (Bode and Vraga 2015; Sethi 2017) are also tools available for unveiling fake news. Recent scholarship has evidenced that false news spreads quicker and deeper than true information (Vosoughi, Roy and Aral 2018). Therefore, *a posteriori* debunking and fact-checking tools might not be adequate to stop the flow of online fake news (Chan et al. 2017; Lewandowsky, Ecker, and Cook 2017). Some researchers are now considering pre-emptive ways of mitigating the problem (van der Linden et al. 2017; Roozenbeek and van der Linden 2019). The main thrust of this research is to prevent false narratives from taking root in memory in the first place, focussing specifically on the process of pre-emptive debunking or so-called 'pre-bunking'.

Any attempt to fight fake news lies at the limen between control and freedom. Control easily provides an excuse for authoritarian states to silence dissenting voices. The fight against fakes opens up another huge political problem: the role of transnational social media companies – e.g. Facebook, YouTube, Instagram and Twitter – which, by aligning with states' and international organisations' instructions, or by filling an international legislative gap, create their own codes of conduct, giving rise to a sort of (informal) governance in the field. By filling the legislative gap, they could become instruments of surveillance and control without any authority or political institution supervising their activity. After having initially downplayed the potential influence of fake news, Facebook has acknowledged the importance of detection and reporting, adding warning labels to untrustworthy pages, and ensuring a crackdown on for-profit fake news pages. Twitter also reacted, developing an experimental prototype feature that allows users to report fake news, and exploring the use of machine learning to detect automated accounts spreading political content (NED 2017).

It is clear that social media companies, by deleting, demonetising or disincentivising content that is deemed problematic, exert a backfiring potential, since algorithms are not yet extremely accurate in deciding what counts as problematic content. Fact-checking organisations such as Snopes, or dedicated task forces who work on debunking viral fake news stories – such as the East StratCom Task Force of the EU's European External Action Service,[6] or the European Parliament Unit in Charge of Disinformation – are also pullulating (Roozenbeek and van der Linden 2019). Lastly, media literacy initiatives are becoming quite widespread, but they only touch upon young people who are currently enrolled in education cycles.[7]

An analytical compass for exploring post-truth politics

In the figure below, we have summarised the main features of the general phenomenon that we call information manipulation in an attempt to cover the different stages of production, diffusion, detection, and counteraction of manipulated information, and point out the nature and identity of the producers and spreaders of manipulated information. Furthermore, the chart outlines the channels and tools used for the construction, diffusion, and detection of manipulated information, as well as the effects produced and the modalities available to fight the phenomenon and neutralise its political implications. The figure should offer readers a cognitive scheme of reference for better placing the phenomenon, while at the same time highlighting the complexity of the information manipulation circuit. It is exactly such a complexity that originates what has been called post-truth politics.

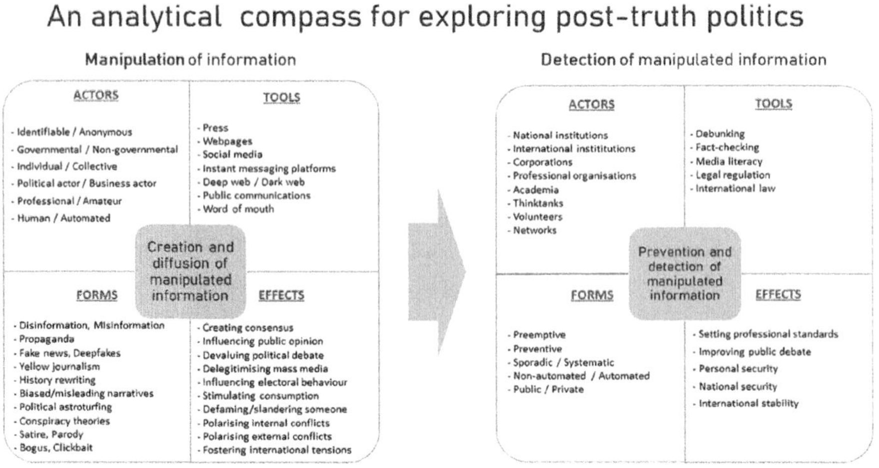

An analytical compass for exploring post-truth politics

Manipulation of information   Detection of manipulated information

ACTORS

- Identifiable / Anonymous
- Governmental / Non-governmental
- Individual / Collective
- Political actor / Business actor
- Professional / Amateur
- Human / Automated

TOOLS

- Press
- Webpages
- Social media
- Instant messaging platforms
- Deep web / Dark web
- Public communications
- Word of mouth

Creation and diffusion of manipulated information

FORMS

- Disinformation, Misinformation
- Propaganda
- Fake news, Deepfakes
- Yellow journalism
- History rewriting
- Biased/misleading narratives
- Political astroturfing
- Conspiracy theories
- Satire, Parody
- Bogus, Clickbait

EFFECTS

- Creating consensus
- Influencing public opinion
- Devaluing political debate
- Delegitimising mass media
- Influencing electoral behaviour
- Stimulating consumption
- Defaming/slandering someone
- Polarising internal conflicts
- Polarising external conflicts
- Fostering international tensions

ACTORS

- National institutions
- International instititutions
- Corporations
- Professional organisations
- Academia
- Thinktanks
- Volunteers
- Networks

TOOLS

- Debunking
- Fact-checking
- Media literacy
- Legal regulation
- International law

Prevention and detection of manipulated information

FORMS

- Preemptive
- Preventive
- Sporadic / Systematic
- Non-automated / Automated
- Public / Private

EFFECTS

- Setting professional standards
- Improving public debate
- Personal security
- National security
- International stability

FIGURE 0.1 Post-truth politics

Outline of the book

In order to navigate our way through the dark forest of disinformation and fake news, we have gathered a group of scholars from various disciplines (political science, law, political philosophy, journalism, and computer science) and practitioners who have contributed to highlight the many aspects of post-truth politics, each inspecting the different phases involved (creation, diffusion, detection) and the challenges they pose to democracy. The volume is articulated in three parts: I) Post-truth politics and the challenges to democracy, II) From disinformation to post-truth politics: Evidences from Russia, III) Dilemmas of contrasting disinformation and fake news.

Part I helps in contextualising the phenomena investigated, offering some definitions and discussing key concepts as well as the aspects linked to the manipulation of information systems, considering in particular its reverberation on democracy. In Chapter 1, Federica Merenda proposes a reflection on relevant concepts and paradigms elaborated in Hannah Arendt's works, which contribute to clarify the relation between (the different kinds of) truth, (the different kinds of) lying and politics in contemporary democracies. In Chapter 2, Elisa Piras addresses the problem of how increasing inequalities affect the public sphere in contemporary democratic societies, reconstructing the main ideas in the ongoing discussions about the transformation of the public sphere and the implications of persistent inequalities for epistemic justice, highlighting the negative effects that spreading fake news, disinformation, and post-truth narratives can have for marginalised individuals and groups. In Chapter 3, Liza Ireni-Saban and Maya Sherman bridge two topical academic discussions, commenting on the potential heuristic value of their interplay: on the one hand, the debate about the intersectional dimension of discrimination and oppression which stemmed from the recent contributions to feminist reflection; on the other hand, the ethical implication of the production and use of artificial intelligence.

In Chapter 4, Jennifer Cassidy shows how fake news and post-truth politics can impact on crucial decisions citizens are called to take, as in the case of the United Kingdom's referendum of 2016 on the country's place in the EU. The link between information and democratic policy-making is further explored in Chapter 5 by Matthew Loveless, who underlines that the Internet, and social media in particular, continues to undermine rather than strengthen any substantive link between information and democracy. The chapter posits that fake news is the description of strategic emotional weapons that cultivate political division in order to maintain the status quo and that, despite this, fake news is merely a covariate, rather than a determinant, of the failed linkage between information and democracy. In Chapter 6, Lugi Curini and Eugenio Pizzimenti investigate the possible impact of fake news on actual electoral outcomes. They argue that this remains a highly contested issue, with scarce empirical evidence to support the claim that the spreading of fake news changes electors' choices. The available scientific literature seems to confirm that people will tend to consume the news (including fake news) that confirms their partisan ideas and, precisely for this reason, the impact of fake news on voting choice will be negligible. Chapter 7, the last of this section, benefits from the experience of Alice Hazelton as a Science Programme Specialist at the World Economic Forum. The author discusses how the Covid-19 pandemic and the related political and economic crisis has highlighted science's vital role in society, also constituting a perfect occasion for the intense production of fake news spurring on new tensions and competition among states.

Part II considers the phenomenon of disinformation, fake news and post-truth politics in the context of Russia – an especially telling case for the present discussion, since it can be considered as a sort of laboratory for discerning the phases of creation and diffusion and for envisaging the ways to counteract disinformation and fake news. In chapter 8, Anna Zafesova argues that, in Russia, the monopoly of the truth is a tool of power and disrupting this monopoly amounts to demolishing the altered version of reality that the regime produces and reproduces daily. The author believes that the disclosure of an alternative truth is the main goal for the anti-Putin opposition in Russia as it was for the Soviet-era dissidents. Fighting the manipulation, the omission, and the ideological interpretation of the truth is the main weapon, not only to defend democracy from Russian attacks, but also to dismantle the Russian regime. On the same line, in Chapter 9 Francesco Bechis explains how the concept of sharp power is well suited for capturing Russia's 'information warfare' as a foreign policy tool. According to the author, government-led propaganda is one of the pillars Russian 'sharp power' stands on. It can take the shape of disinformation campaigns channelled through official media or it can be fuelled through cyber-operations led by hackers affiliated with government agencies. Mara Morini, in Chapter 10, evidences that the post-truth era is based on a variety of elements such as the spreading of fake news and cyberspace attacks that might reinforce Putin's domestic legitimacy while deteriorating the country's external relations. Part II ends with Chapter 11, in which Giorgio Comai points out that, while Russian meddling in other countries has obtained extensive media attention and has led to increased pressure on policy makers and big tech companies to find ways to protect democracy from undue external interference, we must also acknowledge that there is little of specifically foreign (or Russian) in the vulnerabilities that made Russian meddling possible. Russian activism should, in other ways, be an opportunity for other countries to take action against structural vulnerabilities which make them more permeable to any sort of foreign interference. The author underlines that detecting and reacting to external interferences is inextricably intertwined with the broader issue of managing and regulating the privately owned online public spaces that have become a central component of contemporary democracies.

Part III investigates how disinformation and misinformation are affecting Western and Central European political systems. Comparing cases is a difficult task: complete and standard data have yet to be collected, and the complexity of the phenomena poses non-trivial methodological challenges: individuals, groups, and states can easily produce and spread manipulated information from anywhere, and this can be used in a myriad of manners. As a result, contrasting manipulated information is a difficult task and it needs well-framed strategies; those, however, should not endanger the quality of democracy. In Chapter 12, computer scientists and physicians Guido Caldarelli, Rocco De Nicola, Marinella Petrocchi, and Fabio Saracco use Twitter as a benchmark to analyse the flow of information within and between members of different communities and study the dynamics of interaction and the role of automated accounts in such exchanges. Specifically, they consider the propagation of Italian tweets concerned with two topics: migration flows in the Mediterranean and Covid-19. Their analysis shows that bots play a central role in the exchange of significant content, and that the so-called hub nodes (i.e. the most effective accounts in significantly propagating their messages and therefore the most listened to) have high numbers of bots among their followers. This is particularly evident for the migration flows scenario. In Chapter 13, Manuela Caiani and Pál Susánszky focus on how different types of radical right political organisations (both political parties and more informal groups, such as movements) in four Central European countries (Slovakia, Hungary, Czech Republic, and Poland) use the web. By conducting a formalised content analysis of their websites, the authors investigate, from a comparative perspective, the degree and forms of political activism with a particular attention to visual and textual mobilisation and political engagement. The results are presented in a cross-regional perspective, as similarities and differences among the various organisations in the four analysed CEE countries are compared to the radical right cyber activism in Western Europe. In Chapter 14, Mihail Stojanoski examines the effects of recent German legislation regulating the spread of disinformation and fake news by reviewing a recent example involving a prominent German journalist, Claas Relotius, who embellished and invented stories for *Der Spiegel* for years. It then briefly presents the basic elements of the new German piece of legislation which targets the spread of disinformation (NetzDG). The author suggests that individual responsibility of the news consumer should be prevalent and form the basis of any anti-disinformation policy if modern societies are to preserve and promote free press and freedom of expression, especially given the practical and legislative limitations that exist in this field. The reflection on how to fight fake news continues in Chapter 15 as Urban Larssen considers the strengthening of fact-checking routines within the journalistic ranks that is intimately linked with journalistic professional integrity. The chapter builds on ethnographic material gathered in three Swedish news rooms on local, regional, and national level which formed part of a larger project aimed at developing a digital tool that can assist journalists in their everyday fact-checking routines. Through interviews and participant observation, the study enquired about the needs and interests for this kind of tool. The journalists expressed both need and interest, but they also had reservations regarding institutionalised forms of fact-checking, arguing, for example, that it may lead to increased control over the employees from an employer's perspective. Finally, in Chapter 16, Matteo Monti offers a legal point of view on the legal instruments which are currently available for tackling disinformation and misinformation. The author analyses the legal tools enacted by the EU to cope with the spread of fake news on the Internet and to explore the limitations and risks implied. The EU's actions are discussed in light of the question of the free speech constitutional guarantees provided by the member states, which can limit the EU Commission's space of action in this field. The chapter will discuss the genesis as well as the aims of the 'Code of Practice on Disinformation' in regards to the issue of the privatisation of censorship on the Internet. Allowing Internet platforms to censor fake news without their procedure being in any way controlled by public authorities could lead to the emergence of a situation where we could have the 'privatisation of censorship,' as the regime of semi-monopoly in which Google and Facebook are acting in Europe shows.

Notes

1 The fundamental document, which is commonly known as the Action Plan on Disinformation, is the Joint Communication by the European Commission and the High Representative to the European Parliament, the European Council, the Council, the European Economic and Social Committee and the Committee of the Regions (5 December 2018, available at: https://ec.europa.eu/commission/sites/beta-political/files/eu-communication-disinformation-euco-05122018_en.pdf).
2 The banknotes were produced by Bath for Europe – a grassroots group which campaigns to stop Britain leaving the EU – and have already been distributed in thousands at anti-Brexit rallies. They carry the faces of Boris Johnson and Jacob Rees-Mogg: the Johnson design, based on a £10 note, carries the slogan: "I promise not to pay the NHS the sum of £350m pounds," while the "£50 guinea" Rees-Mogg version declares: "I promise to pay myself more than you," and carries the fake motto: "Arrogantus Toffo Posterium".
3 See the video produced by BBC, *Coronavirus: False claims by politicians debunked – BBC News*, www.bbc.com/news/av/52299689/coronavirus-false-claims-by-politicians-debunked, 16 April 2020, reporting some fake news on the origin of the virus and involvement of countries.

4 US intelligence and special counsel Robert Mueller, for the investigation on Russia's interference in the US 2016 presidential race, has affirmed that a broad effort by Russian intelligence and a Russian social media group, the Internet Research Agency, has helped Donald Trump and damaged Democratic candidate Hillary Clinton in the 2016 presidential election. Mueller's report, released in April 2019, documented attempts by Trump's campaign to cooperate with the Russians.

5 It is said that Russian trolls sent thousands of messages with the hashtag #ReasonsTo-LeaveEU on the day of UK's referendum on EU membership. According to Twitter, the fake accounts tweeted 1,102 posts with this hashtag. The Russian-linked accounts tweeted the phrase "Brexit" more than 4,400 times during their period of activity, although mostly after the referendum had taken place.

6 The East StratCom Task Force was created in 2015 with a mandate to combat fake news emanating from Russia, which had been identified as one of the biggest proponents of information warfare against the EU. In 2017, two additional Task Forces were established, focussing on Europe's South and the Western Balkans.

7 There are many programmes run by the EU (see the Media Literacy programme) and other organisations, such as UNESCO (e.g. Coalition of Information and Media Users in South East Europe, www.cimusee.org/mil-resources/organizations-initiatives-projects/european-charter-on-media-literacy/) or UNICEF (www.unicef.org/georgia/press-releases/developing-media-literacy-skills-young-people).

References

Addley E. (2019) 'Fake anti-Brexit banknotes added to British Museum collection', *The Guardian*, 9 August 2019.

Bennett, W.L., S. Livingston (2018) 'The disinformation order: Disruptive communication and the decline of democratic institutions', *European Journal of Communication* 33(2): 122–39.

Bode, L., E.K. Vraga (2015) 'In related news, that was wrong: The correction of misinformation through related stories functionality in social media', *Journal of Communication* 65(4): 619–38.

Borrell, J. (2020) 'Disinformation around the Coronavirus pandemic: Opening statement by the HR/VP Josep Borrell at the European Parliament', Brussels, 30 April, https://eeas.europa.eu/headquarters/headquarters-homepage/78329/disinformation-around-coronavirus-pandemic-opening-statement-hrvp-josep-borrell-european_en.

Bufacchi, V. (2020) 'What's the difference between lies and post-truth in politics? A philosopher explains', *The Conversation*, 24 January 2020, https://theconversation.com/whats-the-difference-between-lies-and-post-truth-in-politics-a-philosopher-explains-130442.

Bull, H. (1977) *The Anarchical Society: A Study of Order in World Politics*, London: Macmillan.

Carlson, M. (2018) 'The information politics of journalism in a post-truth age', *Journalism Studies* 19(13): 1879–88.

Chan, M.S., C.R. Jones, K. Hall Jamieson, D. Albarracín (2017) 'Debunking: A meta-analysis of the psychological efficacy of messages countering misinformation', *Psychological Science* 28(11): 1531–46.

Chesney, R., D. Citron (2019) 'Deepfakes and the new disinformation war: The coming age of post-truth geopolitics', *Foreign Affairs* 98(1): 147–55.

Chinchilla, L. (2019) 'Post-truth politics afflicts the global South, too', *The New York Times*, 15 October 2019, www.nytimes.com/2019/10/15/opinion/politics-global-south.html.

Corner, J. (2017) 'Fake news, post-truth and media–political change', *Media, Culture & Society* 39(7): 1100–07.

Council of the European Union (2016) *Council's Conclusions on Developing Media Literacy and Critical Thinking Through Education and Training*, Brussels.

Egelhofer, J.L., S. Lecheler (2019) 'Fake news as a two-dimensional phenomenon: A framework and research agenda', *Annals of the International Communication Association* 43(2): 97–116.

European Commission (2020) 'Tackling COVID-19 disinformation – Getting the facts rights', Brussels, JOIN(2020) 8 final.

Farhall, K., A. Carson, S. Wright, A. Gibbons, W. Lukamto (2019) 'Political elites' use of fake news discourse across communications platforms', *International Journal of Communication* 13: 4353–75.

Fioriglio, G. (2019) 'Post-verità, paura e controllo dell'informazione. Quale ruolo per il diritto?', *Governare la paura*: 105–24.

Friesem, Y. (2019) 'Teaching truth, lies, and accuracy in the digital age: Media literacy as project-based learning', *Journalism & Mass Communication Educator* 74(2): 185–98.

Fuller, S. (2018) *Post-Truth: Knowledge as a Power Game*, London: Anthem.

Graves, L. (2018). 'Boundaries not drawn. Mapping the institutional roots of the global fact-checking movement', *Journalism Studies* 19(5): 613–31.

Guess, A.M., B. Nyhan, J. Reifler (2018) 'Exposure to untrustworthy websites in the 2016 US election', www.dartmouth.edu/~nyhan/fake-news-2016.pdf.

Hannan, J. (2018) 'Trolling ourselves to death? Social media and post-truth politics', *European Journal of Communication* 33(2): 214–26.

Hopkin, J., B. Rosamond (2017) 'Post-truth politics, bullshit and bad ideas: "Deficit fetishism" in the UK', *New Political Economy* 23(6): 1–15.

Keller, F.B., D. Schoch, S. Stier, J.H. Yang (2020) 'Political astroturfing on Twitter: How to coordinate a disinformation campaign', *Political Communication* 37(2): 256–80.

Kessler, G. (2019) 'The Iraq War and WMDs: An intelligence failure or White House spin?', *The Washington Post*, 22 March 2019.

la Cour, C. (2020) 'Theorising digital disinformation in international relations', *International Politics* 57: 704–23, https://doi.org/10.1057/s41311-020-00215-x.

Lanoszka, A. (2019) 'Disinformation in international politics', *European Journal of International Security* 4(2): 227–48.

Lewandowsky, S., U.K.H. Ecker, J. Cook (2017) 'Beyond misinformation: Understanding and coping with the "post-truth" era', *Journal of Applied Research in Memory and Cognition* 6(4): 353–69.

Lewandowsky, S., U.K.H. Ecker, C.M. Seifert, N. Schwarz, J. Cook (2012) 'Misinformation and its correction: Continued influence and successful debiasing', *Psychological Science in the Public Interest* 13(3): 106–31.

Lippmann, W. (1997) *Public Opinion*, New Brunswick – London: Transaction Publishers.

McIntyre, L. (2018) *Post-Truth*, Cambridge, MA – London: The MIT Press.

National Endowment for Democracy (NED) (2017) 'Distinguishing disinformation from propaganda, misinformation, and "fake news"', 17 October 2017, www.ned.org/issue-brief-distinguishing-disinformation-from-propaganda-misinformation-and-fake-news/.

Nyhan, B., J. Reifler (2010) 'When corrections fail: The persistence of political misperceptions', *Political Behavior* 32: 303–30.

Polyakova, A., C. Meserole (2019) 'Exporting digital authoritarianism', Democracy & Disorder Policy Brief, Foreign Policy at Brookings, www.brookings.edu/wp-content/uploads/2019/08/FP_20190827_digital_authoritarianism_polyakova_meserole.pdf.

Pomerantsev, P. (2019) *This is Not Propaganda*, London: Faber & Faber.

Roozenbeek, J., S. van der Linden (2019) 'Fake news game confers psychological resistance against online misinformation', *Palgrave Communications* 5: 65.

Rose, J. (2017) 'Brexit, Trump, and post-truth politics', *Public Integrity* 19(6): 555–58.

Select Committee on Communications, House of Commons (2019) 'Disinformation and "fake news": Final report', https://publications.parliament.uk/pa/cm201719/cmselect/cmcumeds/1791/179102.htm.

Sethi, R.J. (2017) 'Crowdsourcing the verification of fake news and alternative facts', *Proceedings of the 28th ACM Conference on Hypertext and Social Media (HT '17)*, Association for Computing Machinery, New York, NY, USA: 315–16.

Sky News, 'Coronavirus: "You know you are a fake" – Trump to reporter,' 14 April 2020, https://news.sky.com/video/trump-calls-reporter-a-disgrace-11972861.

van der Linden, S. E. Maibach, J. Cook, A. Leiserowitz, S. Lewandowsky (2017) 'Inoculating against misinformation', *Science* 358(6367): 1141–42.

Vosoughi, S., D. Roy, S. Aral (2018) 'The spread of true and false news online', *Science* 359(6380): 1146–51.

Vosoughi, S., M. Mohsenvand, D. Roy (2017) 'Rumor gauge: Predicting the veracity of rumors on Twitter', *ACM Transactions on Knowledge Discovery from Data* 11(4), article 50.

Waisbord, S. (2018) 'Truth is what happens to news. On journalism, fake news, and post-truth', *Journalism Studies* 19(13): 1866–78.

Wendling, M. (2018) 'The (almost) complete history of "fake news"', BBC Trending, 22 January 2018, www.bbc.com/news/blogs-trending-42724320.

PART I

Post-truth politics and the challenges to democracy

1

READING ARENDT TO RETHINK TRUTH, SCIENCE, AND POLITICS IN THE ERA OF FAKE NEWS

Federica Merenda

Introduction

"No one has ever doubted that truth and politics are on rather bad terms with each other, and no one, as far as I know, has ever counted truthfulness among the political virtues" (Arendt 1967: 295).

In spite of the success of such "commonplace" mentioned by Hannah Arendt at the very beginning of her reflections on *Truth and Politics*, in 21st century contemporary democracies truth, lies, and political opinions are very intertwined concepts. Expressions like "post-truth politics" and "fake news" by now entered the vocabulary of politics, and they are employed more and more to describe relevant dynamics of the contemporary political discourse.

We live in times when it is not easy at all to distinguish between facts, mystification of facts –which contain some truths well-mingled with a high dose of distorted information – blatant lies, and political opinions. While reading the newspaper or scrolling through the social media newsfeeds of politicians directly speaking to "the people" through Facebook live videos – a habit which became particularly massive during the recent outbreak of Covid-19, when Facebook live-streaming in some countries replaced the usual institutional broadcasting on national television – we sometimes feel outraged as we spot blatant lies or traces of wisely hidden truths in political speeches (or tweets), or when we witness political leaders endorse information soon after unveiled as *fake news*.

Sharing Arendt's view that philosophy can help us to understand reality and to reconcile ourselves with the world we live in (Arendt 1994: 308), this chapter will consider relevant concepts and paradigms elaborated in Arendt's works, which have been at the centre of modern and contemporary Western political thought even beyond Arendt. This conceptual toolbox purposely would help to clarify the relation between (the different kinds of) truth, (the different kinds of) lying, and politics in contemporary democracies.

Contextualising Arendt: On truth and politics in Western philosophy

In order to examine the relationship between truth and politics, we move from Arendt's distinction between different kinds of truth and even different degrees of lying. Identifying which truths possess a political value of some sort presupposes pondering even more basic questions that philosophers well before Arendt have tried to respond to: does truth exist as such? In case it exists, is it intelligible? And when it is not, is it dispensable? Can we talk about any knowledge at all beyond objective truths? Which kinds of truths are at odds with democracy and which are necessary for its wellbeing?

The many different answers to these questions gave rise to different approaches to science, philosophy, and political theory. The discussions concerning whether truth can be deemed to exist as such and whether, in that case, it would be accessible to human knowledge are indeed deeply intertwined with the epistemological question of whether natural or philosophical truths could – and/or should – constitute the ultimate object of philosophical or scientific research and of the appropriateness of such pursuit as the qualifying characteristic of science.

While pre-Socratic philosophers looked for the ultimate principle of natural reality, thereafter, spanning from the *Cave* in Plato's myth to Schopenhauer's *Veil of Maya* (Schopenhauer 1995) and through Kant's *Critiques*, the idea that objective truth and the representation of reality by human beings, as a subjective perception or interpretation, may be two different things deeply affected the evolution of philosophical thought, and that of political theory.[1]

In the 18th century, Immanuel Kant shifted the focus of philosophical research from objective truth, as the study of an outer object, to the subject of knowledge and thus to human rationality, morality, and judgment (Kant 2007a; 2007b; 2012), to explore the way in which we, as human beings, perceive ourselves and the outer world. This brief premise shows the relevance of the subject we are treating in all the philosophical production; a philosophical production that our examination has not the ambition to analyse thoroughly but that constitutes the *humus* in which Arendt's reflections on truth and politics – and contemporary further explorations – could emerge.

In order to contextualise Arendt's definition of truth and truths and their relationship with democratic politics, we adopt the distinction drawn by Antonella Besussi (2013; 2015) in her work devoted to the concept of truth in contemporary political philosophy. Besussi usefully distinguishes between those political theories suggesting a *banalisation* of the relationship between truth and politics and those tending towards a *dramatisation*: it is in this second group that we find Arendt.

The perspective of those allegedly *banalising* such relation is quite clear-cut in its premises: according to these thinkers, there is no objective truth at all to be found out beyond our subjective interpretations. To bring this belief to its extreme would mean to say that there is no such thing as objective facts: subjective interpretations of reality are all we have. We can ponder whether it is convenient or not to attribute to our subjective interpretations of the world the characteristics of truth, that is to present them as undisputable. As an objective truth does not exist, to attribute the quality of truth to our subjective interpretations of the world will thus be a decision that we will take considering *what truth does* rather than *what it is*,[2] in a consequentialist perspective.

On the other hand, political theorists who *dramatise* the relationship between truth and politics are not expressly excluding the possibility that an objective truth does exist. Facts do exist. What they point out is rather that, for different reasons, there is an incompatibility between truth and politics, supporting the idea that truth has no place in the political democratic realm, at least in ordinary circumstances. Such dramatisation, in Besussi's taxonomy, assumed two different forms. The former is that of a "realistic conception of truth".[3] In this view, truth does not concern politics in as far as the objective of democratic politics is not to ascertain which human representation of reality does correspond to truth.

More specifically, politics should deliberate which principles a specific society gives priority to in a specific moment of its history, among those embodied in the programmes and policies proposed by the different competing political parties. These philosophers accept that individuals and groups can believe in comprehensive paradigms that give rise to the principles they support within the democratic competition, but once such principles enter the realm of democratic politics they become just alternative policies competing for consensus. As Norberto Bobbio would say, the discourse over the foundations of such principles is left outside the political arena which is just concerned about their possibility to be agreed on (Bobbio 1997).

Quite differently, Hannah Arendt endorses, similarly to John Rawls, a "value-based conception of truth" by refusing to recognise truth as an absolute standard in the public sphere, from an anti-authoritarian stance. In Rawls' *Political Liberalism* (Rawls 2005), the principles of justice of a well-ordered society are proposed not because they are the true right principles *per se*, but because they are the ones that supposedly would be agreed on by individuals finding themselves in an ideal original position. The overlapping consensus is their source of legitimacy, and thus they are political principles, not moral ones. The function used by Rawls to identify them is political consensus, not truth, even if the first is conceived in an abstract way by means of a mental experiment. To accept truth within the well-ordered society would make the overlapping consensus impossible, as truth accepts no compromise.

Such incompatibility between truth and democratic compromise is strongly perceived by Arendt as well: this is the element that will bring her in going deep in elaborating the taxonomy of truth, truths, and lying which we think does constitute a particularly useful conceptual tool for contemporary reflections. We will examine Arendt's conceptualisation thoroughly in our next section, mainly referring to her works on *Truth and Politics* (Arendt 1967) and *Lying in Politics* (Arendt 1969) but having in mind her much wider philosophical production.

Factual truths, philosophical truths, and lying in politics: Arendt's perspective

In her reflection on *Truth and Politics*, Arendt (1967) distinguishes between *factual truths* (facts, events) and *rational truths* (e.g. mathematical, scientific and philosophical truths) to specify the different relations they have with the political debate in a plural society and to investigate the consequences of their negation or mystification.

In Arendt's definition, factual truths are just factual statements which describe facts and events: with reasonable approximation – an approximation justified by common sense, a crucial concept in Arendt's discourse (Arendt 1982) – to say "It rains", when it is actually raining, is a factual truth. Rational truths (a category which also includes philosophical and religious truths) are instead expressed in the form of statements like "two plus two is four" or "God exists".

What they both have in common is that they imply an element of coercion:

> Statements such as 'The three angles of a triangle are equal to two angles of a square,' 'The earth moves around the sun,' 'It is better to suffer wrong than to do wrong', 'In August 1914 Germany invaded Belgium' are very different in the way they are arrived at, but, once perceived as true and pronounced to be so, they have in common that they are beyond agreement, dispute, opinion, or consent
>
> (Arendt 1982: 302).

In Arendt's view, any truth is coercive because it is beyond agreement, dispute, opinion, or consent, which are precisely those elements that, as we found in Rawls, make the democratic politics of the overlapping consensus possible. In this being undisputable and non-negotiable, truth is intrinsically anti-democratic. Yet, the distinction between factual truths and rational ones is crucial.

Factual truths, while being at odds with the political debate, are necessary for the exercise of democratic power in a plural society. Also, this is the category which acquires critical relevance today with reference to the problem of fake news: it is factual truths that fake news denies On the contrary, according to Arendt, rational truths are both generally at odds with the political debate and also at odds with the exercise of democratic power in a plural society: as truth is not democratic, it does not allow for the plurality of opinions which is the essential nourishment of democracy.

The content of rational truths can be admitted to the public sphere of democratic politics only in the form of a mere opinion among other opinions, which does not carry with its coercive value of truthfulness, and as long as it accepts to give up such claim for truthfulness. For instance, a political party can inform its action to religious values but it cannot do so by presenting its policies as the only true actions to take. Such religious values can enter the political arena just as opinions.

On the other hand, factual truths, while being at odds with the political debate in their being uncontroversial, are not only totally compatible with democratic politics but even necessary for it. While this can appear contradictory, it works if we accept that facts belong to another dimension, which is placed underneath that of politics itself. "Facts and events [. . .] constitute the very texture of the political realm" (ibid.: 297), they are the ground political opinions can be built upon. If we do not agree on the facts at hand, we cannot appropriately start any discussion about how to deal with them, exchanging our opinions on the issue.

While science and philosophy are the dimension of rational truths, politics is thus the realm of opinions, which is grounded on an underlying layer of factual truths. This ground is solid as long as it is not put into question, as long as its validity is not doubted. When facts are not universally recognised and their truthfulness is put into question, when the question "Is it really true that it's raining?" is asked, deliberate lying can make its appearance in the public discourse and the ground which the political discourse is built upon, "the ground on which we stand and the sky that stretches above us" (ibid.: 313) starts shaking.

Fake news: Mingling lies, facts, and opinions

While we find Arendt's definitions very useful, it is crucial to note that by driving distinctions between ordinary conditions and moments when "a community has embarked on organized lying on principle" (ibid.: 307) she was referring to totalitarianism. In that context, Arendt was able to identify more clear-cut dynamics and concepts than what are commonly at work today in post-truth democracies where populist forces are operating.

To distinguish between a healthy relation linking truth and politics and the perversion of such relation is more subtle if we want to apply Arendt's categories not in the most radical context of totalitarian states but in the slippery slope between a well-functioning democracy and populist regimes.

Still, rather than making our effort futile, such blurred conditions characterising the contemporary situation on the contrary make any attempt at a conceptual clarification even more necessary. In the public sphere of our contemporary liberal democracies, we can discuss, argue, and compare different opinions about how to deal with a particular fact or event, for instance climate change, only once we agree that climate change is a reality. Once we acknowledge that climate change is happening, each individual and each community involved can do their part to deal with the consequences of such an alarming fact. Experts can help to clarify the facts, identify the causes of the phenomenon, and the practices that are worsening it.

Politicians can then propose different alternatives on how to face climate change in practice, with each alternative endowing competing values, rights, interests, and priorities. There are many possible alternatives to reach the same goal: for instance, according to their priorities and political values, to fight climate change politicians can propose policies on measures that do not disproportionally affect the most vulnerable countries and individuals, or alternative ones that give priority to protecting the interests of the private sector.

Journalists can provide the general public with accurate information both about climate change itself and about the policies currently under consideration by the different political parties and leaders. However, if some authoritative figure, let's say the President of the United States, denies climate change as a fact by releasing declarations like "I don't believe it" and "The concept of global warning was created by and for the Chinese in order to make US manufacturing non-competitive" (Cheung 2020), at least part of the public debate is diverted from the confrontation between the different political options at disposal to fight climate change to a debate on whether climate change is actually happening or whether it is just a total mischief, an exaggeration, a plan of the Chinese government to disrupt the US as an economic power, a lie construed by those enterprises which have invested in green energy, and so on.

This is a clear example of a negation of a fact: in this case, President Trump firstly put climate change into question and then created an alternative version of reality, a plain lie, that once pronounced by such an authoritative source entered in competition with the factual truth of climate change. Though the contemporary political regime in place in the US is not a totalitarian one, having the President releasing such declaration is still worrying for democracy. Unfortunately, we are witnessing similar dynamics in these very days with regards to Covid-19, not only in the US, but also in other Western democracies (Soubhik et al. 2020).

To reflect upon these contemporary cases, an operative way to think about truth which could be particularly useful, and that we find very much in line with Arendt's conceptual toolkit that we have hereby adopted, has been elaborated by Franca D'Agostini in her work *Introduction to Truth* (D'Agostini 2011). Here, she invites the reader to consider truth not as a substantial content *per se* (which would make it correspond to *a specific truth*) but as a conceptual function, a quality that statements may or may not have or acquire. In mathematical language, we would thus represent truth not as a variable x but as a function $f(x)$ – as a question, rather than as an answer. By applying this definition, we can thus generally state that to think about truth means to think about whether the question "Is it true or not?" can be applied to our perceptions, representations, interpretations of reality.

Once we ask such question, irrespective of the answer we get, truth has entered the dimension of our discourse. When, on the contrary, we implicitly assume a statement as uncontroversial, we are considering it a fact, by excluding the possible debate on its truthfulness or falsity from our concern and thus leaving it in the background of our discourse, not applying the function. As an example, we can take the Preamble of the American Declaration of Independence. By writing "we hold these truths to be self-evident",[4] Thomas Jefferson and his peers made the political-philosophical principles included in the Declaration, among which the principle that "all men are created equal", uncontroversial; they transformed them into facts. The question "is it true that all men are equal?" is pre-emptively displaced because such principle is placed in the sphere of facts, which is beyond arguments. Facts are assumed as truths without the question on their truthfulness even being asked, because to ask that question would mean to doubt them.

The question of the relation between truth and politics can thus be translated into the appropriateness of asking this question about statements expressed in the public sphere: is it appropriate to apply truthfulness as a standard in politics, to ask whether what a politician says is true or not? Whether the political solutions suggested are the true answer to political problems? Or should we just focus on whether we would wish those policies to be adopted in view of their consequences? Do facts have a place in politics? And what is the role of other subjects participating in the public debate, spanning from the common citizen to journalists, public figures or intellectuals?

When there are politicians denying facts, truth makes its appearance *within* the political realm, where it does not belong. When political figures and those exercising public powers lie about factual truths, they bring facts from the background of the political sphere to the political arena itself, that as we said is the realm of opinions. In these cases, truth as a function is applied to facts which, as such, should be considered instead uncontroversial and accepted as they are.

As the truthfulness of such facts is doubted or negated, they are brought by their detractors to the political arena, where they are attacked by fake news through the means employed in the competition between different opinions: in order to be chosen among competing ones, they are asked to be convincing.

But truth is seldom convincing in its being accidental. Factual truths are not opinions resulting from accurate reasoning or reflections with a teleological scope. Therefore, facts cannot be exhaustively explained or thoroughly understood. In this sense they are accidental. They can only be witnessed and believed. It is thus more a question of faith, or at least trust, in the source of information than a matter of epistemic resources of the recipients of the information themselves. As Arendt warns us, lies are usually much easier to believe than factual truths and thus they can be far more persuasive:

> Since the liar is free to fashion his 'facts' to fit the profit and pleasure, or even the mere expectations, of his audience, the chances are that he will be more persuasive than the truth-teller. Indeed, he will usually have plausibility on his side; his exposition will sound more logical, as it were, since the element of unexpectedness – one of the outstanding characteristics of all events – has mercifully disappeared
>
> (Arendt 1967: 307).

The more and more scientists, intellectuals, and scholars are called upon in the public debate to present hard data, "neutral" information that the audience can cling on to in such uncertain times when factual truths are blatantly negated by populist leaders and intellectually dishonest politicians. Experts' action is crucial. In ordinary circumstances, stating facts is not to be considered a political action as acknowledging something that already exists does not give origins to anything new, which is the characteristic of human action in Arendt's wording. Still, when a community has embarked upon

> organized lying on principle, and not only with respect to particulars, can truthfulness as such, unsupported by the distorting forces of power and interest, become a political factor of the first order. Where everybody lies about everything of importance, the truth-teller, whether he knows it or not, has begun to act; he, too, has engaged himself in political business, for, in the unlikely event that he survives, he has made a start toward changing the world
>
> (ibid.).

The noblest contribution of intellectual labour: Conclusive remarks

These reflections are deeply intertwined with Arendt's peculiar idea of politics, which is very close to the *isonomía* of the *polis* in Ancient Greece, as she points out in all her works and she particularly explores in *The Human Condition* (Arendt 1958). Such idea of democratic power is in a way the contrary to dominion and totalitarianism and is therefore a good antidote to totalitarian tendencies in weak democracies.[5]

According to Arendt, philosophers, scientists, politicians, and common citizens are part of the same community of human beings precisely in virtue of sharing the common ground of facts, the world of things that connects yet holds us apart. It is the plurality of the human condition itself to be embroidered within "the common world that unites and separates us" (Arendt 1958), the world of facts, events and accidents over and among which human action can be performed. The very existence of such a world makes us a plurality by connecting us through our sharing it. Still, such a world is *common* as long as we share a *common sense* that enables us to understand each other: the common sense that is necessary to name things and to discuss them, trusting the fact that when we say something the person we are talking to gets pretty much a similar idea of what we have in mind while saying the word. When lies are so widespread as to have become undistinguishable from facts, our common sense is lost.

The loss of common sense would be such a radical problem that among contemporary reflections on post-truth politics, there are some that consider it as just a symptom of a more fundamental problem:

> More than cause of the state of crisis of contemporary liberal democracies, post-truth is the visible symptom of a deeper problem, which in

philosophical terms could be rendered as hyper-individualism or radical subjectivism, which is perhaps best expressed using a word from ordinary language: solitude

(Alagna 2019).

When factual truth is put into question, denied and substituted by deliberate lies, we may start to have reasons to worry about the ability of democratic guarantees to prevent any political discourse paving the way for an exercise of power that reminds us more of political dominion than of democratic power.

More radically, when the practice of organised lying becomes systematic and we lose trust in political institutions and in each other as epistemic sources, we may worry that it is thus sociability and, as a result, politics itself that is endangered.

Arendt is quite optimistic about the fact that, as long as there are witnesses and truth-tellers, in the long run truth will outlive organised lying (Arendt 1967). Yet, nowadays, direct confrontations between 'experts' and lying politicians do not too often end with the first category winning the debate and this is not seemingly managing to disrupt lying on factual truths as a political strategy. When thinking about the contemporary fake-news politics scenario as this book is seeking to do, we need to take into account elements which are peculiar to current times, contextual elements which have an impact on the success of the strategies to rebuild a stability for the shaking ground we stand on. First of all, we could provocatively ask how relevant 'the long run' in which Arendt puts her confidence in is in such times of short-sighted political propaganda, which usually aims at winning one debate today with all the arms at its disposal without caring that much about lies being uncovered afterwards. If we go from election to election, we risk 'the long run' to never come.

Secondly, to have experts battling against politicians on social networks or onscreen television debates, extrapolated from their institutional environment, is tangibly bringing factual truth into the political dimension where it does not belong. When Arendt calls upon intellectuals, journalists, historians to be truth-tellers, she does not suggest that they engage in direct competition against the lying politicians, nor that they replace them by calling experts to take political decisions instead of politicians. The risk of further mingling facts with politics is high. This neither helps the authoritativeness of science nor that of politics itself. Experts and politicians have very different roles and even when the former play a 'political' role through their stating of facts, they do not at all exhaust politics as such. On the contrary, experts' role should always be ancillary to that of politicians. For Arendt, stating factual truth is essential in helping us to understand what political actors *should not* do, rather than what they must (Sorrentino 2013: 90).

Once facts are to a certain extent shared – and we are aware, as Arendt herself surely was, that considering factual truths undisputable is simplistic, as there can be disagreements on facts even among 'experts' – it is up to those exercising the political powers to propose policies on how to tackle them by taking into account different concerns at the same time and prioritising over certain values, objectives, issues instead of others. The contribution that the 'science' of political philosophy can offer to politics is to provide citizens, other than politicians, with conceptual instruments aimed at achieving *clarity* in their discourse. This is what Weber calls the "ethical achievement" of science in politics at the end on his lecture on 'Science as vocation' (Weber 2004). Once facts are restated, the democratic debate among different political opinions can – and must, to have a functioning democracy – restart; the responsibility for this stands with politics, not with science.[6]

Notes

1 To contextualise Arendt's reflections, which will be examined in the second section of this chapter, see Sorrentino (2017).
2 In Besussi's recollection, such premise is shared and differently articulated by Richard Rorty, Hilary Putnam, Jürgen Habermas, Michel Foucault, Bernard Williams and Ronald Dworkin. See Besussi (2013: 9–27).
3 According to Besussi (2013), such perspective is shared by Hans Kelsen, Max Weber and Leo Strauss.
4 *Declaration of Independence: a transcription* (1776) US National Archives, available at www.archives.gov/founding-docs/declaration-transcript (last consulted 1 April 2020).
5 See Cavarero (2019).
6 "The objective knowledge of science is not just true, it is useful too: it provides us with notions to orient ourselves in the world and it trains us at thinking, teaching us a logical and methodological accuracy that is valuable notwithstanding the action we intend to perform [...] Also, it defies factual beliefs which are not objective, it unveils value-judgements disguised as factual truths, it solves moral disagreements resulting from lying on facts or reasonings which are logically unsound [...] This ability to achieve clarity through statements which are "true" is the meaning, the significance, the major and noblest contribution of intellectual labour. And that is so mainly as, by fostering a sense of responsibility, it positively influences the behaviour of political actors" (Ferrera 2013: 52).

References

Alagna, M. (2019) 'The ground trembling under our feet. Truth, politics and solitude', *Soft Power* 6(2): 111–29.

Arendt, H. (1958) *The Human Condition*, second edition, Chicago: University of Chicago Press.

Arendt, H. (1967/2005) 'Truth and politics', in J. Medina., D. Wood (eds), *Truth: Engagements Across Philosophical Traditions*, London – New York: Wiley-Blackwell.

Arendt, H. (1969) *Lying in Politics. Reflections on the Pentagon Papers*, New York: Harcourt Brace Jovanovich.

Arendt, H. (1982) *Lectures on Kant's Political Philosophy*, Brighton: Harvester.

Arendt, H. (1994) (or. ed. 1954) 'Understanding and politics', in: Ead., *Essays on Understanding 1930–1954: Formation, Exile and Totalitarianism*, New York: Schoken Books.

Besussi, A. (ed.) (2013) *Verità e politica. Filosofie contemporanee*, Roma: Carocci.

Besussi, A. (ed.) (2015) *Filosofia, verità e politica. Questioni classiche*, Roma: Carocci.

Bobbio, N. (1997) 'Sul fondamento dei diritti dell'uomo?', in: Id., *L'età dei diritti*, Torino: Einaudi.

Castelli, F. (2012) 'Le verità della Politica. Hannah Arendt sul rapporto tra Verità, Menzogna e Potere', in: A. Pirni (ed.), *Verità del potere, potere della verità*, Pisa: ETS.

Cavarero, A. (2019) *Democrazia sorgiva. Note sul pensiero politico di Hannah Arendt*, Milano: Raffaello Cortina Editore.

Cheung, H. (2020) 'What does Trump actually believe on climate change?', BBC, 23 January 2020, www.bbc.com/news/world-us-canada-51213003 (last consulted 1 April 2020).

Cotroneo, G. (2012), 'L'avventura della menzogna politica', *Filosofia Politica*, XXVI(3): 463–70.

D'Agostini, F. (2011) *Intoduzione alla verità*, Torino: Bollati Boringhieri.

D'Agostini, F., M. Ferrera (2019) *La verità al potere. Sei diritti aletici*, Torino: Einaudi.

Ferraris, M. (2017) *Postverità e altri enigmi*, Bologna: Il Mulino.

Ferrera, M. (2013) 'Max Weber: Verità e responsabilità. Il binomio virtuoso', in: A. Besussi (ed.), *Verità e politica*, Roma: Carocci, 48–65.

Kant, I. (2007a) (or. ed. *Kritik der reinen Vernunft*, 1787) *Critique of Pure Reason*, London: Penguin Classics.

Kant, I. (2007b) (or. ed. *Kritik der Urtheilskraft*, 1790) *Critique of Judgement*, Oxford: Oxford University Press.

Kant, I. (2012) (or. ed. *Kritik der praktischen Vernunft*, 1788) *Critique of Practical Reason*, New York: Dover Publications.

Origgi, G. (2015) 'La verità, nient'altro che la verità? Piccola storia filosofica della menzogna', *MicroMega. Almanacco di filosofia*, 2015/2: 83–97.

Rawls, J. (2005) *Political Liberalism*, New York: Columbia University Press.

Schopenhauer, A. (1995) (or. ed. *Die Welt als Wille und Vorstellung*, 1818/19 [I] – 1844 [II] – 1859 [III]) *The World as Will and Representation*, E.F.J. Payne (ed.), New York: Dover Publications.

Sorrentino, V. (2013) 'Hannah Arendt. Verità, politica e mondo comune', in: A. Besussi (ed.), *Verità e politica. Filosofie contemporanee*, Roma: Carocci.

Sorrentino, V. (2017) 'La politica tra visibile e invisibile. Sul concetto di sfera pubblica in Hannah Arendt', *Politica & Società* 2: 259–74.

Soubhik et al. (2020) *Evaluating COVID-19 Public Health Messaging in Italy: Self-Reported Compliance and Growing Mental Health Concerns*, Working paper, 24 March 2020, https://gking.harvard.edu/covid-italy (last consulted 1 April 2020).

Urbinati, N. (2019) *Io, il popolo. Come il populismo trasforma la democrazia*, Bologna: Il Mulino.

Weber, M. (2004) (or. ed. *Wissenschalft als Beruf*, 1919) *The Vocation Lectures*, D. Owen, T.B. Strong (eds), Indianapolis – Cambridge: Hackett Publishing Company.

2

INEQUALITY IN THE PUBLIC SPHERE

Epistemic injustice, discrimination, and violence

Elisa Piras

Introduction

Contemporary democracies rely on the delicate balance between two fundamental principles of politics: as we can read at the beginning of almost every democratic constitution, within a democratic system all citizens are considered free and equal members of the political community. Even if we frame democratic politics in terms of fairness or social justice – setting the bar higher towards a normative definition of democracy, as a large number of contemporary political theorists do – the two principles at the heart of any conception of justice do not change, although their alternative interpretations can produce very different political outcomes. Within the public sphere, communicative interactions between individuals and groups occur daily, alternative opinions interact, and the public debate unfolds as the result of the exchange, influencing the democratic game, i.e. the formation of electoral majorities and the governments. Social and political inequalities affect the structure and functioning of the public sphere – the arena where public opinion emerges as the result of the continuous exchange of information and opinions. Within the public sphere, inequality produces harm and injustice for the members of marginalised groups. Drawing on the contemporary debate among liberal political theorists, the chapter will analyse the formation of public opinion, highlighting its political implications; then, it will explain and connect the concepts of epistemic and structural injustice; eventually, it will advance the concept of dialogic injustice to depict the specific form of epistemic injustice which harms members of marginalised and oppressed groups when they experience credibility deficits or apparently insurmountable difficulties in acceding to the public sphere as free and equal members.

How inequalities affect the public sphere

Liberty and equality, the two principles lying at the heart of liberalism and democracy, do very often meet and at times clash within the relational setting widely known as the public sphere: this is a domain of social life where public opinion is formed and where a *sui generis* social actor, the public, emerges (Habermas 1991: 398).[1] Within the public sphere, information is spread/offered and obtained/consumed. There, communication-based interactions between individuals and groups occur daily; alternative opinions are publicly stated, refuted, supported, and attacked. Moreover, since the public sphere is a filter between state and society, it is the domain of public reason (Rawls 1993; Habermas 1995; Gaus 2011; Forst 2014), where citizens' requests for justifications for state laws and actions arise and justificatory accounts are presented in response by the representatives of state institutions. Every citizen is entitled to ask and receive acceptable answers (reasonable justifications) when they question the *ratio* of political rules, because obedience to any authority is acceptable insofar as this serves the preservation or enhancement of citizens' liberty and equality (Gaus 1999; Forst 2014). The entitlement to justification can be derived also from the conception of the state as the result of a contract, or from the Kantian idea that all citizens are to be considered as co-legislators (Rawls 1999: 135–37). With respect to democracy, the public sphere is not only a filter, but also a fulcrum: allowing continuous communication between government and citizens, it guarantees the equilibrium, stability, and functioning of the system. There, political consensus can be built and eroded as part of the game for achieving political power; also, it is in the public sphere that the formation of electoral majorities occurs.

There are two main assumptions for the existence of a public sphere. First, within a certain society there is a sufficient degree of liberty to allow the proliferation of ideas, opinions, beliefs, and tastes. Second, all these different ideas, opinions, beliefs, and tastes can be publicly spelled out and any citizen has equal right to express her/his own thought or to profess her/his faith. Ideally, a democratic public sphere is characterised by reasonable pluralism: there is a wide variety of doctrines about truth or about what is good, but each of them respects the others and none aims at defeating all alternative doctrines (Rawls 1993: 38 ff.; Gaus 1999). Again, the two assumptions reflect the core principles of liberalism and democracy: liberty and equality. Within the public sphere, from the debate among free and equal citizens, not only the specific policies and laws, but also the constitutional principles of any democracy are periodically discussed and evaluated, making possible the participation of the public to the processes of constitutional reform which make democratic systems stable and resilient over time (Rawls 1993).

Several problems emerge when we shift from the ideal of the public sphere described above to the non-ideal conditions of existing democracies. In the next section, I will investigate how social and political inequalities affect the distribution of epistemic resources and how this unequal distribution negatively affects some individuals because of their belonging to marginalised groups, contributing to perpetuate their unjust marginalisation. However, another problem affecting the public sphere of existing democracies needs to be briefly mentioned here, since it is closely linked to that of epistemic injustice. Pluralism is not always reasonable: precisely because all doctrines and opinions can freely and equally circulate within the public sphere, also discriminatory and violent (non-reasonable) ideas can enter the public discussion. As a matter of fact, they often come together with abusive or insulting language and sometimes they can serve as triggers for actions of violence carried out by individuals or by organised groups. The problematic reconciliation between freedom of expression and equal respect with regard to what is often called *hate speech* or 'group libel' (Waldron 2012) is an especially thorny task, not only for political theorists, but also for politicians and for professionals working in the field of education as well as in the mass media system. Within liberal democracies, there is a trade-off between protecting freedom of expression for all citizens and combating discriminatory attitudes and discourses which are potentially harmful for marginalised minorities. There are at least two main solutions to this conundrum. The first solution is to set the boundaries to free speech and exclude from the public sphere any harmful speech which could undermine the dignity of the targeted people (ibid.). The second solution consists of evaluating on a case-by-case basis whether it is better to place a higher value on freedom of expression rather than on other liberal values (privacy, security, equality, or the prevention of harm), acknowledging the political nature of any limitation to free speech (Fish 1994).

The contemporary public sphere abounds of examples of discriminatory attitudes and discourses – among others, racism, xenophobia, anti-Semitism, anti-Gypsyism, ageism, sexism, homophobia, ableism, etc. – used to frame political narratives and build consensus for implicitly or explicitly discriminatory political projects. As Catharine MacKinnon explained, in similar cases "speech acts"; to put it differently, concern about the political implications of free speech is justified, since there is something hidden behind words: "In the context of social inequality, so-called speech can be an exercise of power which constructs the social reality in which people live, from objectification to genocide. (. . .) Social supremacy is made, inside and between people, through making meanings" (MacKinnon 1993: 31). Discriminatory discourses are powerful political resources, and they are especially easy to exploit within the contemporary public sphere, which is multimedia, fragmented, and rhizomatic.[2] In this environment, pace to Kant (1784) and Habermas (1991), philosophers and public intellectuals are not the only ones who have the ability and authority to influence public opinion and participate in debates about politics. This is so because the public – the community of citizens where public opinion coalesces – is larger and much more composite compared to the past; consequently, both the language, the cultural references, and the messages used to build convincing argumentation have changed. Rationality, reasonableness, reciprocity, and civility, the pillars of the most influential liberal accounts of the public sphere elaborated during the last two centuries and a half, seem to give way to new features of public discourse that we can easily spot in contemporary political debates: unrestrained appeal to emotions, spontaneity, simplicity, refusal of the politically correct (Salmon 2013).

At this point, one might ask: why is it so important how public opinion is formed? It is because in a democracy public opinion grounds political consensus for the actors who can acquire political power. While observing the democratic 'market of opinions', it is paramount to detect which opinions look more appealing to the public, to trace the actors who back up those opinions and to identify the social mechanisms favouring their diffusion.[3] Since they have a crucial role for the formation of individual opinions and then of public opinion and consensus, information and communication deserve special attention. This comes as no news: almost a century ago, John Dewey (1927) convincingly raised this point while he was looking for an answer to the question: why is the US, notwithstanding the military and economic achievements which made its society great, a soulless and defective democracy? The answer is that the institutional mechanisms are not enough if the sense of community is missing. An ideal public sphere would present a fair market of opinions, based on reliable information provided by independent professionals sincerely committed to offer neutral accounts of the facts. Within such a public sphere, there would be an ideal public, capable of distinguishing the quality of the information, to collect it from different sources and to assess it thanks to critical reasoning. Public opinion emerging from the interactions among individual opinions would then support the best political option available, and possibly concur to its definition. Thus, in front of this public, there would be a government sustained by a (well-deserved) consensus, representing the interests of the society, pursuing the common good and reasonably justifying its actions. Both the conditions of reasonable pluralism and public reason would be realised (Rawls 1993). Like contemporary proponents of deliberative and participatory accounts of democracy, Dewey assigned a central importance to discussion, consultation, persuasion, and debate for democratic decision-making; of course, in his theoretical account high-quality education and unbiased information available for all citizens are fundamental prerequisites for the life of a democratic community.

Unfortunately, in non-ideal circumstances unequal access to good education and biased information are two of the reasons why the public sphere is not equally accessible to all the citizens, while it is especially hospitable to the powerful actors who can mobilise resources and know-how to influence public opinion. They do so by producing and spreading biased information and disseminating opinions and narratives which are suitable to further their interests, either to achieve or preserve political power or to maintain the social *status quo*. The new communication media, especially the Internet and the social networks, are very useful in this respect, since they allow the replacement of rational discourses with emotional messages, selecting the information sources and opinions that each citizen is exposed to on the basis of her/his status within society and of her/his social connections. An effect of this would be the transformation of our democracies towards a model of *bubble democracy*: the public dissolves into a myriad of self-referential 'bubbles', each allowing its 'inhabitants' to hear and read only the information and opinions which match their pre-established personal opinion. Thus, the public sphere is more and more fragmented and polarised, and the epistemic fruitfulness of the debate within the bubble is nullified: the ideas circulating within each bubble are homogeneous and they do not change over time (Palano 2020). This explains also why in contemporary democratic societies a vast majority of the citizens are unable to collect information, formulate their own interests, and mobilise; thus, they are governed by a restricted elite who is able to perform this tasks effectively (Goodin and Spiekermann 2015). The first move for marginalised and oppressed groups to take an active part in the public debate could be to develop *epistemic solidarity*, the "strategy of pooling information with selected others" (ibid.: 440). This would help citizens to bypass two paradoxical problems of the insufficient exposure to alternative opinions which characterise contemporary communication: *epistemic bubbles* – the condition of citizens who are limited in their attempts to formulate their own opinions because they have access to a small number of opinions, and *echo chambers* – the condition where some opinions are actively excluded and discredited (Sunstein 2009; Nguyen 2018). To simplify, "epistemic bubbles exclude through omission, while echo chambers exclude by manipulating trust and credence" (Nguyen 2018: 2). The same social epistemic phenomena facilitate the dissemination of fake news, post-truth messages, false or misleading political narratives.[4] These are especially worrisome features of the contemporary public sphere, not only because they hamper the discussion about the common good, but also because in order to do so they tend to exploit and exacerbate existing social inequalities, setting some groups against other groups and reproducing marginalisation and oppression.

Two effects of discrimination: Epistemic and structural injustice

In the previous paragraph, some concepts of social epistemology have been taken into consideration. Social epistemology is a subdiscipline of epistemology which examines and critically evaluates "the processes through which beliefs, decisions and opinions are formed, maintained and revised by individuals, groups, institutions and, in the widest sense, social practices and social systems" (Prijić-Samaržija 2018: 21). Similar investigations are particularly interesting for political philosophers: in 1690, at the outset of liberal thought, John Locke formulated the 'law of opinion or reputation'.[5] This explains how, by approving or disapproving of an individual's ideas and actions, other people exert a pressure on her/him to conform to a certain way of thinking and behaving which is acceptable or mainstream in her/his social environment. Humans are social animals; they fear isolation and peers' reprobation. Therefore, the majority of individuals will express their opinion in public only if they do not risk appearing as social outcast – this, of course, does not mean that divergent opinions cease to exist; they are hidden and in some cases they can resurface. In democratic contexts, we could observe the sudden appearance of hidden political opinions in numerous elections which showed unpredicted results – people use their quasi-statistical sense to understand the prevailing opinion in their social environment and, in case they have a different opinion, they tend to conceal it: this is the so-called spiral of silence theory (Noelle-Neumann 1980).

There are two insights in Locke's reflection on the problem of individual opinions which are relevant for the present discussion: first, the coercive nature of society over the individual; second, the importance of personal reputation and esteem for any citizen who hopes to be integrated.[6] If we consider them carefully, we can see that, again, there are two principles at stake: liberty and equality.

A serious threat to the principle of equality is connected to the importance of reputation and esteem: because of individuals belonging to certain groups, they may experience epistemic harm as a result of a negative identity-based prejudice. *Epistemic injustice*, as it has been defined in an influential essay written by Miranda Fricker (2007), is a form of injustice which may assume two forms: testimonial injustice and hermeneutical injustice. Testimonial injustice means that a person's testimony is not considered reliable or is not taken seriously because of her/his identity, which is read in the light of prejudices and stereotypes that undermine her/his credibility. On the other hand, hermeneutic injustice applies when a person suffers injustice but is not fully aware of it – because of the cultural context in which one is marginalised – and therefore fails to recognise and denounce the injustice. To clarify these two concepts, it is helpful to consider two examples, both taken from the 2011 movie *The Help*, directed by Tate Taylor. The film is set in the US in 1963. One of the African-American service women protagonists, Aibileen Clark, is falsely accused of stealing three silver pieces of cutlery from the house where she works. Although Aibileen tries to prove her honesty by providing a (true and) plausible narrative of what happened, her testimony is not believed and the (white) landlady fires her. In this case, we can talk about witness injustice. Minny Jackson, another African-American maid, is a victim of continuous violence by her husband but has no clear perception of the injustice she is a victim of and the crime that is repeatedly committed by her husband against her, and so fails to improve her condition. She cannot put into words the injustice that she experiences; therefore, she does not consider herself as a victim. This second case falls into the category of hermeneutical injustice.[7]

Epistemic injustice is closely connected with *structural injustice*, a phenomenon which has been investigated by feminist and postcolonial scholars (Young 1990; Lu 2018). This particular kind of injustice pertains to the whole socio-political system:

> A social structure can be said to be unjust when the rules perpetuated through it persistently disadvantage some social groups vis-à-vis others. Whatever baseline is chosen to help identify structural injustice, if the injustice is to count as structural and not merely a result of unfair or unequal distribution, it must express some more persistent or deeper power-differential between social groups
>
> (Jugov and Ypi 2019).

Both forms of injustice are linked to the existence of a structural asymmetry of epistemic power: in society, some people have identities that give them an advantage in cases where credibility comes into play, while others are (consciously or unconsciously) considered as lacking in credibility by a large number of people. In processes where conflicting narratives about a given event are weighed up, epistemic injustice can play a crucial role in the fate of the victim and the accused, and the dynamics of the economy of credibility can be more relevant than the determination of factual truth.

Although Fricker focuses on the trial phase, it should be noticed that epistemic injustice can also have a significant impact in the investigative phase, in media coverage and in public reception of news about a certain criminal event. In other words, in the judgement, rather than an objective evaluation of epistemic credibility, which can be established if there is competence and sincerity in a testimony, an evaluation vitiated by the existence of negative identity-prejudicial stereotypes related to the identity of the witness prevails. This is an implicit epistemic distortion (bias) which may be potentially harmful for the members of marginalised groups and for the groups as such, because instances of "persistent and systematic" epistemic injustice reinforce and perpetuate the systemic marginalisation and discrimination of the whole group (ibid.: 28).

Generalising from the case of testimonial injustice, we could say that in the process of formation of public opinion the members of marginalised groups experience *dialogic injustice*, that means that they are not considered as equal partners in the exchange of information or opinions which lead to the construction of public opinion. They lack the reputation and credibility – and very often the self-esteem – needed to actively take part in discussions concerning the political good. Because of hermeneutical injustice, very often a person who is unjustly marginalised in the public sphere fails to recognise it as an injustice and therefore is unable to react to the injustice. In a similar situation, the person is not 'epistemically aware', but her/his capacity of analysing reality and of acting toward its transformation is reduced because of partial or total 'epistemic opacity' (ibid.: 14–17). Overcoming dialogic injustice is especially challenging, since the contemporary public sphere presents significant obstacles to the participation of members of discriminated and marginalised groups on conditions of equality. In addition to the perceived credibility deficit and the self-censorship that this might bring about, the technological tools and skills needed to access the public sphere on a regular basis, the considerable time needed to acquire reliable information, the difficulty in identifying trustworthy epistemic authorities and the diffusion of discriminatory discourses and narratives, combined with the unbridled resort to hate speech, are some of the challenges ahead. Perhaps the first action needed in order to start a transformative process for changing the public sphere and making it more in line with the principles of liberty and equality is to organise collective action and activate epistemic solidarity in order to influence the formation of public opinion.

Conclusion

Looking at the socio-political implications of epistemic injustice, it is important to notice how it is linked to the unequal distribution of power within the society and how it harms the lives of the marginalised members, not only during police investigation or trials, but in how it reproduces and strengthens their condition of marginalisation and oppression. In particular, this chapter showed that credibility deficits due to negative-identity stereotypes affect members of marginalised groups even when they take part in any public discussion or when they abstain from participating because they think their opinion would not be heard. In analogy with the epistemic injustice, this phenomenon could be called dialogic injustice. The persistent and systematic credibility deficit, together with the lack of time, technological devices and skills, explains why often members of the marginalised groups tend not to enter the public sphere or, when they do so, they do not participate on an equal foot – as Fricker notes, identity power "at once constructs and *distorts* who the subject really is," conditioning her/his own understanding of the self (Fricker 2007: 55).

It is important to point out that the absence or silence of marginalised people within the public sphere has a negative impact not only for their individual lives, but also for the formation of public opinion – which, as seen in the first section of the chapter, matters when it comes to supporting candidates for government positions. Public opinion emerges from the exchange of views about politically relevant issues; if the number of opinions is reduced, the diagnosis of the relevant problems and the search for viable solutions will be based on partial evidence and reflect the interests of a part of the society.

Notes

1 In the final part of his seminal work, Habermas maintains that the public sphere as he defines it has been functioning for a relatively short period in history – from the rise of the *bourgeoisie* during the 18th century to its crisis, which emerged by the half of the 20th century – and that it would have entered a situation of crisis with the advent of globalised capitalism and the simultaneous processes of depoliticisation/cooptation of labour, culture, and education. According to Habermas, public opinion would be more and more politically irrelevant or prey of the manipulations of the powerful actors of the market. Nonetheless, the concept of the public sphere – analysed, criticised, and reassessed – from many perspectives is still widely used by sociologists as well as by political philosophers not only for reflecting about the past, but also about the present (cfr. Fraser 1990; Calhoun 1992; Benhabib 1997; Palano 2020). For a critical reappraisal of the significance of Habermas' contribution for the debate, see Genscher (2006).

2 For a brief reconstruction of the main features of the debate on the conceptualisation of the public sphere for the digital era, see Casadei (2014).

3 As Antonio Gramsci (2014) pointed out, looking at the experience of the coming to power of the Fascist party in Italy during the 1920s, the progressive construction of political consensus requires the widespread dissemination within the public sphere of ideas and ideals (elements which combine to form a worldview, or a comprehensive political doctrine). The final goal is to acquire cultural hegemony and maximise consensus, eventually obtaining political power. Disseminating anti-democratic ideas, which implicitly undermined the principles of liberty and equality, Mussolini and his party won the democratic game and made loot of democratic institutions and laws.

4 A stimulating discussion on the evolving relationship between truth and politics emerges from the different political philosophers' contributions presented in Bistagnino and Fumagalli (2019). In particular, Antonella Besussi, Paolo Gerbaudo, and Valeria Ottonelli look from different angles at one main question that is crucial for the discussion presented

in this book: the change of the truth-authority nexus that is occurring within democratic societies. On the same topic, see also Stuart Sim's discussion of the emergence of post-truth politics and the ambiguous transformation of liberal societies towards a post-liberal condition which might entail progressive or conservative developments (Sim 2019: 139–53). Among the many recent reflections focussing especially on how post-truth affects contemporary philosophical thinking about politics, see Palano (2020) and Newman (2019).

5 The problem of peer pressure and of the effects of conformism produced by the society has been explored more in-depth in 1859 by John Stuart Mill, who looked at its effects both on the cultural and political domain. In the latter, the concept of the law of opinion was translated into that of the tyranny of the majority, in which a democratic majority forces its will on the minority. For a reading of the history of political thought from the perspective of a theory of public opinion, see Noelle-Neumann (1980).

6 Locke presents another thought-provoking idea: the diffusion of certain opinions is (also) a matter of fashion. This means that widely held opinions are more likely to be publicly stated than extravagant opinions. Moreover, as happens with any fashion, there is at least one trend-setter, who, consciously or unconsciously, triggers the diffusion of a certain opinion.

7 In both cases, the discrimination is intersectional: both Aibileen and Minny are victims of discrimination for at least three reasons: because they are African American, because they are women, because they belong to the working class. For a discussion on how intersectionality works for epistemic injustice, see Hill Collins (2017). See Medina (2017) for a discussion of the different forms of hermeneutical injustice.

References

Benhabib, S. (1997) 'The embattled public sphere: Hannah Arendt, Jürgen Habermas and beyond', *Theoria* 44: 1–24.

Bistagnino, G., C. Fumagalli (eds) (2019) *Fake news, post-verità e politica*, Fondazione Feltrinelli ebook.

Calhoun, C. (1992) 'Introduction: Habermas and the public sphere', in: Id. (ed.), *Habermas and the Public Sphere*, Cambridge, MA – London: MIT Press, 1–50.

Casadei, T. (2014) 'La democrazia nell'era di Internet: la filosofia politica di Pierre Lévy e il dibattito contemporaneo sulle reti digitali', *Filosofia Politica* XXVIII(1): 143–54.

Dewey, J. (1927) *The Public and Its Problems*, New York: Holt.

Fraser, N. (1990), 'Rethinking the public sphere: A contribution to the critique of actually existing democracy', *Social Text* 25–6: 56–80.

Fish, S. (1994) *There's No Such Thing as Free Speech . . . and It's a Good Thing Too*, New York: Oxford University Press.

Forst, R. (2014) *Justification and Critique: Towards a Critical Theory of Politics*, Cambridge: Polity Press.

Fricker, M. (2007) *Epistemic Injustice: Power and the Ethics of Knowing*, Oxford: Oxford University Press.

Gaus, G. (1999) 'Reasonable pluralism and the domain of the political: How the weaknesses of John Rawls's political liberalism can be overcome by a justificatory liberalism', *Inquiry. An Interdisciplinary Journal of Philosophy* 42(2): 259–84.

Gaus, G. (2011) *The Order of Public Reason: A Theory of Freedom and Morality in a Diverse and Bounded World*, Cambridge: Cambridge University Press.

Gestrich, A. (2006), 'The public sphere and the Habermas debate', *German History* 24(3): 413–30.

Goodin, R.E, K. Spiekermann (2015) 'Epistemic solidarity as a political strategy', *Episteme* 12(4): 439–57.

Gramsci, A. (2014) *Quaderni dal Carcere*, edizione critica dell'Istituto Gramsci a cura di Valentino Gerratana, Torino: Einaudi.

Habermas, J. (1991) (or. ed. 1962) *The Structural Transformation of the Public Sphere: An Inquiry into a Category of Bourgeois Society*, Cambridge, MA: MIT Press.

Habermas, J. (1995) 'Reconciliation through the public use of reason: Remarks on John Rawls's political liberalism', *The Journal of Philosophy* 92(3): 109–31.

Hill Collins, P. (2017) 'Intersectionality and epistemic injustice', in: J. Kidd, J. Medina, G. Pohlhaus (eds), *The Routledge Handbook of Epistemic Injustice*, Abingdon – New York: Routledge, 115–24.

Jugov, T., L. Ypi (2019) 'Structural injustice, Epistemic opacity, and the responsibilities of the Oppressed', *Journal of Social Philosophy* 50(1): 7–27.

Kant, I. (1784) 'An answer to the question: What is enlightenment?', in Id. (1996), *Practical Philosophy* translated and edited by M.J. Gregor, Cambridge – New York: Cambridge University Press.

Locke, J. (1690) *Essay Concerning Human Understanding*, Book II, chapter 28, 7–13.

Lu, C. (2018) 'Responsibility, structural injustice, and structural transformation', *Ethics & Global Politics* 11(1): 42–57.

MacKinnon, C. (1993) *Only Words*, Cambridge, MA: Harvard University Press.

Medina, J. (2017) 'Varieties of hermeneutical injustice', in: J. Kidd, J. Medina, G. Pohlhaus (eds), *The Routledge Handbook of Epistemic Injustice*, Abingdon – New York: Routledge, 115–24.

Newman, S. (2019) 'Post-truth and the crisis of the political', *Soft Power* 6(2): 91–108.

Nguyen, C.T. (2018) 'Echo chambers and epistemic bubbles', *Episteme*, https://doi.org/10.1017/epi.2018.32

Noelle-Neumann, E. (1980) (or. ed. 1974) *The Spiral of Silence: Public Opinion – Our Social Skin*, Chicago: University of Chicago Press.

Palano, D. (2020) *La fine del pubblico e la nuova polarizzazione*, Brescia: Scholé.

Prijić-Samaržija, S. (2018) *Democracy and Truth. The Conflict Between Political and Epistemic Virtues*, Udine: Mimesis.

Rawls, J. (1993) *Political Liberalism*, New York: Columbia University Press.

Rawls, J. (1999) 'The idea of public reason revisited', in Id., *The Law of Peoples*, Cambridge, MA: Harvard University Press.

Salmon, C. (2013) *La cérémonie cannibale: De la performance politique*, Paris: Librairie Arthème Fayard.

Sim, S. (2019) *Post-Truth, Scepticism & Power*, Cham: Palgrave Macmillan.

Sunstein, C.R. (2009) *Going to Extremes: How Like Minds Unite and Divide*, Oxford: Oxford University Press.

Waldron, J. (2012) *The Harm in Hate Speech*, Cambridge, MA – London: Harvard University Press.

Young I.M. (1990) *Justice and the Politics of Difference*, Princeton: Princeton University Press.

3

INCORPORATING INTERSECTIONALITY INTO AI ETHICS

Liza Ireni-Saban and Maya Sherman

Introduction

AI-driven devices have increasingly become mediators of our social, cultural, economic, and political interactions (Rahwan et al. 2019). Therefore, the appearance of more nuanced and sophisticated aspects of diversity, as well as the emergence of new ways of thinking about identity, require that the notion of AI ethics establishes new tools and strategies for supporting and advocating diversity and inclusion in contemporary AI developments.

Within this notion, it is important to mention that the growing impact of AI technologies in human reality has enabled the strengthening of the scope and scale of disinformation campaigns and fake news dissemination. The scholastic perception of AI in the disinformation sphere is ambiguous, as it accelerates data propagation online via social media platforms but also enables us to automatically detect false content and remove it at a relatively high level of accuracy. Consequently, the alleged nexus between AI and disinformation has amplified the ethical discourse regarding AI usage and implementation.

Moral philosophers and applied ethicists often suggest using a 'deontological' approach to moral norms as a starting point, while others suggest a teleological (consequentialist) ethical approach concerned with whether an action or decision leading to an outcome is good or bad to the society as a whole (Gomila and Amengual 2009). It is argued that for AI as machines with a more limited degree of autonomy, a rule-based approach may be sufficient, or even endorsed. Since these theories are based on explicit rules and norms external to the real world in which they are to be applied, they have limited practical value. In other words, these theories are, from a philosophical perspective, unable to fully explicate the complexities of moral considerations as these complexities are experienced in the world. This chapter suggests that deontological and utilitarian ethics cannot fully address the challenges that AI technological innovations pose to contemporary ethics, which require a more flexible, context-dependent, and case-based approach to morality.

For that, we offer to investigate how AI ethics can be enhanced through critical engagement with intersectionality. Ethical perspectives on intersectionality share normative ideals toward social justice. It is suggested that the development of AI systems has brought forth, with unprecedented clarity, the socioeconomic differences across all identities, and the recognition that the experience of privilege based on social groups and locations is fluid rather than static. The junction of intersectionality theory, ethics, and AI allows us to conceptualise and harness, for the first time, patterns of inequality as redistribution of power, and privilege is a core tenant of deliberative intersectional engagement. An intersectional framework for AI ethics can be used to scrutinise the algorithmic biases and issues rooted in existing AI-driven systems and applications.

This chapter is organised as follows. In the first section, we introduce the theoretical lens of intersectionality and then move to a discussion on how AI ethics can benefit from insights of intersectionality. Finally, we present concrete examples depicting the challenges of AI to underscore the new and different insights intersectionality generates for AI ethics.

Intersectionality: A new paradigm

Albeit a fledgling analytical paradigm, the evolution and development of intersectionality have been long in the making. The concept of intersectionality owes its origins to the feminist movement, which sought to develop a more comprehensive and encompassing schema for recognising and appreciating the converging forces of oppression that affect women on different dimensions of identity. Intersectionality arose from the works by women of colour in the 1960s as a means for expressing the limitations of feminist theory to accurately portray the struggle of women across racial and class boundaries (Samuels and Ross-Sheriff 2008: 5). In fact, in its most essential form, intersectionality theory reflects a criticism of second-wave feminism, which was the preeminent mode of feminism in the 1960s in the US. The second wave of feminism expanded the goals set out by the first wave, which primarily took up the causes of universal suffrage and repealing discriminatory legislation. The second wave of feminism focussed on broadening gender equality by addressing issues like sexuality, domestic rights, reproductive rights, and *de facto* discrimination (Burkett 2016). However, opponents of the emergent movement asserted that the second wave favoured a historical narrative that "whitewashed" and homogenised the feminist struggle and ignored different voices of minority communities such as black women and queer women (Orr and Braithwaite 2012).

The term intersectionality was first coined by Kimberlé Crenshaw (1989), who used the metaphor of intersecting roads to illuminate how differing levels of oppression on the grounds of gender and race interact with one another to create a new and unique experience of marginalisation and discrimination. Crenshaw offered the concept of intersectionality as redress to the singularity and unidimensional consideration of the phenomenon of oppression. Although intersectionality theory's origin is rooted in the struggle of women of colour for recognition within the big-tent feminist movement of the 60s and 70s, as Samuels and Ross-Sheriff (2008: 5) note, it went even further and called on scholars to acknowledge that "for many women of colour, their feminist efforts are simultaneously embedded and woven into their efforts against racism, classism, and other threats to their access to equal opportunities and social justice" (ibid: 5).

The modern definition of intersectionality holds that "gender cannot be used as a single analytic frame without also exploring how issues of race, migration status, history, and social class, in particular, come to bear on one's experience as a woman" (ibid.). Consequently, the methodological approaches of researchers and academics employing an intersectional technique mandate that they explore the multitude of "the overlapping and mutually reinforcing" systems of oppression. The once-accepted universalist approach to the constructs of "woman" or "feminist" as singular, all-encompassing experiences has now been replaced by analyses that consider women as whole individuals whose identities may be informed and reinforced by multiple interlocking structures of oppression. Finally, current intellectual pursuits of intersectional analyses incorporate not only mutually reinforcing systems of oppression but also the myriad of privileges which also inform the feminist experience. Since intersectionality was developed in reaction to and as a criticism of the tendency of feminist narratives to whitewash oppression experiences, the development of intersectionality theory evolved alongside the dialectical evolution of the feminist movement.

Just as important as the subjects of intersectional analysis, one may mention the relationship between the myriad of systems of oppression and structures of power which interact to shape intersectional experiences. This paradigm states that just like different identity layers coalesce to create unique experiences of discrimination, the structures of domination which perpetuate systems of inequality inherently intersect with axes of oppression. Fellows and Razack (1998: 335) suggest this mechanism functions as mutually assimilated networks that "rely on one another" so that "systems of oppression could not be accomplished without gender and racial hierarchies; imperialism could not function without class exploitation, sexism, heterosexism and so on."

In addition to the myriad of levels of oppression, intersectionality acknowledges the varying degrees of privilege, which also inform the unique experiences of women. These privileges occur naturally from the deficits created by the structures of oppression. An example of the symbiotic relationship between privilege and oppression is evident in Samuels and Ross-Sheriff's research (2008) on black or multiracial young children adopted by white parents. Since there was a largely socioeconomic, ethnic, and cultural homogeneity within the interviewees' neighbourhoods, they were inevitably a racial minority in their own community. Here, the interplay between privilege (socioeconomic status) and racism creates the very incubator in which the biracial children experience a unique system of oppression.

Being a biracial or trans-racial adoptee in a white community meant that their experience of structural oppression was unique to their particular set of privileges and oppressions. Although having two white parents meant that they were transmitting the dominant group's culture, and this ultimately allowed the adoptees to operate largely in white race contexts comfortably, few of them reported dating in high school because their appearance was devalued by the dominant "Eurocentric images of beauty" (ibid: 7). In this example, we see that while being raised in a white community endows certain privileges, it simultaneously and inherently creates situations of alienation. Samuels and Ross-Sheriff's anecdotal research demonstrates that not only is oppression an integral component of intersectionality, but in order to fully appreciate the impact of systems of oppression on individual experiences, academics must also consider the networks of privilege.

Although intersectionality theory is intrinsically related to the feminist movement, its methodological contribution reaches far beyond feminist debates. The intersectional methodology encourages researchers to investigate the multilayered effects of experiences of oppression in their unique and varied manifestations. This is a departure from traditional methodological techniques that often pursue a parsimonious quality in both variables and conclusions. The epistemological approaches to the different forms of oppression to this point had been discrete in nature – the exploration of patriarchy was a distinct pursuit, and therefore experiences of victimisation from institutionalised sexism were interpreted as if they existed in a vacuum. Likewise, racism was investigated as a stand-alone system of persecution. In many ways, the methodological inadequacies of research had a deterministic effect on the analysis of the experiences of oppression themselves. Crenshaw put forth that a "single-axis framework" failed to consider the compounded marginalisation that women of colour faced. Crenshaw's foundation offered a theoretical schema for understanding not only bi-level discrimination but multiple layers of oppression (Dhamoon 2011: 231). This differed dramatically from the traditional single-group approach, which attempted to investigate the phenomena "by analyzing the intersection of a subset of dimensions of multiple categories" (McCall 2005: 1787). Single subject design is a subgroup of the categorical comparative approach, and it is useful for streamlining analytical spaces which can become convoluted when multiple groups and levels are compared side-by-side (ibid: 1786). For example, if researchers want to compare specific ethnic groups within broader racial classifications – e.g. Vietnamese, Thai, and Laos subgroups within the more general grouping of Southeast Asian – it becomes necessary to restrict the breadth of analysis for the sake of comprehension. Therefore, a study of this nature would consider these Southeast Asian subgroups independently of gender or class. Naturally, this method has its advantages as it allows researchers to simplify the subject of their research for 'big picture analysis'. However, the very aspect which makes this analytical framework attractive – the ability to disregard intermediary layers of analysis – is also its pitfall. Research which isolates its subject from the multitude of intervening affective torrents of complexity is ultimately reductionist in its analysis.

The Southeast Asian research ignored gender and class in the investigation of Southeast Asians in order to maintain simplicity. However, an intersectionality study of Southeast Asians would employ an ecological model to identify the integrative nature of the myriad of Southeast Asian experiences. For example, it would distinguish the experience of the middle-class, Vietnamese man in comparison to the low-class, Vietnamese woman, and so on and so forth. Although this type of multidimensional, 'interaction effect' modelling makes the research exponentially more complicated, it is arguably the only design equipped to deal with the confluence of multiple systems of oppression and paradigms of power. Furthermore, intersectionality allows researchers to investigate "how multiple and differing sets of interactive processes and systems vary at different levels of life and across time and space" (Dhamoon 2011: 237). This ideation of subjects of oppression and power as dynamic, multilayered, and complex is, of course, antipodal to the positivist tradition which assumes that all phenomena are fixed, generalisable, and fully conceivable. Instead, intersectionality values unpacking and evaluating processes and systems (ibid.).

An additional methodological approach that strives to satisfy this call for complexity is called anti-categorical complexity (McCall 2005). This approach deconstructs the reductionist analytical categories, maintaining that social life and social structures are infinitely too complex and dynamic to be fettered by fixed categorical definitions. Anti-categorical complexity has been applied in deconstructing once-finite categories such as sexuality or gender and examining how they are instead socially designed constructs (Fotopoulou 2012). The anti-categorical approach which emerged from the critique moved to the tendency of white, bigtent feminists to frame women and gender as essential and homogenous categories embracing all women (McCall 2005). The crux of the criticism was that no solitary category could aptly account for the host of experiences of the individual. Additionally, most intersectional experiences did not fit cleanly into these socially constructed categories. Critics also highlighted that the pro-categorisation camp was reinforcing inequalities by excluding experiences that did not fit comfortably into the socially eschewed constructions.

The second approach to complexity is referred to as inter-categorical complexity (ibid.). This approach accepts the socially constructed categories *pro tempore* as a provisional means for tracking the disparities between social groups along multiple lines of intersecting identities, dimensions, and power structures. The fundamental assumption of inter-categorical complexity is that although the relationships and interstices of inequality are fluid and ever-shifting, by adopting categories and simultaneously considering their intersections, researchers are afforded the leverage granted by comparative modes of analysis (Bauerband and Galupo 2014). McCall (2005) puts forth intra-categorical complexity as a last approach to the complexity of intersectionality. Intra-categorical complexity falls somewhere in-between the anti-categorical approach, which wholeheartedly rejects categorisation, and the inter-categorical approach, which provisionally excepts categories, if only for the purpose of comparative analysis. The intra-categorical complexity approach appreciates the methodological potential of categories but tends to focus on "neglected points of intersection – 'people whose identity crosses the boundaries of traditionally constructed groups'" (Dill 2002: 5).

The contribution of intersectional methodologies, although they introduced new obstacles, was paramount for the poststructuralist movement and the larger popular movement to deconstruct social boundaries as a means of combating inequality. Ultimately, the methodological subgroups challenged the then-predominant mode of analysis which suffered from a blatant failure to reflect the *loci* of neglected experiences of oppression.

However, the introduction of intersectionality methodology shall include its limitations. Although intersectionality offers a versatile theoretical basis for researching modes of oppression and privilege, it has simultaneously complicated methods of analysis. In fact, the defining aspect of the methodology of intersectionality studies is "the complexity that arises when the subject of analysis expands to include multiple dimensions of social life" (McCall 2005: 1772). Indeed, most scholars have accepted the legitimacy and necessity of intersectionality to convey the intricacies of intersecting experiences of real life, and yet, intersectionality remains underdeveloped without a practical application.

More recently, Reyes (2017) and Moore (2012) have advocated intersectionality as a useful lens for the shifted focus of code-switching to marginalised factions within society. This stream of research is especially relevant to the social identity framework of intersectionality underlying AI ethics offered in this chapter. We elucidate the development of AI by reference to the basic premises of social interactionism. They include the following assumptions: capturing reality by individuals is a social construction; individuals constantly affect one another as through their interaction over time; individuals are capable of deliberate actions and the way they interact with others and within ourselves; individuals define what exists and decide how to act accordingly. Therefore, we consider social identity as "the self as reflexively understood by the individual in terms of his or her biography" (Giddens 1991: 244). It should be noted that while one's concept of the self may remain consistent over time, social identity is more familiar with a process of shifts and adjustments as it plays out in everyday life. Through a process of social interaction, we work to communicate our identities to others, while we attribute identities to them (Charon 2010; Gecas 1982).

Contemporary issues of AI technologies in the ethical sphere

Following the discussion presented above, we will elaborate upon the contemporary issues relating to AI technologies in the ethical sphere. Although there is no one accepted definition of AI, various scholars address the machine's ability to exhibit intelligent behaviour, react to the environment, and learn from it (Samoili et al. 2020). Nonetheless, this chapter will focus on the AI's twofold functionality within the disinformation sphere. Meaning, AI as referable to complex algorithmic models allowing to automatically generate, detect, and mitigate false contents online and impact on public opinion.

Broadly, there are several disinformation-related affairs that revolve around the evolution of AI technologies. Among these incidents, various scholars highlight the Cambridge Analytica affair and its hidden manipulation of ad targeting (Cadwalladr and Graham-Harrison 2018).[1] Other notable disinformation affairs are the incitement of ethnic cleansing in Myanmar[2] and the emergence of masses of fake Russian accounts (Eidelson 2018; Bloomberg Editorial Board 2017; Weise 2017). Notably, these affairs highlight the unprecedented implications of AI bias in the international community.

One of the most prevalent bias types is the historical bias, which represents an existing inequality and socio-technical issues within the data generation process (Suresh and Guttag 2019). An example emerged in 2015, when academic and media sources revealed a clear gender bias within Google search engine. In the incident, the top results for 'CEO' image search showed mainly photos of men, and when the search engine identified the seeking user as female, it displayed fewer ads for executive positions. It represents a historical bias, since this kind of bias reflects an existing gender inequality in society (Suresh and Guttag 2019; Yapo and Weiss 2018).

The omnipresent spread of AI in the cybernetic and physical spheres has led to a broader discourse regarding its ethical implications. On the one hand, AI-driven interfaces enable the analysis of large sums of data and provide us with a tailored user experience and enhanced personalisation processes, as seen within various fields such as autonomous driving, predictive policing, and language translation. On the other hand, one must consider the ambiguous outcomes of AI usage from the legal, social, and ethical perspectives (Doshi-Velez et al. 2017; Amodei et al. 2016; Sculley et al. 2014; Bostrom 2003; McCarthy 1960). Interesting to note, a Deloitte survey of tech executives in the US (Loucks, Davenport, and Schatsky 2018) highlighted the potential ethical risks of AI, with emphasis on its falsification of contents and imagery and the increase of algorithmic bias.

Therefore, discussing AI and disinformation requires a deeper analysis of the notion of *algorithmic bias*, including its different types as well as its main sources. The literature raises various bias types, which depend both on the data itself and on the user. Data bias may be the result of technical or computational matters, an inappropriate algorithmic deployment, or a user misinterpretation of the algorithm's outputs. Danks and London (2017) highlight notable computational sources of bias, such as the training data bias, and algorithmic processing. For instance, the input data used may be biased and lead to biased outputs for the algorithmic tasks. Furthermore, the algorithm itself may be biased, such as in cases of a statistically biased estimator within the algorithm.

As AI-driven algorithms have become highly prevalent in our decision-making processes and day-to-day practices, the risk of generating discriminatory and offensive outputs rises significantly (ibid). In addition to bias and fake news, one can mention fairness and privacy violations as significant ethical loopholes. From the privacy prism, there is an ongoing conflict between data privacy and efficacy, since AI-driven models enable access to large sums of data and allows it to be analysed with greater accuracy (Whittlestone et al. 2019; Zimmerman 2018). For instance, AI technologies such as sensor networks, social media tracking, and facial recognition enable us to broaden surveillance practices and threaten one's right to privacy. These technologies in use may lead to discriminatory patterns and stigmatisation, even without one's explicit consent or knowledge (Whittaker et al. 2018). In this regard, Mehrabi et al. (2019) suggest:

> like people, algorithms are vulnerable to biases that render their decisions 'unfair' [. . .] fairness is the absence of any prejudice or favoritism toward an individual or a group based on their inherent or acquired characteristics. Thus, an unfair algorithm is one whose decisions are skewed toward a particular group of people
>
> (ibid.: 1).

For example, in the US one can count numerous incidents in which AI usage has exacerbated existing social inequalities, such as the gender bias of the Amazon recruiting tool (Dastin 2018) and the notable discriminatory credit algorithms against minority groups (Bartlett et al. 2018; Glantz and Martinez 2018; Waddell 2016). In addition, the ProPublica investigation found that the risk tool used to create Florida risk scores was biased against black people and led to discriminatory outputs (Angwin et al. 2016).

Interesting to note, several scholars argue that these ethical constraints differ between cultures and languages. For example, Facebook misinterpreted a Palestinian man's post in 2017 due to a machine-translation error, which led to his arrest by the Israeli police (Hagerty and Rubinov 2019; Hern 2017). Therefore, this type of linguistic error might lead to significant implications due to cultural controversies. Another linguistic incident occurred within the ambiguous translation of the 'like' button, leading to algorithmic filtering of an indigenous collective in Brazil (Ochigame and Holston 2016).[3] As Ochigame and Holston suggested in their article on this incident: "AI principles are inevitably value-laden terms, dense with significance. Such terms, even when thoughtfully translated, can have distinct connotations and meanings in different cultures" (ibid.: 10).

Following the cultural perspective, Hagerty and Rubinov (2019) demonstrate that low- and middle-income countries might be more susceptible to ethical implications and not necessarily receive the potential AI benefits. This notion was highlighted by the World Economic Forum (2018), as it claimed that developing countries are prone to great risks of discriminatory patterns when using machine learning methods. From the policy perspective, Hashmi et al. (2019) emphasise the increasing ambiguity revolving around the AI implementation in the public service: "The advent of AI raises a host of ethical issues, related to moral, legal, economic and social aspects of our societies and government officials face challenges and choices pertaining to how to apply AI technologies in the public sector and in governance strategies" (ibid.: 8).

In this regard, it is important to point out that the AI ability to manipulate and deceive human users online turns these ethical issues in the data-driven age into inherent loopholes, which should be properly moderated by policy makers and regulators. Interesting to mention, several scholars consider AI as a countermeasure against the rise of fake news on social media platforms due to its ability to identify fake bot accounts and automated fact-checking. Moreover, current deep learning models enable the enhancement of text classification and analysis of online content (Sharma et al. 2019). According to Facebook, AI tools are responsible for the removal of 99.5% of terrorist-related content and 98.5% of fake accounts (Marsden and Meyer 2019; Kertysova 2018).

Nonetheless, one must consider the monumental contribution of AI to the creation and propagation of disinformation campaigns. With the advance of machine learning and NLP, one's ability to automatically generate content and tailor it for unique users is amplified, and therefore AI enhances the microtargeting of vulnerable audiences (Kertysova 2018). As a result, AI represents an offensive instrument, and not only a defensive component in the detection processes of online bots (Yang et al. 2019). Remian (2019) highlights this dual perception of AI in the disinformation sphere: "Artificial intelligence has the potential to be used for the spread of disinformation, propaganda, and the shaping of social and cultural values. As with security, AI may play a role in both delivering and protecting from misinformation and attempts to manipulate" (ibid.: 31).

These polar AI functions have been analysed by several scholars who look at the AI's ability to create deepfakes, which undermine the authenticity of visual videos (Strickland 2018; Güera and Delp 2018). All the above demonstrates the symbiotic relationships between AI and disinformation, when despite the existing defensive function against bots and automation, one may abuse the inherent AI bias to spread incitement and manipulation within weakened populations.

Conclusion: enhancing AI ethics through intersectionality

According to the review of intersectionality research across disciplinary domains, positioning intersectionality as having an important role within AI ethics highlights two key areas of concern: advocating diversity and inclusion. First, advocating diversity requires that vulnerable and disadvantaged groups and outgroup members of various identity groups will gain a fair and just treatment by ensuring that AI bias will be moderated and diminished.

Second, promoting inclusion contributes to a more appropriate and just representation of disadvantaged individuals' involvement in designing and engineering AI and algorithmic systems. Within AI ethics, the principle of inclusion encourages remedying "situations where people are believed to have been silenced or excluded from decisions which would directly affect them and which do not acknowledge their knowledge or expertise" (Townsend 2013: 36).

Due to the vast phenomena of fake news propagation, there is an urgent need to provide a relevant ethical approach to dealing with the existing technical and moral issues arising from AI technologies. Intersectionality serves as a proper and adaptable mechanism for coping with the AI-augmented falsification processes.

Notes

1 The Cambridge Analytica affair is a salient event in the disinformation sphere, in which a data analytics firm was accused of profiling 50 million Facebook users and targeting them with tailored content in order to influence political outcomes in the 2016 US presidential elections. For a more detailed discussion, see Rehman (2019).
2 In 2017, the publication of fake news imagery has aggravated the conflict between Rohingya Muslims and the military in Rakhine State in Myanmar. This false propaganda fueled the radical hatred of Rohingya Muslims and violence in Myanmar. This incident shows how Facebook has transformed into a platform for hate speech and online falsehoods aimed at vulnerable minorities. For greater detail, see Miles (2018) and Ratcliffe (2017).
3 This algorithmic incident is the result of a semantic loophole of Facebook's 'like' button. The anthropologists Rodrigo Ochigame and James Holston scrutinised an indigenous collective in Mato Grosso do Sul, which uses Facebook as its primary outreach vector to the public and often posts videos against the violence of private agribusiness militias. However, in the Portuguese dialect in Brazil, the button is semantically translated as 'enjoy', and therefore, various users decided not to 'like' certain posts of violence and oppression. As a result, Facebook's filtering algorithm reduced the group's visibility and raised the challenges of the land right activists to spread their message online. For further detail, see Ochigame and Holston (2016).

References

Amodei, D., C. Olah, J. Steinhardt, P. Christiano, J. Schulman, D. Mané (2016) 'Concrete problems in AI safety', *arXiv preprint arXiv:1606.06565*.

Angwin, J., J. Larson, S. Mattu, L. Kirchner (2016) 'Machine bias', *ProPublica*, 23 May 2016, www.propublica.org/article/machine-bias-risk-assessments-in-criminal-sentencing (last consulted 6 May 2020).

Bartlett, R., A. Morse, R. Stanton, N. Wallace (2018) 'Consumer-lending discrimination in the era of fintech', unpublished working paper, Berkeley, University of California.

Bauerband, L.A., M.P. Galupo (2014) 'The gender identity reflection and rumination scale: Development and psychometric evaluation', *Journal of Counseling & Development* 92(2): 219–31.

Bloomberg Editorial Board (2017) 'Think the U.S. has a Facebook problem? Look to Asia', *Bloomberg*, 22 October 2017, https://bloom.bg/3diIXDq (last consulted 6 May 2020).

Bostrom, N. (2003) 'Ethical issues in advanced artificial intelligence', *Science Fiction and Philosophy: From Time Travel to Superintelligence*, 277–84.

Burkett, E. (2016) 'Women's movement', in *Encyclopædia Britannica*, www.britannica.com/topic/womens-movement (last consulted 6 May 2020).

Cadwalladr, C., E. Graham-Harrison (2018) 'Revealed: 50 million Facebook profiles harvested for Cambridge Analytica in major data breach', *The Guardian*, 17 March 2018, www.theguardian.com/news/2018/mar/17/cambridge-analytica-facebook-influence-us-election (last consulted 6 May 2020).

Charon, J.M. (2010) *Symbolic Interactionism: An Introduction, an Interpretation, an Integration*, Upper Saddle River: Prentice Hall.

Crenshaw, K. (1989) 'Demarginalizing the intersection of race and sex: A black feminist critique of antidiscrimination doctrine, feminist theory, and antiracist politics', *University of Chicago Legal Forum*: 139–67.

Danks, D., A.J. London (2017) 'Algorithmic bias in autonomous systems', *IJCAI:*. 4691–97.

Dastin, J. (2018) 'Amazon scraps secret AI recruiting tool that showed bias against women', *Reuters,* 10 October 2018, www.reuters.com/article/us-amazon-com-jobs-automation-insight/amazon-scraps-secret-ai-recruiting-tool-that-showed-bias-against-women-idUSKCN1MK08G (last consulted 6 May 2020).

Dhamoon, R.K. (2011) 'Considerations on mainstreaming intersectionality', *Political Research Quarterly* 64(1): 230–43.

Dill, B.T. (2002) 'Work at the intersections of race, gender, ethnicity, and other dimensions of difference in higher education', *Connections: Newsletter of the Consortium on Race, Gender, and Ethnicity',* 5–7, www.crge.umd.edu/publications/news.pdf (last consulted 6 May 2020).

Doshi-Velez, F., M. Kortz, R. Budish, C. Bavitz, S. Gershman, D. O'Brien, S. Shieber, J. Waldo, D. Weinberger, A. Wood (2017) 'Accountability of AI under the law: The role of explanation', *arXiv preprint arXiv:1711.01134.*

Eidelson, J. (2018) 'Facebook tools are used to screen out older job seekers, lawsuit claims', *Bloomberg*, 29 May 2018, https://bloom.bg/3dm0avO (last consulted 6 May 2020).

Fellows, M.L., S. Razack (1998) 'The race to innocence: Confronting hierarchical relations among women', *Journal of Gender, Race and Justice* 1: 335–52.

Fotopoulou, A. (2012) 'Intersectionality queer studies and hybridity: Methodological frameworks for social research', *Journal of International Women's Studies* 13(2): 19–32.

Gecas, V. (1982) 'The self-concept', *Annual Review of Sociology* 8(1): 1–33.

Giddens, A. (1991) *Modernity and Self-Identity: Self and Society in the Late Modern Age.* Stanford, California: Stanford University Press.

Glantz, A., E. Martinez (2018) 'Kept out: How banks block people of color from home-ownership', *Associated Press*, 15 February 2018, https://apnews.com/ae4b40a720b74ad8a9b0bfe65f7a9c29 (last consulted 4 May 2020).

Gomila, A., A. Amengual (2009) 'Moral emotions for autonomous agents', in J. Vallverdu, D. Casacuberta (eds), *Handbook of Research on Synthetic Emotions and Sociable Robotics: New Applications in Affective Computing and Artificial Intelligence*, New York: IGI Global, 161–74.

Güera, D., E.J. Delp (2018) 'Deepfake video detection using recurrent neural networks', in *2018 15th IEEE International Conference on Advanced Video and Signal Based Surveillance (AVSS)*, 1–6.

Hagerty, A., I. Rubinov (2019) 'Global AI ethics: A review of the social impacts and ethical implications of artificial intelligence', *arXiv preprint arXiv:1907.07892.*

Hashmi, A., R. Lalwani, A. Senatore, C. Perricos (2019) 'AI Ethics: The Next Big Thing in Government', Anticipating the impact of AI Ethics within the Public Sector. *Deloitte Global & World Government Summit.*

Hern, A. (2017) 'Facebook translates "good morning" into "attack them", leading to arrest', *The Guardian*, 24 October 2017, www.theguardian.com/technology/2017/oct/24/facebook-palestine-israel-translates-good-morning-attack-them-arrest (last consulted 6 May 2020).

Kertysova, K. (2018) 'Artificial intelligence and disinformation', *Security and Human Rights* 29(1–4): 55–81.

Loucks, J., T. Davenport, D. Schatsky (2018) 'State of AI in the enterprise', 2nd edition, *Deloitte Insights,* www2.deloitte.com/content/dam/insights/us/articles/4780_State-of-AI-in-the-enterprise/DI_State-of-AI-in-the-enterprise-2nd-ed.pdf.

McCall, L. (2005) 'The complexity of intersectionality', *Signs: Journal of Women in Culture and Society* 30(3): 1771–800.

McCarthy, J. (1960) *Programs With Common Sense*, RLE and MIT Computation Center, 300–07.

Marsden, C., T. Meyer (2019) 'Regulating disinformation with artificial intelligence: Effects of disinformation initiatives on freedom of expression and media pluralism', *European Parliamentary Research Service*, 1–72.

Mehrabi, N., Morstatter, F., Saxena, N., Lerman, K., and Galstyan, A. (2019) 'A survey on bias and fairness in machine learning', *arXiv preprint arXiv:1908.09635*.

Miles, T. (2018) 'U.N. investigators cite Facebook role in Myanmar crisis', *Reuters*, 12 March 2018, https://uk.reuters.com/article/us-myanmar-rohingya-facebook/u-n-investigators-cite-facebook-role-in-myanmar-crisis-idUKKCN1GO2PN (last consulted 13 June 2020).

Moore, M.R. (2012) 'Intersectionality and the study of black, sexual minority women', *Gender & Society* 26(1): 33–39.

Ochigame, R., J. Holston, (2016) 'Filtering dissent: Social media and land struggles in Brazil', *New Left Review* (99): 85–110.

Orr, C.M., A. Braithwaite (eds) (2012) *Rethinking Women's and Gender Studies*, London: Routledge.

Ratcliffe, R. (2017) 'Fake news images add fuel to fire in Myanmar, after more than 400 deaths', *The Guardian*, 5 September 2017, www.theguardian.com/global-development/2017/sep/05/fake-news-images-add-fuel-to-fire-in-myanmar-after-more-than-400-deaths (last consulted 13 June 2020).

Rahwan, I., Cebrian, M., Obradovich, N., Bongard, J., Bonnefon, J.F., Breazeal, C., Crandall, J.W., Christakis, N.A., Couzin, I.D., Jackson, M.O., et al. (2019) 'Machine behaviour', *Nature* 568(7753): 477.

Rehman, I. (2019) 'Facebook-Cambridge Analytica data harvesting: What you need to know', *Library Philosophy and Practice* (e-journal) 2497.

Remian, D. (2019) 'Augmenting education: Ethical considerations for incorporating artificial intelligence in education', *University of Massachusetts at Boston*, https://scholarworks.umb.edu/cgi/viewcontent.cgi?article=1054&context=instruction_capstone (last consulted 6 May 2020).

Reyes, P. (2017) 'Working life inequalities: Do we need intersectionality?', *Society, Health & Vulnerability* 8(1): 14–18.

Samoili, S., M.L. Cobo, E. Gomez, G. De Prato, F. Martinez-Plumed., B. Delipetrev (2020) *AI Watch. Defining Artificial Intelligence. Towards an Operational Definition and Taxonomy of Artificial Intelligence* (No. JRC118163). Joint Research Centre (Seville site).

Samuels, G.M., F. Ross-Sheriff, (2008) 'Identity, oppression and power: Feminisms and intersectionality theory', *Affilia* 23(5): 5–9.

Sculley, D., G. Holt, D. Golovin, E. Davydov, T. Phillips, D. Ebner, V. Chaudhary, M. Young (2014) 'Machine learning: The high interest credit card of technical debt', *SE4ML: Software Engineering for Machine Learning, NIPS'14.*

Sharma, K., F. Qian, H. Jiang, N. Ruchansky, M. Zhang, Y. Liu (2019) 'Combating fake news: A survey on identification and mitigation techniques', *ACM Transactions on Intelligent Systems and Technology (TIST)* 10(3): 1–42.

Strickland, E. (2018) 'AI-human partnerships tackle "fake news": Machine learning can get you only so far – then human judgment is required', *IEEE Spectrum*, 55(9): 12–13.

Suresh, H., J.V. Guttag (2019) 'A framework for understanding unintended consequences of machine learning', *arXiv preprint arXiv:1901.10002.*

Townsend, A.M. (2013) *Smart Cities: Big Data, Civic Hackers, and the Quest for a New Utopia*, New York: W.W. Norton & Company.

Waddell, K. (2016) 'How algorithms can bring down minorities' credit scores', *The Atlantic*, 2 December 2016, www.theatlantic.com/technology/archive/2016/12/how-algorithms-can-bring-down-minorities-credit-scores/509333 (last consulted 4 May 2020).

Weise, E. (2017) 'Russian fake accounts showed posts to 126 Million Facebook users', *USA TODAY*.

Whittaker, M., K. Crawford, R. Dobbe, G. Fried, E. Kaziunas, V. Mathur, O. Schwartz (2018) *AI Now Report 2018*, New York University: AI Now Institute.

Whittlestone, J., R. Nyrup, A. Alexandrova, S. Cave (2019) 'The role and limits of principles in AI ethics: Towards a focus on tensions', Paper presented at the AAAI/ACM Conference on AI, Ethics, and Society, Honolulu, HI, USA, https://doi.org/10.1145/3306618.3314289.

World Economic Forum (2018) 'How to prevent discriminatory outcomes in machine learning', *Global Future Council on Human Rights 2016–2018*, www3.weforum.org/docs/WEF_40065_White_Paper_How_to_Prevent_Discriminatory_Outcomes_in_Machine_Learning.pdf (last consulted 4 May 2020).

Yang, K.C., O. Varol, C.A. Davis, E. Ferrara, A. Flammini, F. Menczer (2019) 'Arming the public with artificial intelligence to counter social bots', *Human Behavior and Emerging Technologies* 1(1): 48–61.

Yapo, A., J. Weiss (2018) 'Ethical implications of bias in machine learning', *Proceedings of the 51st Hawaii International Conference on System Sciences*, 5365–72.

Zimmerman, M. (2018) *Teaching AI: Exploring New Frontiers for Learning*, Portland, OR: International Society for Technology in Education.

4

HOW POST-TRUTH POLITICS TRANSFORMED AND SHAPED THE OUTCOME OF THE 2016 BREXIT REFERENDUM

Jennifer Cassidy

Introduction

One could affirm that the examination of how post-truth politics transformed and shaped the outcome of the 2016 Brexit referendum would never have gained substantial traction as a research question, were it not for the new communication age we now reside in. Especially during times of heightened divides, be it a domestic election, an international political crisis, or a national referendum, popular online platforms such as Twitter, Facebook, Instagram, etc., are widely used by many politicians and commentators.

The case of the Brexit referendum is very much worthy of examination since, over the past 20 years, the UK has crafted a strong reputation for the quality and standard of its scientific advisory system. This is demonstrated by its array of top-level scientific advisers in almost every department of government and by its willingness to experiment and innovate with new approaches to evidence-based policy-making. But this seemingly progressive arc towards the ever-greater uptake of evidence and expertise in decision-making took a major knock in June 2016 with the result of the referendum on UK membership of the European Union (EU) swinging narrowly, 52% to 48%, in favour of Brexit. This happened despite a mountain of evidence and the near unanimous support of experts of all kinds for remaining in the EU. The referendum process itself was marred by exaggeration and the use of dubious facts and figures on both sides, but particularly by the Leave campaign, and by accusations of outside interference in the democratic process by a range of murky and unaccountable actors, including the Russian government.

In short, Brexit quickly became one of the 'ideal-type' case studies when it came to discussing, exploring, and examining the role of post-truth politics in the 21st century. Therefore, the aim and contribution of this chapter to the domains of diplomatic and information studies is three-fold: (1) to expose and confront the historical and present nature of 'post-truth' politics; (2) to shed light onto often overlooked tools and mechanisms used in the 21st century playbook of 'post-truth' politics, with a focus on critical junctures of empirical cases such as the 2016 UK Brexit referendum that allows us to reconceptualise post-truth in an age of real-time governance; (3) to suggest that the current political climate of post-truth politics requires the broad promotion of a sort of *democratic capability*. Drawing on the epistemic aspects of Amartya Sen's work – particularly on his concept of positional objectivity (Sen 1993) – we will discuss and answer the questions, how, why, and should it matter to the challenges faced by our historic, but new, theatre of post-truth politics. This chapter, therefore, aims to offer conceptual and practical tools to help us understand and combat the rise of post-truth politics in the 21st century.

The overall aim and the interconnected character of these three questions is to examine, expand, and illustrate through empirical moments in the Brexit campaign, that the Leave vote was motivated by post-truth politics. Indeed, not only motivated by it, but actively engaging in its processes, mechanisms, and emotional control of the people it sought to influence. This chapter aims to support these claims by developing an argument about the extent to which the UK's Brexit referendum has been shaped and is continuing to be shaped by post-truth politics. As a starting point for the discussion, the definition of post-truth as a type of "politics which seeks to emit messages into the public domain which will lead to emotionally charged reactions, with the goal of having them spread widely and without concern for the accuracy of the messages provided" will be investigated in detail (Marshall and Drieschova 2018: 89).

Post-truth: Historic concept, new theatre

We want to find out if post-truth politics is simply a historical concept. Even if history is repeating itself, this does not mean that we have not learned the lessons of the past. It simply means that we have not recognised its patterns when they returned. That is the reason why we study it, analyse it, explore it, dissect it, scrutinise it: so we can recognise it now, as it is today. This new face of 'post-truth politics' is currently akin to a bad artist seeking to help the police by drawing the suspect who has just robbed them. In short, the suspect's features are ill-defined, and it is almost impossible to distinguish most, if any, detail. Yet despite these challenges surrounding clarity, this does not mean the police should stop looking for the suspect in question. As we have already seen with the new techniques and methods of 21st century post-truth politics, the ones we have seen being actively used by politicians, active governments, and organisations alike come with profuse damage and impact to our national and international governing sphere.

The impact is not simply in the damage done to the elections due to fraud, but due to the polarisation of public discourse, and lies in the inability of many citizens who, bombarded with the terms 'fake news' or 'crisis actors' by governing politics daily, perhaps justifiably simply do not know what to believe anymore. And there is, of course, the issue of credibility. Despite the fact that the term 'post-truth politics' is nothing new, as academics we need to reconceptualise and contextualise it. That is, we need to analyse, individually and comparatively, all new methods, tools, technologies that are challenging, impacting on, and shaping our international political system.

Background to the 2016 Brexit referendum

The UK's referendum on the EU membership, now infamously known as Brexit, took place on 23 June 2016 in the United Kingdom and Gibraltar. The purpose of the vote was to gauge support for the country either remaining a member of, or leaving, the EU. Campaigning began immediately after the referendum's calling. This is a very important thing to note, and indeed a strong variable of why the referendum, its outcome, and continued controversy remain today. Just like the historical roots of post-truth, the tensions connected to the Leave-Remain confrontation within the society and Parliament itself, were and are nothing new. These tensions have presented themselves in many forms since the UK's official entry into the Union in 1973. Yet now the vote had been called. Divides established. With allegiances by politicians and citizens alike, largely known to all.

The underpinnings of controversy, discontentment, and attachment with the UK's continued relationship with Europe are clearly illustrated by a number of instructive examples. First, in 2013 Prime Minister David Cameron stated clearly in a long-awaited speech that if the Conservatives won the next election they would seek to renegotiate the UK's relationship with the EU. Then, by the end of 2017 they would give the British people the "simple choice" between staying in the EU under those terms or leaving the EU. It would be a few years before the election was called, but the seeds of division had certainly not only been sown, but watered. Second, was the creation and emergence of clearly divisive institutions. One such example was the creation of a cross-party, formal group campaigning for Britain to *Remain* a member, called 'Britain Stronger in Europe'. It was established in October 2015, directly after 'The European Union Referendum Bill' was unveiled in the Queen's Speech.[1] Alongside this, there was the creation of two groups promoting exit which sought to be the official *Leave* campaign: Leave.EU (supported by most of the UKIP party, led by Nigel Farage), and Vote Leave (supported by Conservative party Eurosceptics). The Electoral Commission announced on 13 April 2016 that Vote Leave was the official Leave campaign. The UK government's official position was to support the remain option. Before we examine, dissect, and explore the tactics, methods, and challenges faced in a post-truth world in an age of real-time governance, we will conclude by stating what many of us now know to be objective truth. On 23 June 2016, the people of the United Kingdom and Gibraltar were asked: "Should the United Kingdom remain a member of the European Union or leave the European Union?" There were two boxes to answer this complex question: 1) Remain a member of the EU; 2) Leave the EU. The referendum turnout was 71.8%, with more than 30 million people voting. Leave won by 51.9%, while Remain got 48.1% of the votes.

It should be noted that the Brexit campaign was distinct from other referendums or elections because of the unexpectedly high turnout from voters who do not normally vote in British general elections. The voter turnout for the referendum was 72.2%. This is in comparison to a 68.8% turnout in the 2017 General Election, a 66.2% turnout in 2015, 65.1% in 2010, 61.4% in 2005, and 59.4 % in 2001. The referendum was the first major UK vote since 1997 to go above a 70% turnout (Electoral Commission 2017). From YouGov polls, to newspapers, all predicted a Remain vote. The higher turnout, particularly in the north of England, contributed to the miscalculation of the result (YouGov 2016a). People who did not normally vote decided to vote in the EU referendum, and they voted leave. This raises the question of what motivated the high turnout and what led the 1.2 million previously disengaged voters to find the leave message more convincing.

As noted by Moore and Ramsay (2017: 168), the Brexit campaign was "divisive, antagonistic and hyper-partisan (. . .)", as its continued divisive nature and polarising rhetoric, which characterised both sides, has shown before, during and after the vote. To quote Hannah Marshall and Alena Drieschova (2018: 94), "Both 'sides' actively accused each other of dishonesty and scaremongering, and these discursive tactics did little to inspire trust from the public in the debate as a whole. Rather, the public were encouraged to distrust political messaging based on constant back and forth accusations and disparagement." And yet, the two key messages the public remembered from the referendum campaign – that we will directly discuss and examine throughout this chapter – were components of key arguments belonging to Brexiters.

1. "The UK sends £350 m per week to the EU"
2. "Net migration to the UK had hit 333,000"

These key themes of focus during the referendum became rapidly and increasingly significant in the national press (Joyce 2017). The narrative of the Vote Leave campaign, a narrative based on these two core themes, gained traction, and not simply gained traction, but embedded itself in the hearts and minds of the public in a way the Vote Remain campaign did not. What the referendum therefore clearly demonstrated was that two single pieces of pro-Leave campaign material – (1) a slogan on the side of a bus fallaciously implying that leaving the EU would necessarily free up £350 million a week for the NHS; and (2) a poster stating that Britain was at its "Breaking Point" purportedly due to an influx of migrants – proved highly controversial but successful in winning the hearts and minds of the British public.

It is worth noting, particularly in a chapter dedicated to post-truth politics, that these themes, slogans, arenas of deception that won the heart of many voters were at best misleading, and at worst outright false. For example, the Leave side's widely publicised claim that

> [t]he UK sends £350 million per week to the EU is wrong. [. . .]. This figure does not include the rebate, or discount on what the UK has to pay.

In 2014, the UK would have paid £18.8 billion without the rebate but ended up paying £14.4 billion. The estimate for 2015 is £12.9 billion. This is £248 million per week, or £35 million per day

(FullFact 2016b).

Yet, in an opinion poll conducted by "Whatukthinks" (2016c), asking the question "Is It True or False That Britain Sends £350 Million a Week to the European Union?", 47% of respondents thought the former message was accurate (Whatukthinks 2016c). These examples point once again directly to the central thesis at play here: the influence that post-truth politics had on the UK's Brexit 2016 referendum. In the next section, we will examine these cases and sketch the 'key post-truth moment' which ultimately and arguably shaped the voting outcome, not to say the future of Ireland and the resources and agenda setting power of the EU for the next three years.

The NHS bus poster

The now-infamous NHS bus was deployed by Vote Leave, the official campaign group for Brexit as designated by the Electoral Commission. It stated: "We send the EU £350 million a week, let's fund our NHS instead". In defence of this propagandistic slogan, or at best highly misleading statement, many Leave campaigners have argued that they simply used the figure of "the cost of an NHS hospital". The Leave campaigners justified their claims further, stating that the stark slogan was necessary in order to illustrate how expensive remaining in the EU was. Conversely, those standing firmly on the side of Remain, presented the argument that by using this slogan, the Leave side was presenting misleading and false information. Not only did they contend that such an act was morally objectionable, but that the consequence of this act would be momentous for the whole campaign. Their fears proved to be well-founded. The slogan sought to have appeared to convince many voters that Brexit would necessarily free up £350 million to spend on the NHS. Leave campaigners have consistently backed away from this claim since the vote (Griffin 2016).

Indeed, there have been some preliminary challenges to the use of the image. For example, the Advertising Standards Agency received 374 complaints.[2] A group called Vote Leave Watch was formed with the single aim of holding the government and groups like Vote Leave accountable. They also sought to force the government, and as many Leave voters as possible, to admit that the bus was misleading. The group regularly brought up suggestions that the referendum ought to be repeated because of the dishonesty of the Leave side, and the belief that "the leave side won because they . . . promised something that does not exist" (Rothstein 2016).

It is true that calculating the cost of EU membership for any country, let alone the UK, is a complicated task; however, the claim showed on the bus was inaccurate by any reasonable measure. A naïve defence of the Leave campaign emerged that because the figure was hard to reach, thus they went for the best possible figure for their cause. To quote Andrew Reid (2019) on this very point, he writes "A cynic would see it as a lie designed to convince voters of a simple untruth." Such an interpretation would "seem inadequate, especially given that the statements of key Leavers and commentators on the campaign suggest more subtle and nuanced motivations." Dominic Cummings, the political operative who acted as the campaign chief for Vote Leave, also noted in a personal blog that: "Pundits and MPs kept saying 'why isn't Leave arguing about the economy and living standards'. They did not realise that for millions of people, £350m/NHS was about the economy and living standards . . . It was clearly the most effective argument . . . with almost every demographic" (Cummings 2017).

It should be noted that Cummings' journal entry was not intended as a tool for convincing the people of his commitment to his 'truth'. Instead, he denoted in tone and contested ideas to the aged-old act of telling "compelling stories"; in this case, connecting the EU to a general dissatisfaction with the economic state of the country (ibid.). The idea behind the slogan on the bus was arguably on reflection, to exploit a widespread prejudicial belief about the costs of EU membership, deviating the public's attention from considering its benefits. As Shipman puts it in his account of the campaign, "[e]very time there was a row about the size of the cost to taxpayers of EU membership, it simply reinforced in voters' minds that there was a high cost" (2017: 259). As Reid (2019) writes so clearly: "The idea here was that as soon as any Remainer responded to the NHS bus with a response of the kind: 'actually, EU membership costs £X million instead', they were already on the back foot because they were talking about costs not benefits." Indeed, in a post-truth environment, none of these asserted points depended upon people being convinced of the specifics of the claim. Despite this, acts of this nature, falsehoods (whether contested or not) spread like wildfire through a nation, and are proved to have damaging effects on democratic discourse by 'muddying the waters' in factual deliberations.

The key axes in the 2016 Brexit referendum can therefore be thought of as an example of what Yale philosopher Jason Stanley calls "undermining propaganda". This refers explicitly to acts of speech that involve "erecting difficult epistemic obstacles to recognising tendencies of goals to misalign with certain ideals" (2015: 57). The idea itself of "undermining propaganda" is applied broadly to the study and analysis of Stanley's work, referring in many instances to the deeper ideological or moral commitments that underpin society. We can arguably draw on its conceptual underpinnings to examine the factual deliberations in this case. The key phrase in Stanley's definition is "epistemic obstacle". We can link this clearly to the NHS bus being introduced as such an obstacle, due to resulting consequences for members of the public to establish what the costs and benefits of Brexit truly were. The act of the slogan, and the creators behind it, did this by wrongly problematising the epistemic authority of some bodies and figures, and as a practical consequence eroded the set of common factual reference points in what should have been a fair, free, and open debate.

The words of Andrew Reid (2019) on his work on Brexit and disinformation conclude it best when he writes:

> The troublesome function of the NHS bus, then, is to neutralise the discussion of the economic impact of Brexit by increasing scepticism of all factual claims, and presenting all predictions as equally bad. It nullifies the issue by reducing the set of commonly accepted, relevant facts and therefore making it harder to come to judgments about the effects of different policy option.

The Breaking Point

The Vote Leave campaign was led by individuals like Boris Johnson, who created a narrative, or historic reflection, of re-establishing Britain as a global hegemon. Indeed, many of the key leaders of the Vote Leave campaign articulated a narrative of British nationalism that was more insular and Powellite in tone. At the centre of this perspective lay the concerns and increasingly stirred fears surrounding immigration. According to Nigel Farage, the figurehead of Leave.EU, the EU had done insurmountable harm to Britain by facilitating uncontrolled immigration: "Open-door migration has suppressed wages in the unskilled labour market, meant that living standards have failed and that life has become a lot tougher for so many in our country" (Farage 2016).

This actively and carefully constructed narrative creation played on people's fears, whilst weaving perfectly into the nationalistic tone of 'Britain First' that the Leave leaders were exalting across the country. Comparatively, this is not too dissimilar from what is occurring across the water, where we see slogans of 'Make America Great Again' capture voters in their droves, changing the landscape of the 'shining city on the hill' forever. Furthermore, according to what Virdee and McGeever (2018: 1806) argued in their article entitled 'Racism, Crisis, Brexit': "the construction of the migrant as economic threat to the domestic working class was married to a second set of representations that understood the migrant as security threat to the British population." The authors conceptualise this process of misrepresentation into three distinct elements. First, the terrorist attacks in France and Belgium and the onset of the migration to Europe of displaced Syrians and others escaping war in 2015 and 2016 were purposely linked by Farage to make the argument that the "EU's open borders make us less safe" (Farage 2016). This created a gateway for him to imply that by getting "our borders back, our democracy back" through exiting the EU we could also restrict the entry of such "undesirables" and make Britain safe again. According to Virdee and McGeever, the second element integral to this construction of migrant as security threat was that leaving the EU would effectively prevent refugees from seeking sanctuary in Britain, since it would no longer be party to the EU's central benefit freedom of movement between EU member countries. This argument reached its zenith with the creation and posting of the Leave.EU's "Breaking Point" poster. A poster showing Middle Eastern refugees queuing at Europe's borders. The subheading read: "We must break free of the EU and take back control." This was a message of 'island retreat' (Winter 2016): if Britons voted Leave, they could successfully keep such people from entering the country. Finally, the third component conceptualised by Virdee and McGeever on the nature of post-truth narratives of racism, was highlighted when recently arrived migrants were alleged to have committed a series of sexual assaults in Germany – the EU country which had accepted almost a million refugees in 2015. Leave.EU "campaigners contributed to a moral panic that understood refugees as 'sexual predators', reinforcing the message that remaining in the EU would place British women at risk" (Virdee and McGeever 2018).

While the Breaking Point poster, and the integrated narratives and acts surrounding it, may lie at the margins of hateful speech, they have not been subject to criminal sanction. However, according to Reid (2019), although it may not be regarded as hate speech, he justifiably writes:

> [Such acts do] transgress the norms expected of political campaigns because of [their] potential effect on political voice, so should be subject to limited sanctions within this sphere. Such hate speech can, when practiced by political elites, have harmful effects on the democratic forum, and as such might be subject to measures that amount to partial censorship when practised by political parties or recognised campaign groups.

Indeed, although recent migrants would not have been able to vote in the referendum, it remains evident that their voice is valuable and warranted on this subject matter. Thus, the persistent use of nationalistic and discriminatory imagery like that of the Breaking Point poster by those in positions of relative authority can, and do, invariably cause a shift in public perceptions that leads to certain target groups being silenced, their voices not being heard, or when they do choose to speak up, the consequence is that they are not taken seriously in political deliberation. This amounts to what is deemed a *de facto* exclusion from the process of deliberating over laws due to the loss of an effective political voice.

These consequences have been discussed in other works on hate speech, for example when Jeremy Waldron, in a very influential essay on the issue, discusses "group defamation" or "group libel" (2012: 39–40). This is the spreading of mistruths about groups within society that causes them to be treated unfairly or unjustly. Waldron also emphasises the loss of dignity that occurs when we are frequently part of a "disfiguring social environment" where such ideas persist (ibid.: 117). The "disfiguring social environment" I am concerned with is one that contributes to a situation where some are treated as inferiors in political deliberation: this undermines their effective political voice, because it causes others to treat them differently. The loss of esteem in the eyes of other citizens can lead to members of groups targeted by hate speech suffering epistemic injustices (Fricker 2007). One manifestation of epistemic injustice is "testimonial injustice", the injustice of being doubted as a knower, or of having the integrity of one's knowledge challenged (ibid.: 1–2). Minority groups can therefore be forced to deliberate as if such stereotypes are true in order to facilitate a productive dialogue; Stanley uses the example of African Americans who end up participating in debates where racist stereotypes that they are lazy or violent persist (2015: 163). This analysis can be applied to the Breaking Point poster, which depicts non-white citizens and recent migrants as a hostile force, and a drain on the national community's resources. Deliberating when these traits are assumed at the outset means accepting disrespectful falsehoods, and a concurrent loss of perceived credibility. It is to deliberate at a disadvantage, as it requires the internalisation of a norm that the speaker is less trustworthy or able. Such is the world of post-truth politics in the 21st century.

Conclusion

By referring to Brexit as an 'ideal-type' case study for understanding the mechanisms and the effects of post-truth politics, the chapter has shown how the Vote Leave campaign around the referendum was built on misleading narratives that touched very sensitive topics such as the NHS and immigration control. Though neither of the two topics are directly related to EU membership, some of their aspects were exaggerated and framed as though they were part of the overall discourse on permanence in the EU.

The referendum was a quite divisive political instrument *per se*, and by appealing directly to the people it favoured the diffusion of manipulated narratives for pure electoral ends, neglecting the overall good of the country. The themes, slogans, and arenas of deception that won the heart of many voters were misleading at best, and outright false at worst. Furthermore, both factions actively accused each other of dishonesty and scaremongering, nourishing confusion and distrust among the electorate. And yet, the two key messages the public remembered from the referendum campaign were components of key arguments belonging to Brexiters: a slogan on the side of a bus that fallaciously implied that leaving the EU would as a direct consequence free up money for the NHS, and a poster stating that Britain was at a "Breaking Point" because of an immigration crisis. The path to the Brexit referendum was thus riddled with difficult epistemic obstacles that kept the people from understanding the real implications of their choice.

Notes

1 Before the vote had cleared Parliament and become law, the serving government twice saw off attempts in the House of Lords to lower the proposed voting age in the in-out poll to 16. Their attempts, as history has shown us, proved unsuccessful.
2 See Parker (2016) for a journalistic discussion of this issue.

References

Arendt, H. (1973) *The Origins of Totalitarianism*, New York: Harcourt Brace Jovanovich.
Crilley, R. (2018) 'Book review essay: International relations in the age of "post-truth" politics', *International Affairs* 94(2): 417–25.

Cummings, D. (2016) 'On the referendum #2.0: The campaign, physics and data science – Vote Leave's "Voter Intention Collection System" (VICS) now available for all', https://dominiccummings.com/2016/10/29/on-the-referendum-20-the-campaign-physics-and-data-science-voteleaves-voter-intention-collection-system-vics-now-available-for-all/ (last consulted 5 May 2020).

DeCesare, A. (2018) 'Working toward transpositional objectivity: The promotion of democratic capability for an age of post-truth politics', *The Good Society* 26(2–3): 218–33.

The Economist (2016) 'Art of the lie', 10 September 2016, www.economist.com/leaders/2016/09/10/art-of-the-lie (last consulted 5 May 2020).

Electoral Commission (2017) 'The 2016 EU referendum: Report on the regulation of campaigners at the referendum on the UK's membership of the European Union held on 23 June 2016', www.electoralcommission.org.uk.

European Commission (2018) 'Tackling online disinformation: Commission proposes an EU-wide code of practice', http://europa.eu/rapid/press-release_IP-1 8-337 0 _en.htm (last consulted 5 May 2020).

Farage, N. (2016) 'NIGEL FARAGE: Why we must vote LEAVE in the EU referendum', *Express*, 21 June 2016, www.express.co.uk/comment/expresscomment/681776/nigel-farage-eu-referendum-brexit-vote-leave-independence-ukip.

Fricker, M. (2007) *Epistemic Injustice: Power and the Ethics of Knowing*, Oxford: Oxford University Press.

FullFact (2016a) 'False claims, forecasts, and the EU referendum', https://fullfact.org/europe/false-claims-forecasts-eu-referendum/ (last consulted 5 May 2020).

FullFact (2016b) 'Vote leave "facts" leaflet: Membership fee', https://fullfact.org/europe/vote-leave-facts-leaflet-membership-fee/ (last consulted 5 May 2020).

Griffin, A. (2016) 'Brexit: Vote leave wipes NHS £350 claim . . .', *The Independent*, 27 June 2016, www.independent.co.uk/news/uk/home-news/brexit-vote-leave-wipes-nhs-350m-claim-and-rest-of-its-website-after-eu-referendum-a7105546.html (last consulted 5 May 2020).

Joyce, B. (2017) 'Brexit data: Post-truth politics and the EU referendum', *Brandwatch*, www.brandwatch.com/blog/react-brexit-post-truth/.

Marshall, H., A. Drieschova (2018) 'Post-truth politics in the UK's Brexit referendum', *New Perspectives Interdisciplinary Journal of Central & East European Politics and International Relations* 26(3).

Moore, M., G. Ramsay (2017) 'UK media coverage of the 2016 EU referendum campaign', *Centre for the Study of Media, Communication and Power.*

Parker, G. (2016) 'The ASA can't regulate political advertisements. Here's why', *The Guardian*, 6 July 2016, www.theguardian.com/commentisfree/2016/jul/06/advertising-standards-authority-political-advertisements (last consulted 5 May 2020).

Reid, A. (2019) 'Buses and breaking point: Freedom of expression and the "Brexit" campaign', *Ethical Theory and Moral Practice* 22: 623–37.

Rothstein, B. (2016) 'It's perfectly sensible to want a second referendum. Here's why', *New Statesman*, 7 September 2016, www.newstatesman.com/politics/staggers/2016/09/its-perfectly-sensible-want-second-eu-referendum-heres-why.

Sen, A. (1993) 'Positional objectivity, *Philosophy & Public Affairs* 22(2): 126–45.

Shipman, T. (2017) *All Out War: The Full Story of Brexit* (revised edition), London: William Collins.

Stanley, J. (2015) *How Propaganda Works*, Princeton: Princeton University Press.

Virdee, S., B. McGeever (2018) 'Racism, crisis, Brexit', *Ethnic and Racial Studies* 41(10): 1802–19.

Waldron, J. (2012) *The Harm in Hate Speech*, London: Harvard University Press.

whatukthinks (2016a) 'Are politicians from both the Leave and Remain campaign mostly telling truth or lies?', https://whatukthinks.org/eu/questions/8070/ (last consulted 5 May 2020).

whatukthinks (2016b) 'How likely or unlikely do you think it is that Turkey will join the EU in the next 10 years?', https://whatukthinks.org/eu/questions/how-likely-or-unlikely-do-you-think-it-isthat-turkey-will-join-the-eu-in-the-next-10-years/ (last consulted 5 May 2020).

whatukthinks (2016c) 'Is it true or false that Britain sends £350 Million a week to the European Union?', https://whatukthinks.org/eu/questions/is-it-true-or-false-that-britain-sends-350-million-a-week-to-the-european-union/ (last consulted 5 May 2020).

whatukthinks (2016d) 'To what extent is the way you intend to vote in the EU Referendum based on your heart or your head?', https://whatukthinks.org/eu/questions/to-what-extent-is-the-way-youintend-to-vote-in-the-eu-referendum-based-on-your-heart-or-your-head/ (last consulted 5 May 2020).

whatukthinks (2016e) 'Whose opinions have influenced your decision on how to vote in the referendum?', https://whatukthinks.org/eu/questions/whose-opinions-have-influenced-yourdecision-on-how-to-vote-in-the-referendum/ (last consulted 5 May 2020).

Winter, A. (2016) 'Island retreat: On hate, violence and the murder of Jo Cox', *Open Democracy*, 20 June 2016, www.opendemocracy.net/uk/aaron-winter/island-retreat-on-hate-violence-and-murder-of-jo-cox.

Wise, D. (1973) *The Politics of Lying*, New York: Random House.

YouGov (2016a) 'Unexpectedly high turnout in Leave areas pushed the campaign to victory', 24 June 2016, https://yougov.co.uk/news/2016/06/24 /brexit-follows-close-run-campaign/ (last consulted 5 May 2020).

YouGov (2016b) 'YouGov on the day poll: Remain 52%, Leave 48%', 23 June 2016, https://yougov.co.uk/news/2016 /06/23/yougov-day-poll/ (last consulted 5 May 2020).

Younge, Gary (2016) 'Brexit: A disaster decade in the making', *The Guardian*, 30 June 2016, www.theguardian.com/politics/2016/jun/30/brexit-disaster-decades-in-the-making (last consulted 5 May 2020).

5

INFORMATION AND DEMOCRACY

Fake news as an emotional weapon

Matthew Loveless

Introduction

In the field of Political Science, the role of information – whether through education, exposure, content availability – has been taken, normatively, as a linchpin of a democratic society (Dahl 1989). A quote widely, if erroneously, attributed to Thomas Jefferson is often used to underscore this important relationship, "An educated citizenry is a vital requisite for our survival as a free people."[1] This is an intuitive and widely shared notion within Political Science, Sociology, Economics, and Psychology – as well as in popular culture. It makes intuitive sense that an individual or collection of individuals are better able to make appropriate decisions for themselves by understanding what is happening around them. In the field of politics, having both a sense of the ideological landscape and the positions of parties and their policies can only serve to improve the quality of democratic governance. Better and more information produces better individual and, in turn, collective decisions.

Yet, the evidence does not appear to bear this out. In the late 1950s, a team at the University of Michigan – Campbell, Converse, Miller, and Stokes – set out to survey the American public and to assess their political attitudes, choices, and behaviours. The resultant publication, *The American Voter* (1960), showed that Americans' political attitudes appeared to originate from such profoundly unstructured political beliefs that the authors reported a stunning lack of sophistication and rationality. Key's book, *Public Opinion and American Democracy,* the following year (1961) as well as Butler and Stokes' book, *Political Change in Britain* (1969) did little to challenge these findings, showing that, in the latter case, Americans were not unique in such under-informed political states.

Political Science has taken one of two approaches to deal with this 'discovery'. One approach has been to either say that democratic outcomes appear – at least in the aggregate – 'rational' (Page and Shapiro 1992) or to call individual political choices 'reasoned' to the extent that individuals must have some process through which information is both gathered and (more importantly) incorporated to make decisions (Lupia and McCubbins 1998). Others searched for answers at the individual level. Zaller (1992) was among the first and most influential scholars to argue that *how* individuals process information explains how they formulate their opinion but that most of the information used to do so was heuristically driven; that is, more or less directly from elites and media. In other words, internal processes and external cues compensate for low concrete and specific political knowledge in the same way that knowing *how* to do multiplication saves you from having to memorise all possible combinations of any two numbers (Lodge and McGraw 1995). Yet, and still, Americans and Europeans continue to show low levels of both political knowledge and sophisticated processing skills (Sniderman, Brody, and Tetlock 1991; Lupia, McCubbins, and Popkin 2000).

In terms of information and democracy, while attention is scarce and the ability to process information is low, the sources of information have increased. The exponential growth in the availability of information stresses the need for individuals to develop some method for sorting the growing torrent of information. In addition to the ability of legacy media to broadcast to a near comprehensive audience over the past 40 years, a (slim) majority of the world's population has had at least some access to the largest repository of collected knowledge: the Internet.[2] Yet, over precisely the same period, the once solid footing of post-war democratic institutions has begun to deteriorate. In other words, greater availability to greater absolute amounts of information does not appear to resolve the information and democracy dilemma. In fact, it appears to have made it worse.

Fake news is a key debate in this dilemma. Fake news is an emotional weapon which refers not to discrete instances or stories, but rather to the strategic effort to cloud current debates with the aim of manipulating audience's feelings to undercut any potential for collective (political) action. As increasingly recognised by the mainstream literature on political sophistication and cognition, such emotive appeals often overwhelm individuals' attempts to reason with political topics (Druckman 2012; Edelson et al. 2017; Flynn, Nyhan, and Reifler 2017; Karp, Nai, and Norris, 2018; Prior, Sood, and Khanna, 2015; Redlawsk 2002; Suhay et al. 2015). Fake news is weaponised by appealing directly to people's emotions rather than their intellect. The driving force for using and supporting fake news is to scramble and divide public opinion in order to benefit from the resultant chaos, whether financially or politically.

How fake news disrupts democracy

In addition to greater availability of information, the Internet has opened up greater opportunities for misinformation. One of its most common forms is fake news. The term 'fake news' is both specific and broad. Fake news is not propaganda or 'spin' in which a group, such as a political party, might try to reframe events so that the group is seen in a more positive light (Uscinski 2019). Fake news is similar to a hoax, in that it is a deliberately fabricated falsehood made to masquerade as truth (ibid.). Although presented as being factually accurate, fake news has little or no basis in fact (or is a dissembled fusion of bits and pieces of factual things). Its distinguishing feature is that fake news is strategically deployed with an ostensive financial incentive or damaging purpose (Walker 2018). As such, it is a weapon.

The efficacy of this weapon corresponds with the transition of citizens from passive consumers to active selectors of political cues (Prior 2007). This self-selecting exposure depends on previous patterns and goes by names that vary by discipline: selective exposure, informational congeniality, pro-attitudinal information search, or confirmation bias, *inter alia*. Simply, in a sea of information, consumers cling to what they know. In terms of searching for information, this process has led to the silo-ification of consumers, informational bubbles, filter bubbles, echo chambers in which individuals' understandings of the world are decreasingly exposed to counter-narratives, critiques, and outright challenges.

Information silo-ification originated with the idea that the information systems could be constrained from freely communicating with other information systems, i.e. operate in a silo. Applied to individuals, information silo-ification refers to a situation in which that person is unable to freely communicate with – or be exposed to – alternative information sources (Garrett 2017). Silo-ification is commonly the result of Internet search filters and histories that increasingly narrow online searches, in turn developing decreasingly varied algorithmic selectivity and thus lower exposure to other (i.e. unlike) information sources. The individual is thus increasingly constrained to an informational environment in which one's own beliefs about the world are amplified and reinforced in a closed communication system. While the various steps of the process overlap, they refer to the decrease in alternative information and the increase in the repetition and fortification of one's own worldview. In this environment, fake news finds a fertile field of targets.

Polls show that conspiracy theories and fake news are popular everywhere, including Europe, in which popular perceptions of the extent of both in the public sphere are similar if not greater than in the US (Uscinski 2018). At the same time, public attention to fake news and misinformation has grown, because of recent controversial and divisive events such as Brexit and the 2016 US presidential election (Allcott and Gentzkow 2017; Karp, Nai, and Norris 2018; Flynn, Nyhan, and Reifler 2017; Lazer et al. 2018; Lewandowsky, Ullrich, and Cook 2017). Yet, the crucial issue is less about the consumption but rather the strategic deployment of fake news as a weapon to shape politics. That is, fake news offers a means for some to circumvent a reality which disallows others' preferred outcome. For democratic politics, this is deeply problematic.

One of the core tenets of early Internet evangelism was the democratisation of voices (Dahlgren 2000; Shirky 2011; Valenzuela, Park, and Kee 2009; Ward, Gibson, and Lusoli 2003; Weber, Loumakis, and Bergman 2003; Zhang et al. 2010; Gil de Zúñiga, Jung, and Valenzuela 2012). However, this has had the unintended consequence of undermining the role of expertise. Information and data are, on their own, not equal to knowledge. There must be some process by which information and data become useable, and that process is the competent application of knowledge (i.e. expertise). The equalisation of all voices – the deterioration of expertise – does not naturally transform into a free market of ideas in which ideas compete for constituents. Not all ideas have equal standing. There must be a justifiable process for distinguishing between ideas that are allowed into the market and those that must be discounted and possibly excluded. The Internet has introduced previously unforeseen issues that have created a difficult landscape on which to fight fake news. Thus, the use of fake news finds a welcome home on the Internet as many of the traditional definitions associated with media have melted away: Who is a 'reporter'? Who is an 'expert'? What constitutes 'news'?

This atrophy of expertise corresponds to the rise of emotional politics, in which facts are allowed to be replaced by what one believes or feels to be true. There is a growing body of scholarly work that shows that knowledge – i.e. information about the world – is simply less important in determining individual choices than what individuals believe it to be (Druckman, Peterson, and Slothuus 2013; Hart and Nisbet 2012; Suhay et al. 2015; Druckman 2012; Kunda 1990; Kahan 2016; Lodge and Taber 2000; Redlawsk 2002).[3] As the distance between political sophistication and political behaviour grows, that is, as people rely less on key and reliable information sources, they tend to base political decision-making on feelings and emotions (Lau, Andersen, and Redlawsk 2008; Luskin 1987; Sniderman, Brody, and Tetlock 1991; Taber and Lodge 2006). Simply, facts have become either secondary, debatable, or ultimately inconsequential to what one believes – or feels – to be true. The loss of expertise and concomitant rise in preferring feelings to facts converge to create an environment in which fake news – as a strategic, emotional weapon – can thrive.

The implications of competing subjective realities as the basis for orienting oneself to the world are not hard to imagine. At the broadest level, it has been observed that greater numbers of citizens are acting against their own (observable) self-interest (Achen and Bartels 2016). Yet the deterioration of the ability for – small 't' – truth to outweigh fiction fits a broader pattern that has been more recently formalised. Kavanagh and Rich (2018) call this phenomenon "truth decay".[4] From the Introduction to their book, they define it as a set of four connected and observable trends (2018: 3):

1. Increasing disagreement about facts and analytical interpretations of facts and data;
2. A blurring of the line between opinion and fact;
3. The increasing relative volume, and resulting influence, of opinion and personal experience over facts;
4. Declining trust in formerly respected sources of factual information.

Each on its own represents an independent challenge to distinguishing fact from fiction (or, opinion). However, as the authors point out, it is their synergistic convergence and *strategic deployment*, with increasingly sophisticated means such as message micro-targeting in social media, that has allowed for truth decay to grow rather than be contained.

The message from Kavanagh and Rich is that, while the contest between facts, opinion, and outright fiction has a long history (in their examination, in the US, but with clear application to Europe), it is the ability to outright control information flows and target the most susceptible that distinguishes the present from previous periods. That is, fictions and opinions are used as weapons to actively challenge what may seem to be demonstrable reality. And the means most appropriate, and what Kavanagh and Rich (ibid.) cite as drivers in the US, are employing means to manipulate individuals' psychologies via cognitive processing and built-in biases (e.g. which concepts, beliefs, and rules one applies to the evaluation, Kunda 1990; Sniderman 2000) as well as their emotional profiles (i.e. galvanising individual partisanship as well as cultivating negative partisanship) in the context of greater political polarisation.

The US is not alone. The rise of regional autonomy movements, Brexit, the rise of soft dictators in Eastern Europe, the migration question, the rise of both extreme and new parties, and terrorism represent only the most visible contemporary and concurrent events that directly challenge democratic states' abilities to respond. Thus, the most insidious effect of fake news' impact on the weak bond between information and democracy is the negative downstream effect it has had on democratic political culture by de-legitimising democratic institutions.

In the context of European democratic systems, and specific to the relationship between information and democracy, the limitlessness of digital platforms in the age of fake news/disinformation is a substantive problem. At minimum, it has created more opportunities for financially or ideologically motivated producers. Non-state political actors have the capacity not only to initiate cross-national links with like-minded parties but also to roll out coordinated public 'information' campaigns.

As mentioned earlier in the chapter, early Internet evangelists promised that by making social media widely available – that is, democratic, inasmuch as anyone can participate equally – we would not only strengthen our own democratic cultures but spread democratic inspiration to non-democratic countries (Dahlgren 2000; Shirky 2011; Valenzuela, Park, and Kee 2009; Ward, Gibson, and Lusoli 2003; Weber, Loumakis, and Bergman 2003; Zhang et al. 2010; Gil de Zúñiga, Jung, and Valenzuela 2012). More Internet, more social media, more democracy. However, over the past two decades, the only coherent social media effect to have been clearly identified is the silo-ification of information provision and the construction of echo chambers. This has led, instead of in the direction of more democracy, towards greater polarisation and separation.

A broader perspective suggests that the loss of expertise and the ability to speak with one another about the same set of facts is the results of the strategic deployment of the emotional weapon of fake news. Namely, rather than simply individuals' information silo-ification, we can see a torrent of half-truths, conspiracy theory, and misdirection in the news-sphere. The strategic goal is to drown any signal with an over-abundance of noise.[5] In this way, the inundation of the public space with every variety of specious 'news' results in an emotional toll on the consumer who begins to not only question every story – true or fake – but also considers resigning from the increasingly difficult task of differentiating real from fake news altogether.[6] At the individual level, exposure to and acceptance of misinformation, fake news, and conspiracy theories correspond with individual negative epistemic motives (e.g. seeing self-reinforcing patterns where none exist) or negative existential motives (e.g. alienation, Douglas et al. 2019; Clarke 2007); a deficiency in the ability to reason clearly or apply logic (Ståhl and van Prooijen 2018); a propensity toward delusional (Freeman 2007) or dogmatic thinking (Berinsky 2012); or even experiences of hallucinations (Dagnall et al. 2015).[7] Thus, fake news is emotional in the sense that it has very real, negative individual psychological correlates, creating individual disincentives to the collective action that meaningful democratic politics requires.

Fake news threatens the democratic process in myriad ways but none so effectively as being aimed at influencing outcomes counter to popular will (Uscinski 2019). There are those who benefit from using fake news *despite* its impact on information and democracy, one might argue, precisely *because* of its impact on information and democracy. We should recognise that periods in which economics and politics merge have historically all been followed by popular anger, extreme politics, indiscriminate and racial violence, economic sluggishness, and a sapping of any collective energy to achieve anything civil or ambitious or necessary (such as punish the culprits). In addition, and possibly more disconcerting, is the discernible difference from previous periods in the increasing amount of fake news found in governmental information or national news outlets which 'benefits' from the speed at which fake news can travel (Lazer et al. 2018; Vosoughi, Roy, and Aral 2018). As such, fake news can be used in a manner resembling propaganda (Radnitz 2018; Garrett 2017; Oliver and Wood 2014; Weeks, Ardèvol-Abreu, and Gil de Zúñiga 2017; Oreskes and Conway 2010).

The motive for perpetuating quasi-truths, half-truths, non-truths is not particularly obscure. Wielding an emotional weapon to cloud clear thinking and objective observation is motivated in order to achieve an outcome. The political, social, and economic shifts that have taken place over the past several decades – such as more openly hostile and polarised politics, growing economic burdens on greater numbers of citizens – open up new, potentially unimagined areas for generating money. Conflict, uncertainty, and having mechanisms in place for extracting any remaining profits from a politically weak and divided country are the goal. Those who stand to profit (in the strictest sense of the word) understand this. As fake news sows discord and division, this keeps broad-based political action, such as redistribution or coordinated responses to climate change, at arm's length and undermines attempts to change the *status quo*. In an environment in which the strategic deployment of fake news profits political and economic incumbents, an effective 'top-down' institutional response is unlikely.

Such a development is a fair description of the three-year process of Brexit, the recent 2016 US elections, and even the immigration issue during the refugee crisis of 2015–17 in the EU. Demobilising swaths of voters by emotional attrition and mobilising others to a reality designed to distort actually existing problems accrues power to those already in place. Thus, if and when fake news floods the newssphere, the resulting inability to have even-footed discussions benefits the political and economic incumbents.

What is to be done?

Our defenses against such deployment are weak. As the Center for Media Pluralism and Media Freedom at the European University Institute in Florence has pointed out, at present, most EU countries do not have specific requirements that ensure transparency and fair play in online campaigning.[8] Attempts have been made to measure, at a minimum, the enactment/enforcement of new neutrality law(s) and active (public) efforts to confront fake news/disinformation. However, as acknowledged by the European Commission, what are national and supranational governments to do about the rise of new problems, such as the exposure of citizens to large-scale online disinformation efforts and micro-targeting of voters based on the unlawful processing of personal data?

However, there are reasons to be confident in a collective and individual response to fake news. Most news in general, including fake news, is consumed by a minority of politically active people who already have highly skewed information diets. Both conspiracy theories and fake news attract their own customers as those predisposed to them will actively search for them (Edelson et al. 2017; Clarke 2007; Uscinski, DeWitt, and Atkinson 2018; Uscinski, Klofstad, and Atkinson 2016). For an institutional response, one might propose to identify a means to regulate the Internet on impartiality, transparency, equal opportunities in media access, political advertising, and labelling political ads. At the same time, providing more information or 'facts' does not appear to have had a significant impact on the levels of political information or knowledge. Research in Political Science and Psychology has shown that providing evidence, even motivating that information with incentives, provides only occasional change and little lasting impression (see Bolsen and Druckman 2015; Lewandowsky et al. 2012; Nyhan and Reifler 2015; Prior, Sood, and Khanna 2015). More challengingly, if we are to support the idea of regulating the Internet, we require an answer to the question: who should be the arbiter of what is real and what is not? That question may be too difficult to answer and any resulting gatekeeper derived from asking this question would be too powerful.

Thus, an institutional response to fake news is likely to be ineffective and demonstrate an incomplete understanding of the problem. If this is the case, one might propose individual immunisation; that is, to cultivate individual immunisation from the intended effects of 'fake news'/disinformation through the promotion

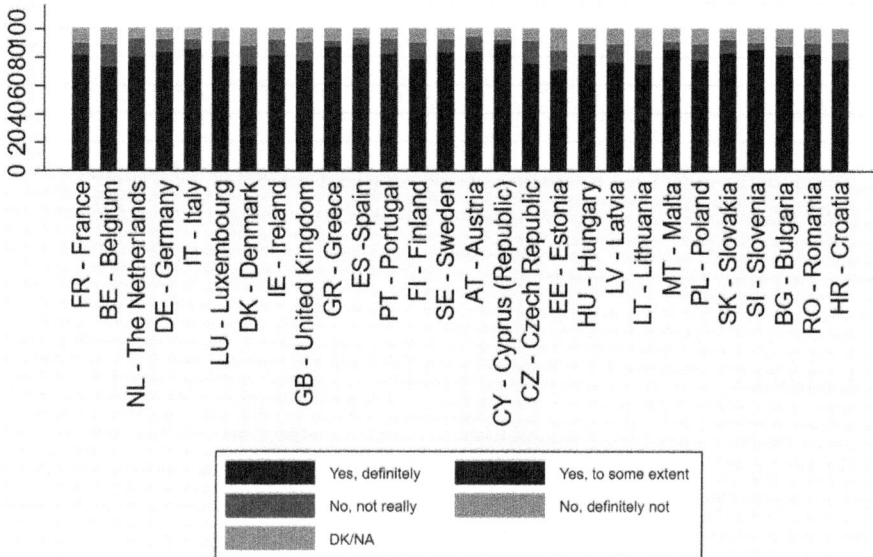

FIGURE 5.1 Is fake news a problem?[9]

Source: Eurobarometer 464: Feb–Mar 2018.

of 'media and digital literacy' courses; raising public awareness about the existence and dangers of 'fake news'/disinformation; and building human resilience (Roozenbeek and van der Linden 2018). Which may in turn help us make better policy choices.

In the case of Europe, how do citizens of the EU see fake news? Using the question, "In your opinion, is the existence of news or information that misrepresent reality, or is even false, a problem? (Response categories: Yes, definitely; Yes, to some extent; No, not really; No, definitely not) from the Eurobarometer 464 (2018, Question 4), we can see the EU citizens' answers to this question (Figure 5.1). In every country, more than 50% say, "Yes, Definitely" and "Yes, to some extent".

However, one disquieting aspect of the results in Figure 5.1 is that in Greece, Malta, Italy, Cyprus, Spain (almost Portugal), more than 50% responded *only* 'Yes, definitely". That is, despite five response categories ranging from a strong disagreement to strong agreement, the majority responded with fake news is 'definitely' a problem. Lowering the threshold to 45% of respondents, these Southern European countries are joined by Hungary, Bulgaria, Romania, Poland, Czech Republic, Slovenia, and Slovakia. Remarkably, estimating a simple model with this question as the dependent variable,[10] there is very little correlation with socio-demographic or socio-economic profiles of respondents. What is more important is the regionality of these perceived issues. Southern and Eastern European countries rank lower on measures of democracy, such as civil liberties and political rights.[11] Taken together, we can see that countries with shorter histories of democracy, less well-developed civil societies, and recent national economic struggles also have majorities (or solid pluralities) of citizens responding that fake news is a problem. This correlation is troubling. However, in the same survey, not only does every single EU member state country exhibit concern about fake news, but a vast majority of respondents report having seen fake news at least once a week,[12] and most are somewhat to very confident that they can identify it.[13] This may offer a faint positive note that not only do European citizens report that that they see a lot of fake news but rather that they think they can.

Conclusion

Fake news has exposed the disconnect between information and democracy and highlighted the importance of the relationship between feelings and information and democracy. Our normative theories of democracy require a great deal from citizens. It feels 'more correct' to say that people should be more intelligent and try to understand politics. Yet, even the amount of staggering political unsophistication previously observed in the US (Campbell et al. 1960), corresponded to a time considered by many a golden era of US politics. The use of fake news has taken advantage of the delivery system of the Internet and how it connects us to sow discord and create disunity. It exploits and amplifies our fears and concerns, appealing to how the world makes us feel rather than how it is. Yet, this strategy rests neatly on the tectonic fault lines of social, political, and economic shifts, which have been growing for the past several decades. In this way, while a challenge, it is predominantly an unfortunate covariate rather than a determinant of the problem between information and democracy.

Notes

1 While the exact quote may not have been written by Thomas Jefferson, the widely 'quoted' sentiment underpins his views on education, knowledge, and republican self-governance (*Source*: The UNESCO World Heritage Thomas Jefferson Monticello, www.monticello.org/site/research-and-collections/educated-citizenry-vital-requisite-our-survival-free-people-spurious).
2 53.6% of the global population has access to the Internet. For Europe, it is 82.5% (*Source:* International Telecommunications Union; https://www.itu.int/en/ITU-D/Statistics/Documents/facts/FactsFigures2019.pdf).
3 I call this the George Costanza defense: "It's not *fake news* if you believe it."
4 Kavanagh and Rich (2018, 4): "It is worth noting that although we are calling the phenomenon "truth decay," we are not talking about "truth" in the philosophical sense . . . Instead, . . . the term "Truth Decay" [is] a shorthand for . . . the importance of facts and fact-based analysis rather than on "truth".
5 In an interview with Michael Lewis, Steve Bannon said, "The real opposition is the media. And the way to deal with them is to flood the zone with shit." (Lewis 2018)
6 The Russian dissident and chess champion, Garry Kasparov, once commented on Soviet 'news' thusly, "the point of modern propaganda isn't only to misinform or push an agenda. It is *to exhaust your critical thinking*, to annihilate truth" (*emphasis mine*).

7 Put differently, if a citizen of a democratic country is genuinely upset by the 'news' that 'George Soros eats Christian babies', fake news is not the number one problem for that person, nor for us.

8 Their own Digital Monitor provides an inverse media pluralism measure, the Resilience Index, defined by the availability of and access to informational options. The digital monitor identifies macro- and individual-level measures that distinguish the availability of and access to informational options of the Internet by nations.

9 Data sourced from Eurobarometer Flash Survey 464, European Commission, Brussels (2018) Flash Eurobarometer 464 (Fake News and Disinformation Online). TNS opinion, Brussels [producer]. GESIS Data Archive, Cologne. ZA6934 Data file Version 1.0.0, https://doi.org/10.4232/1.13019

10 The Ordinary Least Squares (OLS) model is not shown for space but is available from the author.

11 Freedom House: Freedom in the Worlds. *Source:* https://freedomhouse.org/reports.

12 (Q3) "How often do you come across news or information that you believe misrepresent reality or is even false?" Response categories: Every day or almost every day, At least once a week, Several times a month, Seldom or Never.

13 (Q2): "How confident or not are you that you are able to identify news or information that misrepresent reality or is even false?" Response categories: Very confident, Somewhat confident, Not very confident, Not at all confident.

References

Achen, C.H., L.M. Bartels (2016) *Democracy for Realists: Why Elections Do Not Produce Responsive Government*, Princeton, NJ: Princeton University Press.

Allcott, H., M. Gentzkow (2017) 'Social media and fake news in the 2016 election', *Journal of Economic Perspectives* 31: 211–36.

Berinsky, A. (2012) 'Rumors, truths, and reality: A study of political misinformation', *MIT*, http://web.mit.edu/berinsky/www/files/rumor.pdf.

Bolsen, T., J.N. Druckman (2015) 'Counteracting the politicization of science', *Political Communication* 65(5): 745–69.

Butler, D.H.E., D.E. Stokes (1969) *Political Change in Britain: Forces Shaping Electoral Choice*, New York: St. Martin's Press.

Campbell, A., P.E. Converse, W.E. Miller, D.E. Stokes (1960) *The American Voter*, Chicago: University of Chicago Press.

Clarke, S. (2007) 'Conspiracy theories and the internet: Controlled demolition and arrested development', *Episteme* 4: 167–80.

Dagnall, N., K. Drinkwater, A. Parker, A. Denovan, M. Parton (2015) 'Conspiracy theory and cognitive style: A worldview', *Frontiers in Psychology* 6: 206.

Dahl, R.A. (1989) *Democracy and Its Critics*, New Haven: Yale University Press.

Dahlgren P. (2000) 'The Internet and the democratization of civic culture', *Political Communication,* 31(3): 329–84.

Douglas, K.M., J.E. Uscinski, R.M. Sutton, A. Cichocka, T. Nefes, C.S. Ang, F. Deravi (2019) "Understanding conspiracy theories" *Political Psychology,* 40: 3–35. doi:10.1111/pops.12568.

Downs, A. (1957) *An Economic Theory of Democracy*. London: Harper Collins.

Druckman, J.N. (2012) "The politics of motivation', *Critical Review* 24(2): 199–216.

Druckman, J.N., E. Peterson, R. Slothuus (2013) 'How elite partisan polarization affects public opinion formation', *American Political Science Review* 107(1): 57–79.

Edelson, J., A. Alduncin, C. Krewson, J.A. Sieja, J.E. Uscinski (2017) 'The effect of conspiratorial thinking and motivated reasoning on belief in election fraud', *Political Research Quarterly* 70: 933–46.

Flynn, D.J., B. Nyhan, J. Reifler (2017) "The nature and origins of misperceptions: under-standing false and unsupported beliefs about politics", *Political Psychology* 38: 127–50.

Frank, T. (2004) *What's the Matter with Kansas? How Conservatives Won the Heart of America*, New York: Metropolitan Books.

Freeman, D. (2007) 'Suspicious minds: The psychology of persecutory delusions', *Clinical Psychology Review* 27: 425–57.

Garrett, R.K. (2017) 'The "echo chamber" distraction: Disinformation campaigns are the problem, not audience fragmentation', *Journal of Applied Research in Memory and Cognition* 6: 370–76.

Gil de Zúñiga, H., N. Jung, S. Valenzuela (2012) 'Social media use for news and individuals' social capital, civic engagement and political participation, *Journal of Computer-Mediated Communication* 17(3): 319–36.

Hart, P.S., E.C. Nisbet (2012) 'Boomerang effects in science communication: How moti-vated reasoning and identity cues amplify opinion polarization about climate mitigation policies', *Communication Research* 39(6): 701–23, doi 10.1177/0093650211416646.

Kahan, D.M. (2016) 'The politically motivated reasoning paradigm, part 1: What politically motivated reasoning is and how to measure it', *Emerging Trends in the Social and Behavioral Sciences: An Interdisciplinary, Searchable, and Linkable Resource*, 1–16.

Karp, J.A., A. Nai, P. Norris (2018) 'Dial "F" for fraud: Explaining citizens suspicions about elections', *Electoral Studies* 53: 11–19.

Kavanagh, J., M.D. Rich (2018) *Truth Decay: An Initial Exploration of the Diminishing Role of Facts and Analysis in American Public Life*, Santa Monica, CA: RAND Corporation.

Key, V.O. Jr. (1961) *Public Opinion and American Democracy*, New York: Alfred A. Knopf.

Kunda, Z. (1990) 'The Case for motivated reasoning', *Psychological Bulletin* 108: 480–98, doi: 10.1037/0033-2909.108.3.480.

Lau, R., D.J. Andersen, D.P. Redlawsk (2008) 'An exploration of correct voting in recent US presidential elections', *American Journal of Political Science* 52 (2): 395–411.

Lazer, D.M.J., M.A. Baum, Y. Benkler, A.J. Berinsky, K.M. Greenhill, F. Menczer (2018) "The science of fake news', *Science* 359: 1094–96.

Lewandowsky, S., K.H.E. Ullrich, J. Cook (2017) 'Beyond misinformation: Understand-ing and coping with the 'post-truth' era', *Journal of Applied Research in Memory and Cognition* 6: 353–69.

Lewandowsky, S., K.H.E. Ullrich, C. Seifert, N. Schwarz, J. Cook (2012) 'Misinformation and its correction', *Psychological Science in the Public Interest* 13(3): 106–31.

Lewis, M. (2018) 'Has anyone seen the president?', *Bloomberg*, 9 February 2018, www.bloomberg.com/opinion/articles/2018-02-09/has-anyone-seen-the-president (last con-sulted 12 January 2020).

Lodge, M., C. Taber (2000) "Three steps toward a theory of motivated political reasoning', in: A. Lupia, M.D. McCubbins, S.L. Popkin (eds) *Elements of Reason: Cognition, Choice, and the Bounds of Rationality*, Cambridge: Cambridge University Press, 183–213.

Lodge, M., K.M. McGraw (eds) (1995) *Political Judgment: Structure and Process*, Michigan: University of Michigan Press.

Lupia, A., M.D. McCubbins (1998) *The Democratic Dilemma: Can Citizens Learn What They Need to Know?* Cambridge: Cambridge University Press.

Lupia, A., M.D. McCubbins, S.L. Popkin (eds) (2000) *Elements of Reason: Cognition, Choice, and the Bounds of Rationality*, Cambridge: Cambridge University Press.

Luskin, R.C. (1987) 'Measuring political sophistication', *American Journal of Political Science*, 856–99.

Nisbet, E.C., E. Stoycheff, K.E. Pearce (2012) 'Internet use and democratic demands: A multinational, multilevel model of internet use and citizen attitudes about democracy', *Journal of Communication* 62(2): 249–65.

Nyhan, B., J. Reifler (2015) "The effect of fact-checking on elites: A field experiment on us state legislators", *American Journal of Political Science* 59(3): 628–40.

Oliver, E., T. Wood (2014) "Conspiracy theories and the paranoid style(s) of mass opinion", *American Journal of Political Science* 58: 952–66.

Olson, M. (1965) *The Logic of Collective Action: Public Goods and the Theory of Groups*, Cambridge, MA: Harvard University Press.

Oreskes, N., E.M. Conway (2010) *Merchants of Doubt*, London: Bloomsbury Publishing.

Page, B.I., R.Y. Shapiro (1992) *The Rational Public: Fifty Years of Trends in American Policy Preferences*, Chicago: University of Chicago Press.

Prior, M. (2007) *Post-Broadcast Democracy: How Media Choice Increases Inequality in Political Involvement and Polarizes Elections*, Cambridge: Cambridge University Press.

Prior, M., G. Sood, K. Khanna (2015) "You cannot be serious: The impact of accuracy incentives on partisan bias in reports of economic perceptions", *Quarterly Journal of Political Science* 10: 489–518.

Przeworski, A., H. Teune (1970) *The Logic of Comparative Social Inquiry*, Hoboken, NJ: Wiley.

Radnitz, S. (2018) 'Why the powerful (in weak states) prefer conspiracy theories', in: J.E. Uscinski (ed.) *Conspiracy Theories and the People Who Believe Them*, New York: Oxford University Press, 347–59.

Redlawsk, D.P. (2002) 'Hot cognition or cool consideration? Testing the effects of motivated reasoning on political decision making', *Journal of Politics* 64(4): 1021–44.

Roozenbeek, J., S. van der Linden (2018) 'The fake news game: actively inoculating against the risk of misinformation', *Journal of Risk Research* 1–11, doi: 10.1080/13669877.2018.1443491.

Shirky, C. (2011) 'the political power of social media: Technology, the public sphere, and political change', *Foreign Affairs* 90(1): 28–41.

Sniderman, P.M. (2000) 'Taking sides: A fixed choice theory of political reasoning', in: A. Lupia, M.D. McCubbins, S.L. Popkin (eds) *Elements of Reason: Cognition, Choice, and the Bounds of Rationality*, Cambridge: Cambridge University Press, 67–84.

Sniderman, P.M., R.A. Brody, P.E. Tetlock (1991) *Reasoning and Choice: Explorations in Political Psychology*, Cambridge: Cambridge University Press.

Ståhl, T., J-W van Prooijen (2018) 'Epistemic rationality: Skepticism toward unfounded beliefs requires sufficient cognitive ability and motivation to be rational', *Personality and Individual Differences* 122: 155–63.

Suhay, E., J.N. Druckman, P.W. Kraft, M. Lodge, C.S. Taber (2015) 'Why people don't trust the evidence', *The Annals of the American Academy of Political and Social Science* 658(1): 121–33.

Taber, C., M. Lodge (2006) 'Motivated skepticism in the evaluation of political beliefs', *American Journal of Political Science* 50(3): 755–69.

Uscinski, J.E. (ed.) (2018) *Conspiracy Theories and the People Who Believe Them*, New York: Oxford University Press.

Uscinski, J.E. (2020) 'Conspiracy theories', in: E. Suhay, B. Grofman, A.H. Trechsel (eds) *The Oxford Handbook of Electoral Persuasion*, Oxford: Oxford University Press, 523–53.

Uscinski, J.E., C. Klofstad, M. Atkinson (2016) 'Why do people believe in conspiracy theories? The role of informational cues and predispositions', *Political Research Quarterly* 69: 57–71.

Uscinski, J.E., D. DeWitt, M. Atkinson (2018) "A web of conspiracy? Internet and conspiracy theory', in: A. Dyrendal, D. Robinson, E. Asprem (eds), *The Brill Handbook of Conspiracy Theory and Contemporary Religion*, Boston, MA: Brill.

Valenzuela, S., N. Park, K.F. Kee (2009) 'Is there social capital in a social network site?: Facebook use and college students' life satisfaction, trust, and participation', *Journal of Computer-Mediated Communication* 14(4): 875–901.

Vosoughi, S., D. Roy, S. Aral (2018) 'The spread of true and false news online', *Science* 359: 1146–51.

Walker, J. (2018) 'What we mean when we say "conspiracy theory"' in: J. E. Uscinski (ed.), *Conspiracy Theories and the People Who Believe Them*, New York: Oxford University Press, 53–61.

Ward, S., R. Gibson, W. Lusoli (2003) 'Online participation and mobilisation in Britain: Hype, hope and reality', *Parliamentary Affairs* 56: 652–68.

Weber, L. M., A. Loumakis, J. Bergman (2003) 'Who participates and why? An analysis of citizens on the internet and the mass public', *Social Science Computer Review* 21(1): 26–42.

Weeks, B. E., A. Ardèvol-Abreu, H. Gil de Zúñiga (2017) 'Online influence? Social media use, opinion leadership, and political persuasion', *International Journal of Public Opinion Research* 29: 214–39.

Zaller, J. (1992) *The Nature and Origins of Mass Opinion*, Cambridge: Cambridge University Press.

Zhang, W., T. J. Johnson, T. Seltzer, S. L. Bichard (2010) 'The revolution will be networked: The influence of social networking sites on political attitudes and behavior', *Social Science Computer Review* 28(1): 75–92.

6

SEARCHING FOR A UNICORN

Fake news and electoral behaviour

Luigi Curini and Eugenio Pizzimenti

Introduction

Recent evidence shows that: (1) elections across the globe have been characterised by a swing towards populism – from the 2016 US presidential elections to the 2018 Italian parliamentary elections; (2) populist politicians appear to rely more on their online communication on fake news than any political counterpart. Putting these two facts together, a number of commentators have suggested that the spread of fake news is somehow responsible for affecting electoral results (for examples, see Parkinson 2016; Read 2016; Hall Jamieson 2018). Still, it remains unclear if we are witnessing a causal relationship between two distinct phenomena or merely a temporal correlation that does not imply any causation. In fact, while numerous studies analyse different types of fake news campaigning, including their relative spread, their impact on the public remains an open question (Guess et al. 2020b). Our aim in this chapter is to give a critical review of the current literature, by focusing on a specific issue: can the exposure to false news actually affect people's attitudes and behaviour, and especially voting?

A definition of fake news

Today's fake news furore should be evaluated against the backdrop of long-standing political and commercial efforts to persuade and influence citizens through propaganda and political marketing (Bakir and McStay 2018). Fake news in some form has in other words long been with us (Pennycook and Rand 2019).

However, fake news seems to have gained an unprecedented level of prominence through the rise of social media. Thanks to some distinguishing features characterising the latter (low barriers to entry and reliance on user-generated content), the digital media ecology has in fact proliferated, democratized, and intensified the scale of this phenomenon (Allcott and Gentzkow 2017).

Two main motivations appear as the main engine for producing fake news. The first one is pecuniary: there is a growing number of people that financially capitalise on algorithms used by social media platforms and Internet search engines. Fake news articles that go viral can in fact draw significant advertising revenue or increase the value of one's own domain. The second motivation is ideological. Some fake news providers seek to advance politicians they favour. Regardless of the reason, we define fake news as either wholly false or containing deliberately misleading elements incorporated within its content or context (Rampersad and Turki 2020). That is, we intend fake news as intentionally fabricated information characterised by its politically charged content.

Understanding the causal path

To understand the possible causal linkage between fake news and voting, we need to better understand at least three aspects that are directly interrelated among themselves: the voting determinants, the psychological reasons behind consuming news, and the role of campaigning in affecting voting. As we will see, reviewing such aspects allow us to develop our expectations linking fake news with voting decisions.

The voting determinants

First, we need to develop a manageable map to orient readers on the steep terrain of the determinants of voting behaviours: this preliminary step will allow us to assess the (potential) weight of fake news and to place their (eventual) impact among the classical factors raised by the literature.

Voting behaviour is a core topic in contemporary Political Science. The detection and the study of the determinants *behind* people's electoral attitudes and voting choices gave birth to a vast literature, which is virtually impossible to summarise in this contribution (Fisher et al. 2017). However, to a merely heuristic aim it is possible to classify the classical theories of voting into three main approaches: (1) Sociological; (2) Psychological; (3) Rational Choice. According to the Sociological Approach (SA) – whose main pillar rests on the classic book by Lazarsfeld, Berelson, and Gaudet (1944) – voting behaviour is deeply entrenched in people's belonging to social groups. From this perspective, the sociographic properties of individuals (such as religion, race, gender, generation, occupation, class, geographical location) have an impact in orienting and stabilising, in time, their electoral preferences. Also the Psychological Approach (PA) emphasises the role played by individuals' characteristics – in particular: childhood, social background, and adult socialisation – in determining their *party identification* (Campbell et al 1960), which is considered the main cognitive map through which people frame politics and cast their vote accordingly. Finally, the Rational Choice Approach (RCA) builds on the assumptions of methodological individualism and on an economic theory of democracy (Downs 1957). Individuals are expected to behave *rationally*: once translated into the study of voting behaviour, this implies that citizens choose candidates/parties like consumers choose commercial products, by selecting the one whose policies best fit their preferences.

As this brief and incomplete introduction to voting behaviour theories should have suggested, there is no single way to address the puzzle of voting determinants, which proves more counter-intuitive than commonly expected. To deal with such a complicated issue, we opt to resort to the bi-dimensional approach elaborated by Rokkan (1970) and refined by Bellucci and Whiteley (2005). This analytical framework considers two different dimensions: a *Macro-Micro* dimension for the study of the characteristics of the political system on the one hand, and those of the voters on the other; and a *Temporal* dimension along which it is possible to distinguish between *Distant* and *Contextual* processes/factors that impact on voting behaviour (see also Bellucci and Segatti 2010).

By combining these two dimensions, we obtain four different quadrants within which it is possible to place the most recurring factors that impact on voters' final decision (at the centre of Figure 6.1). The quadrants placed on the left refer to the long-term determinants of voting behaviour. In the left-upper quadrant (*Macro-Distant*) we find the main characteristics of the political system: the structure of socio-political cleavages, the format and mechanics of the party system, the

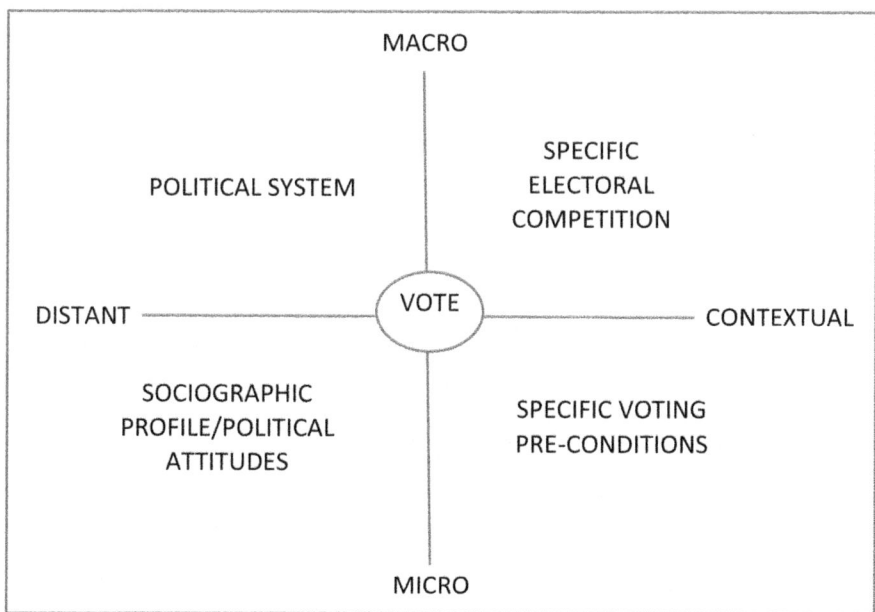

FIGURE 6.1 The analytical framework

'rules of the game' of the political-institutional arenas, etc. These determinants are exogenous, as they represent the set of systemic constraints and opportunities that bind voters' choices. In the left-lower quadrant *(Micro-Distant)*, the sociographic properties, the social position, the moral and political values, and the political pre-dispositions of the individuals are included. Here we find those social/economic/religious characteristics that are supposed to have an impact on voters' political attitudes. On the right side of the figure, the quadrants contain the contextual factors that shape a specific election and the related individual's voting decision. In the upper quadrant *(Macro-Contextual)*, the main determinants of voting refer to the specificities of the electoral competition: the state of the economy, the patterns of parties' alignment/strategies, the most debated political themes and policy issues, the role of the political leaders during the electoral campaign, the prevailing campaigning style, etc. In this respect, voters are expected to be driven *also* by their own evaluations about these aspects, such as the quality of the political class, the representativeness/cohesion of parties, the performances of the outgoing government, as well as by their expectations about the future and the reliability of the debated issues. Finally, in the lower quadrant *(Micro-Contextual)* we find a number of individual behaviours (exposure to campaigning, social interactions) and cognitive processes at the basis of a specific voting decision. Different voters adopt different decision-making heuristics through which they frame the political messages they are exposed to, according to their emotional involvement. In this respect, the role of mass-media – as well as that of other intermediation agencies, whether collective or individual (Gunther, Montero, and Puhle 2007) – is crucial. This does not mean that other factors – such as the kind of campaigning exposure, the informal debates within the circle of relatives, friends, and colleagues – are irrelevant; on the contrary, they constitute powerful filters between political news (whether fake or not) and voters.

As we will discuss more in depth in the following sections, the recent debate on the impact of fake news on voting behaviour tends to emphasise the relevance of the determinants placed on the right side of the figure, while overlooking the others. In particular, the underlying idea that peoples' votes are largely conditioned by the *contextual* information they gather during each specific electoral campaign seems to be consistent with the hypothesis of the 'individualisation' of voting (Dalton 1996). According to this interpretation, as far as traditional social pillars and partisan identifications have progressively evaporated, citizens tend to adopt personal decision-making schemes based on their own assessments and perceptions of the political environment. No longer determined by traditional social/political identities (which represented powerful constraints in orienting voting decisions), voters are now considered *free* to select the information that best fits with their *individual* preferences and to vote accordingly. If this is the case, voters will be more 'contestable' by competing parties and, in general, more willing to change their preferences depending on the contextual characteristics of the electoral campaign. Within this scenario, the weight of the fake news seems to be crucial, as deliberately false information that circulates during the electoral campaign is supposed to produce relevant impacts on voters, whose social and political background is considered a sort of *tabula rasa*.

However, neither the socially determined nor the hyper-individualised model of voting are satisfactory. In fact, if it seems undisputable that the de-freezing of the long-standing socio-economic-cultural cleavages (Dalton 1996), the decline of the traditional party organisational models (Katz and Mair 1995; 2009), the parallel erosion of the traditional social pillars (Dalton and Wattenberg 2002), as well as the information technology revolution (Ward and Gibson 2009) have contributed to the individualisation of political participation, it does not necessarily follow that contemporary voters are completely deprived of any social identity and/or that they are insensitive to the influences of the wider groups they still belong to. If voters were completely individualised and impressionable by contextual factors we should register exorbitant levels of volatility at every election, everywhere, which is not the case in liberal democracies. Thus, as (substantial) stability continues to prevail, it seems plausible that voters' choice is still affected by their socially constructed and rather homogeneous social networks (Dalton 1996), whose boundaries do not vary dramatically over time.

The psychological reasons behind consuming a news

Rather than confining the debate on voting determinants to the clash between socially determined and individualised voters, we probably should build our assumptions on a model of voters' behaviour that stands "in between: for sure more strong-willed and strategic in choosing his/her affiliations, but still identified and socially situated" (Corbetta and Cavazza 2009: 371, our translation). On this basis, it is possible to elaborate an analytical framework on the relevance of fake news that eschews the widespread (deterministic) conventional wisdom about its impact. First, we need to examine whether exposure to fake news actually affects voting behavior or if it only reinforces predetermined political beliefs. To this aim we will focus on how ordinary citizens experience misinformation on social media platforms.

That sizable populations reading fake news on social media doesn't, in fact, necessarily mean that such messages influenced public attitudes. The concept of 'selective exposure' is enlightening in this respect. Research shows that people tend to prefer congenial information, including political news, when given the choice (Iyengar and Hahn 2009; Iyengar et al. 2008). Why does it happen? Because selective exposure enables people to defend their attitudes, beliefs, and behaviours by avoiding information likely to challenge them and seeking information likely to support them (Hart et al. 2009). Moreover, such 'defense' motivation is strengthened by individuals' commitment to such pre-existing attitude, belief, or behaviour (Kiesler 1971). This creates a linkage with the world of politics. In contrast to other topics, those individuals with strong political leanings may in fact be particularly likely to engage in selective exposure because their political beliefs are accessible and personally relevant (Hart et al. 2009). Politics, on the other side, often yields an affective response, and this is another factor that has been shown to matter to inspire selective exposure (Stroud 2008).

Today, it is moreover far easier engaging in selective exposure, i.e. in the selection of media sharing one's political predispositions, compared to times past (Stroud 2008). The existence of social media has, of course, just further strengthened this dynamic, not only on a quantitative but also on a qualitative basis. In particular, the human confirmation bias discussed above is favoured by the algorithm employed by social networks, which reinforces the creation of 'filter bubbles' where users are subjected to a limited exposure to, and lack of engagement with, different ideas and other people's viewpoints (Bessi et al. 2016; Sunstein 2001).[1]

The role of campaigning in affecting voting

The previous two sections should warn us about the complex mixture between consolidated attitudes and contextual factors in orienting peoples' behaviour. Among the latter, the role of political advertising deserves specific attention. Research suggests two broad reasons why campaign advertising might have effects on voters' choices (see Kalla and Broockman 2018): (1) by providing voters new arguments and/or (2) by heightening the salience of existing arguments. Still, there are reasons to take both aspects with care.

When it comes to providing voters with new arguments and information, by the time election day arrives, voters are likely to have already absorbed all the arguments and information they care to retain from the media and other sources beyond the political campaigns themselves (Gelman and King 1993). This is not to say that voters will know all the relevant information campaigns could provide them, but that they are likely to have been exposed to all this information and that they will have chosen to retain nearly all they care to (Kalla and Broockman 2018). In such an environment, it may be difficult for campaigns to change voters' minds by informing them about a party's positions, as voters are likely to agree with their party on any issues on which they have opinions in the first place (Berinsky 2009; Lauderdale 2016). Accordingly, there are few considerations campaigns can provide that would lead voters to abandon their party, in particular as election day is approaching (Kalla and Broockman 2018).

What about the possibility for a campaign to make certain considerations more salient as people decide what they think (Zaller 1992)? The salience-raising effects of communication diminish in the presence of clear cues (Druckman, Peterson, and Slothuus 2013) and when individuals are exposed to competing arguments and information (Druckman 2004). This is, however, the typical situation we meet in general elections wherein a partisan perspective makes generally other frames irrelevant to many voters.

In this sense, what a campaign typically does – providing information voters are already being exposed to and attempting to increase the salience of this information – is very unlikely to lead voters to cross partisan lines. And, in fact, Kalla and Broockman (2018) convincingly show in their meta-analysis that campaigns have "minimal effects;" actually an effect that is not statistically different from zero. Field experiments testing the effects of online ads on political candidates and issues have also found such null effects (Nyhan 2018).[2] In sum, such findings offer an important caveat to the widespread notion that people can easily manipulate citizens' political choices. By building on the three sections discussed, we can advance two main expectations:

E1) *people will tend to consume the news that confirms their partisan ideas. This also should happen within social media, and, most notably, with respect to fake news;*
E2) *precisely for this, the impact of fake news on voting choice will be negligible.*

These considerations bring us to the review of the main findings of the literature on fake news and voting.

Much ado for nothing? Fake news and empirical evidence

Spreading and consumption of fake news

Many statistics have been produced about how many times fake news was shared on Facebook or Twitter. These statistics, however, should be taken with care. First, they obscure the fact that the content being shared may not reach many voters (most people are not, for example, on Twitter and consume relatively little political news). Second, and most important, they do not adopt a relative framework, i.e., they do not consider how much these numbers mean when compared to the statistics related to the consumption of more typical mainstream news. Our review of some of the most quoted works with respect to the 'consumption' of fake news on social media shows results that are quite consistent among themselves in their conclusions, irrespective of the specific social media platform considered.[3]

Let's start with Twitter. Vosoughi, Roy, and Aral (2018) have studied the spread of false stories on this platform between 2006 and 2017 by following 126,000 distinct stories covering different topics. They show that these stories were tweeted and retweeted over 4.5 million times by three million people. Among these stories, those that were false diffused significantly faster, more broadly (to a larger number of users), and deeper (with a larger number of re-shares) than those that were true. The difference between the speed and the width of spreading false vs. true stories was particularly pronounced for political news. The authors suggest that the degree of novelty (higher for false news) and the extent to which the news is emotionally charged (also higher for false news) may be responsible for why Twitter users retweet fakes more.

In a related study, Törnberg (2018) models fake news as a complex contagion highlighting the role played by the echo chamber effect. He uses a metaphor in this respect: if we think of the viral spread of fake news in a social network as akin to a wildfire, an echo chamber has the same effect as a dry pile of tinder in the forest; it provides the fuel for an initial small flame that can spread to larger sticks, branches, trees, to finally engulf the forest. In other words, fake news spreads easier in networks where there is a presence of an echo chamber. This 'trigger' that helps us to explain why fake news spreads fast, however, is also the key to understanding who is reading this type of news.

Grinberg et al. (2019), for example, studied the exposure of Twitter users to false news during the 2016 US presidential election. They found that false political stories constituted a significant share of all news consumption (about 6%) on Twitter. For the average Twitter user, however, content from fake news sources constituted only 1.2% of political exposures. Finally, the circulation of false news was highly concentrated, with 1% of all users exposed to about 80% of false news exposure. The retweeting of false news was even more concentrated, with about 0.1% of all users responsible for 80% of the retweets of fake political stories. Individuals most likely to engage with fake news sources were conservative leaning and highly engaged with political news. Moreover, despite the significant presence of false stories on Twitter, for people across the political spectrum, most political news exposure still came from mainstream media outlets.

A similar story appears if we focus on a study that analyses the interaction with Russian Internet Research Agency (IRA) accounts on Twitter, that have been considered as one of the major sources of fake news during the 2016 US presidential elections (Hall Jamieson 2018). Twitter reported that 1.4 million of its 69 million monthly active users had interacted with IRA accounts in early 2018, or approximately 2%. In their study Baila et al. (2020) show the vast majority (80%) of active partisan Twitter users did not interact with any IRA account. And for those who did, these interactions represented a minuscule share of their Twitter activity – on average, just 0.1% of their liking, mentioning, and retweeting on Twitter. The trait that turned out to be the best predictor of interaction with Russian trolls on Twitter was, by far, the strength of a user's pre-existing echo chamber. That is, Twitter users who followed political figures almost entirely from their own party were the ones most likely to engage with IRA agents on the platform.

Let's turn now to Facebook. Guess, Nagler, and Tucker (2019) studied the characteristics of the sharers of false news on Facebook during the 2016 US presidential election campaign. They merged survey data with respondents' Facebook profiles to measure sharing activity. First and foremost, they found that sharing this content was a relatively rare activity. The vast majority of Facebook users in their data did not share any articles from fake news domains in 2016, and this is not because people generally do not share links. While 3.4% of respondents included in the authors' data shared 10 or fewer links of any kind, 310 (26.1%) respondents shared 10 to 100 links during the period of data collection, and 729 (61.3%) respondents shared 100 to 1000 links. On the contrary, over 90% of the respondents in this study shared no stories from fake news domains. Moreover, and once again, the sharing activities were partisan. Indeed, the authors find evidence that the most conservative users were more likely to share this content.

If we now turn on fake news consumption, Guess, Nagler and Tucker (2019) find that approximately one in four Americans visited a fake news website (27.4%)

during the final weeks of the 2016 election campaign. Fake news has been defined in this research as recently created sites that frequently published false or misleading claims that overwhelmingly favour one of the presidential candidates in the weeks before the 2016 election. The previous percentage seems impressive, but these visits overall made up only about 2% of the information people consumed from websites focussing on hard news topics. The consumption was disproportionately observed among Trump supporters for whom its largely pro-Trump content was attitude-consistent. However, this pattern of selective exposure was heavily concentrated among a small subset of people – almost six in ten visits to fake news websites came from the 10% of Americans with the most conservative information diets who were responsible for approximately six in 10 visits to fake news websites during this period. Even in that group, however, fake news made up less than 8% of their total news 'diet'.

Moreover, the reach of fake news declines dramatically in the period before the 2018 midterm elections (see Guess at al. 2020b). In fall 2018, only 7% of the public read an article from a fake news site. The only thing that remains constant if we compare the 2016 and 2018 campaigns is related to who does consume fake news. As in fall 2016, fake news consumption in fall 2018 is disproportionately concentrated among the 10% of Americans with the most conservative news diets.

Summing up, the above reviewed articles arrive at the same conclusion, which can be summarised in two main points. First, the prevalence of fake news on social media seems to be overstated, which would suggest that it is unlikely to cause massive changes in public opinion that many commentators have feared. Second, the results suggest that fake news sources seem to have been a niche interest. In other words, their impact on political discourse might be limited by the same mechanism that helps their posts find traction and spread: the algorithms and filter bubbles that ensure people see political content they were already inclined to agree with. The citizens most likely to interact with Russian trolls or to consume fake news were those the least likely to be influenced by them – because of their more entrenched political views.

Fake news and voting behaviour

Compared to studies focussing on fake news spread and consumption, the studies linking fake news exposure with voting are far fewer. Usually, the discussion brings forward an indirect evidence rather than a direct one. With respect to former studies, for example, Nyhan (2019) illustrates how there remains no evidence that fake news changed the result of the 2016 election. The reason is that any such claim must take into account not just the reach of fake news, but also the proportion of those exposed to it whose behaviour could be changed. As noted above, approximately six in 10 visits to fake news websites came from the 10% of Americans with the most conservative news diets – a group that was already especially likely to vote for Donald Trump.

Similarly, Allcott and Gentzkow (2017) stress that even assuming that a fake news article is as persuasive as a TV campaign ad, which is *per se* a very strong assumption, the effect of fake news exposure was most certainly not enough to be decisive to the 2016 election outcome given the total amount of consumption of fake news in that election (and, once again, the specific type of users that most heavily consumed such news).

More indirect evidence of the scarce impact of fake news consumption on voter decisions, comes from fact-checking literature. Several studies (Nyhan et al. 2019; Swire et al. 2017) based on an experimental framework show that journalistic fact-checks can reduce belief in fake news items. However, supporters of a specific politician appear not to change their attitudes towards him/her after receiving fact-checks, suggesting that voters' preferences are not contingent on their perceptions of the factual accuracy of the candidates (being it true or just fake). In other words, factual corrections can achieve the limited objective of creating a more informed citizenry but struggle to change citizens' minds about whom to support.

One of the few studies focussing on the direct relationship between fake news and voting is the work by Cantarella, Fraccaroli, and Volpe (2019). Interestingly, this study is not based on the US case, but on the Italian one, i.e. it looks at a country where populist parties are strong, and wherein fake news seem to have been largely consumed.[4] For example, a survey about the 2018 elections showed that the likelihood of sharing so-called fake news was found to be higher for voters of two Italian populist parties (Movimento 5 Stelle and Lega) than for voters of other parties. Second, this is one of the few attempts to study the phenomenon of fake news using a quasi-experimental methodology in order to account for the possible reverse causality issues between voting preferences and exposition to misinformation.

In particular the authors compares two different provinces located in the Trentino Alto-Adige/Südtirol region in Italy. This region, which is located on the border with Austria, is home to a German-speaking linguistic minority and features some degree of language segregation: a parallel German-language media market exists, and effective bilingualism is not particularly widespread (Ebner 2016). In this respect, the authors select the province of Trento and the province of Bolzano. In this latter province, German-speaking citizens are by far the majority. Therefore, we have two different areas next to each other, comparable in terms of economic and demographic conditions, but wherein one province (contrary to the other one) is exposed to a peculiar filter bubble where exposure to fake news concerning Italian politics is limited. In fact, it can be reasonably assumed that fake news disseminators may have little or no incentive to produce fake news especially targeted to the (small) German-speaking population living in Italy. Through that, it becomes possible to exploit the language differences across the two provinces as an exogenous source of variation in exposure to fake news. The authors then gathered municipality-level data on electoral outcomes, demographics, and social media usage from the two provinces and exploited a natural experiment occurring in the region to randomise exposition to fake news.

The authors' main finding was that the persistence of very similar differences in voting behaviour, especially as far as the support for populist parties is considered, conditioned by linguistic grouping and broadband penetration, indicates that exposure to fake news is entirely dictated by self-selection, meaning that the causal channel between voting and fake news goes in a single direction, with individuals being exposed to fake news because of their prior political presences. A result, once again, consistent with the previous studies that we have discussed.

Conclusion

How easy is it to change people's votes in an election by disseminating fake news? Much remains to be learnt about the effects of these types of online activities, but people should not assume they have huge effects. This is at least the conclusion of our review. A conclusion that is coherent, *inter alia*, with our starting expectations grounded in the literature on voting behaviour, psychology, and campaigning.

We have highlighted how voting behaviour cannot be just considered the by-product of contextual factors, limited to the peculiarities of an electoral campaign, in a specific moment in history. On the contrary, despite the declining impact of the traditional social, cultural, and partisan identities on voting, and the parallel 'self-determination' of voters, the sociographic factors are still relevant in tracing voters' profile and political attitudes, as they constitute the pre-conditions of their contextual decision-making heuristics. Unsurprisingly, then, people tend to consume the news that confirms their pre-established partisan ideas and the impact of campaign advertising (including fake news) on voting seems rather poor. Note that the sociographic factors developed in the 1950s could be easily extended as a category to include also the current 'online life'.

Accordingly, social media information bubbles can matter independently of the presence of fake news precisely for their being an incarnation of shared narrations within groups of citizens with extended (virtual) social interactions. The ironic thing about all the fake news discussion would be therefore our 'rediscovering' of the important role of a classic issue very well known in the literature on voting behaviour.

This conclusion may sound jarring at a time when people are concerned about the effects of fake news that flooded social media. Observers speculated that these so-called fake news articles swung the election to Trump. Similar suggestions of large persuasion effects have been made about Brexit and the rising of populist parties (in Italy as elsewhere). So why did it happen? Probably for the same reasons that determine the success of the hoaxes: it offers a simplistic explanation (a kind of straw-man concept) for a complex problem and lends itself to be an effective propaganda tool.

None of these findings indicate that fake news isn't a worrisome sign for a democracy. Fake news can have negative effects that extend beyond election outcomes. It can mislead and polarise citizens, undermine trust in the media,[5] and distort the content of public debate. But we need (more) evidence and data, not hype or speculation. Measuring the causal effect of exposition to fake news is indeed far from trivial, as simple correlations do not provide much information on their effect on voting. If people with given political views both vote and consume news accordingly, there is much of the raw correlation that is not causal from fake news to vote.

We end this chapter by highlighting a possible further avenue for the research on fake news and politics. Influencing vote choice is very difficult because likely voters have strong prior beliefs as we discussed. However, experiments demonstrate that persuasive interventions can affect voter turnout (albeit the evidence here is also not so straightforward: see Kalla and Broockman 2018). That is, campaigns can also aim to influence whether voters bother to vote at all (Ansolabehere 2006).

Of course, when assessing the possible relationship between fake news and turnout, it is important to remember that voting is habitual. Effective manipulation, therefore, likely requires targeting occasional rather than regular voters. In social media, however, this type of targeting is possible and, according to some observers, it took place during the 2016 US presidential election. Analysis of the precision of targeting efforts is, therefore, essential to understanding voter turnout effects, in particular to identify both the possible direct effects of fake news consumption on turnout and indirect spillover effects (e.g., word of mouth from recipients to peers). However, studying the relationship between fake news and turnout requires a sophisticated causal approach (Aral and Eckles 2019), rather than an analysis based upon qualitative analyses or anecdotal evidence; something that quite often has been lacking in the public discussion.

Notes

1 Note, however, that the fears of widespread online 'echo chambers' remain a highly discussed topic. Behavioural data indicates, for example, that only a subset of users – once again characterised by their degree of strong political leaning – have heavily skewed media consumption patterns (Gentzkow and Shapiro 2011; Barberá 2015).

2 This, of course, does not imply that political campaigns are not important. See Kalla and Broockman (2018) for a discussion.

3 We are presenting in this section only works based on the USA case, given the relevance that the 2016 US presidential elections has generated when it comes to the possible role played by fake news. See for example Hall Jamieson (2018).

4 *Il Sole 24 Ore* (2018) 'Fake news: quando le bugie hanno le gambe lunghe', 4 May 2018, www.infodata.ilsole24ore.com/2018/05/04/fake-news-le-bugie-le-gambe-lunghe/. Note, however, that we should be aware of the results we get when focussing on surveys alone, in particular post-election survey recall. For example, Allcott and Gentzkow (2017) show that 15% of survey respondents recalled seeing false news stories during the campaign and 8% recalled both seeing a false story and acknowledging that they believed it. However, a question about exposure to placebo false news stories – untrue but plausible headlines that the authors invented which never actually circulated – gives almost the same responses as a question about false news stories that actually did circulate: 14% of people reported seeing placebo stories and 8% reported seeing and believing them. This highlights the limitations of recall-based surveys about fake news consumption.

5 This outcome can also be the by-product of an unintended process. Indeed, it has been shown that when people are exposed to tweets and press articles containing the term 'fake news', their ability to tell real from fraudulent stories decreases (see Van Duyn and Collier 2018).

References

Allcott, H., M. Gentzkow (2017) 'Social media and fake news in the 2016 election', *Journal of Economic Perspectives* 31(2): 211–36.

Ansolabehere, S. (2006) 'The paradox of minimal effects', in: H.E. Brady, R. Johnston (eds), *Capturing Campaign Effects*, Ann Arbor: University of Michigan Press, 29–44.

Aral, S., D. Eckles (2019) 'Protecting elections from social media manipulation', *Science* 365(6456): 858–61.

Baila, C.A., B. Guaya, E. Maloneya, A. Combsa, D.S. Hillygusa, F. Merhouta, D. Freelonf, A. Volfovskya (2020) 'Assessing the Russian Internet Research Agency's impact on the political attitudes and behaviors of American Twitter users in late 2017', *Proceedings of the National Academy of Sciences* 117(1): 243–50.

Bakir, V., A. McStay (2018) 'Fake news and the economy of emotions', *Digital Journalism* 6(2): 154–75.

Barberá, P. (2015) 'How social media reduces mass political polarization: Evidence from Germany, Spain, and the US', *Mimeo*, New York University.

Bellucci P., P. Segatti (eds) (2010) *Votare in Italia: 1968–2018*, Bologna: Il Mulino.

Bellucci P., P. Whiteley (2005) 'Modelling electoral choice in the twenty-first century: An introduction', *Electoral Studies* 25: 319–24.

Berinsky, A.J. (2017) 'Measuring public opinion with surveys', *Annual Review of Political Science* 20: 309–29.

Bessi, A., F. Zollo, M. Del Vicario, M. Puliga, A. Scala, G. Caldarelli (2016) 'Users polarization on Facebook and Youtube', *PLoS ONE* 11(8): e0159641.

Campbell A., P.E. Converse, W.E. Miller, D.E. Stokes (1960) *The American Voter*, New York: Wiley.

Cantarella M., N. Fraccaroli, R. Volpe (2019) *Does Fake News Affect Voting Behaviour?*, DEMB Working Paper Series 146.

Corbetta, P., N. Cavazza (2009) 'Capire il comportamento di voto: dalla debolezza dei fattori sociologici all'insostenibile tesi dell'individualizzazione', *Polis* 3, https://doi.org/10.1424/31134.

Dalton, R.J. (1996) 'Political cleavages, issues and electoral change', in: L. Le Duc, R.G. Niemi, P. Norris (eds), *Comparing Democracies: Elections and Voting in Global Perspectives*, London –Thousand Oaks: Sage, 319–42.

Dalton R.J., P.M. Wattenberg (eds) (2002) *Parties without Partisans: Political Change in Advanced Industrial Democracies*, New York: Oxford University Press.

Downs A. (1957) *An Economic Theory of Democracy*, New York: Harper.

Druckman, J.N. (2004) 'Political preference formation: Competition, deliberation, and the (ir) relevance of framing effects', *American Political Science Review* 98(4): 671–86.

Druckman, J.N., E. Peterson, R. Slothuus (2013) 'How elite partisan polarization affects public opinion formation', *American Political Science Review* 107(01): 57–79.

Ebner, C.V. (2016) 'The long way to bilingualism: The peculiar case of multilingual South Tyrol', *International Journal for 21st Century Education* 3(2): 25.

Fisher, J., E. Fieldhouse, M.N. Franklin, R. Gibson, M. Cantijoch, C. Wlezien (2017) *The Routledge Handbook of Elections, Voting Behaviour and Public Opinion*, London: Routledge.

Gelman, A., G. King (1993) 'Why are American presidential election campaign polls so variable when votes are so predictable?', *British Journal of Political Science* 23(4): 409–51.

Gentzkow, M., J.M. Shapiro (2011) 'Ideological segregation online and offline', *Quarterly Journal of Economics*, 126(4): 1799–839.

Grinberg, N., K. Joseph, L. Friedland, B. Swire-Thompson, D. Lazer (2019) 'Fake News on Twitter during the 2016 U.S. presidential election', *Science*, 363(6425): 374–78.

Guess, A., J. Nagler, J. Tucker (2019) 'Less than you think: Prevalence and predictors of fake news dissemination on Facebook', *Science Advances*, 5(1): eaau4586.

Guess, A., S. Lach, J. Reifler (2020a) 'Exposure to untrustworthy websites in the 2016 U.S. election', *Nature Human Behaviour*, forthcoming.

Guess, A., B. Lyons, J.M. Montgomery, B. Nyhan (2020b) 'Fake news, Facebook ads, and misperceptions: Assessing information quality in the 2018 U.S. midterm election campaign', *Mimeo*, Princeton University.

Gunther, R., J.R. Montero, H.J. Puhle (2007) *Democracy, Intermediation, and Voting on Four Continents*, Oxford: Oxford University Press.

Hall Jamieson, K. (2018) *Cyberwar: How Russian Hackers and Trolls Helped Elect a President: What We Don't, Can't, and Do Know*, Oxford: Oxford University Press.

Hart, W., D. Albarracin, A.H. Eagly, I. Brechan, M.J. Lindberg, L. Merrill (2009) 'Feeling validated versus being correct: A meta-analysis of selective exposure to information', *Psychological Bulletin* 135(4): 555.

Iyengar, S., K.S. Hahn, J.A. Krosnick, J. Walker (2008) 'Selective exposure to campaign communication: The role of anticipated agreement and issue public membership', *Journal of Politics* 70(1): 186–200.

Iyengar, S., K.S. Hahn (2009) 'Red media, blue media: Evidence of ideological selectivity in media use', *Journal of Communication* 59(1): 19–39.

Kalla, J.L., D.E. Broockman (2018) 'The minimal persuasive effects of campaign contact in general elections: Evidence from 49 field experiments', *American Political Science Review* 112(1): 148–66

Katz, R., P. Mair (1995) 'Changing models of party organisation and party democracy: The emergence of the Cartel party', *Party Politics*, 1(1): 5–28.

Katz, R., P. Mair (2009) 'The Cartel party thesis revisited', *Perspective on Politics* 7(4): 753–66.

Kiesler, C.A. (1971) *The Psychology of Commitment*, New York: Academic Press.

Lauderdale, B.E. (2016) 'Partisan disagreements arising from rationalization of common information', *Political Science Research and Methods* 4(3): 477–92.

Lazarsfeld, P., B. Berelson, H. Gaudet (1944) *The People's Choice: How the Voter Makes Up His Mind in Presidential Campaign*, New York: CUP.

Lazer, D.M.J. et al. (2018) 'The science of fake news', *Science* 359(6380): 1094–96.

Nyhan, B. (2018) 'Fake news and bots may be worrisome, but their political power is overblown', *The New York Times*, 13 February 2018.

Nyhan, B. (2019) 'Why fears of fake news Are overhyped', *Medium*, 4 February 2019, https://gen.medium.com/why-fears-of-fake-news-are-overhyped-2ed9ca0a52c9.

Nyhan, B., E. Porterz, J. Reifler, T.J. Wood (2019) 'Taking fact-checks literally but not seriously? The effects of journalistic fact-checking on factual beliefs and candidate favorability', *Political Behavior* 42(3): 939–60.

Parkinson, H.J. (2016) 'Click and elect: How fake news helped Donald Trump win a real election', *The Guardian*, 14 November 2016.

Pennycook, G., D.G. Rand (2019) 'Lazy, not biased: Susceptibility to partisan fake news is better explained by lack of reasoning than by motivated reasoning', *Cognition* 188: 39–50.

Rampersad, G., A. Turki (2020) 'Fake news: Acceptance by demographics and culture on social media', *Journal of Information Technology & Politics* 17(1): 1–11.

Read, M. (2016) 'Donald Trump won because of Facebook', *New York Magazine*, 9 November 2016.

Rokkan, S. (1970) *Citizens, Elections, Parties: Approaches to the Comparative Study of the Processes of Development*, New York: David McKay.

Sinan, A., D. Eckles (2019) 'Protecting elections from social media manipulation', *Science* 365: 6456.

Stroud, N.J. (2008) 'Media use and political predispositions: Revisiting the concept of selective exposure', *Political Behavior* 30(3): 341–66.

Sunstein, C. (2001) *Echo Chambers: Bush Vs. Gore, Impeachment, and Beyond*, Princeton, NJ: Princeton University Press.

Swire, B., A.J. Berinsky, S. Lewandowsky, U.K.H. Ecke (2017) 'Processing political misinformation: Comprehending the Trump phenomenon', *Royal Society Open Science* 4: 160802.

Törnberg, P. (2018) 'Echo chambers and viral misinformation: Modeling fake news as complex contagion', *PLOS ONE* 13(9): e0203958.

Van Duyn, E., J. Collier (2018) 'Priming and fake news: The effects of elite discourse on evaluations of news media', *Mass Communication and Society* 22: 29–48.

Vosoughi, S., R. Deb, A. Sinan (2018) 'The spread of true and false news online', *Science* 359(6380): 1146–51.

Vosoughi, S., D. Roy, S. Aral (2018) 'The spread of true and false news online', *Science* 359: 1146–51.

Ward, S.J., R.K. Gibson (2009) 'European political organizations and the Internet: Mobilization, participation, and change', in: A. Chadwick, P.N. Howard (eds), *The Routledge Handbook of Internet Politics,* London: Routledge, 25–39.

Zaller, J.R. (1992) *The Nature and Origins of Mass Opinion*, New York: Cambridge University Press.

7

ONCE UPON COVID-19

A tale of misleading information going viral

Alice Hazelton

Introduction

First detected in Wuhan, China, a pneumonia of an unknown cause was reported to the World Health Organization (WHO) country office in China on 31 December 2019. The outbreak was declared a Public Health Emergency of International Concern on 30 January 2020 and on 11 February 2020, the WHO announced a name for the new coronavirus disease: Covid-19, the word that will define 2020 for many of us. One month later, "deeply concerned both by the alarming levels of spread and severity", the WHO declared Covid-19 a pandemic (World Health Organization 2020a).

Covid-19 is the name of the infectious disease caused by the virus known as severe acute respiratory syndrome coronavirus 2 (Sars-CoV-2). At the time of writing, on 6 June 2020, the virus has infected over 6.75 million people in almost every country and claimed the lives of 395,328 people. Almost three million people have recovered after the infection (Johns Hopkins University 2020). With differing testing capabilities across different jurisdictions, the true toll of the virus on human lives will not be known for some time, if ever.

Along with an escalation of cases and deaths, life as we know it has ground to a halt. Millions of people around the world have found themselves under lockdown measures and quarantined to their own homes. Border closures and travel bans have severely disrupted supply chains, businesses are teetering on the brink of collapse, and record levels of unemployment loom. The magnitude and speed of collapse in economic activity is unlike anything ever experienced for many of us and, as long as containment measures are necessary to further prevent the spread of Covid-19 or the development of therapeutics and vaccines comes about, the worse are the prospects for economic recovery. The 'Great Lockdown' will see the world economy experience the worst recession since the Great Depression (Gopinath 2020).

As the virus has spread around the planet affecting both lives and livelihoods, so too has an overload of information, including misinformation – incorrect but not deliberately misleading – and disinformation – purposefully misleading (UNESCO 2018). Day-to-day conversation, social media feeds, front page news, television, and radio are dominated by stories about Covid-19 and it is becoming increasingly difficult to look past sensational headlines and separate facts from fiction. From tales of the virus starting with a woman eating bat soup, to the President of the United States touting drinking bleach as a cure (Taylor 2020), how does one know what to believe and what not to?

"We're not just fighting an epidemic; we're fighting an infodemic", Tedros Adhanom Ghebreyesus, Director-General of the WHO, said on 11 February 2020 at the Munich Security Conference in Germany, referring to the fact that fake news "spreads faster and more easily than this virus" (World Health Organization 2020b). Indeed, a lack of reliable information and trusted sources can be as danger-ous as the virus itself. Inaccurate information does not only mislead people, but it can endanger lives by encouraging people to ignore public health advice, take unproven drugs, or refuse a vaccine, should one become available.

Written during the midst of the pandemic, this chapter aims to briefly docu-ment the rise of misinformation and disinformation related to Covid-19 to date and to consider some attempts to thwart it, along with offering suggestions for future work and discussion. As the situation is rapidly evolving and changing on a day-to-day basis, it is by no means an exhaustive account but instead showcases several illustrative examples. A thorough analysis should be undertaken if and when the pandemic subsides.

History repeats itself: Disease narratives

"We know that every outbreak will be accompanied by a kind of tsunami of infor-mation, but also within this information you always have misinformation, rumours, etc. We know that even in the Middle Ages there was this phenomenon," said Sylvie Briand of WHO's Health Emergencies Programme (Zarocostas 2020).

Misleading information is nothing new. Before diving into the details of the Covid-19 pandemic, it is perhaps worth briefly looking at what history tells us about the way news travels during outbreaks, why falsehoods originate, and how they spread. While a scientific approach is vital to helping us understand the virus itself, lessons from folklore – the study of culture – can offer an understanding of the reasons behind human behaviour; in this case, how and why inaccurate infor-mation spreads during disease outbreaks. Both approaches are equally important to the study of information dissemination, but it is often the difference between how the scientific world views or tells the story of an epidemic event – the evidence – and the story that circulates in public discourse where rumours begin.

Only humans tell stories. In his unified theory of storytelling, Gottschall (2012) argues that stories help us navigate life's complex problems and have evolved over time to ensure our survival. He notes that, "Of course, our story instinct has a darker side. It makes us vulnerable to conspiracy theories, advertisements, and narratives about ourselves that are more 'truthy' than true" (Gotschall 2012).

Looking back at past epidemics reveals a similar truth about the role of storytelling and the ability of humankind to believe one story over another. In his 2014 book, *An Epidemic of Rumours: How Stories Shape Our Perceptions of Disease*, folklorist Jon D. Lee sets out to examine the story-making process that underlies the narratives which circulate, and draws an unparalleled similarity between historical and modern disease narratives.

Lee (2014) uses the severe acute respiratory syndrome (Sars) as a case study but suggests that one could easily replace the words Sars and China with H1N1 and Mexico and the same narratives would hold. Unsurprisingly, doing the same thing today with Covid-19 reveals that, once again, the same narratives have been recycled, modified only by specific details that are necessary to link the narrative to the current situation.

Where did it come from? How does it spread? How can it be prevented? How can it be treated? Why do we not have a cure? In the absence of scientific evidence as answers to such questions, humans have a natural tendency to create their own answers in the form of stories in a bid to fill the void. For example, to date, scientists have not determined the exact origins of the Sars-CoV-2 virus yet numerous stories are filling the void, including that the virus escaped from a laboratory at the Wuhan Institute of Virology (Singh et al. 2020) or that the United States military brought the virus to Wuhan (Sardarizadeh and Robinson 2020). During the Sars epidemic in 2003, in the absence of scientific evidence regarding the origins of the virus, similar narratives circulated, including that Saddam Hussein had released Sars as part of a biological warfare campaign (Lee 2014: 58).

Some studies on disease narratives have revealed the common themes that one is already seeing during the Covid-19 pandemic and that we can expect to see used again in future outbreaks. Rooted in how different social groups perceive and represent reality, themes of xenophobia, racism, government deception, secrecy, and misconduct are commonplace. All revolve around the emotion of fear, which fuels the spread of rumours as individuals within a particular group sharing a common belief system are likely to pass it on to members of the same group in order to warn them of danger and protect them (ibid.: 171). "Rumours are often grounded in prejudices and misunderstandings so old that they are not recognised as inaccurate, so any attempt to challenge the rumour inherently challenges deeply ingrained belief systems and ideas," states Lee (2014: 172).

In the absence of scientific evidence, rumours and disinformation serve the purpose of filling an information vacuum and this in itself is strong enough to continue to support the existence of the narrative. Eradicating false narratives is likely to take as long as it takes to eradicate the disease and this is evidenced from Lee's study on the Sars epidemic: "As soon as the virus disappeared and ceased to make headlines, the stories died" (ibid.: 173).

It goes without saying that during public health emergencies this approach is not useful when evidence-based information is essential to contain the disease and ensure public safety. Unfortunately, there are already instances from the Covid-19 pandemic where misleading information has resulted in unnecessary death. Just one example is that of a couple in Arizona, United States, who ingested chloroquine phosphate that they had left over from treating their koi fish, after seeing a televised briefing where President Trump talked about the benefits of chloroquine as a treatment for Covid-19. Chloroquine remains unproven as a treatment for Covid-19 and to great regret, the man died and the woman was left in a critical condition (BBC 2020).

If eradicating misleading information does not seem possible, then containment strategies are necessary, just like with the virus itself. When Lee wrote the book *An Epidemic of Rumours* in 2014, some previous studies had already shown that historical methods of controlling rumours were generally ineffective and resulted in further spread of the misleading information. Initial research at the time pointed to repeating evidence-based information rather than denying the misleading information: "For best results, the accurate, positive information should be repeated frequently to help solidify its public recognition and familiarity" (Lee 2014: 179). Certainly, organisations that disseminate information through society, such as the media, have a role to play in adopting this approach, but, as the next section will show, the rise in social media use makes this task ever-more challenging.

Social media as a disease vector

While many of the themes surrounding disease narratives and the associated misleading information undoubtedly appear to remain the same during the Covid-19 pandemic as in the past, the mediums by which such information spreads are different. Take the Internet, for example. One of our most transformative technologies had just 413 million active users in 2000, a number which has now grown to 4.57 billion people, encompassing 59% of the global population (Clement 2020).

Just over a decade after the creation of the Internet, 2004 marked the shift to Web 2.0 – a shift towards user-generated content – and with it, the dawn of social media. At the time, MySpace was the first social media site to reach one million active monthly users but fast-forward to today and Facebook, established in 2004, is the dominant social media platform with 2.3 billion users. YouTube, Instagram, and WeChat follow, with more than a billion users. Tumblr and TikTok come next, with over half a billion users (Roser et al. 2020). Note that during the Sars epidemic that formed the case study for Lee's (2014) book, social media was nascent.

As well as increased access to the Internet, the proliferation in the rise of smartphones around the world has led to a growing number of people spending time online and using social media platforms. In fact, one in three people worldwide and two thirds of all Internet users are on such platforms (Roser et al. 2020).

It is not hard to imagine how misleading information can go viral with an increased use in social media, exacerbated by more time at home online due to lockdown situations around the world. One example from the current Covid-19 pandemic is that dubbed the 'Uncle with master's degree' post. The earliest version of the post was found on Facebook on 7 February and read, "My classmate's uncle and nephew, graduated with a master's degree, and work in Shenzhen Hospital. He is being transferred to study Wuhan pneumonia virus. He just called me and told me to tell my friends . . .". It was shared with a group called Happy People that had nearly 2000 members. The post included advice that is not scientifically or medically proven. Several days later, the same post was shared with minor modifications by a man in India and then again several weeks later by a man called Peter in the UK who had also altered the post to include new information. This time it caught the attention of fact-checking organisations but by then it was too late. The post had already been shared 350,000 times and contained false information like the virus hates the sun but also included factually accurate information about the importance of hand-washing. Since then, the post has spread across languages and the source has changed from the Uncle with the master's degree to board members of Stanford hospital and a friend's nephew in the military (Robinson and Spring 2020).

As we know from past studies of rumour formation and spread, it is likely that the post was not shared with bad intention but indeed through fear and with the intention to protect friends and family. After all, social media platforms allow like-minded people to connect from anywhere in the world. Therefore, the spread of misleading information can be faster and go further than ever before, especially when taking into consideration that platforms take account of user preferences and attitudes, and rely on algorithms to mediate and facilitate information, thus perpetuating the polarisation of views. Studies have shown that when polarisation is high, misleading information is high and can spread faster and further than evidence-based information (Vosoughi et al. 2018).

Recognising the extent of the 'infodemic' in hampering an effective public health response, the WHO, businesses, and governments around the world have united in their response to provide the public with trustworthy sources, reliable guidance, and evidence-based information. Specifically, the WHO established the Information Network for Epidemics (EPI-WIN) to "unite technical and social media teams working closely to track and respond to misinformation, myths and rumours and provide tailored information and evidence for action" (World Health Organization 2020c).

The WHO is tackling the infodemic under the four themes listed below:

1. The causes of the disease: How did it emerge and what is the reason?
2. The illness: what are the symptoms and how is it transmitted?
3. The treatment: How can it be cured?
4. The interventions: what is being done by health authorities or other institutions?

Working with some of the world's biggest search and social media companies, such as Facebook, Google, Tencent, Twitter, and others, the WHO is trying to counter the spread of rumours including that consuming ginger and garlic can prevent the virus, that the virus cannot survive hot weather, and that introducing bleach to your body will protect against Covid-19 (World Health Organization 2020d).

Over the last weeks and months, it's not been unusual to be directed to official guidance (based on evidence) when undertaking an Internet search for "Covid-19" or logging on to social media platforms. Facebook includes an 'Information Center' sharing official medical advice, Instagram delivers a pop-up urging US users to go to the website for the Centers for Disease Control and Prevention (CDC) – or UK users to the NHS – rather than look at the memes and pictures tagged with #coronavirus, and on Pinterest, the only memes and infographics to be found related to Covid-19 are those made by internationally recognised organisations (Wong 2020). In an unprecedented move, Facebook and Twitter have both removed content from a head of state falsely stating that a drug could treat Covid-19 (Ball and Maxmen 2020). As of 5 March, Twitter introduced a new labelling system for tweets containing synthetic and manipulated media and, more recently, tweets containing potentially harmful, misleading information related to Covid-19 are also labelled (Roth and Pickles 2020).

All these efforts rely on fact-checkers at independent media organisations to verify and raise the alarm on misleading information. Back in January, 88 media organisations joined together to record their fact-checking activities with regards to information related to Covid-19. The database, which contained more than 6000 samples in May, is maintained by the International Fact-Checking Information Network – the Network is part of the Poynter Institute for Media Studies in St Petersburg, Florida (Ball and Maxmen 2020), and it is just one group among many which are banded together to sift through countless claims in a bid to weed out accurate, evidence-based information.

Despite the valiant efforts of social media platforms to control the narrative on Covid-19, misleading information continues to spread mostly on social media compared to other sources. An analysis conducted by Brennen and colleagues (2020) which looked at 225 pieces of information considered misleading by independent fact-checkers showed that, while the social media companies have removed or labelled misleading content, 58% of false posts remained active on Twitter, 27% on YouTube, and 24% on Facebook. It should also be noted that while independent fact-checking can go some way in identifying misleading sources of information, fact-checkers are limited in their resources and cannot assess the veracity of information that spreads in private channels, closed groups, and messaging applications; a phenomenon that misinformation scholar Joan Donovan refers to as 'hidden virality' (Donovan 2020). She states that researchers have access to less than 2% of the spaces where misleading information circulates; this makes it impossible to investigate, let alone counter, the huge influx of misleading information that is circulating.

While we know that misleading information is exacerbated by social media, it is not limited to these platforms. It should be noted that Brennen's (2020) analysis found that 20% of claims known to be false came 'top-down' from high-level politicians, celebrities, and prominent public figures, and 36% of these instances included speaking publicly or to the media.

Although the public is increasingly aware, and increasingly concerned, about the problem of misleading information (Fletcher et al. 2020), this new attitude does not equate to an ability to be less susceptible to misleading information. For that, science and scientists can help.

Flattening the curve of misleading information through science

While the Covid-19 pandemic to date has shown that a myriad of stakeholders – from social media platforms to governments and public health authorities – are willing to step up their efforts to combat the spread of misleading information, raising the profile of evidence-based information can only go as far as how much individuals trust the source it is coming from.

"If people think the WHO is anti-American, or Anthony Fauci is corrupt, or that Bill Gates is evil, then elevating an alternative source does not do much – it just makes people think that platform is colluding with that source," says Renée diResta from the Stanford Internet Observatory in California (Ball and Maxmen 2020).

Some suggest that those sharing evidence-based information, such as public health authorities, could do a better job at explaining how the evidence base that ultimately resulted in public health recommendations was built up (Ball and Maxmen 2020). For example, rather than just sharing the results of scientific assessments, it would help to explain how and why the evidence was collected and evaluated. Indeed, Lee (2014: 186) concludes the final paragraph of his book by stating that, "Unfortunately no herbal remedies can fix the media; no vaccines can cure racism. Only concerted, intelligent efforts to educate people in the delicate intricacies of cause-and-effect relationships stand any chance of succeeding." Therefore, the need to increase scientific literacy among different publics could not be a more urgent and important task.

Doing so could avoid widespread phenomena such as 'vaccine hesitancy', which has gained momentum over the years despite evidence that vaccines are effective in preventing infections by deadly diseases. (This indeed is an especially worrying trend considering that a vaccine, when developed, will likely contain the Covid-19 pandemic). Misleading information is also slowing prior momentum towards an international agreement on climate change, which will likely have disastrous consequences worldwide later this century (Hopf et al. 2019). The Covid-19 pandemic is just another instance in this string of recent examples where misleading information can result in harm. Indeed, in a 'post-truth' era, experts are also questioned and opinions towards some scientific issues remain polarised among religious and political lines. Without equipping individuals with the knowledge and skills necessary to be able to autonomously evaluate scientific evidence, we risk undermining trust in science and evidence-based decision-making for better outcomes.

But why should we trust scientific evidence? Since its introduction by Francis Bacon in the 17th century, the scientific method has evolved but is guided by unbiased observations that are evaluated for reproducibility and subjected to careful self-criticism before being offered for scrutiny by the scientific community through the peer review process and publication in scientific journals. If disproved, prevailing models and theories would be replaced by new ones more consistent with the contemporary state of knowledge (Hopf et al. 2019). More recently, historian of science Naomi Oreskes (2019) has argued that it is not necessarily the scientific method that makes science trustworthy, as many of us assume, but it's the 'social character' of science that makes it trustworthy: "All scientific claims are subject to tough scrutiny, and it's only the claims that pass this scrutiny that we can say constitute scientific knowledge." Scientific authority is not based on any individual, but rather on the collective wisdom of the community (Oreskes 2019).[1]

Science will provide us with an 'exit strategy' from the pandemic when a vaccine is finally developed, but until then researchers around the world are working to help understand the origins of the Sars-CoV-2 virus, how it spreads, what treatments are most effective, and indeed if a cure is possible. Sure, there are no definite answers to these questions yet but as more evidence is gathered and consensus built through the collective wisdom of the scientific community, public health advice is likely to change and adapt. As Hopf et al. (2019) note, "this provisional character of science is not a weakness but is one of the key reasons for its strength."

As purveyors of evidence, scientists and members of the broader scientific ecosystem have multiple roles to play when it comes to fighting both the Covid-19 pandemic and associated infodemic:

- *Contributing to knowledge and evidence*

Scientists around the world have mobilised, formed new collaborations and redirected their research agendas to help support the response to Covid-19. In fact, processes that normally take months or years have moved at lightning speed and researchers have already made progress in identifying the virus, deciphering its structure, testing treatments, and trialling a vaccine. In January, the first scientific paper related to Covid-19 was published but since then, scientific literature relating to Covid-19 has reached more than 23,000 papers and is doubling every 20 days according to one count (Brainard 2020).

As well as contributing to evidence to inform the public health response, research has an important role to play in charting the spread of misleading information related to the infodemic. Numerous studies are already underway including, for example, a team at the University of Southern California in Los Angeles sharing a data set containing more than 120 million tweets about Covid-19, and in Trento, Italy, a team at the Bruno Kessler Institute using automated software to track

4.7 million tweets a day about Covid-19 to evaluate the content, determine where they were sent from, and to estimate their reliability (Ball and Maxmen 2020).

Finally, there is a need for a new research agenda into 'the science of science communication'. Future research should study the measures put in place by social media platforms and health authorities during Covid-19 to combat misleading information to see what effect they had. As we know, susceptibility to any information, whether evidence-based or not, is highly driven by cultural context, and scientists and scientific institutions need to use cultural literacy to better engage communities with science and its evidence. These communication and engagement strategies should themselves also be subject to analysis to better understand what works and what doesn't.

- *Communicating and engaging the public*

Just as important as explaining the evidence itself, is explaining the process it took to get there. It is also no secret that explaining science is complicated and unintentional communication errors can result in misleading information. One such example from the COVID-19 pandemic is when a German newspaper reported a study that was yet to undergo scientific peer review and ultimately led to a change in policy (Lahrtz and Serrao 2020).

During a time when we need individuals who can critically evaluate and clearly communicate evidence, it is discouraging to take note of the decline in both professional fact-checkers and science journalists in newsrooms around the world (Scheufele and Krause 2019). As such, coverage of scientific issues has become the responsibility of political reporters, business writers, and journalists in non-scientific beats, sometimes leading to the dangerous phenomenon of "balance as bias" coined by Boykoff and Boykoff (2004): equal coverage and weighting is given to opposing views according to journalistic norms; this contributes to further exacerbate views not based on evidence, resulting in a biased account of the situation. For example, reporting on US elections involves giving equal weighting to opposing parties but reporting on climate change should not give equal weighting to climate scientists and those who do not believe in anthropogenic climate change. Science communicators and science journalists are well placed to undertake this job as they have been trained in how to properly evaluate evidence, interpret jargon, or report on statistics. Investment in these professions is urgently needed, as well as the upskilling of scientists in order to represent their own work in an accurate, engaging, and easy-to-understand manner.

Education systems should also be reformed to place more emphasis on the culture and values of science and its processes. Durant and Ibrahim (2001) also make an important point about the power of informal outreach and engagement with science and suggest that nations should celebrate the culture of science and its values of reasoning, openness, tolerance, and respect for scientific evidence, just as they celebrate the arts and humanities that enrich peoples' lives. With this in mind, it should not go unnoticed that traditional channels of science communication outside of the education system included newspapers, television, and science museums, which tend to reach more educated and higher income audiences. Going forward, it will be crucial to make sure that under-served audiences are also reached.

- *Advocating for science and science literacy*

As well as contributing to scientific knowledge and communicating the 'what' and 'how', scientists must advocate for science and be ambassadors for the scientific community at large. Scientists must be ready to stand up against misleading information and call out those who dismiss valid scientific evidence when they see it (Hopf et al. 2019). Increased and improved capacity for science communication and public engagement will help with this, but scientists remain important stakeholders in upholding and sharing these values with society at large.

Conclusion

Seven months on from when the first cases of Covid-19 were reported, the pandemic is far from over. A week before the end of June 2020 and the world is seeing some of the biggest numbers of daily cases while countries remove lockdown measures in a bid to restart their economies. The aims of this chapter were to briefly document the rise of misinformation and disinformation related to Covid-19 along with some of the attempts to-date to thwart it. It finished by offering thoughts on steps forward, which may well end up being undertaken in the time that it takes to publish this book. When the pandemic finally subsides, I look forward to working with others from different fields to analyse the story of Covid-19 in further detail, take note, and share the lessons learned in the hope that history will not repeat itself in the same way again.

Note

1 It should not go unmentioned that during the Covid-19 pandemic there have been instances of influential scientific papers being retracted. For example, a study into the efficacy of hydroxychloroquine – touted as a treatment by several public figures – was found to be flawed, retracted, and clinical trials were halted (Davey and Kirschgaessner 2020). One can only assume that the pressure to find a treatment resulted in some editorial oversight and in normal circumstances this would not, and should not, happen. The chapter is written on the assumption that proper checks and balances are in place to avoid these sorts of instances.

References

Ball, P., A. Maxmen (2020) 'The epic battle against coronavirus misinformation and conspiracy theories', *Nature* [online], 27 May 2020, www.nature.com/articles/d41586-020-01452-z (last consulted on 5 June 2020).

BBC (2020) 'Coronavirus: Man dies taking fish tank cleaner as virus drug', *BBC News*, 24 March 2020 https://www.bbc.com/news/52012242 (last consulted on 7 June 2020).

Boykoff, M., J. Boykoff (2004) 'Balance as bias: global warming and the US prestige press', *Global Environmental Change* 14(2): 125–36.

Brainard, J. (2020) 'Scientists are drowning in COVID-19 papers. Can new tools keep them afloat?', *Science*, 13 May 2020, www.sciencemag.org/news/2020/05/scientists-are-drowning-covid-19-papers-can-new-tools-keep-them-afloat (last consulted on 8 June 2020).

Brennen, J. et al. (2020) 'Types, sources, and claims of COVID-19 misinformation' *Reuters Institute, University of Oxford*, 7 April 2020, https://reutersinstitute.politics.ox.ac.uk/types-sources-and-claims-covid-19-misinformation#sources (last consulted on 6 June 2020).

Clement, J. (2020) 'Worldwide digital population as of April 2020', *Statista*, 4 June 2020, www.statista.com/statistics/617136/digital-population-worldwide/ (last consulted on 6 June 2020).

Conway, E., N. Oreskes (2010) *Merchants of Doubt: How a Handful of Scientists Obscured the Truth on Issues from Tobacco Smoke to Global Warming*, New York: Bloomsbury Press.

Davey, M., S. Kirschgaessner (2020) 'Surgisphere: Mass audit of papers linked to firm behind hydroxychloroquine Lancet study scandal', *The Guardian*, 10 June 2020, www.theguardian.com/world/2020/jun/10/surgisphere-sapan-desai-lancet-study-hydroxychloroquine-mass-audit-scientific-papers (last consulted on 19 June 2020).

Donovan, J. (2020) 'Covid hoaxes are using a loophole to stay alive – even after content is deleted', *MIT Technology Review*, 30 April 2020, www.technologyreview.com/2020/04/30/1000881/covid-hoaxes-zombie-content-wayback-machine-disinformation/ (last consulted on 7 June 2020).

Durant, J., A. Ibrahim (2011), 'Celebrating the culture of science', *Science* 331(6022): 1242.

Fletcher, R. et al. (2020) 'Trust in UK government and news media COVID-19 information down, concerns over misinformation from government and politicians up', *Reuters Institute, University of Oxford*, 1 June 2020, https://reutersinstitute.politics.ox.ac.uk/trust-uk-government-and-news-media-covid-19-information-down-concerns-over-misinformation (last consulted on 7 June 2020).

Gopinath, G. (2020) 'The Great Lockdown: Worst economic downturn since the Great Depression', *IMFBlog*, 14 April 2020, https://blogs.imf.org/2020/04/14/the-great-lockdown-worst-economic-downturn-since-the-great-depression/ (last consulted on 6 June 2020).

Gottschall, J. (2012) *The Storytelling Animal: How Stories Make Us Human*, Boston: Houghton Mifflin Harcourt.

Hopf, H. et al. (2019) 'Fake science and the knowledge crisis: Ignorance can be fatal', *Royal Society Open Science* 6: 190161, http://doi.org/10.1098/rsos.190161.

Johns Hopkins University (2020) 'COVID-19 Dashboard by the Center for Systems Science and Engineering (CSSE) at Johns Hopkins University (JHU)' *Johns Hopkins University*, https://coronavirus.jhu.edu/map.html (last consulted on 6 June 2020).

Lahrtz, S., M. F. Serrao (2020) 'Drosten, kekulé und Corona: Hahnenkampf ohne gewinner', *Neue Zürcher Zeitung*, 28 May 2020, www.nzz.ch/international/drosten-kekule-und-corona-hahnenkampf-ohne-gewinner-ld.1558276 (last consulted on 8 June 2020).

Lee, J. D. (2014) *An Epidemic of Rumours: How Stories Shape Our Perceptions of Disease*, Boulder: University Press of Colorado.

Oreskes, N. (2014) 'Why we should trust scientists', *TEDSalon NY2014*, available from: www.ted.com/talks/naomi_oreskes_why_we_should_trust_scientists (last consulted on 6 June 2020).

Oreskes, N. et al. (2019) 'Naomi Oreskes on *Why Trust Science?*' [online], 13 November 2019, https://press.princeton.edu/ideas/naomi-oreskes-on-why-trust-science (last consulted on 6 June 2020).

Robinson, O., M. Spring (2020) 'Coronavirus: How bad information goes viral', *BBC Trending*, 19 March 2020 https://www.bbc.com/news/blogs-trending-51931394 (last consulted 4 June 2020).

Roser, M., H. Ritchie, E. Ortiz-Ospina, J. Hasell (2020) 'Coronavirus pandemic (COVID-19)', https://ourworldindata.org/coronavirus (last consulted on 6 June 2020).

Roth, Y., N. Pickles (2020) 'Updating our approach to misleading information', *Twitter*, 11 May 2020, https://blog.twitter.com/en_us/topics/product/2020/updating-our-approach-to-misleading-information.html (last consulted on 6 June 2020).

Sardarizadeh, S., O. Robinson (2020) 'Coronavirus: US and China trade conspiracy theories', *BBC News*, 26 April 2020, www.bbc.com/news/world-52224331 (last consulted on 6 June 2020).

Scheufele, D. A., N. M. Krause (2019), 'Science audiences, misinformation and fake news', *Proceedings of the National Academy of Sciences* 116(16): 7662–69.

Singh, M. et al. (2020) 'Trump claims to have evidence coronavirus started in Chinese lab but offers no details', *The Guardian*, 1 May 2020, www.theguardian.com/us-news/2020/apr/30/donald-trump-coronavirus-chinese-lab-claim (last consulted on 6 June 2020).

Taylor, J. (2020) 'Bat soup, dodgy cures and "diseasology": The spread of coronavirus misinformation', *The Guardian*, 31 January 2020, www.theguardian.com/world/2020/jan/31/bat-soup-dodgy-cures-and-diseasology-the-spread-of-coronavirus-bunkum (last consulted on 6 June 2020).

UNESCO (2018) *Journalism, Fake News & Disinformation: Handbook for Journalism Education and Training* [online], Paris: UNESCO – Communication and Information Sector, https://en.unesco.org/fightfakenews (last consulted on 6 June 2020).

Vosoughi, S. et al. (2018) 'The spread of true and false news online', *Science* 359(6380): 1146–51.

Wong, C. (2020) 'Tech giants struggle to stem "infodemic" of false coronavirus claims', *The Guardian*, 10 April 2020, www.theguardian.com/world/2020/apr/10/tech-giants-struggle-stem-infodemic-false-coronavirus-claims (last consulted on 6 June 2020).

World Health Organization (2020a) 'WHO Timeline – COVID-19', *World Health Organization,* 27 April 2020, https://www.who.int/news-room/detail/27-04-2020-who-timeline---covid-19 (last consulted on 5 June 2020).

World Health Organization (2020b) 'Munich Security Conference', *World Health Organization,* www.who.int/dg/speeches/detail/munich-security-conference (last consulted on 6 June 2020).

World Health Organization (2020c) 'EPI-WIN: WHO information network for epidemics', *World Health Organization,* www.who.int/teams/risk-communication (last consulted on 6 June 2020).

World Health Organization (2020d) 'Coronavirus disease (COVID-19) advice for the public: Myth busters', *World Health Organization* www.who.int/emergencies/diseases/novel-coronavirus-2019/advice-for-public/myth-busters (last consulted on 6 June 2020).

Zarocostas, J. (2020) 'How to fight an infodemic', *The Lancet* 395(10225): 676, https://doi.org/10.1016/S0140-6736(20)30461-X.

PART II

From disinformation to post-truth politics

Evidences from Russia

8

LIE TO LIVE

The production of a faked reality as an existential function of Putin's regime

Anna Zafesova

The need to be believed

Once upon a time, a delegation of the Italian Communist Party went to Moscow and, as it was customary at the time, the Italian comrades were to meet the Soviet comrades. They were received by comrade Boris Ponomariov, the head of the Foreign department of the Central Committee of the Communist party of the Soviet Union, and they told him about their concern about the Soviet invasion of Afghanistan. They told him it was really difficult, nearly impossible, for them to justify this invasion before their followers and voters, that it was a brutal and completely counterproductive move. In response, comrade Ponomariov repeated to them all the explanations of the Soviet propaganda, such as the need to respond to a call of international solidarity from Kabul, and the urge to occupy Afghanistan before the US did. The Italian comrades expressed their disappointment to be treated like fools and objected to the obvious piece of propaganda. At that point, Ponomariov looked them intensely in the eyes and said gravely: "You must believe us."[1]

More than 30 years later, in the autumn of 2014, the Italian government made an attempt to bring Vladimir Putin to negotiate the Ukrainian crisis with his Western counterparts, inviting him to an international summit in Milan. As a former East German citizen and somebody who learned Russian at school, Angela Merkel was chosen as the chief negotiator for the West. Mrs. Merkel waited for Putin almost until midnight. The Russian president was late as usual: he went to Belgrade, where he was welcomed with a military parade, and he was still awaited for a truffle dinner at the country villa of Silvio Berlusconi (Yardley and Herszenhorn 2014). When he finally appeared, Mrs. Merkel, a little bit annoyed, asked him to expose his 'real' reasons and requests about Crimea and Ukraine (Buckley et al. 2015). Putin, at 2 a.m., being alone with the most powerful woman in Europe, a unique opportunity to negotiate without witnesses and restraints, started again to expose his usual propaganda: the 'Nazi coup' in Kiev backed by the West, the danger to the Russian-speaking population in Crimea, and so on (Dempsey 2014). He did not ask for any realpolitik concessions, for example, to exchange the recognition of Crimea and the Donbass as Russian territories for some guarantees against Russian missiles aiming at Europe, or oil and gas discounts, or other potentially tradable issues. Putin was in need of something entirely different: "You have to admit we are right," he told the chancellor. The two leaders had more or less the same conversation again a month later, at the G20 summit in Brisbane (Barkin and Rinke 2014). Then, Angela Merkel called Barack Obama and told him that it is impossible to negotiate with Putin because he "lives in another world," as she put it (Baker 2014).

These two little true stories help to define better the problems we are facing in our newsrooms. There are many recent researches about the strategy and the tactics of the fake news interference inspired by Russians in the Western politics and media environment, which present them as a tool of a 'hybrid war' against the West; something invented and promoted specifically to undermine the enemy. For fake news we usually mean altered or completely wrong facts, and we suppose that people who are spreading them do so intentionally. In other words, they lie and they know it. From the fact-checker's point of view, it is quite simple: you consider a statement, you research it, you find out it is a fake, you tell it, and people open their eyes. The reality is much more complex, as we are starting to find out now that fake news is becoming an issue of concern in the West. We Westerners have our own trolls, both on payroll of some political forces and volunteers, and while they can be linked in some ways to their Moscow colleagues, they are an expression of our homegrown disease and vulnerabilities.

Telling the truth from lies

When we are speaking about Russia, however, we are dealing with something we are not prepared for: an entire alternative reality, for which being believed and promoting the regime's very own different truth is one of the main goals, one of the tools of survival. The fake news Moscow's agents are spreading in the West is not a byproduct of Putin's regime; rather, it is the main staple Russia produces and consumes. The main target of the faked picture are not the Westerners, but Russians themselves, even the same members of the power system that produces it. As Dr. House would say, everybody lies: to their voters, to their diplomatic counterparts, to the Western public, but first of all to themselves. Some of them, sometimes, know they are lying: somebody obviously knew the truth about the Malaysian Boeing,[2] for example, about who shot it down and how. But a lot of opinion makers – Russian journalists, Duma members, diplomats etc. – do believe what they are saying, at least to some degree. For them, fake news is not fake at all. Instead, they think and affirm that Western information is entirely and intentionally faked, or at least biased. The lies they are telling to the world are the same they are telling to themselves. In a way, they are not lying: they may be wrong, but they think they are right.

Sometimes we can doubt that even Vladimir Putin can always tell the truth from the false: when he showed Oliver Stone on his phone a video of a Russian raid in Syria that later was revealed by the fact-checkers as being a footage of an American raid,[3] or when he cited as a crucial witness for the Russian version of the Malaysian Boeing disaster a "Spanish air traffic controller," a fake Twitter account that at the time of the interview was already debunked as fake (Schreck 2018), was he consciously lying to the American filmmaker, or was he an unconscious victim of his own masters of fakes? And who was responsible: the Minister of Defense Sergey Shoigu? Some smart people from the army's press service? Some trolls from the St Petersburg 'factory of trolls' created by Evgeny Prigozhin, the so-called 'Putin's cook'? Did Putin just see the video on the web? And how do we have to deal with it? Must we consider a fake statement from the Russian president that Crimea was not annexed by Moscow but 'reunited' with its homeland (Golubeva, Chernous, Ehrman 2019)? The journalists of free media in a world of free speech may have a problem reporting statements of propaganda without commenting on them, although we also cannot just call a head of a foreign state a liar. But, if we explain that it's just his own opinion, are we giving a lie a more honorable status? Do we need to stop interviewing Russian officials so that we do not help them spread fake news? Would it be correct to object to things they are telling us without forgetting the rules of the objective interview? How do you quote somebody who is part of a system in which the main product is fake news, in a way the crucial exporting Russian industry sector?

But the relationship of the Russian – and before, of the Soviet – regime with the truth is not only its beating heart and its strongest weapon; it is also its weakest point. The Soviet Union collapsed when it became impossible not to face the obvious truth of its failure. It is a system without negative feedback: if you're not allowing the existence of a truth that contradicts the official one, if sticking to the right truth becomes a matter of loyalty, and career, for the members of the establishment as well as for the ordinary people, then the very meaning of the fake disappears. This self-destructive behaviour was most obvious during the Chernobyl disaster, for example, when the long habit of hiding unpleasant truths from high-ranking officials delayed rescue operations in the affected area and put millions of Soviet and Western citizens in danger. The truth about Chernobyl, mostly revealed in the following months by increasingly free press of the *perestroika*, was a relevant component of the loss of trust in the regime, and it is really odd to see that, even more than 30 years later, the Russian officials can still become angry at the critical depiction of the Chernobyl incident in the HBO series (Meduza 2019), considering this TV fiction as yet another attack on contemporary Russia, which wants to identify itself with the late Soviet Union rather than see it as belonging to the past.

Another example of this attitude to defend the one and only official truth as a political weapon is President Putin's campaign to "defend the truth on the Second World War," which was even included in the amendments of the new version of the Constitution (Interfax 2020). Russian leadership sees the imposition of its rhetoric on Moscow's special rights as one of the winners in the war as a legitimisation of its own ambitions to former Soviet zones of influence, and wants to simply ban any theories that dismantle this narrative, like the resolution of the European Parliament on the 80th anniversary of the beginning of WWII (European Parliament 2019). Again, it is very difficult to understand how much the Kremlin is manipulating the historical truth and to what extent Putin and most of his fellow citizens truly believe something they were taught for half a century.

Truth as a prized asset

The truth in the Soviet Union was something of a privilege, reserved to the happy few: even Mikhail Gorbachev was absolutely convinced that the Katyn massacre was perpetrated by the Nazis, until his chief of staff Valery Boldin showed him the top secret file. The legend that newly sworn US presidents receive a thick file with the ultimate truths – who shot JFK, were there really aliens at Roswell, and is Elvis still alive – was true in the Soviet Union. Gorbachev, the first and last Soviet president, already the Secretary General of the one and only ruling party, the leader of the country, the plenipotentiary who went to negotiate the end of the nuclear threat with US presidents, even he was ignoring a lot of hidden truths (Taubman 2018), included the Katyn reports and even the secret protocols on the partition of Europe signed together with the Molotov-Ribbentrop Pact. Who did know them? Boldin? The archive employees? High-ranking KGB people? Not even them, as it seems Vladimir Kriuchkov, in his very first days as KGB chairman, launched an inquiry on the 'real' state of things in the country, asserting after his mentor Yuri Andropov that "We ignore the country we live in" (Bondarenko 2004). Later, in August 1991, both Boldin and Kriuchkov became leaders of a doomed hardliners' coup against Gorbachev,[4] which ultimately led to the collapse of the Soviet Union instead of saving it: it seems that they were not so well informed after all.

As the abovementioned examples from Soviet history show, when lying is systematic within an authoritarian regime, lies become more than lies – to stay in power the removal of truth is necessary, and the same is true for contemporary Russia, which becomes more and more like a late-Soviet regime, rather than a post-Soviet one. People inside the system, from the lower levels up, are not encouraged to tell the truth to their superiors: they risk being dismissed and substituted with plenty of officials ready to stick with the desired truth in exchange for the benefits of being a high-ranking member of the regime's *nomenklatura*. The sanctions imposed by the West against the more prominent among Putin's oligarchs, businessmen, and opinion-makers, were in some way an attempt to force the Kremlin to face the truth, to change its mind about its own power and impunity, to see the limits of its narrative about Russia "rising from its knees" (Manaeva 2019), and the partial failure of these sanctions derives from a system where acknowledging a truth is equal to failure. The side-effect of this mindset is that the system is gradually cleared of the most bright people, i.e. those capable of critical and analytical thinking, and then it lacks the resources to correct the mistakes, which is the first rule of a functioning system, and the first and only condition to survive in the long term. We see that the priority of Russian politics is not to achieve concrete goals of any kind – we saw it in Ukraine and in Syria, two wars that are very expensive for the Kremlin from any point of view –, but rather to impose its own truth, to show they were right: defining reality through an official narrative is something that is seen as a source of legitimisation.

One of the most beloved taglines for Russian nationalists is 'Truth is with us', 'Our strength lies in the truth'. The main Soviet newspaper was even called *Pravda* – the truth, nothing less – while the greatest dissident to challenge the regime, Alexandr Solzhenitsyn, gave one of his political manifestos the title *Live Not By Lies* (Solzhenitsyn 1974). Having access to an alternative version of the events, which often meant knowing the truth, was something thousands of Soviet citizens were searching for, listening to Western radio broadcasts or reading banned books in the *samizdat* network. In a way, the fight between the regime and its adversaries, in USSR and abroad, had at its heart the collision between two alternative versions of reality, the clash between truth and false, and hiding the truth was one of the main activities of the repressive branches of the government. The Communist regime collapsed when the truth about it was gradually revealed, when the perception of a faked history, faked success, faked superiority, of a country-sized myth, became widespread, especially when confronted with the much more easily available information about life in the Western countries.

The problem in the Soviet Union was the censorship, the physical unavailability of the truth, which was the most prized and hard to find in the Soviet world of perennial shortages of anything. Having the truth on your side was seen as quintessential to win. Starting with a president who proudly described himself as 'pragmatic', in 20 years Putin's leadership evolved into a quasi-Soviet regime which feeds on ideology and assertions, almost religious in their being undebatable. The current Russian regime uses the old tools of propaganda and censorship together with a very modern and smart implementation of the contemporary tools of media manipulation, including television and social networks (Pomerantsev 2019; 2015). Information manipulation is a mainly domestic product, whose export is a side-activity of the government's core business of building a reality that voters would like and vote for.

Under Vladimir Putin, Russian public opinion has been shaped for 20 years to stick with an alternate version of facts concerning the Soviet and post-Soviet history, which at some point also became a diplomatic issue. A case in point was the short-lived Commission in charge of fighting the 'distortions' of the history of the Second World War,[5] founded by the Russian government[6] to impose its own vision internationally in order to justify Moscow's claims to control former Soviet territories and parts of Eastern Europe, something hardly possible once the Red Army was considered an occupation rather than liberation force. Something, again, that a wide majority of Russians, voters and politicians alike still believe, considering it a truth quintessential to assert the 'greatness' of their country. Putin's obsession with the annual Victory parade, which the Kremlin was reluctant to postpone even in the middle of the Covid-19 pandemic, has transformed it into one of the main moments of the political year in Russia, and the list of the preferences for the foreign leaders depends greatly on the ones who accepted the invitation to join the show in the Red Square (and the ones who didn't). These differences in the interpretation of the past (and of the present), eventually, have produced a diplomatic stall in the relations between Russia and most Western diplomacies: it is nearly impossible to have a negotiation or a deal if you disagree even on the basics, and in recent years the role of the head of Russian diplomacy, Sergey Lavrov, has become more of a spokesperson than a Foreign minister, coming to international meeting just to state his government's position and express his indignation towards whomever stays on different grounds.

The truth as a battlefield

In this Orwellian context where words and narratives take on supreme importance while facts and evidence are devalued, the efforts of opposition leaders, first of all Alexey Navalny, are concentrated on the demolition of the faked version of reality offered by the regime. Navalny is the most vivid example of this battle line between false and true: his main activity is the debunking of the propaganda myths and the spreading of revelations about corruption and illicit conduct of the members of the power elite in Russia. Born as a 'classical' politician, an activist of the then parliamentary party Yabloko, he later became a blogger, then went offline for some months during the street protests in the winter of 2011–2012. He has emerged again in the last four years as the founder and head of something that we can call a sort of opposition media holding;[7] an alternative television show working on the YouTube platform, with even a weekly news broadcast where the opposition leader acts as an anchorman, telling people news they wouldn't hear in the official media. His 'offline' projects – the Anti-Corruption Foundation[8] and the party Russia of the Future – would not exist without this media communication, which to some extent is (at least in present Russia) its main goal.

The battle to impose its own truth and hold the monopoly on its own version of the reality is still central to the survival of Putin's power in the Kremlin, as it was in the USSR. But there are two substantial differences. The first one is that Russia is now formally a democracy and it holds regular elections. Rigged, manipulated, or forbidden to the opposition, the vote is still something to conquer, as the source of the 20-year-long reign of Putin was in the first place his overwhelming popularity, obtained in an undisputed context of propaganda and censorship, but still authentic. Putin's Kremlin is eager to be recognised in the West, Putin's oligarchs want to live, shop, and invest in the West, so the option of becoming a closed totalitarian regime, like the Soviet Union or contemporary North Korea, is not attractive to the leader, nor to his supporters. In a system that somebody called a 'managed democracy', or an 'illiberal democracy', the carrot is more important than the stick, and you have to convince – even by deception – your voters, instead of just threatening them. We saw Putin bringing the media under his control, especially television, much earlier than the oil assets: his rule would be impossible without the monopoly on the news, including faked and manipulated news.

The second difference, which Russia shares with the Western world, is that today a lot of people, the so called 'ordinary people' – which means readers and voters – refuse the truth even when confronted with it. The problem in contemporary Russia, and now also in the West, is that all the facts are readily available, at least on the web, but people do not want to look for them. Instead, they search for comfortable lies. The *perestroika* was, in a way, an eye-opening political process, and both in Russia and in the West this moment of revelation was seen as crucial and self-sufficient: once you saw the truth, everything else would work in the right way. This magic does not work anymore. If we look closer at the discontent of the Russian public, which has become widespread in the last two years (Kolesnikov and Volkov 2020), we can see that there is a share of voters who would desire a shift towards the Western standards of democracy – freedom of speech and assembly, free elections, and rule of law. This desire is increasing within the society and it has been expressed mainly by the most wealthy part of the middle class, the intellectuals, the youngest generations of westernised Russians. During the street protest of the 2011–2012 Vladislav Surkov, Putin's ideologist, called the people belonging to those groups "angry urban communities" (Earl 2011). These 'angry urban' young people are growing in numbers, because of a natural generational turnover, but also because they don't see many opportunities in the increasingly conservative Russian society. They are mostly immune to the language and to the cultural codes Putin shares with their parents, they have not experienced the shock of the collapse of the Soviet Union, and they are not susceptible to the narrative that 'anything is better than going back to the '90s'. They don't watch TV, they are digital natives, and Internet taught them not to trust anything and anybody, at least not unconditionally. They are the Millennials that we have recently seen leading protests against unfair elections and unjustified arrests, searching and spreading alternative information on the web. We saw them also becoming the main targets of the police and of judiciary repression (Dixon 2020).

Other Russians, the majority, just protest against widespread poverty, corruption, and other social issues, without a clear political programme they would trust and support. But reading on social media, for now one of the few measurement tools of a submerged discontent in Russia, you can see also a lot of people violently criticising Putin for not being Putin anymore, willing for a return of a paternalist and powerful national leader – in other words, willing to have back the narrative of the 'Russia great again' that they have started to perceive as fake. They do not like the way Putin and his court are managing the reality they live in, but they still stick with the myths and narratives the government has created in the past years, included the one of Western malevolence and interference. Essentially, they are asking to remain inside the fake propaganda picture, even when confronted with facts.

We see the same weakness of the facts in Western public opinion. Stating what is considered as a fact did not work with the Anti-Vax movement, for example, and it doesn't work well in the debates on the economy – as a former vice minister of the Italian populist Five Star Movement put it when confronted with risks of inflation and growing debt burden by a professional economist, "It's your words," cancelling with one sentence years of research and empirical experience on a highly specialistic field.[9] The psychological and political mechanism of Western populists and sovereignists is similar to that adopted by the Russian regime: you have to create an alternate reality, to leave rational grounds and make potential voters believe it, because otherwise it would be impossible to play on the adversary's ground where you can differ in opinions or interests you advocate, but not on the basic principles of what is rational and possible.

This brings us to the possible solution of the fake news problem, which is not only a problem for journalists and politicians. In the first Cold War, the goal was to let the truth about the regime slip across the border: the fake reality of Communism would shatter in pieces and the 'evil empire' would fall. It worked. During the new Cold War of fake news, we have to fight simultaneously on two fronts, because we have the same problem at home. We are finding out that the immune defenses of European and Western democracies are weaker than we had thought and the vaccination must come from the school system, from cultural institutions, from governments. But these are all long-term processes while we are dealing with the news, so we have to respond quickly. What do we have to do as journalists? We have to do our job: verifying our sources, crosschecking information, trying to be impartial, and using less adjectives and more data. It can sound too simple, but if in a lot of Western countries we are facing the risk of a potential interference of the Russian official and unofficial media actors aiming at conquering a share of the public, and the risk of domestic political forces using the same method (aided or not by Moscow), it is because we didn't do our job well enough. Legal tools to stop possible Russian interferences are needed, to be applied by governments, media outlets, and social networks, but they will be not enough without a solid counter-narrative. Again, during the Cold War Moscow invested a lot in the propaganda, sustaining news outlets like Novosti agency (of which the RIA Novosti is the heir) or Communist newspapers, courting influential opinion-makers (writers, filmmakers, painters) and moving puppet parties, movements, and NGOs. But the Soviet propaganda efforts were efficiently blocked by a widespread information on the crimes of the Communist regime and on the hard life most of the Soviet citizens led, which resulted in appealing to only a minority of Western public opinion.

Russia has this strange role of being a sort of mythical place to part of the Western audience, something to look at as an alternative to the existing order, but from a distance (Applebaum 2019). Today the pro-Russian public in the West is no longer a network of left-wing sympathisers; Putin's supporters in the West mainly support right-wing parties and movements. Instead of a realm of equality, welfare, and wellbeing for the ordinary people, Russia is perceived today as a rich, powerful nation, invulnerable to the problems of the contemporary world – globalisation, migration, and secularisation. Instead of being seen as the radiant future of Communism, Putin's Russia is now perceived by many Westerners as a heaven where the good old past still survives, where there are no immigrants, LGBT people, pacifists, feminists, and environmental activists; a country which is faithful to the 'traditional Christian values', with white males still firmly in control of their families, and clear and undisputed hierarchies. Both narratives are nothing more than propaganda myths, or fakes, as they could be called nowadays. The only way to fight them is to tell the truth. Cognitive dissonance is the most powerful weapon against ideology.

What to do? Some final remarks

Informed people are harder to force into believing without questioning. However, it is hard to see how information, critical analysis, and propaganda interact in a horizontal world, where everybody can create and spread information and opinions. Journalists must convince the public to listen to them because they have an expertise. This is what makes them different, this is what makes them professionals. Even if they do not know everything, they are trained to deal with information and to recognise it as fake or true, and to know whom and how to ask when they do not know something. They have to attract the public's attention on relevant issues; nothing is given anymore as a birthright, journalists of long-established media outlets are no longer considered as particularly trustworthy. They have to train their readers not to trust anybody blindly, not even journalists. This task requires a good dose of old-school journalism: not infotainment, not partisan spirit, not gossips, not click-baiting. Journalists must use as a rule of thumb – for example, not considering politicians' tweets as news, especially when it comes to the populist and authoritarian ones. Doing this just helps them to reach a larger audience. Media must learn what to tell and what not to tell, not because of a censorship, but to set rules: pulp news, TV shows that rise their ratings by inviting political freaks, fear and hate speech and morbid passion for disasters and catastrophes – it might sound out of fashion, but our media shares the responsibility for the fake news epidemic and we have to acknowledge it. At least in Italy, we do. In a world of perfect journalism, why would people look for fakes and believe them to be true?

What media and journalists must do is not only to debunk, find out, and expose fakes. In this way, they will be only following others' initiative. Speaking of Russia, they have to produce and propose alternative facts and views, to inform, to show different aspects of Russian life. For example, speaking more about the reform of the Russian retirement system or of the healthcare system than about Putin's new car or the last military parade – showing more grim reality and less Kremlin glamour, in other words, to avoid falling for the propaganda that media professionals are supposed to fight against. As hard as this may be, we need to clearly distinguish between fakes and facts, facts and opinions, opinions and propaganda. A clear set of rules for dealing with information must distinguish certified journalists from other media and paramedia producers. We have to be there not only to fight fakes; we need to be there before fakes arrive, and do our job.

Notes

1 From a private conversation between the author and one of the members of the delegation, at the time a high-ranking member of the Italian Communist Party (PCI).

2 On 17 July 2014, a Boeing-777 of Malaysian Airlines was shot down over Donbass while performing a flight from Amsterdam to Kuala Lumpur (MH17). All 283 passengers and 15 crew were killed. The Dutch-led international Joint Investigation Team concluded that the aircraft was downed by a Buk surface-to-air missile fired from the territory controlled by the Russian-backed separatists, been brought and controlled by Russian military from the 53rd Anti-Missile Brigade of the Russian Federation. After years of investigation, the Dutch Public Prosecution Service started a trial hearing in March 2020, with several of the Russian military being charged for the downing of the MH17. The Russian government always denied any responsibility and/or involvement. Moscow didn't offer an alternative explanation. Instead, from the very first hours after the disaster, different officials and commentators suggested a different hypothesis, attributing the guilt to a Ukrainian fight jet, Ukrainian surface-to-air missile, a bomb placed on board, and even a statement that the aircraft was filled with dead bodies by some Western intelligence service which then shot at it to put the blame on Donbass separatists (a plot clearly borrowed from the *Sherlock* series).

3 See on YouTube the video shared in 2018, 'Vladimir Putin Shows Oliver Stone a Fake Video', www.youtube.com/watch?v=-ZGx9XtPUrw

4 On 18 August 1991, a group of conservative high-ranking Communist Party officials, ministers, and intelligence officers launched a coup against Mikhail Gorbachev and his plan to sign a new Union Treaty that would decentralise power in USSR. The coup's leaders formed a State Committee on the State of Emergency, imprisoned Soviet President Gorbachev in his Crimea *dacha*, suppressed freedom of speech and gathering, brought tanks into Moscow, and tried to arrest liberal politicians and Russian Federation President Boris Yeltsin. The widespread campaigning of civil resistance in Moscow, led by Yeltsin, and the refusal of special units commanders to assault the Russian Parliament which became the headquarters of the resistance, brought the attempted coup to collapse. Gorbachev returned to Moscow and was reinstated in power on 21 August. The coup discredited the Communist leadership and the Communist party was outlawed. The coup leaders were arrested. In the three days of turmoil in Moscow most Soviet republics declared independence, and the coup that aimed to save the Soviet Union instead accelerated its collapse, formalised by the Supreme Soviet of the USSR on 26 December 1991.

5 The Presidential Commission of the Russian Federation to Counter Attempts to Falsify History to the Detriment of Russia's Interests was founded by a decree from the then Russian President Dmitry Medvedev in 2009, and included several top-ranking government officials, members of Parliament, military and intelligence officers, and historians heading the State research centres. The Commission's goal was to counteract 'revisionist' attempts from foreign countries and Russian opposition to 're-write' the history of the Second World War, especially in regard to the Soviet role in Eastern Europe. The Commission was disbanded in 2012, but Russian diplomacy continues to vehemently attack any statement which goes against the 'official version' of history.

6 See the official news on the webpage of the Russian President: http://en.kremlin.ru/events/president/news/4121.

7 Navalny.com, Navalny Live YouTube channel, FBK (Anti-Corruption Foundation) social accounts, and some other online resources are all expressions of the opposition group led by Alexey Navalny. They function both as a political platform and as alternative media outlets which produce documentaries, shows, and news critical of the official propaganda version, with special attention to exposing the corruption of the Russian government and governors. Navalny himself stars in different videos and is the host of a weekly show commenting on the main news, while explaining to his followers how to organise themselves to counteract the wrong-doing he reveals. For further reading and watching, www.navalny.com blog contains all the activities of Alexey Navalny and his allies and links to

all other resources of the group, which acts only on the web, the last partially free media environment in Russia.

8 This is the website of the Anti-Corruption Foundation: https://fbk.info/english/about/.

9 This is the video of the discussion, broadcasted by a popular TV show on Italian national television. The video of the confrontation between Laura Castelli and Pier Carlo Padoan became viral for its grotesque tone: www.youtube.com/watch?v=Z7f2imlR6xI.

References

Applebaum, A. (2019) 'The false romance of Russia', *The Atlantic*, 12 December 2019, www.theatlantic.com/ideas/archive/2019/12/false-romance-russia/603433/.

Baker, P. (2014) 'Pressure rising as Obama works to rein In Russia', *The New York Times*, 2 March 2014, www.nytimes.com/2014/03/03/world/europe/pressure-rising-as-obama-works-to-rein-in-russia.html?.

Barkin, N., A. Rinke (2014) 'Merkel hits diplomatic dead-end with Putin', *Reuters*, 25 November 2014, www.reuters.com/article/us-ukraine-crisis-germany-insight/merkel-hits-diplomatic-dead-end-with-putin-idUSKCN0J91EN20141125.

Bondarenko, A. (2004) 'Vladimir KRYUCHKOV: "I did everything I could to save the power"', *Krasnaia Svezda*, 28 February 2004, http://old.redstar.ru/2004/02/28_02/5_01.html.

Buckley, N. et al. (2015) 'Battle for Ukraine: How the West lost Putin', *Financial Times*, 2 February 2015, www.ft.com/content/e3ace220-a252-11e4-9630-00144feab7de.

Dempsey, J. (2014) 'Can Merkel deal with Putin's myths?', *Carnegie Europe*, 20 October 2014, https://carnegieeurope.eu/strategiceurope/56962.

Dixon, R. (2020) 'They were Russian vegans, environmentalists, antifascists and airsoft players. Then they were accused of terrorism', *The Washington Post*, 10 February 2020, https://www.washingtonpost.com/world/they-were-russian-vegans-environmentalists-antifascists-and-airsoft-players-then-they-were-accused-of-terrorism/2020/02/10/1197d95e-4c19-11ea-a4ab-9f389ce8ad30_story.html.

Earl, J. (2011) 'Surkov and Prokhorov spin election', *The Moscow Times*, 6 December 2011, https://www.themoscowtimes.com/2011/12/06/surkov-and-prokhorov-spin-election-a11270.

European Parliament (2019) *Resolution on the Importance of European Remembrance For the Future of Europe*, 19 September 2019, www.europarl.europa.eu/doceo/document/TA-9-2019-0021_EN.html.

Golubeva, A., A. Chernous, G. Ehrman (2019) '"Return" or "power grab"? The crisis in Ukraine in Russian and Ukrainian history textbooks', *BBC Russia*, 15 March 2019, www.bbc.com/russian/features-47442536.

Interfax (2020), 'Putin considered it appropriate to "carefully reflect" the prohibition on falsification of history in the Constitution', 26 February 2020, www.interfax.ru/russia/696798.

Kolesnikov, A., D. Volkov (2020) 'Russians' growing appetite for change', *Carnegie Moscow Center*, 30 January 2020, https://carnegie.ru/2020/01/30/russians-growing-appetite-for-change-pub-80926.

Manaeva, N. (2019) 'Kadyrov congratulated Putin on his 20th anniversary: "He has lifted Russia from its knees"', *Znak*, 17 August 2019, www.znak.com/2019-08-17/kadyrov_pozdravil_putina_s_20_letiem_u_vlasti_on_podnyal_rossiyu_s_kolen.

Meduza (2019) '"Illiterate, stupid, uninquiring idiots". HBO's "Chernobyl" miniseries has enraged Russia's state media and pro-Kremlin reporters. Here's why they hate it', 6 June 2019, https://meduza.io/en/slides/illiterate-stupid-uninquiring-idiots.

Pomerantsev, P. (2015) *Nothing Is True and Everything Is Possible: The Surreal Heart of the New Russia*, London: Faber & Faber.

Pomerantsev, P. (2019) *This Is Not Propaganda: Adventures in the War Against Reality*, London: Faber & Faber.

Schreck, C. (2018) '"That awkward moment": Putin cited debunked MH17 claims in Oliver Stone interview', *Radio Free Europe/Radio Liberty*, 5 March 2018, www.rferl.org/a/putin-debunked-spanish-air-traffic-controller-claims-oliver-stone-interview/28709936.html.

Solzhenitsyn, A. (1974) *Live Not By Lies*, 12 February 1974, full text in English available at: https://archive.org/stream/LiveNotByLies/Live%20Not%20By%20Lies_djvu.txt.

Taubman, W. (2018) *Gorbachev: His Life and Times*, New York: Simon & Schuster.

Yardley, J., D.M. Herszenhorn (2014) 'Making Merkel wait, finding time for truffles', *The New York Times*, 17 October 2014, www.nytimes.com/2014/10/18/world/unbowed-putin-chews-the-scenery-in-milan.html.

9

PLAYING THE RUSSIAN DISINFORMATION GAME

Information operations from Soviet tactics to Putin's sharp power

Francesco Bechis

Information operations (IO): a review of the doctrine

Like any other major power, Russia has become an efficient actor in the cyber-domain. Information operations (IOs) and state-led propaganda play a primary role in Russian cyber warfare. This is not surprising, given the fact that state-sponsored disinformation has been in place as long as there have been State-actors. Yet during the last two decades, the digital revolution has provided Russia with new tools and tactics that have put the country at the forefront of global information warfare. This process has been accompanied by a continuous evolution of Russian military doctrine on unconventional warfare that has considerably accelerated throughout the last decade.[1] State-guided weaponisation of information has often been referred to by Western academics as 'hybrid warfare'.[2] When it comes to definitions, though, one cannot but note how slightly Russian and Western military doctrines over IOs differ from each other. Terms like 'hybrid warfare', 'new-generation warfare', and 'cyberwarfare' have little room in the Russian military science glossary and sometimes are even at odds with it. There are two main reasons why in Moscow one hardly hears discussion of 'cyberwarfare' (*kibervoyna*) or IOs in the same way as Western academics and pundits. First, Russia has a truly different view of IOs than the United States or Europe. As Rand Waltzman (2017: 4) has noted, Russian military elites conceive IOs as a "continuous activity, regardless of the state of relations with any government." This means that they see information warfare as an endless state of warfare that is non-reliant on any *casus belli*, but instead is a pillar of a long-term power strategy. Western states, a glossary provided by the Russian Military Academy of the General Staff explains, rather tend to think of IOs as tactical activities that need to be undertaken in case of hostilities. The second difference lies in the attribution of this kind of operation. Russian military and political élites tend to refer to hybrid warfare as a Western-rooted strategy aimed at undermining its enemies' cohesion. Stating that key elements of the Russian military doctrine are instead part of the Western vocabulary seems to be a recurrent method that dates back to the Soviet times. In fact, the Russian government's attention to hybrid warfare came to be world-known after one of those articles Russian top generals wrote seven years ago. The author was General of the Army Valery Gerasimov, Chief of the General Staff of the Russian Federation Armed Forces, still one of the most prominent figures in the Russian military establishment. Since the 21st century had seen a tendency "toward blurring the lines between the states of war and peace", Gerasimov (2016: 24) noted at the time, traditional warfare had to be re-thought by exploring the possibilities of the new information warfare, which provides States with a competitive against their adversaries. "The role of non-military means of achieving political and strategic goals has grown", the general observed, "and, in many cases, they have exceeded the power of force of weapons in their effectiveness."

The 'Gerasimov doctrine' in the Western debate

The article soon sparked a lively debate in Western academies over a supposed 'Gerasimov doctrine'. Some scholars like Keir Giles referred to it as one of the turning points in the recent evolution of Russian military doctrine, others argued it was no more than a resumé of Soviet-style military theories (Giles 2016). In an article published in the magazine *Foreign Policy*, Mark Galeotti claimed to have been the real 'inventor' of the expression back in 2013 (Galeotti 2018). Truth may lie beneath. Whilst Gerasimov's impact on Russian strategic thought must not be overrated, Galeotti's article nonetheless showed the world how deeply rooted hybrid warfare was in Moscow's military doctrine and how the debate had grown inside the Military Academy. Moreover, Gerasimov's references to a new kind of asymmetric warfare in the information space that paved the way to "wide asymmetrical possibilities for reducing the fighting potential of the enemy" revealed the Russian government already had a clear idea on how to use information as a strategic weapon in the cyber-domain (Gerasimov 2016: 27). Russian doctrine on IOs has since passed through a significant evolution. Other terms, like new generation warfare (NGW) or new-type wars (NTW), have taken the stage in public debates and studies promoted by the General Staff (Thomas 2016: 555).

During the last decade, the Western debate over Russian IOs and asymmetrical warfare has grown remarkably. Among the hundreds of prominent scholars who gave an in-depth description of how Russian State-led disinformation and cyberwarfare work today, there is a group of US researchers from the NED (National Endowment for Democracy) who coined a new term to address Russian attempts to exert influence in the information space: 'sharp power' (Cardenal et al. 2017). Presented at first in a report in 2017, this interpretation has gained ground throughout the academic world and had a vast media echo (Messa 2019). While 'soft power'[3] means the ability to attract and co-opt through appeal and attraction, sharp power, the authors argued, is the ability to wield influence that "pierces, penetrates, or perforates the political and information environments in the targeted countries" (Cardenal et al. 2017: 6). This seems to be a regular practice for authoritarian states, which came to learn how to turn the advantages of globalisation into a weapon. More precisely, they managed to exploit a 'glaring asymmetry'. Globalisation and the digital revolution have widened the openness of democratic systems. Major authoritarian powers like Russia and China, though, have exploited these spaces on a global scale, while raising barriers and narrowing communication and information spaces at home. Russia has been particularly active in taking advantage of the opportunities provided by the globalisation era and, as mentioned, has learned how to turn this asymmetry into strategic leverage in the information war.

The information sphere, though, is not the only domain where authoritarian states' sharp power comes into action: trade, foreign direct investments, energy supplies, schools and universities, international political and cultural institutions, think tanks, foundations. Mastering control and coercion in all these domains is useful to win over the public opinion of a foreign country and getting leverage in its political system is a valid weapon for sharp power. As the name suggests, it is a 'sharp' form of influence, as it penetrates the targeted national system just as a dagger penetrates flesh. Form and method might even perfectly resemble a classic 'soft power' operation, but sharp power has its own distinctive features, as argued by Cardenal and his colleagues: whatever the tool used, the final goal has little to do with cultural exchanges or public image (Cardenal et al. 2017). Sharp power aims at maximising political leverage.

Even though the NED's work has faced some opposition from top scholars, like soft power's father Joseph Nye, who disputes the idea that sharp power represents a new form of influence (Nye 2018), it deserves credit for having shed light on the ongoing challenge posed by authoritarian states with a new face of the information competition through conventional and unconventional means that is not 'soft' nor comes close to what Joshua Kurlantzick called a "charm offensive." [4]

Russia's 'active measures'

As noted before, the concept of information warfare is not new to Russia's strategic thought. Indeed, it has always been a key component of what Russian intelligence officers, military chiefs, and policy makers have historically referred to as 'active measures' (*aktivnye meropriyatiya*), or, to cite a well-known definition by American Kremlinologist George Kennan, "measures short of war" (MSW), a set of measures aimed at undermining the enemy's resilience through covert operations in the economic, military, cyber, and information fields. Nevertheless, the tools and tactics that the digital revolution has introduced demand a new theoretical framework to read Russian IOs. Before entering into details about the Russian government's approach to information warfare, it is worth noting how it fits a well-established practice.

Since Soviet times, in Russian military doctrine active measures have been indicated as a set of three main concepts: disinformation (*dezinformatsiya*), deception (*maskirovka*), and reflexive control (*refleksivnoe upravlenie*) (Connable et al.

2020: 25). None of these is a stand-alone tactic, as they concur to create a holistic approach to warfare within the field of information. Among the three, *maskirovka* is the oldest, as it first appeared in Russian military academia around 1904, when the Czar and his family were still alive and in charge. To understand how deeply institutionalised this notion is, it suffices to recall that from 1904 to 1929 there has been a school, the Higher School of Maskirovka, where Russian military officials were provided with the basics of this tactic through textbooks and dedicated lessons (Thomas 2004: 239). A comprehensive definition can be found in the work of Roger Beaumont, one of the leading scholars who has studied Soviet disinformation techniques in depth. *Maskirovka*, he argued, "encompasses a diverse spectrum of stratagems employed to warp the enemy's view of Soviet positions, designs and missions, and to alter the perceptions of their own side and their clients as well" (Beaumont 1982: 3). Recently, Keir Giles has defined it as "the complex of measures devised to confuse the enemy regarding the presence and disposition of forces, their condition, readiness, actions and plans" (Giles 2018: 10). Deception and camouflage are two recurrent elements of any country's military doctrine and hitherto should not be overlooked. What has really made *maskirovka* a peculiar feature of Russian State action though is its transversal use both in the military and in the political and civilian world. Born in the military academia, the concept has become a State paradigm that encompasses the whole spectrum of government activities. Even though *maskirovka* is an old-fashioned Soviet-era strategy, some authors maintain that it still has its place in Russian hostile measures. Galeotti, for instance, has described the operations of the 'little green men' who fled Crimea in 2014 before it was annexed by Russia as a classic case of *maskirovka*, as the confusion and fear they sowed among the Ukrainian military establishment and forces bought time to the Russians and to their local allies, allowing them to gain the commanding positions in Crimea.[5]

Disinformation and reflexive control

Russian *dezinformatsiya* is "the practice of misinforming or misleading adversaries (and others) with false information, typically to slow, degrade, or stop effective responses to an associated Russian activity, such as sabotage, cyberattack, or limited military incursion" (Connable et al. 2020: 27). Despite building on Cold War tactics, contemporary Russia's State-led disinformation presents unique features. This is not just due to the use of social media and new technologies, but also because it has changed scope, speed, and volume. Today Russian disinformation campaigns can count on a wholly new set of tools. Social media platforms and the pro-government media environment provide them with a much higher level of discretion than the Soviet ones, making it more difficult to trace them back to government agencies. Christopher Paul and Miriam Matthews (2016) have defined the contemporary model of Russian disinformation as a "Firehose of falsehood", as it presents two distinctive features: "high number of channels and messages and a shameless willingness to disseminate partial truths or outright factions." Multiple sources and channels help today's Russian government disinformation efforts reach their targets with much greater efficiency and speed than before. The simultaneous use of government-related media outlets, social networks, and automated bots and trolls grants these campaigns an audience once inconceivable. Moreover, unlike Soviet-era propaganda operations, present disinformation campaigns do not come out as a response to isolated events or threats, but instead they are part of a continuous flow of information channelled both through official and unofficial means. As several studies in the experimental psychology field have shown, repetition helps a message to be successful and accepted by the targeted audience (Petty et al. 2005). In the words of Paul and Matthews, "repetition leads to familiarity, and familiarity leads to acceptance" (Paul and Matthews 2016: 4).

While *dezinformatsiya* is a relatively recent concept, *refleksivnoe upravlenie* or 'reflexive control', has much deeper roots in Russian military literature. Its first appearances date back more than 30 years ago. Maria Snegovaya has described it as the ability to force a "stronger adversary voluntarily to choose the actions most advantageous to Russian objectives by shaping the adversary's perceptions of the situation decisively" (Snegovaya 2015: 7). A similar interpretation has been offered by Timothy Thomas, who defined reflexive control as "a means of conveying to a partner or an opponent specially prepared information to incline him to voluntarily make the predetermined decision desired by the initiator of the action" (Thomas 2004: 237). Both definitions insist on the same aspect: Russian reflexive control operations are aimed at altering the enemy's perceptions, in order to make him think what they want him to think and do what they want him to do. These operations can leverage different tactics, from isolated military measures to acts of disinformation and diversion (*diversiya*), which is the tactic of diverting the adversary's attention to divide its forces. To be successful, they usually need to exploit pre-existing vulnerabilities in their targets, which can be individuals (i.e. decision-makers, military chiefs, influential personalities) or wide sections of the population. In the words of Thomas, "chief task of reflexive control is to locate the weak link of the filter, and exploit it" (ibid.: 241). Several cases can be borrowed, both from past and recent times. During the Cold War, the Soviet Union used to set up parades of fake-ICBMs in Moscow to convince the US the Soviets had the latest generation nuclear missiles, altering the enemy's perception of their nuclear arsenal. Knowing dozens of US diplomats, attachés, and undercover agents used to attend these parades, as they provided them with public information over Russian military capabilities, the Russian government filled them with fake missiles, hoping the attendants would then report to domestic intelligence agencies (ibid.: 253).

When theory meets practice: The war with Georgia and Ukraine

Concrete examples of how the tactics described above have been translated into actions can be drawn from the Russia-Georgia war in 2008, a conflict which is considered the first and most significant test bench for Putin's hybrid warfare and Russian IO. As stressed by Giles, the way this confrontation ended provides a clear example of how Russian reflexive control works and can be effective (Giles and Seaboyer 2018: 13). Tensions arose after the maxi-military drill Kavkaz-2008 ended on 4 August. The ongoing movement of Russian troops at the border unrelated to the Russian contingents of the CIS (collective peacekeeping forces), along with the evacuation of civilians in South Ossetia to Russia, let the Georgian government led by President Mikheil Saakashvili, as well as most of the international community, believe Russians were on the edge of storming Tbilisi and overthrowing the government. Rumours and fears eventually led to the evacuation of the city on 9 August. This contributed to the creation of a sense of urgency among EU countries, which ultimately led to the ceasefire agreement signed on the 12 August. Thus, the terms dictated in the peace plan, Giles and Seaboyer wrote, "resulted from a false perception that Georgia could be lost altogether" (ibid.). French President Nicolas Sarkozy's mediation helped Russia get away with an unexpected set of concessions: not only was Moscow allowed to keep its troops on the ground, but it was also given an additional 'security-zone' across the borders of South Ossetia and Abkhazia. This was a textbook case of Russian reflexive control. By letting its adversaries believe a military invasion of Tbilisi was about to happen, Russia got away with more concessions that it could have ever hoped for.

A more recent case where the Russian government has made extensive use of reflexive control techniques is the ongoing war in Ukraine, which started with the annexation of Crimea in 2014. As Snegovaya (2015: 7) pointed out, "the Ukrainian war may well turn into the most relevant testing ground for Russian reflexive control tactics ever." Although not all of the objectives set by Moscow have been accomplished so far, it is undeniable that Putin has achieved some considerable results, notably the decision taken by Western countries to avoid a direct intervention into the conflict, not to mention the divisions sown among NATO allies in one of the toughest tests for the Alliance cohesion.[6] As in the previous cases, the Ukrainian crisis has seen the deployment of a wide range of strategies from Russian authorities. Denying the presence of Russian forces on the ground and of any link between the Federation and the 'little green men' who poured into the Ukrainian territory six years ago; convincing EU countries that Russia's tools and resources were scarce and therefore the Russian army presence in Ukraine was somehow tolerable; at the same time, promoting an unprecedented set of disinformation campaigns and cyber-warfare operations to spread the narrative of Russia as a 'saviour', the only actor capable of allowing Crimean citizens to rightfully reclaim sovereignty from a corrupt country.

Social media: The disinformation chain

After this brief overview of the Russian disinformation strategic pillars, it is worth noting how theory meets practice today. Whether the cited notions are still acknowledged by the Russian military and political elites or not, what allows the reinterpretation and the putting of these old Soviet-fashioned approaches into practice is the range of new techniques and tools that digitalisation and the Internet have brought. Among these, social media plays a central role in modern Russian State-led IOs. This seems nothing extraordinary at a first glance. Yet, things change when one looks at how institutionalised the Russian government has made its use of media outlets and social media for propaganda and targeted disinformation purposes. Of course, this institutionalisation did not happen overnight. Rather, it is part of a well-established strategy that reflects President Putin's perception of the information landscape as well as his ideas about how it should be controlled. Back in 2013, Putin gave an unambiguous explanation of his long-term plans to put Russia at the forefront of the information competition worldwide. While visiting the new RT (one of the major Russian broadcasters, previously known as Russia Today) headquarters in Moscow, he expressed his hope that Russian media could soon manage to "break the Anglo-Saxon monopoly on the global information streams" (Messa 2019: 43). Later that same year, at the annual news conference, commenting on the future of State media outlets, Putin left no doubts about how he conceives the freedom of information: "There should be patriotically minded people at the head of state information resources" – he told reporters – "people who uphold the interests of the Russian Federation. These are state resources. That is the way it is going to be" (Dougherty 2015). As Paolo Messa (2019: 43) noted, "Post-Soviet Russia's media strategy is a case that is well-known (and very relevant today) of how subtle the boundary can be between political propaganda and information."

There are many reasons why today's social media allows a government to target its adversary in a way that was inconceivable before. First of all, their target is much wider than any information campaign in the past. As Giles pointed out, they can hit entire populations, and reach people "in their natural environment" (Giles and Seaboyer 2018: 34). Second, social media campaigns are far harder to be exposed. Last but not least, they are relatively low-cost compared to the old kinetic techniques through which IOs were carried out. All these features made Putin bet heavily on the social media potential in the information war. The difference between Russia and other major Western countries is the scale, the extent, and the sophistication behind its social media State-led disinformation strategy.

A recent report from RAND Corporation describes the "disinformation chain" underpinning the Kremlin's use of social media to achieve its foreign policy objectives (Connable et al. 2020). On top of the chain is the Russian government. This indeed is what emerged in July 2018 from US special counsel Robert Mueller's 'Russiagate' final report, where 12 Russian agents from the GRU (Main Intelligence Directorate of the General Staff), a long-established Russian foreign military intelligence agency, were indicted for the massive hacking of the National Democratic Committee and US presidential candidate Hillary Clinton's campaign staff. Intelligence agencies, however, are not the only players in the Russian disinformation game. Evidence shows that the majority of the disinformation campaigns channelled through social media are pursued by entities that are not formally linked to the government. This category, which represents the second ring of the chain and includes popular media outlets like RT and press agencies like Sputnik, is formed by actors which receive public support from the government and have a key role in conveying the Kremlin's disinformation campaigns, both domestically and abroad. A third ring is then represented by a wide set of entities whose links to the Russian government are often hard to find without an intelligence inquiry. This group includes thousands of webpages and blogs committed to shaping the Russian government's disinformation efforts spreading fake or misinformed stories and injecting fake news into the targeted audiences. The Internet Research Agency (IRA), a well-known troll factory (i.e. an agency specialising in the creation and diffusion of fake social media accounts) based in St. Petersburg, with dozens of employees working daily to fabricate false stories and spread them online, is a major player at this level (Chen 2015). It was cited in the final report of the 'Russiagate' investigation by the US Special Counsel Robert Mueller, which was delivered to the Attorney General William Barr on 22 March 2019. The report defined it as "a Russian organization funded by Yevgeniy Viktorovich Prigozhin", then one of the most prominent Russian oligarchs, and accused it of having conducted "social media operations targeted at large US audiences with the goal of sowing discord in the U.S. political system."[7]

Who did what? The attribution dilemma

Another lens through which the Russian disinformation scheme can be understood is deniability. Disinformation is fuelled by a wide range of actors, going from those whose attribution is easy to those that are much harder to relate. State-media giants such as Sputnik News, Channel One, Ruptly, and the All-Russia State Television and Radio Broadcasting Company (VGTRK) belong to the first group. Some of these government-related media outlets, alongside officially independent media like RT, can rely on an amount of resources second to none of the many other world-known broadcasters. RT, for instance, has an outstanding presence on social media, especially on YouTube, where it counts more subscribers than BBC or Fox News and broadcasts in various languages such as German, French, Arabic, and even Mandarin. However, their level of independence has little to do with the one enjoyed by other global media outlets. To put it in Daniel Fried and Alina Polyakova's (2018: 4) words, "they are arms of the Russian State no more independent than *Pravda* was during the Soviet period." As a matter of fact, despite a broad offer, the Russian State media environment does not seem to have much room for challenging views of the government's action. This is also due to a strict legal framework that has recently been tightened by a new set of laws introduced in March 2019 establishing fines up to 1.5 million roubles (20,500 euros, approximately) for those who disseminate 'false information' through the media landscape and do not remove it at the request of the Federal Service for Supervision of Communications, Information Technology and Mass Media (*Roskomnadzor*). These laws allow for "the censorship of online journalism and online speech", OSCE Representative on Freedom of the Media Harlem Désir noted.[8]

As noted above, official media outlets are just the tip of the iceberg. Their strength comes from a broad audience. Their weakness lies in their easy attribution. Hence, a second link of the disinformation chain is needed. Blogs, websites, and online newspapers that are not officially affiliated to the Russian government but that nonetheless clearly side with it can prove to be very effective force multipliers of disinformation campaigns. These include news aggregators, data-dump websites, far-right and far-left blogs, often easily recognisable by conspiracy theories and click-bait headlines. Together, they form a 'grey zone': useful for inflating propaganda, they lack direct links to Russian public authorities and yet play a key role in shaping their views and disinformation. Records show that the great majority of these outlets is active in the dissemination of divisive content, mostly with a strong anti-Western bias. Depending on the geographical context, they can exploit different pre-existing cultural and political divisions. For instance, in the so-called 'near abroad', a term that has historically indicated ex-Soviet States such as Ukraine, Belarus, Moldova, Lithuania, Estonia, Latvia, but also states of the Trans-Caucasus region such as Georgia or Armenia, these sites usually insist on the widespread discontent of local populations towards the Western, US-led cultural model and the presence of strong, deeply rooted Russian speaking communities. On the other side, in Europe, they frequently use issues such as immigration, Islam, and sovereignty as leverage against an elitist EU or a declining NATO.

Force multipliers: When bots come into action

Finally, the lowest level of attribution is reached by the last link of the chain: a network of fake social media accounts, both human-led (trolls) or automated (bots), which are especially useful for amplifying the disinformation and for spreading it on the web while keeping their cover. Here the lines between the information and the cyberspace become blurred. Trolls and bots carry different tasks. The former have a more consolidate presence in the Russian information space. Their main objective is to create content, not just to spread it. In recent years, notably after Putin's return to Kremlin in 2012 and the impressive wave of mass protests that followed, there has been a continuous record of pro-government trolls targeting opposition leaders, opinion-makers, and bloggers. Content created by trolls does not necessarily have to be faked. Indeed, it can well consist of a mixture of realistic claims and fiction, so long as it is presented as credible to the targeted audience. Records show that several disinformation campaigns carried out by pro-Kremlin trolls were built on highly detailed information that was hacked from their victims. This was the case for Sergei Maksimov, a Russian hacker known through the name of 'Torquemada Hell', who, for years, has attacked anti-government bloggers, stealing data and information through spear-phishing and then spreading it with the help of trolls and bots. He was convicted for his crimes in Germany (Sanovich 2017: 10).

Unlike trolls, the core task of bots is to act as force multipliers of disinformation. Their distinguishing feature, as the name explains, is to be fully automated. They usually consist of fake social media accounts, especially on Twitter, and act simultaneously, publishing content on a schedule and expanding the reach of Russian trolls as well as State-media content. As previously noted, the more coordinated the disinformation chain, the higher the chance for the message to reach its target. Not surprisingly, most Russian IOs that have been unmasked by Western intelligence in recent years have shown a high degree of coordination between the three levels of the chain. A celebrated textbook case is the 'Lisa case'. On 11 January 2016, in Berlin, during mass migrant public unrest in the city of Cologne, Lisa, a 13-year-old German girl with Russian origins, did not come home from school. Soon after her disappearance was reported to the media by her parents, a journalist from Channel One, a Russian-language Kremlin TV broadcasting in Germany, suggested that the girl had been raped by migrants while she was out. Once Russian outlets, such as RT Deutsch and Sputnik, picked up the news, it quickly broke through the mainstream media. Eventually it prompted the Russian Minister of Foreign Affairs Sergey Lavrov to condemn Germany's reluctance to investigate the case. In a few hours, a diplomatic case broke out, and the story rapidly entered social media, relaunched by pro-Kremlin Twitter users and Facebook groups and igniting a street protest from hard-right groups in Cologne. The day after the German police revealed that the whole story was fake: Lisa had spent the night at her friend's home. Other examples can be drawn from recent events. The Covid-19 virus worldwide outbreak in February 2020 offered another chance for a widespread disinformation campaign carried on by Russian State media and social media accounts. A report from the EEAS (European Union External Action Service) noticed an increase of disinformation efforts from providers based in Russia or linked to the Kremlin (Rankin 2020). Conspiracy theories describing the virus as a Western plot to benefit pharmaceutical companies appeared on the website of RIA FAN federal agency, while the pro-Kremlin REN TV claimed the virus could be a 'biological weapon' used by US forces against China. This seems to be part of a new path that Russian State media have taken to disseminate false claims against Western countries. Instead of fabricating the fake contents themselves, the EU report shows, they increasingly tend to refer to conspiracy theories originated elsewhere, to avoid accusations. It is a new form of *maskirovka* but translated into the media sphere. After all, some good old Soviet tactics never get old.

Conclusion

One of the most common arguments the disinformation 'skeptics' tend to resort to goes as follows: 'should we really care?' Why should we fear that a few Twitter bot accounts or a handful of conspiracy blogs might really have a visible impact on one state's political and information environment? While the question is no doubt legitimate, it is also misplaced. As our review tried to demonstrate, websites, blogs, and social network accounts are just the tip of the iceberg. Or, in other words, they are nothing but the last links of the disinformation chain. At the top of it, there often might be a highly sophisticated direction from state actors. No one could be so naïve as to believe that every worldwide state-led disinformation campaign has the Kremlin's stamp on it. As we recalled, disinformation has been in place as long as there have been states. However, the Russian case is one worth studying, for two main reasons. First: it can count on an institutional architecture no other state can claim today. Second: as we showed, today's Russian disinformation relies on a long-standing tradition of Soviet-era military tactics. This has become even clearer after Mr Putin came to power. Proof is the extraordinary attention Russian military élites have increasingly devolved to the reinterpretation of the old Soviet 'active measures' during the last decade, and the impressive sophistication of Moscow's 'sharp power' techniques in the social media landscape. This, along with the progressive disintegration of some of the pillars that govern globalisation and multilateralism due to the global Covid-19 pandemic and, therefore, the increasing danger for the resilience of democratic states and their institutions, should be enough for a clear, ultimate answer to the question above: we should definitely care.

Notes

1 See, for example: Chekinov and Bogdanov (2012); Kartapolov (2015); Andrianov and Loyko (2015).
2 The term 'hybrid warfare' describes a strategy that builds both on conventional military force and irregular and cyber warfare tactics. For an overview, see Murray and Mansoor (2012) and Lanoszka (2016).
3 Soft power is the ability to affect others to obtain the outcomes one wants through attraction rather than coercion or payment. A country's soft power is built on its culture, values, and policies. The first definition of soft power was coined by Harvard scholar Joseph Nye in 1990. See Nye (1990).
4 In his book, Kurlantzick describes "charm offensive" as the way China uses soft power to appeal to its neighbours and to distant countries alike. The author contends China has wooed the world with a "charm offensive" that has largely escaped the attention of American policy makers, thus allowing Beijing to take advantage of American foreign policy mistakes. See Kurlantzick (2007).
5 The phrase "Little green men" indicates masked soldiers of the Russian Federation wearing unmarked green uniforms who entered Crimea in February–March 2014. While the Russian government initially denied they belonged to the Russian Armed Forces, it eventually confirmed its military presence in Crimea. See Galeotti (2015).
6 On 3 March 2014, two weeks after the Russian invasion of Crimea, EU foreign ministers met in Brussels but could reach no clear agreement on a shared road map to sanction Moscow. Polish Foreign Minister Radoslaw Sikorski told reporters that "the rest of the Europe is sometimes half a phase behind us" (Faiola 2014).
7 See the full report: https://edition.cnn.com/2019/04/18/politics/full-mueller-report-pdf/index.html.
8 Full text of the OSCE press release: www.osce.org/representative-on-freedom-of-media/414770.

References

Andrianov, V.V., V.V. Loyko (2015) 'Questions regarding the use of the armed forces of the Russian federation in crisis situations in peacetime', *Voennaya Mysl'* (*Military Thought*) 1: 68.

Beaumont, R. (1982) *Maskirovka: Soviet Camouflage, Concealment and Deception*, College Station: Center for Strategic Technology, Texas A&M University.

Cardenal, J.P., J. Kucharczyk, G. Mesežnikov, G. Pleschová (2017) *Sharp Power*, Washington DC: National Endowment for Democracy.

Chekinov, S.G., S.A. Bogdanov (2012) 'The initial period of war and its influence on the preparation of the country for future wars, *Military Thought* 11: 16.

Chen, A. (2015) 'The agency', *The New York Times*, 7 June 2015.

Connable, B., S. Young, S. Pezard, A. Radin, R.S. Cohen, K. Migacheva, J. Sladden (2020) *Russia's Hostile Measures*, Santa Monica: RAND Corporation.

Dougherty, J. (2015) 'How the media became one of Putin's most powerful weapons', *The Atlantic*, 21 April 2015.

Faiola, A. (2014) 'Europe divided over Russia as NATO meets on Ukraine crisis', *The Washington Post*, 4 March 2014.

Fried, D., A. Polyakova (2018) 'Democratic defense against disinformation' *Atlantic Council*.

Galeotti, M. (2015) '"Hybrid war" and "little green men": How it works and how it doesn't', in: A. Pikulicka, R. Sakwa (eds), *Ukraine and Russia: People, Politics, Propaganda and Perspectives*, Bristol: E-International Relations Publishing.

Galeotti, M. (2018) 'I'm sorry for creating Gerasimov doctrine', *Foreign Policy*, 5 March 2018.

Gerasimov, V. (2016) 'The value of science is in the foresight: New challenges demand rethinking the forms and methods of carrying out combat operations', *Military Review*, January–February issue.

Giles, K. (2016) 'The next phase of Russian information warfare', *NATO Strategic Communications Centre of Excellence*.

Giles, K., A. Seaboyer (2018) *Russian Reflexive Control*, Kingston: Royal Military College of Canada.

Kartapolov, A.V. (2015) 'Lessons of military conflicts, prospects for the development of means and methods of administering them, direct and indirect actions in contemporary international conflicts', *Journal of the Academy of Military Science* 2(51).

Kurlantzick, J. (2007) *Charm Offensive: How China's Soft Power is Transforming the World*, New Haven: Yale University Press.

Lanoszka, A. (2016) 'Russian hybrid warfare and extended deterrence in eastern Europe', *International Affairs* 92(1): 175–95.

Messa, P. (2019) *The Age of Sharp Power*, Milan: Bocconi University Press.

Murray, W., P.R. Mansoor (eds) (2012) *Hybrid Warfare: Fighting Complex Opponents From the Ancient World to the Present*, Cambridge: Cambridge University Press.

Nye, J. (1990) 'Soft power', *Foreign Policy* 80: 153–71.

Nye, J. (2018) 'How sharp power threatens soft power', *Foreign Affairs*, 24 January 2018.

Paul, C., M. Matthews (2016) *The Russian 'Firehose of Falsehood' Propaganda Model*, Santa Monica: RAND Corporation.

Petty, R.E., J.T. Cacioppo, A.J. Strathman, J.R. Priester (2005) 'To think or not to think: Exploring two routes to persuasion', in: T.C. Brock, M.C. Green (eds), *Persuasion: Psychological Insights and Perspectives*, Thousand Oaks: Sage Publications.

Rankin, J. (2020) 'Russian media "spreading Covid-19 disinformation"', *The Guardian*, 18 March 2020.

Sanovich, S. (2017) 'Computational propaganda in Russia: The origins of digital misinformation', in: S. Wolley, P. Howard (eds), *Working Paper 3. Oxford: Project on Computational Propaganda*, Oxford: Oxford University Press.

Snegovaya, M. (2015) 'Putin's information warfare in Ukraine', *Russia Report*.

Thomas, T. (2004) 'Russia's reflexive control: Theory and the military', *Journal of Slavic Military Studies*, 17(2): 237–56.

Thomas, T. (2016) 'The evolution of Russian military thought: Integrating hybrid, new-generation, and new-type thinking', *Journal of Slavic Military Studies*.

Waltzman, R. (2017) *The Weaponization of Information*, Santa Monica: RAND Corporation.

10

MYTHS AND REALITIES OF PUTINISM IN POST-TRUTH POLITICS

Mara Morini

Introduction

In 2016 the *Oxford Dictionaries* selected the term "post-truth" as the "word of the year" to describe the emergence of "an era of boundless virtual communication" which characterises a battle between facts and lies in different arenas and policies.[1] Post-truth politics has been defined by *The Economist* as "reliance on assertions that 'feel true' but have no basis in fact" and are based more on emotions than rationality.[2] In contemporary democracies this term also refer to the use of fake news and populist protest/movements as a reaction to the establishment's policies which are considered unaccountable and unresponsive in comparison with citizens' needs and demands. These new political movements try to delegitimise democratic institutions in order to pave the way to a new political order so that elements of deception and misinformation can be considered as a potential and effective threat to liberal democracies.

In the early 2000s, the Internet was considered a tool for more participation, freedom, and democratisation. Nowadays, the Internet has become a real threat due to the increased number of people who prefer getting information online, where fake news and fake accounts are more present than in newspapers. The post-truth era is also characterised by the repudiation of science-based facts, objectivity, expertise, evidence, and statistics which undermines the community of scientists.

The main effects of fake news are political and social polarised debates which shed light on moral crisis, individuality, reinforcing people's beliefs among those who share the same opinion, and the rejection of scientific principles, analyses, research dealing with health, environment, education policies, and so on. Nowadays, the Internet has revealed the dark side of the online community, i.e. a large amount of web-based information that could be harmful and dangerous for the audience who are more oriented to believe information that appeals to their beliefs and emotions. The 'production of confusion'[3] is a real problem for governments, industries, and private firms which must implement literacy skills for better meaningful learning and understanding of information consumption.

In foreign and domestic policies this attitude against the truth based on evidence has determined the growing feeling of anti-globalisation, xenophobic attitudes, and nationalist politicians who challenge the liberal order and create fake news in order to make people anxious and insecure about their own future. So, fake news can determine a sort of distrust in political elites and democratic decision-making. We have some examples with the false claim on the extortion of money by the EU which paved the way to the Brexit decision, as well as the news that the Ukrainian government crucified a child which was spread on social media by the Russian government (Oates and Steiner 2018: 2–5).

Nevertheless, we share Ostrovsky's opinion (2017) about the importance of a conceptual distinction between 'post-truth politics' and 'fake news'. While the two terms seem interchangeable, there is a need for clarification in regard to what they mean and involve in non-democratic political regimes, and in the Russian political environment in particular. In doing so, this chapter aims to provide an analysis of the Kremlin's role in taking advantage of the post-fact/post-truth sphere, both in the domestic policies dealing with social, political, and economic issues and as a political/strategic tool in the international setting. As far as the latter is concerned, in the aftermath of the Ukraine crisis in 2014, and particularly since the election of Donald Trump as President of the US, many scholars and journalists are exploring Moscow's manipulations of the Western mediascape (Orttung and Nelson 2018). Its foreign manipulations range from biased coverage of events, taking sides in political controversies, intentional securitisation of narratives, hacking, information warfare (cyber politics), and direct lies.

Secondly, a description of the Russian media landscape and peculiarity and its rapid change in recent years, influenced especially by the rise of digital media across the globe, is necessary to better understand *who* the main actors able to influence the political debate are and *how* this develops. Special attention will be also devoted to Internet governance policy and to its role in weaponising lies to face the domestic/foreign political dimensions between the matters of fact and the matters of concern in Russian politics.

Fake news and Russian propaganda

Strategic narratives have always been used in Soviet times. Miskimmon, O'Loughlin, and Roselle (2017: 3) define strategic narratives as "tools that political actors employ to promote their interests, values, and aspirations for international order by managing expectations and altering the discursive environment." They are based on a system of stories that in politics represent the intersection of communication and power. Kenez in his work on Soviet propaganda, *The Birth of the Propaganda State* (1985), underlines that propaganda was part of the larger Soviet system.

Contemporary Russia has also invested in mass media propaganda because Russia's government relies on high domestic consensus to maintain its legitimacy (Petrov, Lipman, and Hale 2014). Although there are still some independent voices such as *Ekho Moskvy* radio station, *Novaya Gazeta*, an alternative newspaper, and online video producer *Telekanal Dozhd*, the analysis made by "Reporters Without Borders" ranked Russia as only 148 out of 180 countries assessed for its "World Press Freedom Index" in 2016. Journalism became deprofessionalised in Russia, while in the past it had always been considered a truthful speech based on accuracy, willingness to stand by one's words, sincerity, seriousness, and courage.

Roudakova admits that "what we are observing in Russia today is what the world looks like when journalism is made superfluous" (2017: 219). Nowadays, propaganda is more dynamic and organic and takes advantage of new channels of communication (the Internet and social media, such as Facebook and Twitter). After the election of Vladimir Putin in 2000, the narrative maintained the legacy of the past, i.e. the struggle against the West which does not respect and recognise Russia as a global player in the international setting. The West against Russia narrative has been used to make people aware of the fact that the West does not want "Russia resurgent as a Great Nation" (Oates and Steiner 2018: 3).

Consequently, Russian media construct modern narratives based on some specific stories of the West against Russia. The most famous concerns the term *Russophobia*, which was created by a Tsarist diplomat in the 19th century to stress that Russia was marginalised by the West in every political affair (Darczewska and Zochowski 2015: 9). Nowadays this term is used by Putin to underline the Western attempt to make Russia weaker in the international setting, focussing on the emergence of a Western prejudice against Russia. We can find some examples in the hashtag #Russophobia on Twitter, as well as the publishing of "Russophobia Digest" articles and opinions.[4] As of 1 December 2018, the phrase "Russophobia" appeared 790 times on the *RT* website and 855 times on the *Sputnik News* website.[5]

A recent verbal meme used on Russian Twitter narratives is "highly likely". This hashtag derives from a sentence pronounced by Theresa May's after the poisoning case involving Sergey and Yulia Skripal: she asserted that "it is highly likely that Russia is responsible." Foreign Minister Lavrov responded this was "highly likely as a new invention of the British diplomacy to describe why they punish people – because these people are highly likely guilty, like in Alice in Wonderland."[6] The divergence of media narratives between Western and Eastern media is a crucial part of a new kind of hybrid warfare, or postmodern warfare, where military actions, propaganda, political activity, and online campaigns are combined. In 2017, Lavrov stated that "propaganda needs to be clever, smart and efficient" (Isachenkov 2017: 5). Another example is the campaign started by Rossotrudnichestvo, the state agency responsible for Russians living abroad, titled "Highly Likely Welcome Back" to invite Russian students studying in foreign universities to go back home, in order protect them from "the negative influence of Russophobic attitudes".

Another analysis elaborated by Tatiana Dubrovskaya shows how media debate on sanctions imposed on Russia as punitive measures have been represented and have contributed to the construction of an IR debate:[7] "The debate on the sanctions in Russian media exemplifies how ideologically opposed forces make sense of the facts and attach different meanings to them, at the same time as contributing to the construction of Russia's international relations as a whole" (Dubrovskaya 2018: 11). Consequently, this narrative of the West against Russia is very dynamic and characterises the legacies of the past in contemporary foreign affairs.

While policy analysts, journalists, and governmental agencies are trying to understand to what extent Russian hackers were able to influence the 2016 US presidential election campaign and many speculations and official investigations took place, it is also noteworthy that television remains the Russian public's primary source to get information.[8] Television news is trusted by 49% of Russians, while only 24% trust online publications, and 15% social media.[9] So, the narratives Russian broadcasters use are extremely important in influencing domestic and international perceptions of the Unites States and the EU, for instance.

Nevertheless, Sarah Oates stresses the fact that "we need audience studies to determine the degree to which these narratives have a direct effect on citizens in the West." As a matter of fact, "this discussion of Russian strategic narratives cannot offer any evidence of the audience reception of these messages. While we can observe the nature of Russian strategic narrative, trace its flow through the media ecosystem through key words and even computational linguistics" (Oates, Barrow, and Foster 2018). In such a context, Russian media play a critical role in spreading half-truths and non-truths related to the dissemination of the Kremlin's viewpoints in order to face any attempt to destabilise the regime's stability. As Mejias and Vokuev (2017: 1) underline: "Citizens themselves actively participate in their own disenfranchisement by using social media to generate, consume or distribute false information." This sort of 'peer-to-peer propaganda' is produced by ordinary people sharing posts and comments.

In March 2019, the Russian State Duma passed a set of controversial laws targeting journalists and Internet users for 'spreading fake news' and 'disrespecting the authorities'. The penalty for publishing false information ranges from 30,000 rubles (450 dollars) to one million rubles (15,000 dollars), while for disrespect it is 300,000 rubles (4500 dollars) and 15 days in jail for repeat offenders. As a matter of fact, Russian Public Opinion Research Center (VCIOM) presents the findings of a survey on "life without Internet".[10] The share of Russians using Internet in 2019 is around 84%, and 64% of them on a daily basis. Younger people (18–24) with higher education, high income, and living in Moscow and St Petersburg are the main users. On the contrary, 16% of respondents do not use any online resources. 11% of users cannot imagine their life without Internet while half of them would be able to adapt their life.

In April 2019, a second survey was based on the spreading of fake news in Russia: 31% of respondents have come across fake news, especially on television (20%), newspapers (7%), and radio (5%).[11] When confronted with fake news, most of respondents (62%) thought that they might be fake stories; 31% realised that they were probably wrong only later. According to the survey, 74% of Russians think that fake news is published deliberately (84% of 33–44 year olds), and 17% think that fake stories are journalists' mistakes (especially among youngsters).

And what about Russians' opinion on a new 'fake news' law? The survey shows that 78% of the respondents are aware of the fake news law and 42% think that it is impossible to distinguish reliable from unreliable information. Nevertheless, 83% of Russians consider that this law is extremely important for the country in order to face threats to human life.[12] Moreover, 57% of respondents believe that after the law will be implemented the amount of fake news will be reduced; on the contrary, 29% do not believe that anything will change.

The Russian hybrid warfare

The attempt to introduce order and political/economic stability in Russia has been translated into a new 'ideology' (Putinism), able to strengthen the relationship between politics and people. The starting point of this new "ideology to the people" rather than "by the people" dates back to the legacies of Soviet history, such as patriotism, claims related to the Soviet power, political order, and the idea of a nation able to leave "Russia's doors shut on the Soviet Union's sins" (Sakwa 2008), and paves the way to the charismatic leadership appealing to the myths of the past.

The politics of memory through the narrative based on re-Stalinisation and the securitisation of societal identity played a crucial role in reformatting Russia's relations with various others – be they internal others, designated as the 'fifth column', 'national traitors', 'enemies of the people', 'Western spies', or external others, firmly identified with the West in general and the US in particular. The divergence of media narratives between Western and Eastern media is a crucial part of a new kind of hybrid warfare, or postmodern warfare, which combines military actions, propaganda, political activity, and online campaigns (Mitrokhin 2015).[13]

There are different terms used to describe hybrid warfare,[14] such as 'Fourth Generation Warfare' or 'Full Spectrum Warfare' in respect to the description on how Russian military forces conducted operations in Ukraine in 2014 and in Syria in 2015.[15] Many scholars agree with the fact that it is time for a reevaluation of Russia's place in the world, where new forms of power are used as cyber tactics as well as the use of energy politics. "Russian cyber power is considered to be one of the savviest and most technologically advanced in the world. Along with China and the United States, Russia is considered one of the 'heavyweights' in its abilities to deface websites, steal information, and cripple states' infrastructure via the web" (Maness and Valeriano 2015: 1).

Cyber conflict is the least costly tool for Russian foreign policy. Cyberspace is a new dimension of conflict and Russia has applied it in the realm of foreign policy.

The downing of Malaysia Airlines Flight 17 flying over Eastern Ukrainian territory on 17 July 2014 with 298 passengers led to severe reactions in the international setting. The Ukrainian issue is very important for Russia because the shift of Ukraine towards Western institutions and influence would be considered a threat to the great power identity of the Russian modern state since Russian origins are traced back to the Kievan Rus' clan.[16] Consequently, coercive measures were adopted to avoid such a path, ensuring that Ukraine remains in Russia's political orbit.

Although the use of cyber warfare has been increasing during the last decade, it has had some noticeable antecedents during the previous decade. In April 2007, the Estonian government put "The Bronze Soldier of Tallinn", a Soviet era grave marker, in a new place far from the city centre where it used to be. This statue represented the Soviet struggle against Nazi invaders during World War II and is a symbol of Russians' pride. The Kremlin reacted, relying on well-organised cyber operations attacking the private and public Estonian networks which provoked a two-week offline status of banks, businesses, and social networking. Many observers declared that this Russian operation was one of the most sophisticated to date. As a matter of fact, Estonia became the international leader in developing cyber norms and defense tools. While the international community condemned this attack, the Estonian government hosted the International Conference on Cyber Conflict, becoming a global leader in the field.

A similar cyberattack took place one year later in Georgia, where – during the South Ossetian crisis – Georgian government websites were hacked, with pictures of President Mikheil Saakashvili appearing as Hitler, and many other services were shut down. The main consequences were to reveal the Georgians' incapacity to decipher what was actually going on with the movement of soldiers and military hardware. It was the first time that such a cyber action was implemented during a military campaign. Analysts state that Russia does not use cyberattacks very often, and when it does, they are usually aimed at preventing retaliation in post-Soviet states. Cyberattacks can be defined either as "hostile actions in cyberspace that have effects that amplify or are equivalent to major kinetic violence" or as actions of "penetration of foreign networks for the purpose of disrupting or dismantling those networks, and making them inoperable" (Nye 2011: 20–21).

So, Russia is reemerging with new forms of power which are summarised in Table 10.1.

The Russian General Staff defines cyberattacks as "disruption of the key enemy military, industrial and administrative facilities and systems, as well as bringing information-psychological pressure to bear on the adversary's military-political leadership, troops and population, something to be achieved primarily through the use of state-of-the-art information technologies and assets" (Maness and Valeriano 2015: 87). Russia's offensive capabilities are also impressive since it was a Russian firm labelled Kaspersky Labs that funded the infamous Stuxnet and Flame malware incidents in Iran. Despite the Soviet system, which did not pay much attention to the cyber capabilities, Putin's administration invested in the cyber sector and implemented the 'Doctrine of Information Security of Russia' in 2016. According

TABLE 10.1 Summary of cyber incidents involving Russia 2001–11

Dyad (Initiator first)	Name (Duration)	Type	Severity score	Explanation
Russia – Estonia	Bronze Soldier Retaliation (4/27/2007–5/10/2007)	Vandalism, DDoS	2	Response to Estonian removal of a Soviet-era war memorial, widespread DDoS and vandalism
Russia – Georgia	Before the gunfire (4/20/2008–8/16/2008)	DDoS	1	Ongoing DDoS tatics before the Russo-Georgian conflict
Georgia – Russia	Osinform.ru website (8/4/2008–8/4/2008)	DDoS	1	Russian 'hacktivist' networks shut down after Georgian troops killed
Russia – Georgia	VoiP Phone system (8/4/2008–8/8/2008)	DDoS	1	Infiltration of major Georgian mobile network
Russia – Georgia	Georgian Government Site Defacements (8/7/2008–8/16/2008)	Vandalism	1	Widespread vandalism on Georgian government sites before conflict
Russia – US	US Identities stolen in hack (8/6/2008–8/12/2008)	Infiltration	1	US government sites hacked to steal identities and vandalise Georgian sites
Russia – US	US Central Command in Iraq and Afghanistan hacked (11/26/2008–11/28/2008)	Infiltration	2	Information stolen from US Central Command, origins in Russia
Russia – US	US power grid hack (8/24/2009 – ongoing)	Infiltration	3	Eastern Seaboard power grid hacked but no damage, origins in Russia
Russia – US	Dragonfly energy grid hack (1/15/2013–ongoing)	Infiltration	3	Hacker group originating from Russia infects the US energy grid

Source: Maness and Valeriano (2015:110)

to this doctrine, "The national security of the Russian Federation depends on a substantial degree on ensuring information security, a dependence that will increase with technological progress."

In this respect, the FSB (Federal Security Service) monitors all Internet users within Russian borders: it requires service providers to install hardware; also, companies such as Microsoft are asked to share source codes with the FSB. The FSB relies on Kaspersky Labs, which has over 300 million customers worldwide, but tracing the origins of its hackers is difficult; as a matter of fact, it is still a matter of discussion whether or not Russia was involved in the Estonian and Georgian incidents. Russia is considered one of the most dangerous states operating in cyberspace, competing with the USA, China, Iran, North and South Korea, Great Britain, Israel, and Germany, although its ranking in the Global Cybersecurity Index declined from 12 in 2014, to 10 in 2017, and then 26 in 2018. General Valery Gerasimov stated the "the very rules of war" changed, especially the role of nonmilitary means. Without a clear declaration of war, it seems that Clausewitz concept of the 'Fog of War' applies: while originally it referred to the context of the battlefield, it can be used in different contexts, such as a virtual environment. Nevertheless, there is a shared opinion that "Russia is not a 'geopolitical' threat. It is a regional power that challenges United States in its sphere of influence, which is post-Soviet space" (Maness and Valeriano 2015: 88).

Conclusion

As Holzscheiter (2014: 144) notes, "facts do not speak for themselves", and "facts have to be represented . . . to become socially real." The Russian representation of both international events and domestic issues which can be related to the Russian public opinion towards the West is based on the main tools that the post-truth era has given birth to: fake news as the legacy of the Soviet propaganda and hybrid warfare measures aiming at weakening contemporary democracies. Both of them are strongly related thanks also to the role played by Russian mass media.

In Western societies, post-truth represents a dangerous surge of populism with implications that are not 'just' ethical but also destabilising for domestic politics and geopolitics: it is an emerging security challenge and governments must cooperate to cope with it.[17] Taking advantage of new technological tools, populists have come up with new strategies in the framework of post-truth politics. It is also true that some Western populist leaders (Orbán, Le Pen, Salvini, Voigt) see Putin's Russia as a model, where "Putinism and populism are mutually reinforcing phenomena with some shared components" (Oliker 2017: 16–20).

Putin was able to attract people's trust thanks to the evolution of a new Russian nationalism, which combines both historical tradition and the Russian Orthodox Church and advocates conservative values, opposing them to the values characterising European liberalism (equal rights for LGBTQ people, women, religious minorities, and so on), which are considered to be disruptive for the social order. Putin is considered as an embodiment of "strength, racial purity and traditional Christian values in a world under threat from Islam, immigrants, and rootless cosmopolitan elites."[18] Therefore, it does not come as a surprise that analysts and observers have underlined the relationship between the Kremlin and many extremist right and left parties in Europe. Russia challenges the United States interfering in elections and influencing public opinion with a new narrative based on anti-Western attitudes, to do so, it relies on Internet and social media campaigns.

The question to be better explored is whether Russia is using fake news and supporting populist opposition movements in Europe in order to determine the crisis of liberal democracies in the hope they will give birth to new types of regimes which are more similar to the Russian one. On the contrary, Russia could try to position itself in the international setting in such a way that Western populism is a tool to threaten the cohesiveness of NATO and the EU (Oliker 2017: 19).

Notes

1 See: www.oxforddictionaries.com/press/news/2016/12/11/WOTY-16. The Oxford Dictionaries dates the first use of the term to 1992 and an essay by Steve Tesich, a Serbian-American playwright writing in *The Nation* following the Iran/Contra scandal. It was also used by a journalist stressing the way politicians deny scientific claims about climate change more than 20 years ago. In 2004, a book written by Ralph Keyes, *The Post-Truth Era*, warned that lies are told without any fear of impunity, arguing that this is the new social and human challenge to be defeated for the future of democracy.

2 See www.economist.com/leaders/2016/09/10/art-of-the-lie; www.economist.com/brief ing/2016/09/10/yes- id-lie-to-you.

3 To better understand the effects of the 'production of confusion' it is necessary to analyse the role of journalism in the sphere of fake news as suggested by Jay Rosen, a professor of journalism who describes the attempt by Trump's White House to manipulate news outlets and the administration's knowledge of the 'deep grammar' of journalism. See: Cooke (2018).

4 'Russophobia: RT Rates the Top 10 Kremlin Critics & Their Hilarious Hate Campaigns', *RT International,* 28 September 2017, www.rt.com/uk/404930-russophobia-kremlin-critics-paranoia/ (last consulted on 29 November 2018).

5 Google search within the domains: www.rt.com/ and www.sputniknews.com/, conducted on 1 December 2018.

6 Lavrov, S. (2018) 'Foreign Minister Sergey Lavrov's interview with BBC HardTalk' 4 April 2018. See a transcript here: http://rusisworld.com/en/interview/transcript-ser gey-lavrovs-interview-bbc-hardtalk/, in Oates and Steiner (2018).

7 These sanctions were introduced in 2014 and extended till 31 January 2019 after the Ukraine crisis and the 'annexation' (term used by Westerners)/ reunification (term used by Russians) of Crimea.

8 An August 2018 survey by the Levada Center found that 73% of Russians consult television news more than any other information source.

9 In August 2009, this question was formulated as follows: "Other Internet sources". Source: representative opinion polls by Levada Center, August 2009 to 23–30 August 2018, www.levada.ru/2018/09/13/kanaly-informatsii/, published on 13 September 2018

10 See https://wciom.com/index.php?id=61&uid=1659.

11 See https://wciom.com/index.php?id=61&uid=1654.

12 See https://wciom.com/index.php?id=61&uid=1644.

13 "The term 'war' is not meant as a war in the traditional sense but as a tool to use in foreign policy" to alter behaviour (Maness and Valeriano 2015: 87).

14 So these terms are used to describe conventional and non-conventional conflicts (conventional, irregular, terrorist, criminal, cyber, economic, diplomatic, political, social).
15 It was also used following the aftermath of the 2006 Israeli war in Lebanon against Hezbollah.
16 Kievan Rus' is the first East Slavic state which consisted of several clans struggling for the princely throne of Kiev.
17 So far, numerous countries have tried to tackle this independently. The Spanish and American governments have arrested a Russian hacker (alias Severa) for his involvement in the US 2016 elections with his fake antivirus software which functioned as a spam, infecting between 70,000 and 90,000 computers and sending up to 1.5 billion spam messages a day
18 See Feuer and Higgins (2016).

References

Cooke, N. A. (2018) *Fake News and Alternative Facts: Information Literacy in a Post-Truth Era*, Ala Edition: Chicago.

Darczewska, J., P. Zochowski (2015) *Russophobia in the Kremlin's Strategy: A Weapon of Mass Destruction*, Warsaw, Poland: Centre for Eastern Studies.

Feuer A., A. Higgins (2016) 'Extremist turn to a leader to protect Western values: Vladimir Putin', *New York Times*, 3 December 2016, www.nytimes.com/2016/12/03/world/americas/alt-right-vladimir-putin.

Dubrovskaya, T. (2018) 'How Russian media represent the sanctions imposed on Russia by the West in relation to wider international relations issues', *Russian Analytical Digest* 229: 9–12.

Hale, H. (2014) *Patronal Politics: Eurasian Regime Dynamics in Comparative Perspective*, New York: Cambridge University Press.

Hinck, R. S., R. Kluver, S. Cooley (2018) 'Russia re-envisions the world: Strategic narratives in Russian broadcast and news media during 2015', *Russian Journal of Communication* 10(1): 21–37.

Holzscheiter, A. (2014) 'Between communicative interaction and structures of signification: Discourse theory and analysis in international telations', *International Studies Perspectives* 15(2): 142–62.

Hutchings, S., V. Tolz (2015) *Nation, Ethnicity and Race on Russian Television*, London – New York: Routledge.

Isachenkov, V. (2017) 'Russia announces new branch of military to focus on information warfare amid hacking allegations', *The Independent*, 22 February 2017, www.independent.co.uk/news/world/europe/russia-military-information-warfare-hacking-allegations-a7594456.html

Kenez, P. (1985) *The Birth of the Propaganda State. Soviet Methods of Mass Mobilization*, Cambridge: Cambridge University Press.

Keyes, R. (2004) *The Post-truth Era: Dishonesty And Deception In Contemporary Life*, New York: St. Martin's Press.

Maness, R., B. Valeriano (2015) *Russia's Coercive Diplomacy: Energy, Cyber, and Maritime Policy as New Sources of Power*, London: Palgrave Macmillan.

Mejias U. A., N. E. Vokuev (2017) 'Disinformation and the media: The case of Russia and Ukraine', *Media, Culture & Society* 39(7): 1027–42.

Miskimmon, A., B. O'Loughlin, L. Roselle (eds) (2017) *Forging the World – Strategic Narratives and International Relations*, Ann Arbor: University of Michigan Press.

Neumann, I. B. (2008) 'Russia as a great power', *Journal of International Relations and Development*, 11(2): 128–51.

Mitrokhin, N. (2015) 'Infiltration, instruction, invasion: Russia's war in the Donbass', *Journal of Soviet and Post-Soviet Politics and Society* 1 (1): 219–49.

Nye, J.S. (2011) *The Future of Power*, New York: PublicAffairs.

Oates, S. (2014) 'Russian state narrative in the digital age: Rewired propaganda in Russian television news framing of Malaysia Airlines Flight 17', Presented at the 2014 American Political Science Association Annual Meeting, Washington, DC, Available at: https://papers.ssrn.com/sol3/papers.cfm?abstract_id=2941192.

Oates S., J. Barrow, B. Foster (2018) 'From network to narrative: understanding the nature and trajectory of Russian disinformation in the U.S. news', Presented at the International Journal of Press/Politics Conference, Oxford, UK.

Oates S., S. Steiner (2018) 'Projecting power: Understanding Russian strategic narrative, *Russian Analytical Digest* 229: 2–5.

Oliker, O. (2017) 'Putinism, populism and the defence of liberal democracy', *Survival Global Politics and Strategy* 59(1): 7–24.

Orttung, R.W., E. Nelson (2018) 'Russia Today's strategy and effectiveness on Youtube', *Post-Soviet Affairs* 35(2): 77–92.

Ostrovsky, A. (2017) *The Invention of Russia: the Rise of Putin and the Age of Fake News*, London: Penguin Books.

Petrov, N., M. Lipman, H.E. Hale. (2014) 'Three dilemmas of hybrid regime governance: Russia from Putin to Putin', *Post-Soviet Affairs* 30(1): 1–26.

Roselle. L., A. Miskimmon, B. O'Loughlin (2014) 'Strategic narrative: A new means to understand soft power', *Media, War & Conflict* 7(1): 70–84

Roudakova N. (2017) *Losing Pravda: Ethics and the Pre in Post-Truth Russia*, New York: Cambridge University Press.

Sakwa, R. (2008) 'Putin's leadership: Character and consequences', *Europe-Asia Studies* 60(6): 879–97.

Schafer, B. (2018) 'A view from the digital trenches: Lessons from year one of Hamilton', Alliance for Securing Democracy, GMF Report 33, www.gmfus.org/publications/a-view-from-the-digital-trenches-lessons-from-year-one-of-hamilton-68.

Simons, G. (2017) 'Fake news: As the problem or a symptom of a deeper problem?', *Соціокомунікативне середовище: теорія та історія*: 33–44.

Szostek, J. (2017) 'Defence and promotion of desired state identity in Russia's strategic narrative', *Geopolitics* 22(3): 571–93.

11

RESPONDING TO ALLEGED RUSSIAN INTERFERENCE BY FOCUSSING ON THE VULNERABILITIES THAT MAKE IT POSSIBLE

Giorgio Comai

Introduction

In recent years, the legitimacy of electoral processes in Western democracies has been repeatedly put into question by alleged Russian interference. As abundantly described in journalistic reporting and official investigations, actors associated with Russia have been involved in the production and spreading of disinformation as well as in social media manipulation; moreover, they have waged cyberattacks in the run-up to the US presidential elections of November 2016 (Mueller 2019). Even if the direct impact of Russian efforts has likely been minor, the very fact that meddling was both plausible and possible has been cause for significant concern in Europe and North America. The events associated with Russian meddling have not only highlighted the increased willingness of the Kremlin to use a wide variety of tools in its geopolitical confrontation with the West, but have also served to expose in vivid form newly shaped structural vulnerabilities of contemporary democracies: vulnerability of our information environment to the spread of disinformation and the vulnerability of computer systems of political campaigners to hacking by malicious actors. Widespread calls for policy responses duly ensued (e.g. Cherto and Rasmussen 2019).

This chapter firstly defines 'Russian meddling' as a distinct phenomenon that emerged at the time of the US presidential elections in November 2016 based on a media analysis of mainstream Western media.[1] It then proceeds by putting the preoccupation with Russian interference in the context of contemporary West-Russia relations and it discusses what is specifically Russian about Russian meddling. Finally, it outlines the work conducted by expert groups and dedicated committees to find policy responses to the vulnerabilities exposed by alleged Russian interference. As will be argued, there is a growing consensus on the structural nature of these vulnerabilities, and an appreciation of the fact that they must be approached without unduly focussing on the Russian component.

Defining Russian meddling

The events surrounding the election of Donald Trump to the presidency of the United States in November 2016 generated a significant and unprecedented media hype around 'Russian interference'/'Russian meddling' (the two expressions will be used interchangeably hereafter). The confrontation between Russia and the West has become increasingly apparent since Vladimir Putin first became president of the Russian Federation in 2000, but before 2016 the issue of 'Russian interference' simply did not exist as a consolidated discourse in Western media. As appears from a quantitative analysis of mainstream English-language media such as *The New York Times* and *The Guardian,* mentions of 'Russian meddling' were uncommon before 2016, and almost without exception referred to events in Ukraine and Georgia rather than in established Western democracies. References to 'Russian meddling' became less frequent in *The New York Times* after the release of the Mueller report in April 2019, while on *The Guardian* they had a new surge in the run-up to the UK general elections of December 2019 in relation to a new set of scandals.[2]

An analysis of publications on German weekly *Der Spiegel* and Italian daily *La Repubblica* point at similar patterns: references to Russian meddling appear almost exclusively starting in 2016, and mostly in reference to US politics or to domestic scandals associated with the same narrative.[3] In the full online archive of *Der Spiegel*, available from the year 2000, there is a grand total of three articles mentioning Russian interference (*russische Einmischung*) before 2016, in reference to the 2008 war in Georgia, the 2014 annexation of Crimea, and the war in Syria in 2015; almost all others (about 30) refer to the fallout of events related to the 2016 US presidential elections.

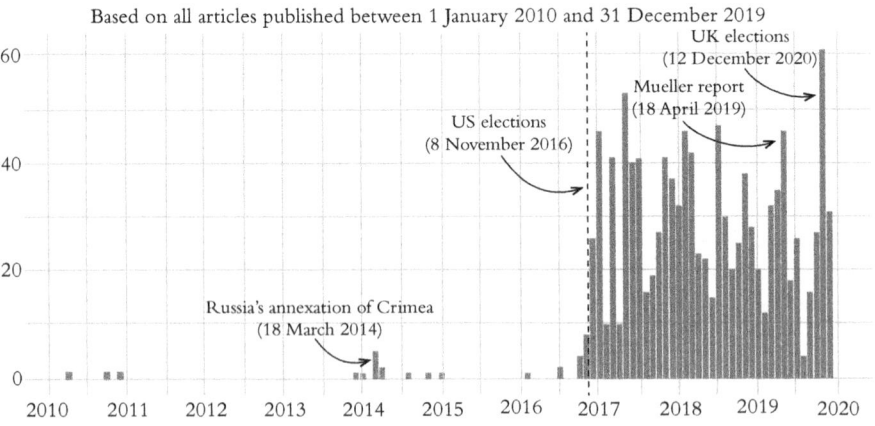

Based on all articles published between 1 January 2010 and 31 December 2019

Data collected using *The Guardian's* own APIs; data processing: Giorgio Comai

FIGURE 11.1 Articles mentioning 'Russian interference' or 'Russian meddling' in a month in *The Guardian*

It is too early to tell if the media attention toward Russian meddling/interference will wane; what this brief media analysis shows, however, is that the preoccupation with 'Russian meddling' is a distinct phenomenon which appeared in late 2016, largely in relation to the US presidential elections. There is scant indication of any continuity between the discourse around Russian meddling and the growing tension between Russia and the West that has become increasingly apparent, in particular after Russia's annexation of Crimea in 2014 (Trenin 2016); 'Russian meddling' as a media discourse is specifically linked to interference into *domestic* political processes in Western democracies and on both sides of the Atlantic has been heavily influenced by the framing established by US media. Before dissecting the main components of 'Russian meddling' and possible responses to them, the following section places them in the context of West-Russia relations.

What is specifically Russian about Russian meddling?

The fact that an external state actor may have successfully interfered in domestic political processes has come as a shock to the United States in 2016. On the contrary, concern with foreign meddling has been a major issue in Russia for a long time. The whole concept of 'sovereign democracy' formalised by Vladislav Surkov in 2006 and strongly associated with Vladimir Putin's tightening grip on power has been widely understood as a response to the preoccupation with Western interference in domestic politics in its 'near abroad' and in Russia itself (McFaul and Spector 2009).[4]

There is an established narrative in Russia according to which all activities associated with 'Russian meddling' were ultimately reactive or defensive in nature. After all, even the infamous article that gave the name to the non-existing 'Gerasimov doctrine' – a troubled expression often used as a shorthand for Russia's supposedly new hybrid war tactics – ultimately described what it perceived as the Western approach to interfering with domestic affairs in other countries (Galeotti 2019). By using and perfecting similar tactics, Russia would simply be updating its repertoire to include practices that the US had been using for a long time not only in Central or South America, but also in other regions, such as the Middle East, especially during the Arab Spring and, most importantly from the Kremlin's point of view, in Russia's 'near abroad' and in Russia itself.[5]

As Russia's neighbours know all too well, Russian interference in the domestic affairs of other countries did not start in 2016. Even the West's preoccupation with the specific tactics at the core of the post-2016 Russian meddling narrative is not new. In 2015, the EU launched its East StratCom Task Force known for its controversial "EU vs. Disinfo" project targeting Russian disinformation, well before Donald Trump's election in the United States.[6] Yablokov (2015) published an academic article on conspiracy theories as a Russian public diplomacy tool: promoting controversial points of view to instil distrust in liberal elites was not a new idea for Russia in the fall of 2016. Politically motivated, large-scale cyberattacks had been used by Russia in its neighbourhood for a decade before they became a major issue in the US (Pernik 2018) and they continue to be a source of concern (UK Foreign Office 2020).[7]

The vulnerabilities exposed by Russian meddling

What is actually new about the post-2016 preoccupation with Russian meddling is a widespread realisation that modern technologies have brought newly shaped structural vulnerabilities to established Western democracies themselves. In one form or another, disinformation may be as old as humanity and it certainly had nefarious and even violent consequences at different point in times in history, but social media and the current model of the Internet have turned it into a fundamentally new challenge for liberal democracies. The increasing ubiquity of digital technologies in everyday life and communication has immensely increased the potential impact of cyberattacks even in comparison to only a few years ago. Indeed, even if Russia did exploit these vulnerabilities, there is little that ties them specifically to Russia.

As argued by Tufekci (2018), Russian meddling is only a symptom: "to heal, we need the correct diagnosis followed by action that treats the underlying diseases." In other words, rather then focus on Russia, it may be more sensible to take a more comprehensive approach that mitigates the vulnerabilities exposed by the scandals concerning Russian meddling. The Mueller investigation confirmed, providing abundant details, the existence of Russian attempts at interfering in the US 2016 presidential elections. Two operations were undertaken: a campaign of disinformation conducted through social media and a hacking-and-dumping operation against the Clinton campaign. The following sections will consider these two components and outline some of the responses that have been proposed in recent years to tackle these issues.

Information operations, disinformation, and social media

Given the sheer amount of resources poured into presidential campaigns in the United States, it is close to impossible that a (relatively speaking) tiny information operation run from the outskirts of St Petersburg in Russia had a substantial impact on the outcome of the vote.[8] Yet, the way that social media facilitates the spread of polarising contents has been cause for concern well beyond that much debated operation. Indeed, if the object of that campaign was "to provoke and amplify political and social discord" (Mueller 2019: 4), it may have just contributed to what social media had already been doing for years (Neudert and Marchal 2019: 15).[9] In this specific instance, disinformation may have been spread by Russian actors, but profit motives have proved to be powerful drivers, pushing both domestic and foreign actors to produce junk news on many other occasions (e.g. Burger et al. 2019; Bradshaw et al. 2019). More broadly, the current model of the Internet – averse to privacy and largely relying on unaccountable platforms – has come under increased scrutiny, in particular after new scandals such as that related to Cambridge Analytica and its mishandling of private data obtained through Facebook (Cadwalladr and Graham-Harrison 2018).

As appears from this brief overview, the concern with foreign meddling in time of elections quickly escalates to systemic consideration about the challenges to democratic societies coming from the increased digitalisation and privatisation of our public arena. The complexity of these issues, as well as the real risk that rushed regulation may cause more harm than good, should, however, not serve as an excuse for inaction. Indeed, researchers, working groups, and committees at various levels have worked to develop sensible policy proposals that mitigate these vulnerabilities. The devil may well be in the details, but at least on some aspects there is a broad consensus. For example, in many countries regulation on political campaigning has never been updated to include digital spaces, and, as a consequence, many of the transparency and accountability requirements that traditionally accompany elections do not currently stand online; well-meaning legislators should start from there, including comprehensive transparency obligations as well as limits on micro-targeting (Dobber, Fathaigh, and Borgesius 2019).

Comprehensive policy-oriented reports such as 'Protecting electoral integrity in the digital age' written by the Kofi Annan Commission on Elections and Democracy in the Digital Age (2020) serve as key points of reference and envisage sensible policies that would not only contribute to mitigate the risk of foreign interference, but also to foster an enabling environment for domestic democratic processes. Calls for stronger transparency requirements and considerable efforts to promote digital and media literacy are included, among other things, in official recommendations issued by the European Commission (2018), in reports for the European Parliament (Neudert and Marchal 2019), or in studies resulting from the work of parliamentary committees conducted at the national level (e.g. UK House of Commons 2019; Canada House of Commons 2018). Even when they refer to foreign interference or specifically to Russian meddling, all these reports argue in favour of structural responses, rather than focus on a specific external actor such as Russia.

Hacking and dumping

The second component of Russian meddling, as characterised by the Mueller report, is the hacking-and-dumping operation against the Clinton campaign. The coordinated efforts at maximising the visibility of the exfiltrated materials has fundamentally contributed to the impact of the operation, and it is no less important than the hacking operation itself. Readers who do not have a keen interest in cyber-security issues may well not even have heard that Chinese hackers violated the computer system of both the Obama and McCain campaign in

2008 (Isikoff 2013) or that Russian hackers exfiltrated data from the computer networks of the German Parliament (Beuth et al. 2017): what is particularly new about the hacking of the US Democrats and the Clinton campaign in 2016 is, ultimately, its very notoriety.

Even when hackers do publish online the private communication of politicians they have illicitly obtained, the media reaction may be muted. For example, when more than 20 GB of emails from the servers of Lega, a prominent right-wing party in Italy, were hacked about a month before the Italian political elections of May 2018, the news barely featured in the media (Martelli 2018). Other scandals involving hacked personal communications of politicians in Europe did achieve some visibility in the media, but they had hardly any political impact (Soesanto 2017; Franceschi-Bicchierai, Koebler, and Maiberg 2019). Insisting that journalists fully consider the ethical implications of reporting on illicitly obtained materials may be relevant, but explicit regulations on this issue may be both useless (i.e. ineffective in the age of social media) and damaging (i.e. used to silence investigative journalists).

Also, in the case of cyber-security in time of elections there is a considerable consensus on viable policy options that should be pursued, as summarised for example in the relevant report by ENISA, the European Union cyber-security agency (ENISA 2019). The first basic concern in this context is to ensure high cyber-security standards for the very infrastructure used to conduct elections. At its core, this is a technical and organisational issue to be approached through established best practices (NIS Cooperation Group 2018), enhanced cooperation between government agencies (van der Staak and Wolf 2019), and further exchange of experiences and information among partners (ENISA 2019: 11; Pope 2018).

A second specific vulnerability relates to the computer systems and the internal communication of political parties and campaigns. Although they are extremely high-value targets for both domestic and foreign actors, they do not seem to take their own cyber-security seriously enough. This is not necessarily by ill will: in comparison with corporate environments, decentralised organisations that involve volunteers may find it more difficult to enforce tight cyber-security practices. Even if they may eventually hold the keys to the state coffers and manage considerable resources, many political organisations operate on a shoe-string budget: having to decide between more electoral posters and expensive cyber-security consultants, they have strong incentives to prefer the former. For that reason, ENISA (2019) argues in favour of the introduction of mandatory high cyber-security standards for political organisations and proposes to assist them throughout the adaptation process. Such initiatives are already taking place in various European country (Maurer and Brattberg 2018), and previous experience may well serve as a source of inspiration in other countries, keeping in consideration local needs and sensitivities. Guides for practitioners (Belfer Center for Science and International Affairs 2017) are useful tools and educating individuals is indeed an important element of a comprehensive cyber-security strategy, but political campaigners should not be left alone to fend off attacks from advanced, state-sponsored malicious actors. Assistance should come with the understanding that widespread default solutions, such as relying on foreign big tech companies, may be politically unacceptable.[10]

Finally, Russian meddling has once again highlighted the importance of defining a framework for reacting if a cyber-attack can be convincingly attributed to a foreign actor.[11] The European Union has been working for a few years on its cyber-diplomacy toolbox which may become a useful point of reference in time of need (Moret and Pawlak 2017; Ivan 2019), and more dialogue along these lines is needed at the international level. Any such initiative should, however, include mechanisms that prevent quick escalation, also considering Russia's own aggressive use of cyber-operations in recent years (Greenberg 2019).

Secret deals and illicit funding

This chapter deliberately focussed on aspects that were directly related to the impact of new technologies on the information space due to their prominence in the Russian meddling narrative as epitomised by the Mueller report. However, perhaps the most hotly debated part of that investigation was aimed at determining – as it turned out, inconclusively – if the Trump campaign actively "conspired or coordinated with the Russian government in its election interference activities" (Mueller 2019; Bullough 2019).

In continental Europe, somewhat similar shenanigans involving Russia have revolved around actual or attempted transfers of money from Kremlin-related actors to friendly political forces. For instance, in 2014 Marine Le Pen's National Front obtained a loan for 9.4 million euro from a Prague-based, Kremlin-linked bank that had been used for unrelated money-laundering operations, in a deal that according to media reports was related to the Russia-friendly stance Le Pen took on Russia's annexation of Crimea (Gatehouse 2017). In what turned out to be an elaborate set-up, in July 2017 Austria's Freedom Party leader Heinz-Christian Strache was recorded on camera as he negotiated support from a woman he believed to be the niece of a Russian oligarch (Al-Serori et al. 2019). In July 2019, *Buzzfeed News* released secretly recorded audio of a meeting which took place in Moscow in October 2018, reported in a cover story published on the Italian weekly *L'Espresso*. During the meeting, three Russian and three Italian individuals were conspiring to use an oil deal to syphon off 65 million USD to be used to finance the political campaign of Lega (Tizian and Vergine 2019; Nardelli 2019). The issue of funds of dubious origins flooding political campaigns obtained particular prominence in the UK in recent years (e.g. Ramsay and Geoghegan 2017) and there may indeed be a Russian connection: a dedicated report by the UK Intelligence and Security Committee of Parliament is due to be published in 2020 (Bullough 2019).

Scandals related to specific individuals make for media-grabbing headlines, but do not lend themselves as easily to more generalisable patterns. Yet, even these stories shed some new light on contemporary vulnerabilities to Western democracies. In the case of the UK, its role as a cornerstone for the global offshore industry makes it particularly vulnerable to the corrupting influence of 'dark money'; kleptocratic regimes in the post-Soviet space are a well-known source of such funds (Cooley and Heathershaw 2017; Bullough 2018a), but this is a global problem – an under-appreciated "dark side of globalisation" (Bullough 2018b) – rather than anything Russia-specific. Elsewhere, concerns about illicit funding may well serve as a reminder of the importance of transparency requirements for political campaigns and other actors such as foundations and thinktanks that in many countries are playing an increasing prominent role in domestic politics.

Fundamentally, the recent preoccupation with Russian meddling that emerged in late 2016 is not related to the cosy relationship between leading politicians and the Kremlin; For example, the explicit pro-Russian stance of leading figures such as former German Chancellor Gerhard Schröder or former Italian Prime Minister Silvio Berlusconi, as well as their flaunted friendship with Russian president Vladimir Putin have called for some criticism, but they have not been denounced as a case of Russian interference. There is also no sensible policy proposal that could (or should) deal with the personal preferences and political choices of politicians, as long as they remain within the boundaries of the law. There are, however, sensible policies that would reduce the risk that dark money interferes with domestic political processes.

More broadly, when thinking of policy responses to the concerns stemming from stories about 'Russian meddling', looking beyond the Kremlin is the safest approach for making democracies less vulnerable to foreign interference (from Russia or elsewhere) as well as more resilient to the challenges of domestic spoilers.

Conclusion

In recent years, Russian meddling has obtained extensive media attention and has led to increased pressure on policy makers and big tech companies to find ways to protect democracy from undue external interference. The preoccupation with foreign meddling is understandable, but it should also come with an appreciation of the fact that there is little of specifically foreign (or Russian) in the vulnerabilities that made Russian meddling possible, or at least plausible. Domestic spoilers – motivated by politics or by profit – have used and will likely continue using some of the same techniques to a much greater extent.

Liberal democracies have no acceptable way to protect themselves from these kinds of operations without dealing with the newly shaped structural vulnerabilities that have come with the uptake of digital technologies. Fortunately, expert groups as well as national and international committees tasked to investigate these issues have put forward a number of meaningful policy proposals. At least on some of them, there is an extraordinary degree of consensus. Policy makers should know where to start and ensure that the preoccupation about these matters that emerged with Russian meddling isn't wasted.

Of course, Western governments would also do well to reason on a sensible course of action to manage the current confrontation with Russia (Trenin 2016). Countries bordering the Russian Federation should consider adequate measures to deal with Russia's much more pervasive presence in their information spaces while resisting the temptation of outright censorship even under extreme pressure (Mijatović 2014). These are, however, quite separate matters. When thinking of policy responses to Russian meddling into domestic political processes in Western countries, the better course of action is to focus on the vulnerabilities that make such interference possible.

Notes

1 This operationalisation of external – specifically Russian – meddling makes it possible to concentrate on a distinct subset of problematic instances of external interference. As a consequence, this chapter does not analyse other forms of external influence that are generally perceived as legitimate (e.g. transnational networks or regional cooperation mechanisms), nor others phenomena that, depending on the context, can be more problematic (e.g. different understandings of public diplomacy or democracy promotion).

2 These include the delayed release of an official dossier on Russian meddling in the UK and new revelations about Russian donors to the Tory party; other articles were related to the impeachment of Donald Trump in the United States.

3 The analysis of *Spiegel* and *Repubblica* was based on their online archives. For a debate on the usefulness of applying basic word frequency analysis to better define a case study, see Comai (2017).

4 Russia vividly denounced the West's active interference at the time of the "Orange Revolution" in Ukraine in 2004 (Ambrosio 2010). It should be acknowledged that external interference from both Russia and the West was perceived to be improper by large swathes of Ukrainian residents (Shulman and Bloom 2012).

5 To counter this narrative based on false equivalence, the Kofi Annan Commission on Elections and Democracy in the Digital Age (2020: 87) argues in favour of establishing an international convention to "develop international norms that distinguish legitimate cross-border assistance from illicit or unlawful interventions."

6 On criticism of "EU vs. Disinfo", see for example Nijeboer (2018).

7 Given both the significant change of context and the distinct temporal hiatus between those phenomena and present events, the affinities between recent events and Soviet-time practices with some contiguity with them are not discussed. An incomplete list of references would include disinformation activities (United States 1981; Martin 1982), "active measures" (Godson and Shultz 1985), as well as a specific attention to collect and use compromising materials (*kompromat*) on opponents.

8 For a debate on the meaning of 'information operation' and of alternative concepts, see in particular Wanless and Pamment (2019).

9 As pointed out by Neudert and Marchal (2019: 15), the attention economy and the pressure to increase engagement on these platforms had already proved to be powerful incentives for "the dissemination of partisan and emotionally-charged content that reinforces tensions between users."

10 On top of a strong security record for all their users, big tech companies such as Google and Microsoft provide premium services with additional security to political campaigns for free, see Google's "Protect your election" (https://protectyourelection.withgoogle.com/), and Microsoft's "Defending democracy program" (https://m365forcampaigns.

microsoft.com.). However, using services offered by US-based conglomerates with dubious records on matters such as so-called 'tax optimisation', abuse of monopoly power, and privacy, may be problematic for political campaigns.

11 On the issue of attribution of cyberattacks, see in particular Rid and Buchanan (2015).

References

Al-Serori, L., O. Das Gupta, P. Münch, F. Obermaier, B. Obermayer (2019) 'Caught in the trap', *Süddeutsche.De*, 17 May 2019, https://projekte.sueddeutsche.de/artikel/politik/caught-in-the-trap-e675751/.

Ambrosio, T. (2010) 'Russia', in: D. Ó Beacháin, A. Polese (eds), *The Colour Revolutions in the Former Soviet Republics: Successes and Failures*, London – New York: Routledge, 136–55.

Belfer Center for Science and International Affairs (2017) 'Cybersecurity campaign playbook', Belfer Center for Science and International Affairs, November 2017, https://www.belfercenter.org/CyberPlaybook.

Beuth, P., K. Biermann, M. Klingst, H. Stark (2017) 'Cyberattack on the Bundestag: Merkel and the Fancy Bear', *Die Zeit*, 12 May 2017, https://www.zeit.de/digital/2017-05/cyberattack-bundestag-angela-merkel-fancy-bear-hacker-russia.

Bradshaw, S., P.N. Howard, B. Kollanyi, L.-M. Neudert (2020) 'Sourcing and automation of political news and information over social media in the United States, 2016–2018', *Political Communication* 37(2): 173–93.

Bullough, O. (2018a) *Moneyland: Why Thieves & Crooks Now Rule the World & How to Take It Back*, London: Profile Books.

Bullough, O. (2018b) 'The dark side of globalization', *Journal of Democracy* 29(1): 25–38.

Bullough, O. (2019) 'The toxic relationship between Britain and Russia has to be exposed', *The Guardian*, 13 November 2019, www.theguardian.com/commentisfree/2019/nov/13/relationship-britain-russia-money-report.

Burger, P., S. Kanhai, A. Pleijter, S. Verberne (2019) 'The Reach of Commercially Motivated Junk News on Facebook', edited by Sabrina Gaito, *PLOS ONE* 14(8): e0220446, available from: https://doi.org/10.1371/journal.pone.0220446.

Cadwalladr, C., E. Graham-Harrison (2018) 'Revealed: 50 Million Facebook profiles harvested for Cambridge Analytica in major data breach', *The Guardian*, 17 March 2018, www.theguardian.com/news/2018/mar/17/cambridge-analytica-facebook-influence-us-election.

Canada House of Commons (2018) 'Democracy under threat: Risks and solutions in the era of disinformation and data monopoly', Report of the Standing Committee on Access to Information, Privacy and Ethics, House of Commons,: www.ourcommons.ca/Content/Committee/421/ETHI/Reports/RP10242267/ethirp17/ethirp17-e.pdf.

Cherto, M., A.F. Rasmussen (2019) 'The unhackable election – what it takes to defend democracy', *Foreign Affairs*, January/February: 156–64.

Comai, G. (2017) 'Quantitative analysis of web content in support of qualitative research. examples from the study of post-Soviet de facto states', *Studies of Transition States and Societies* 9(1), http://publications.tlu.ee/index.php/stss/article/view/346.

Cooley, A.A., J. Heathershaw (2017) *Dictators Without Borders: Power and Money in Central Asia*, New Haven, CT: Yale University Press.

Dobber, T., R.Ó. Fathaigh, F.J. Zuiderveen Borgesius (2019) 'The regulation of online political micro-targeting in Europe', *Internet Policy Review* 8(4), https://policyreview.info/articles/analysis/regulation-online-political-micro-targeting-europe.

ENISA (2019) 'Election cybersecurity: Challenges and opportunities', Brussels: ENISA – EU Cybersecurity Agency, www.enisa.europa.eu/publications/enisa-position-papers-and-opinions/election-cybersecurity-challenges-and-opportunities.

European Commission (2018) 'Commission recommendation of 12.9.2018 on election cooperation networks, online transparency, protection against cybersecurity incidents and fighting disinformation campaigns in the context of elections to the European Parliament', C(2018) 5949 final. Brussels: European Commission, available from: https://ec.europa.eu/commission/sites/beta-political/files/soteu2018-cybersecurity-elections-recommendation-5949_en.pdf.

Franceschi-Bicchierai, L., J. Koebler, E. Maiberg (2019) 'Before Germany's massive hack, we learned what not to do with sensitive stolen information', *Motherboard*, 4 January 2019, https://motherboard.vice.com/en_us/article/xwjj4a/germany-politicians-hack-and-leak-what-not-to-do-with-sensitive-stolen-data.

Galeotti, M. (2019) 'The mythical "Gerasimov doctrine" and the language of threat', *Critical Studies on Security* 7(2): 157–61.

Gatehouse, G. (2017) 'Who's funding France's far right?', *BBC News*, 3 April 2017, available from: https://www.bbc.com/news/world-europe-39478066.

Godson, R., R. Shultz (1985) 'Soviet Active Measures: Distinctions and Definitions', *Defense Analysis* 1(2): 101–10.

Greenberg, A. (2019) *Sandworm: A New Era of Cyberwar and the Hunt for the Kremlin's Most Dangerous Hackers*, New York: Doubleday.

Isikoff, M. (2013) 'Chinese hacked Obama, McCain campaigns, took internal documents, officials say', *NBC Investigations*, 6 June 2013, http://investigations.nbcnews.com/_news/2013/06/06/18807056-chinese-hacked-obama-mccain-campaigns-took-internal-documents-officials-say.

Ivan, P. (2019) 'Responding to cyberattacks: Prospects for the EU Cyber Diplomacy Toolbox', Brussels: European Policy Center, https://www.epc.eu/en/publications/Responding-to-cyberattacks-EU-Cyber-Diplomacy-Toolbox~218414.

Kofi Annan Commission on Elections and Democracy in the Digital Age (2020) 'Protecting electoral integrity in the digital age', www.kofiannanfoundation.org/app/uploads/2020/01/f035dd8e-kaf_kacedda_report_2019_web.pdf.

Martelli, F. (2018) 'Anonymous ha pubblicato online 70.000 email della Lega', *Vice* [online], 23 February, www.vice.com/it/article/evmqgn/anonymous-ha-pubblicato-online-70000-email-della-lega.

Martin, L.J. (1982) 'Disinformation: An instrumentality in the propaganda arsenal', *Political Communication* 2(1): 47–64.

Maurer, T., E. Brattberg (2018) 'Russian election interference: Europe's counter to fake news and cyber attacks', Washington DC: Carnegie Endowment, https://carnegieendowment.org/2018/05/23/russian-election-interference-europe-s-counter-to-fake-news-and-cyber-attacks-pub-76435.

McFaul, M., R.A. Spector (2009) 'External sources and consequences of Russia's "sovereign democracy"', in: P. Burnell, R. Youngs (eds), *New Challenges to Democratization*, New York: Routledge.

Mijatović, D. (2014) 'Communiqué by OSCE representative on freedom of the media on propaganda in times of conflict', OSCE Representative on Freedom of the Media, 15 April, available from: https://www.osce.org/fom/117701.

Moret, E., P. Pawlak (2017) 'The EU Cyber Diplomacy Toolbox: Towards a cyber sanctions regime?', Paris: European Union Institute for Security Studies (EUISS), www.iss.europa.eu/uploads/media/Brief_24_Cyber_sanctions.pdf.

Mueller, R.S. (2019) 'Report on the investigation into Russian interference in the 2016 presidential election', Washington DC, www.justice.gov/storage/report.pdf.

Nardelli, A. (2019) 'Revealed: The explosive secret recording that shows how Russia tried to funnel millions to the "European Trump"', *BuzzFeed News*, 10 July 2019, www.buzzfeednews.com/article/albertonardelli/salvini-russia-oil-deal-secret-recording.

Neudert, L.M., N. Marchal (2019) *Polarisation and the Use of Technology in Political Campaigns and Communication*, Brussels: European Parliamentary Research Service, www.europarl.europa.eu/RegData/etudes/STUD/2019/634414/EPRS_STU(2019)634414_EN.pdf.

Nijeboer, A. (2018) '[Opinion] Why the EU Must Close EUvsDisinfo', *EUobserver*, 28 March 2018, https://euobserver.com/opinion/141458.

NIS Cooperation Group (2018) 'Compendium on cyber security of election technology', CG Publication 03/2018, www.ria.ee/sites/default/files/content-editors/kuberturve/cyber_security_of_election_technology.pdf.

Pernik, P. (2018) 'The early days of cyberattacks: The cases of Estonia, Georgia and Ukraine', in: N. Popescu, S. Secrieru (eds), *Hacks, Leaks and Disruptions – Russian Cyber Strategies*, Paris: European Union Institute for Security Studies, www.iss.europa.eu/content/hacks-leaks-and-disruptions-%E2%80%93-russian-cyber-strategies.

Pope, A.E. (2018) 'Cyber-securing our elections', *Journal of Cyber Policy* 3(1): 24–38.

Ramsay, A., P. Geoghegan (2017) 'The "dark money" that paid for Brexit', *OpenDemocracy*, 15 February 2017, www.opendemocracy.net/en/dark-money-investigations/you-aren-t-allowed-to-know-who-paid-for-key-leave-campaign-adverts/.

Rid, T., B. Buchanan (2015), 'Attributing cyber attacks', *Journal of Strategic Studies* 38(1–2): 4–37.

Shulman, S., S. Bloom (2012) 'The legitimacy of foreign intervention in elections: The Ukrainian response', *Review of International Studies* 38(2): 445–71.

Soesanto, S. (2017) 'The Macron leak that wasn't', *ECFR*, 9 May 2017, www.ecfr.eu/article/commentary_the_macron_leak_that_wasnt_7285.

Tizian, G., S. Vergine (2019) 'Quei 3 milioni russi per Matteo Salvini: ecco l'inchiesta che fa tremare la Lega', *L'Espresso*, 21 February 2019, http://espresso.repubblica.it/plus/articoli/2019/02/21/news/tre-milioni-matteo-salvini-russia-1.331924.

Trenin, D. (2016) *Should We Fear Russia?*, Malden, MA: Polity Press.

Tufekci, Z. (2018) 'Russian meddling is a symptom, not the disease', *The New York Times*, 5 October 2018, www.nytimes.com/2018/10/03/opinion/midterms-facebook-foreign-meddling.html.

U.K. Foreign Office (2020) 'UK condemns Russia's GRU over Georgia cyber-attacks', *Gov.Uk.*, 20 February 2020, www.gov.uk/government/news/uk-condemns-russias-gru-over-georgia-cyber-attacks.

UK House of Commons (2019) 'Disinformation and "fake news": Final report', Eighth Report of Session 2017–19, London, UK: House of Commons, https://publications.parliament.uk/pa/cm201719/cmselect/cmcumeds/1791/1791.pdf.

United States (ed.) (1981) *The Origins, Direction, and Support of Terrorism: Hearing Before the Subcommittee on Security and Terrorism of the Committee on the Judiciary, United States Senate*, Vol. Serial no. J-97-17, Washington: US G.P.O., www.ncjrs.gov/pdffiles1/Digitization/82825NCJRS.pdf.

van der Staak, S., P. Wolf (2019) *Cybersecurity in Elections: Models of Interagency Collaboration*, International Institute for Democracy and Electoral Assistance, https://doi.org/10.31752/idea.2019.23.

Wanless, A., J. Pamment (2019) 'How do you define a problem like influence?', *Journal of Information Warfare* 18(3): 14.

Yablokov, I. (2015) 'Conspiracy theories as a Russian public diplomacy tool: The case of *Russia Today* (RT)', *Politics* 35(3–4): 301–15.

PART III

Dilemmas of contrasting disinformation and fake news

12

INFORMATION SPREADING AND THE ROLE OF AUTOMATED ACCOUNTS ON TWITTER

Two case studies

*Guido Caldarelli, Rocco De Nicola,
Marinella Petrocchi, and Fabio Saracco*

Introduction

Disruptive Innovation: a term that perfectly sums up the impact of social media on people's everyday life. Crucial information can be produced and disseminated among millions of people in a flash, even information concerned with real-time updates on important events. Unfortunately, new technologies have not only revolutionised traditional sectors such as retail and advertising, but they have also been fertile and ground-breaking even on a much more slippery ground: misinformation, hoaxes, and propaganda (National Endowment for Democracy 2017). Disinformation, widely defined as "the purposeful dissemination of false information intended to mislead or harm" (National Endowment for Democracy 2017), is probably as old as human relationships – in the 5th century B.C., the Chinese military theoretician Sun Tzu wrote that "all warfare is based on deception."[1] However, the advent and easiness of use of social media has served to enhance the scale (capability to reach billions of people), scope (capability to achieve a focussed objective, e.g. in terms of a particular audience group), and effectiveness of disinformation (Bradshaw and Howard 2018).

Moreover, the dis/information diffusion on social media is often supported by automated accounts, controlled totally or in part by computer algorithms, called bots. Designed to mimic human behaviour online, a dominant and worrisome use of automated accounts is far from being benign: they have been often used to amplify narratives or drown out political dissent (Yang et al. 2019). Recent studies demonstrate that bots are particularly active in spreading false information. Among other examples, Shao et al. (2018) report of a highly viral fabricated news story titled 'Spirit cooking', which claimed Clinton's campaign chairman practiced bizarre occult rituals, and was published four days before the 2016 US election, subsequently shared in over 30,000 tweets. Even more worryingly, the Global Inventory of Organised Social Media Manipulation reports that bot accounts are being used in 50 out of 70 investigated countries which make use of organised social media manipulation campaigns (Bradshaw and Howard 2019).

According to the 2019 report 'Weapons of mass distraction' (Gangware and Nemr 2019), strategists of false news can exploit – at least – three significant targets of the online information ecosystem: (1) the medium: the platforms on which fake news creeps in and expands; (2) the message: what is the information that one wants to convey?; (3) the audience: who consumes (and contributes to diffuse) this information. The work presented in this chapter focussed on the three mentioned aspects. Relying on two huge Twitter corpora about (1) migration in the Mediterranean Sea from North Africa to Italy, and (2) Covid-19-related discussions, the authors analyse the relevant (i.e. those not compatible with users' random activity) communication and interaction patterns, spotting out the accounts that contribute to the effective dissemination of messages.

Our main results are the following: first, after cleaning the system from the random activity of users, we detect the main hubs of the two networks, i.e. the most effective accounts in significantly propagating their messages, and we observe that those accounts have a higher number of bots among their followers than average. Second, for the migration topic, the strongest hubs in the network share a relatively high number of bots as followers, which most probably aim at further increasing the visibility of the hubs' messages via following and retweeting. As far as the Covid-19 topic is concerned, at least at the time of our investigation, the presence of bots is more limited, but we expect it will grow when the issue stops being only medical and starts becoming political.

To the best of our knowledge, the existence of formations of bots shared by a group of human-operated accounts has never been reported in the literature before.

Datasets

Our study is based on two large corpora of Twitter data, generated by collecting tweets in Italian concerned with migrations and Covid-19-related discussions. For data collection, we developed specific programmes which, by exploiting Twitter public filter API,[2] provided real-time tweet delivery and allowed the collection of sets of data filtered according to specified keywords. For both datasets, we selected a set of keywords compatible with recent chronicles.

The keywords for the dataset about migration have been selected because they are commonly used in Italy when talking and writing about immigration flows from Northern Africa to the Italian coasts, including the dispute about the holder of jurisdiction for handling emergencies involving European countries and NGOs.[3] We collected 1,082,029 tweets, posted by 127,275 unique account IDs over a period of one month (from 23 January to 22 February 2019). By relying on the bot detector classifier developed by Cresci et al. (2015), all the accounts have been classified either as human-operated or as bots. This classification led to 117,879 genuine accounts and 9396 social bots, representing around 7% of all accounts.

It may be worth pointing out that the period over which the data was collected was characterised by a lively political debate in Italy about the landing of the *Diciotti* ship, which was operated by NGOs and rescued migrants fleeing from North Africa to Italy. Rescuing almost 200 migrants on 16 August 2018, it initially received a veto to land from the Italian government; it was allowed to do so only after ten days. Mr. Matteo Salvini, at that time Minister of Internal Affairs, was afterwards investigated for kidnapping and abuse of office; the case was stopped on 19 February 2019, when the Italian Senate did not grant judges the possibility to prosecute him. Right before and after the Senate's decision, there was an intense debate on social networks about migrants and NGOs, and about the role of the Italian government and of the European Union (EU).

The collected tweets concerned with Covid-19 had hashtags related to the coronavirus contagion in the text of the tweet.[4] We collected almost 2.5 million tweets in Italian, from 21 February 2020 to 10 March 2020.[5] By relying on Botometer, the bot detector/classifier developed at the Indiana University (Varol et al. 2017), all the accounts have been classified either as human-operated or as bots. This classification led to 265,910 genuine accounts and 16,973 bots, representing 6% of all accounts. Also in this case, it is important to notice that the timing of the data collection is significant, as far as the topic and the Italian scenario are concerned. In fact, on 21 February the case of the so-called patient one in Lombardy broke out, giving rise to the escalation of the epidemic in Italy.

Users' affiliation

Following previous studies (Becatti et al. 2019; Caldarelli et al. 2020), we used the official certification of one account's authenticity, provided by Twitter, in order to get the polarisation of users. Indeed, upon request from its owner, an account can be certified by the platform and tagged as verified once its authenticity is confirmed. On the official portal, the verified accounts display a blue circle with a white tick at the centre, close to their name.

The intuition behind recent researches on Italian Twitter users' polarisation (Becatti et al. 2019; Caldarelli et al. 2020) is that two verified users are perceived as similar if their messages are retweeted by the same (unverified) users. In order to translate this intuition into a measure, we consider the bipartite network formed by verified users (on one layer) and unverified users (on the other layer). A link is present in the network if one of the two users retweeted the other one at least one time, no matter if the unverified user retweeted the verified one or vice-versa. We chose to focus on retweets since they represent the preferred way through which users spread messages they agree with (Conover et al. 2011).

Figures 12.1 and 12.2 show, respectively, the communities of verified users found for the migration flows scenario and the Covid-19 one. In particular, the network in Figure 12.1 presents a strong community structure. The accounts tied

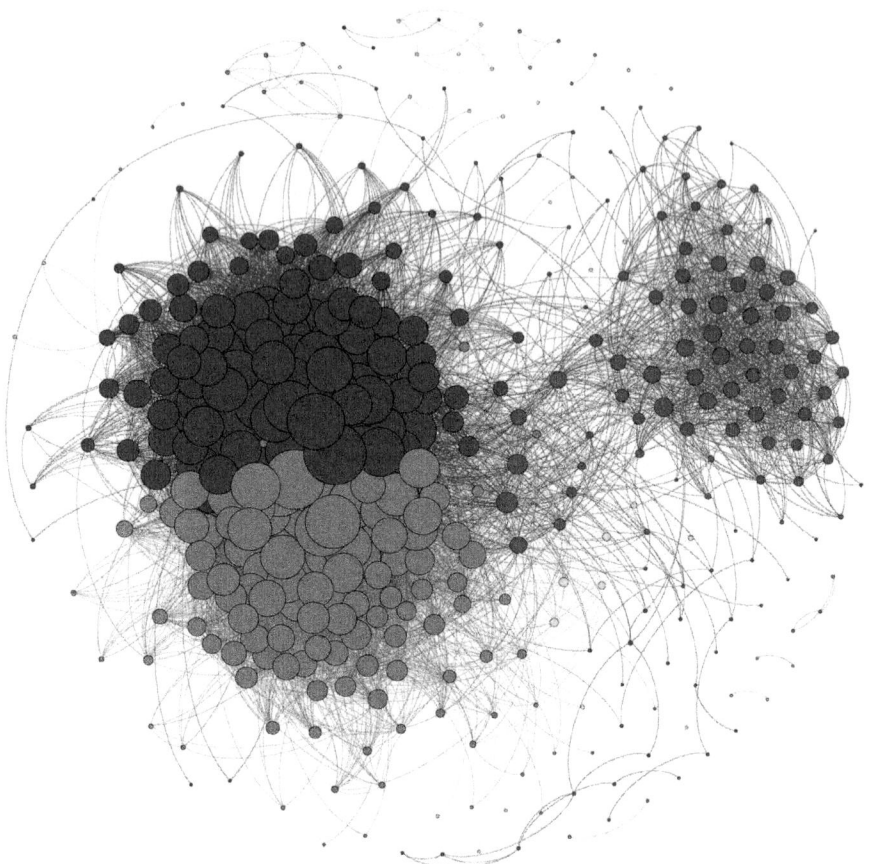

FIGURE 12.1 The communities of verified users in the migration flows dataset

to the Italian government – in office at the time of data collection (Lega and Movimento 5 Stelle) – and other right-wing parties are in blue. The accounts of the centre-left-wing parties (e.g. the Italian Democratic Party, PD) are in red. The violet group includes official media accounts, several NGOs, and left-wing politicians. Some official accounts related to the Catholic Church are in orange. In turquoise, we represent some smaller groups involved in the debate, such as the Maltese Prime Minister Joseph Muscat and some of his ministers, and in green we represent a soccer commentators' community.

As can be seen, the communities are mostly based on their political inclinations. In fact, it is well known that Twitter users tend to be strongly clustered in communities sharing similar ideas (Bessi et al. 2016; Del Vicario et al. 2016; Schmidt et al. 2018). Figure 12.2 shows a pretty clear correlation with respect to political ideas. Orange represents the accounts of the Movimento 5 Stelle. Light blue (on the left) are accounts of Forza Italia. The red vertices are those of the Democratic Party, the institutional users (embassies, police, *carabinieri*, ministers, local governments) are

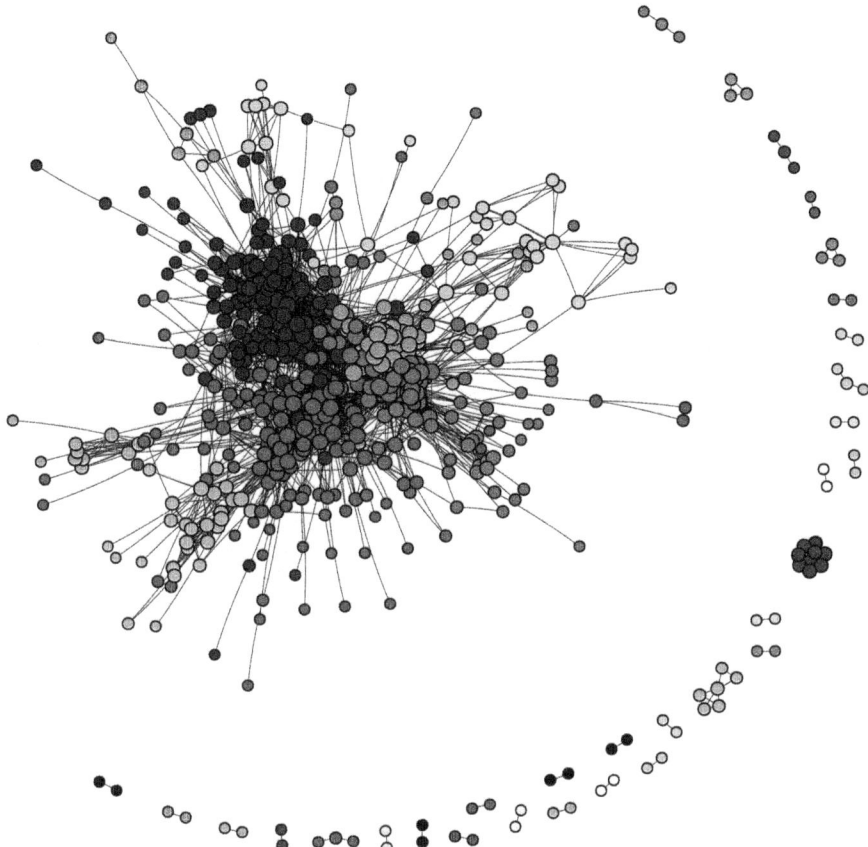

FIGURE 12.2 The communities of verified users in the Covid-19 dataset

represented by blue vertices. Purple vertices are related to Fratelli di Italia, Lega, and newspapers. Finally, the light green vertices on the right are related to TV pundits, journalists, actors, or theatres accounts, while the yellow community on the left is composed mainly by sport journals and journalists.

Verified accounts of politicians can be easily associated with a political party; thus, ideological inclination of unverified users can be guessed by considering their interactions with the communities of verified ones. Figures 12.3 and 12.4 show the matrix of online interactions between verified and unverified users. In Figure 12.3, we report the matrix describing the interactions between verified and unverified users for the migration flows dataset. Nodes are coloured according to their communities, i.e. violet for NGOs, media accounts, left-wing politicians, and for the Democratic Party community, orange for Catholic Church-related accounts, and blue for the pro-government users. In grey, there are users with lower values of polarisation. Figure 12.4 describes the interactions between verified and unverified users for the Covid-19 dataset. Also in this case,

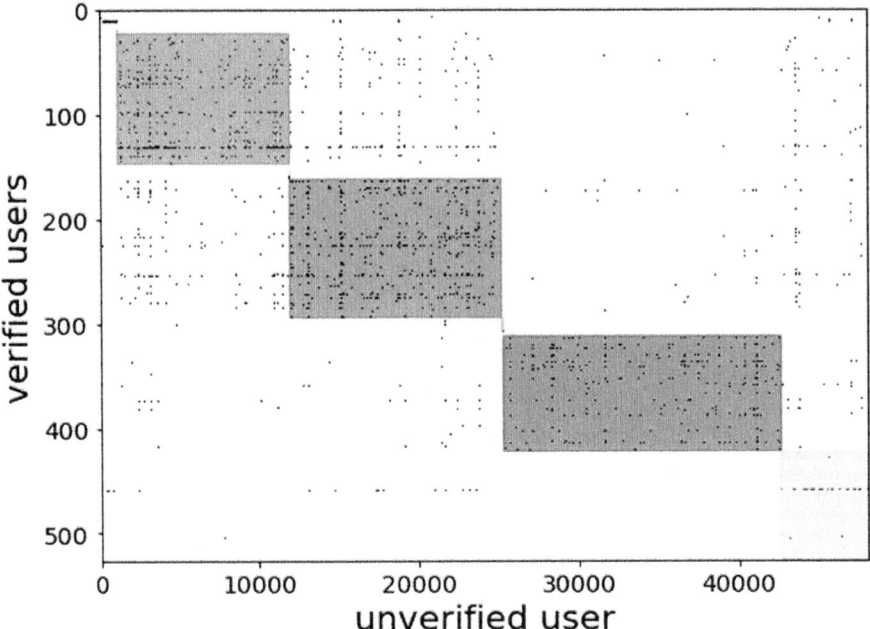

FIGURE 12.3 Interactions between verified and unverified users for the migration flows dataset

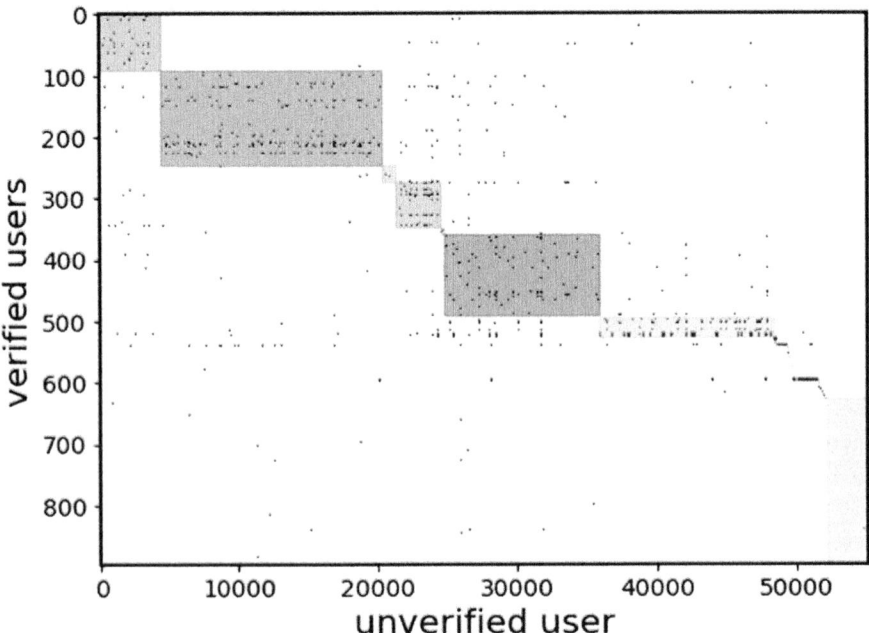

FIGURE 12.4 Interactions between verified and unverified users for the Covid-19 dataset

the community structure clearly reproduces the cluster of verified users with similar political background. Even in a situation of crisis, people tend to follow advice from experts only from a particular side of the political parties (Bessi et al. 2016; Del Vicario et al. 2016). A striking case is that of medical doctor Roberto Burioni, a physician with expertise in infectious diseases (Starr 2020), whose messages are retweeted only by the red community.

Like in a previous study (Becatti at al. 2019), even for the two case studies the community structure is strong.

Significant content exchange

As anticipated in the Introduction, in the analysis of a complex information system, one of the main issues is to skim relevant information from 'noise' (Cimini et al. 2019). Of course, the definition of noise itself depends on the system. In the previous section, we obtained the political affiliation of verified users by projecting the information in the bipartite network describing the interactions between verified and unverified users.

By applying the procedure proposed by van Lidth de Jeude et al. (2019), we filter the total exchange of content in our datasets after discounting the information regarding the activity of users and the virality of messages. Following the approach of Becatti et al. (2019) and Caldarelli et al. (2020), we build the network of users and messages. A link from a user to a message is present if the user authored the message, while there is a link from the message to the user if the latter retweeted the message. This network of users and messages is then used to determine the connections between the users: for every (ordered) couple of users u and w, we consider how many times w retweeted a message authored by u, compared to the activity of u as an author, the retweeting activity of w, and the virality of the messages.

At the end of the procedure, we obtain a 'validated' network: users in such a network contribute to spread the messages in a statistically significant way. The filtering procedure returns a directed network in which the arrows go from the authors to the retweeters. For the migration dataset, the number of nodes reduces to 14,883 users and the number of links reduces to 34,302. For the Covid-19 dataset, the final network contains 10,412 different users and 14,105 links.

Figures 12.5 and 12.6 show the structure of the validated networks in terms of communities for the two scenarios, respectively. The former figure describes the directed validated projection of the retweet activity network. Nodes are violet for NGOs, media accounts, and left-wing politicians, red for the Democratic Party community, and blue for the pro-government users; other colours identify smaller communities. An arrow between a source node and a target node is present if the target is a significant retweeter of the source. The dimension of each node is proportional to its hub score: the biggest node (in blue) is the account of Matteo Salvini, i.e. the leader of a major right-wing party and the Minister of Internal Affairs at the time of the data collection. The latter figure describes the directed

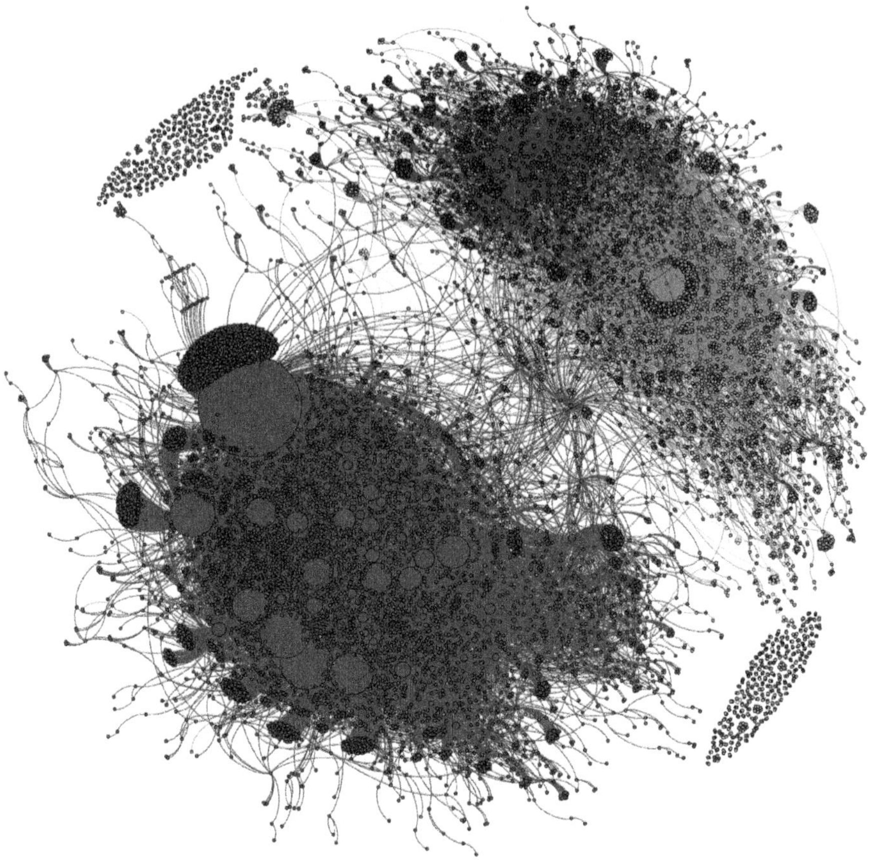

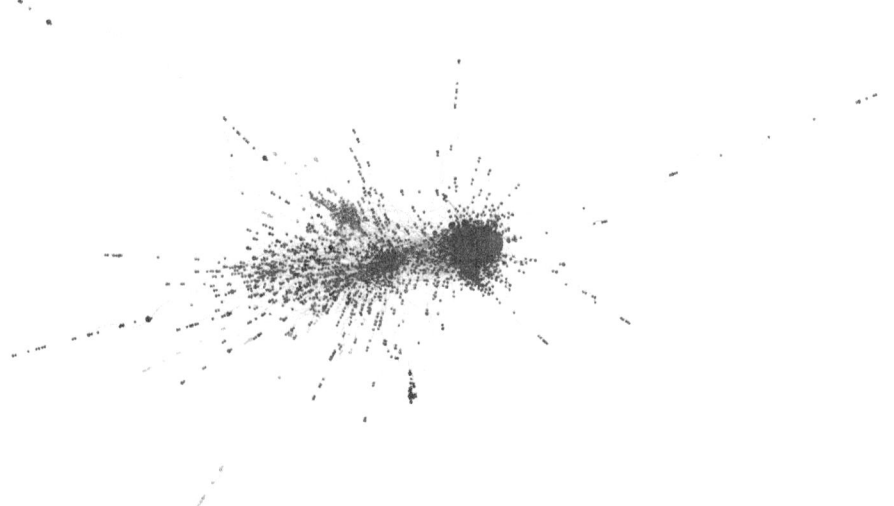

FIGURE 12.5 Mediterranean flows

FIGURE 12.6 Covid-19

validated projection of the retweet activity network. In red, the Italian Democratic Party, in orange, accounts of politicians and journalists close to Movimento 5 Stelle. The violet cluster is divided into two poles: the one of media (in the centre) and the one of the extreme right parties (on the right). Interestingly, all communities are extremely linked to the core of the media.

Results

The effectiveness of a hub can be derived by its ability to reach a high number of relevant nodes: this principle is finely implemented in the Hubs–Authorities algorithm, originally introduced in Kleinberg (1999) to rate webpages. In the original version, the paradigm assigns two scores for each webpage: its authority, which estimates the value of the content of the page from the pages linking to it, and its hub value, which estimates the ability to redirect to the most relevant pages. In the scenario currently under investigation, hubs and authorities are Twitter accounts. In the following we will focus on hubs, because they represent the driving force of the discussion and are relatively popular users, and even if they are not verified by Twitter, we often have reliable information about their accounts.

Migration flows scenario

Among the top 20 nodes, in terms of hub scores, the first account is owned by Matteo Salvini, leader of the right-wing party Lega. The second and the third ones belong to two journalists of a news website supported by Casa Pound, a neo-fascist Italian party. The fourth is owned by Giorgia Meloni, leader of the right-wing party Fratelli d'Italia and former ally, during the 2018 Italian electoral campaign, of Lega. Salvini and Meloni have similar opinions on how to deal with migration in the Mediterranean. The fifth and sixth accounts belong, respectively, to a journalist of *Il Fatto Quotidiano* (a newspaper close to M5S) and an unverified user with opinions in line with the ones of the two above mentioned politicians. Notably, the top nodes belong to the blue community. The first account with a different membership (*TgLa7*, a popular newscast by a private TV channel, whose account belongs to the purple community) ranks 176th in the hub score ranking.

Remarkably, we observe a non-zero overlap among the bots in the lists of the validated followers of human-operated accounts. To the best of our knowledge, this is the first time that such a phenomenon is detected. In our opinion, the use of bot squads, retweeting the messages of two or more strong hubs, aims at increasing the visibility of their tweets. We have detected two main groups of such accounts, the other being composed by a maximum of two common bots. The first one includes 22 genuine accounts (nine of which are in the top 10 hubs), sharing 22 bots. In this set, some users share a relatively high fraction of bots; there is one right-wing account that shares all its automated followers with both Meloni and Salvini (see Figure 12.7).

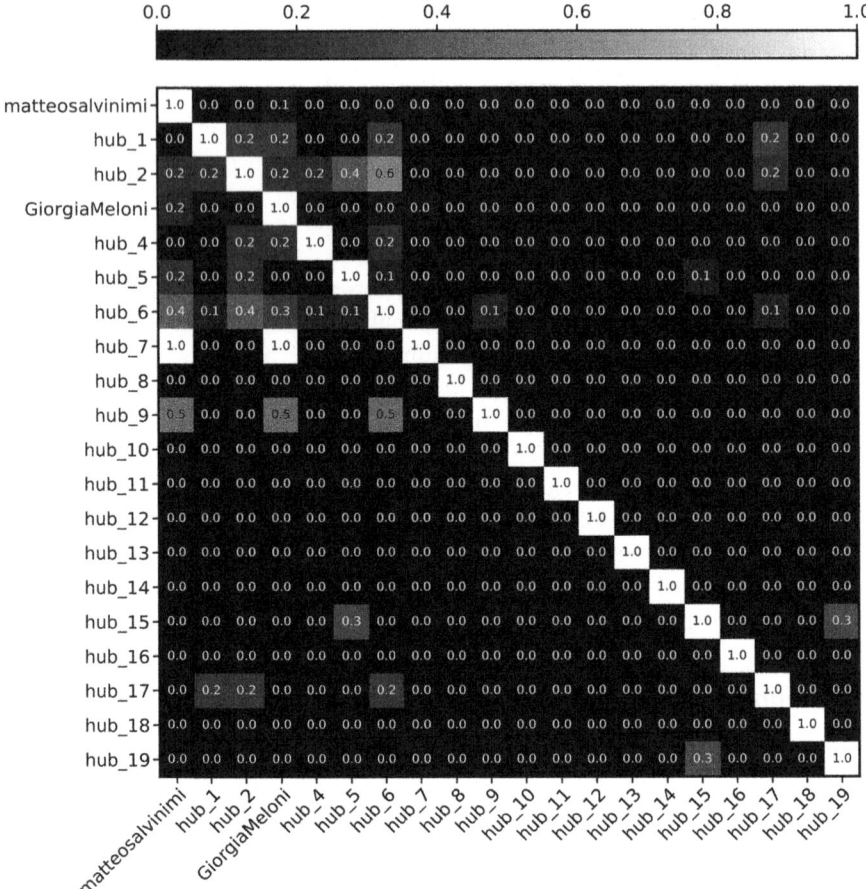

FIGURE 12.7   The relative overlap matrix among the list of bots following the top 20 hubs. A matrix entry represents the percentage of shared bots between users i and j over the number of bots following node i. There are 12 accounts sharing a relatively high number of bots

Figure 12.8 shows the first group of genuine accounts sharing bots and all their bot followers. The subgraph includes genuine accounts (in dark blue) and all the bots following them (in magenta). The dimension of the nodes is proportional to their hub score but normalised on the subgraph. The biggest node represents Salvini's account. In the picture, there are 22 bots shared by 22 humans. Among the latter, nine accounts are among the top 10 hubs. The subgraph contains 172 nodes. Notably, the accounts belong almost exclusively to the blue, i.e., pro-government community. The genuine accounts sharing bots and all their bot followers belong almost exclusively to the blue community, thus we can notice that in this community there is a strong cooperation between bots and humans. The hub scores, represented by the dimensions of the nodes, are nearly homogeneous among the hubs.

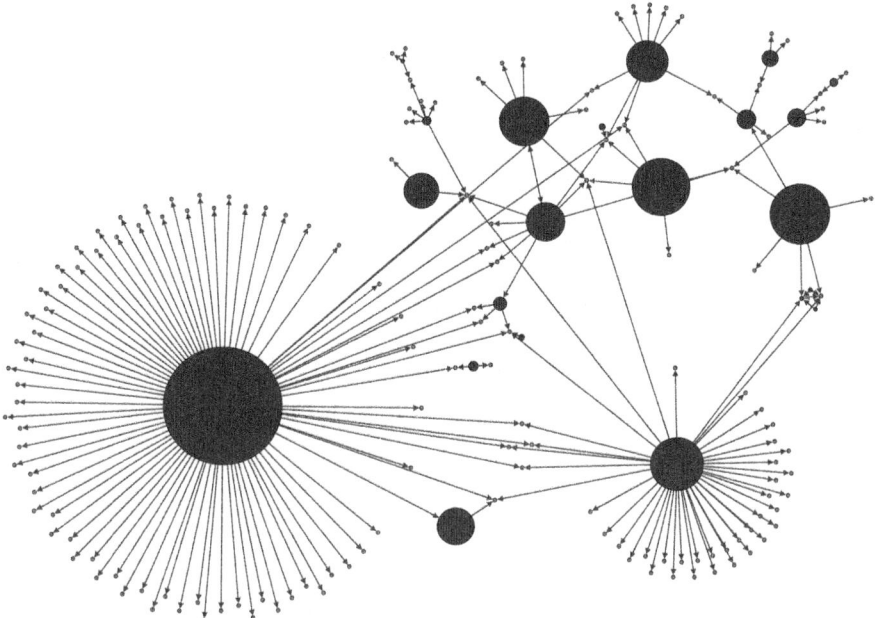

FIGURE 12.8   Subgraph of the largest group of users sharing bots

The incidence of bots in the subgraph of Figure 12.8 is 87%. The number of shared bots over the total number of genuine users is exactly 1. Interestingly, the hubs rarely retweet between each other in a significant way (in fact, only three links can be found among them). They leave it to the bots to spread the content of their partners.

The topmost panel of Figure 12.9 shows that the main activity of the bots in the largest bot squad is retweeting. As expected, they mostly retweet human-operated accounts connected to them (see the central panel of Figure 12.9). The same cannot be said for mentions that may be used either to provoke or to involve the target in a discussion. Accounts from different political sides are mentioned by bot squads; in fact, the bot accounts with more than 30 mentions point to members of the blue community as well as to the official account of the Italian Democratic Party (pdnetwork), a centre-left party. It is worth noticing that other 'non-partisan' verified accounts, e.g. the one of the President of the Republic (Quirinale) and the one of the President of the Chamber of the Deputies, are mentioned there and that, in most cases, the messages containing those mentions are sort of invites for the institutional figures to intervene in the management of migration flows (bottom panel, Figure 12.9). The most striking outcome of the analysis, however, concerns the sources cited by the bots in the blue squads: 89% of their original tweets (i.e. not replies, nor retweets or quoted tweets), contain a URL, and 97% of those URLs refers to www.voxnews.info, a website blacklisted as a source of political disinformation by two popular fact-checking websites, namely www.butac.it and www.bufale.net.

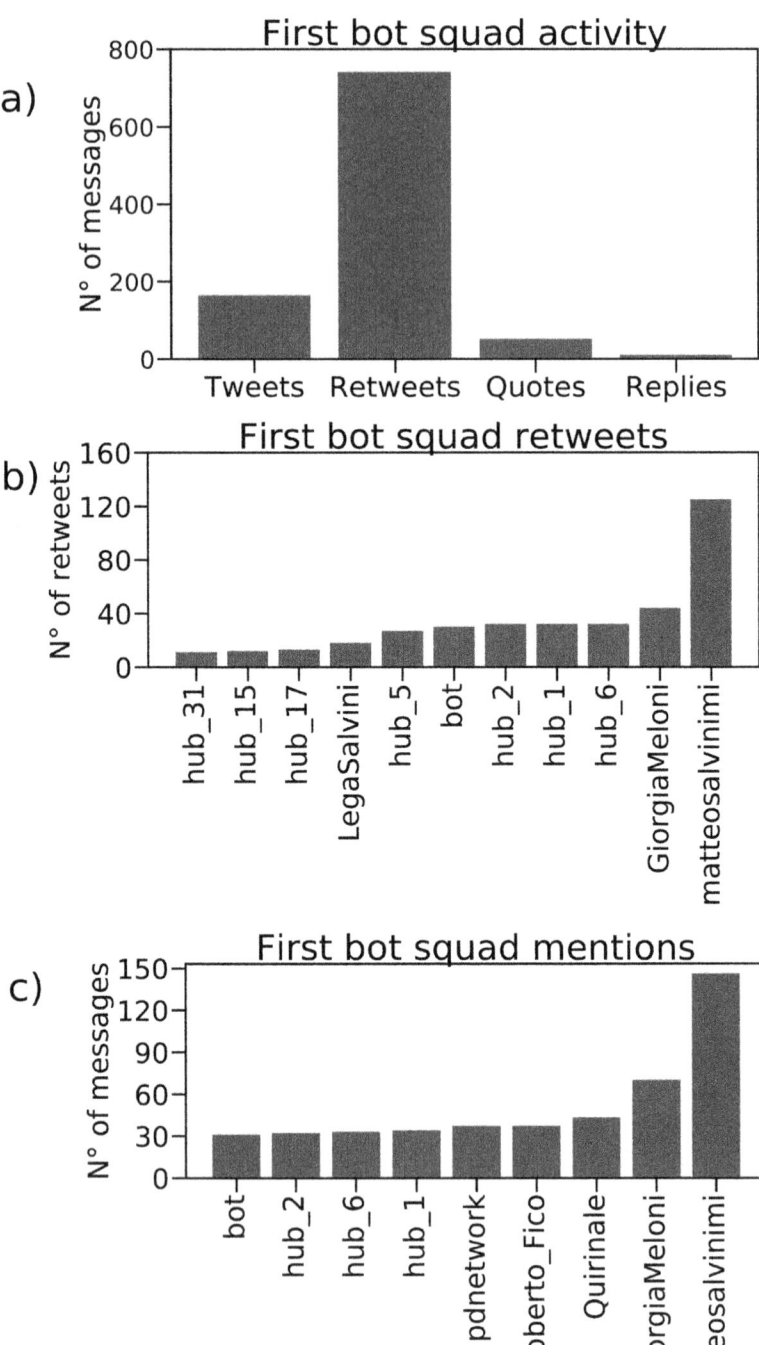

FIGURE 12.9 Statistics of the largest bot squad

Covid-19 scenario

The top 20 hubs are mostly unverified accounts, all from the right wing and the extreme right wing of the political spectrum (exactly as in the above scenario). Among the verified accounts, we have Matteo Salvini, Giorgia Meloni, two right-wing journalists, Salvini's political party, and a politician from the same party; all of them belong to the purple community. In the first position we have an unverified user that we did not spot in the previous analysis, with hub score = 1: this is an unverified account that can be put in relation with extreme right-wing parties. Interestingly enough, in the top 10 hubs, we found four accounts already present

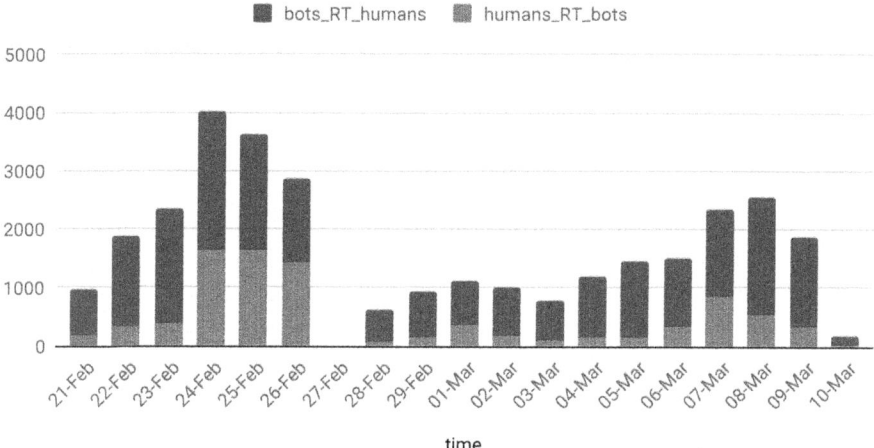

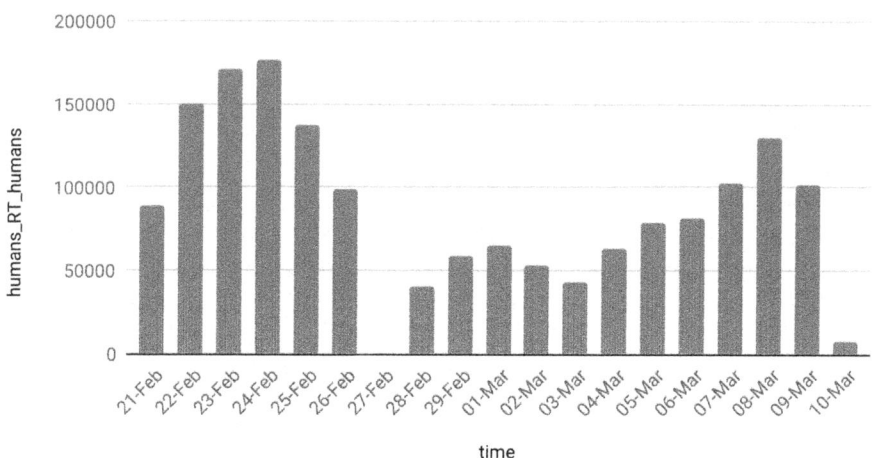

FIGURE 12.10 The retweeting activity of genuine and automated accounts

in the previous study on migration flows. Salvini and Meloni are respectively in the third and fifth places. It should be noticed that the distribution of the hub scores is very peaked (the second place in the ranking accounts for a hub score of 0.45, and it drops down to less than 0.10 for the 10th place).

The activity of bots consists mostly of retweeting human users, although there is a non-negligible activity of genuine accounts in retweeting automated ones (see Figure 12.10). Figure 12.10 shows the retweeting activity of genuine users in the top panel, while the bottom panel reports the the retweeting activity for bots. As it can be seen, the trend of the retweeting activity of automated accounts closely follows the one of genuine users. Looking at the scales, the interaction between human users and bots is limited. Furthermore, the number of genuine users retweeting bots is even smaller.

Amongst these bots, 300 also appeared in the analysis of the political discussion about migration flows. Only 1.7% of all detected bots passed the filtering procedure, thereby representing about 2.8% of validated accounts. Differently from the previous analysis, no bot is shared by the first 500 hubs in the network.

Conclusion

In this chapter, using Twitter as a benchmark, we have analysed the flow of information within and between members of different communities, studying the dynamics of their interactions and the role of automated accounts in such exchanges. For our study, we have relied on techniques developed by physicists and computer scientists. In particular, we have filtered the network of connections and focussed on the most effective accounts in tweets propagation by taking advantage of statistical physics techniques, and we have used machine learning techniques to single out the automatic accounts operating on the network. We have demonstrated the impact of our approach by considering the propagation of Italian tweets concerned with two topics: migration flows in the Mediterranean and Covid-19 related discussion. The analysis has shown that bots play a central role in the exchange of significant content, and that the so-called hub nodes (the most effective accounts in propagating messages) have, among their followers, a high number of bots. This is particularly evident for the migration flows discussion. In the Covid-19 discussion, at least at the time of our investigation, the presence of bots is more limited, but we expect it will grow when the issue stops being only medical and starts becoming political.

The conclusions we can now draw from our analysis do indeed depend on the specific topic of the discussion. As expected, the debate on migrants is dominated by the interplay of several communities strongly related to political parties and alliances operating in the Italian political arena. In this scenario, a rather clear structure of bot squads is present and its effect on the debate is evident. The total presence of bots represents 7% of all users, while their contribution to the backbone of content exchange reduces to the 2.5% of all validated users.

For the Covid-19 discussion, a preliminary analysis showed the presence of echo chambers too. Interestingly enough, those chambers are related to political opinions, even if the subject is mostly scientific. This is not completely unexpected. Indeed, the political countermeasures in order to face the Covid-19 contagion strongly influenced the public debate; by converse, the already present political echo chambers still shape the activity of users on Twitter. The total presence of bots represents 6% of all users, while their contribution to the backbone of content exchange reduces them to 2.8% of all validated users. In contrast to the migration case, we find no signs of a coherent squad of automated accounts acting in the discussion.

Notes

1 Geoff Nunberg (2019) '"Disinformation" is the word of the year – and a sign of what's to come', *NPR*, 30 December 2019.
2 https://developer.twitter.com/en/docs/tweets/filter-realtime/api-reference/post-statuses-filter.html.
3 We searched for the Italian translation of the following keywords: immigrants, migrants, ngo, boat drivers as human smugglers, seawatch, barges, illegal immigrants, Libyan coast guard, shipwreck, disembarkation.
4 #coronavirus, #WuhanCoronavirus, #CoronavirusOutbreak, #coronaviruschina, #coronaviruswuhan, #ChinaCoronaVirus, #nCoV, #coronaviruses, #ChinaWuHan, #nCoV2020, #nCov2019, coronavirus, coronaviruses, ncov, ncov2020, ncov2019, covid2019, covid-19, SARS-CoV2, #SARS_CoV2, #SARSCoV2, #COVID19.
5 We had an interruption of one day and four hours on 27 February due to connection breakdown.

References

Becatti, C., G. Caldarelli, R. Lambiotte, F. Saracco (2019) 'Extracting significant signal of news consumption from social networks: The case of Twitter in Italian political elections', *Palgrave Communications* 5, https://doi.org/10.1057/s41599-019-0300-3.
Bessi, A., F. Zollo, M. Del Vicario, M. Puliga, A. Scala, G. Caldarelli, B. Uzzi, W. Quattrociocchi (2016) 'Users polarization on Facebook and Youtube', *PLoS One* 11(8), doi:10.1371/journal.pone.0159641.
Bradshaw, S., P. N. Howard (2018) 'How does junk news spread so quickly across social media? Algorithms, advertising and exposure in public life', Knight Foundation.
Bradshaw, S., P. N. Howard (2019) 'The global disinformation order: 2019 Global Inventory of Organised Social Media Manipulation', Oxford Internet Institute.
Caldarelli, G., R. De Nicola, F. Del Vigna, M. Petrocchi, F. Saracco (2020) 'The role of bot squads in the political propaganda on Twitter', *Communication Physics* 3(81).
Cimini, G., T. Squartini, F. Saracco, D. Garlaschelli, Andrea Gabrielli & Guido Caldarelli (2019) 'The statistical physics of real-world networks', *Nature Physics Reviews* 1: 52–70.
Conover, M. D., J. Ratkiewicz, M. Francisco, B. Gonçalves, A. Flammini, F. Menczer (2011) 'Political polarization on Twitter', *ICSWM*, doi:10.1021/ja202932e.
Cresci, S., R. Di Pietro, M. Petrocchi, A. Spognardi, M. Tesconi (2015) 'Fame for sale: Efficient detection of fake Twitter followers', *Decision Support Systems* 80: 56–71, doi: 10.1016/j.dss.2015.09.003.

Del Vicario, M., G. Vivaldo, A. Bessi, F. Zollo, A. Scala, G. Caldarelli, W. Quattrociocchi (2016) 'Echo chambers: Emotional contagion and group polarization on Facebook', *Scientific Reports* 6, doi:10.1038/srep37825.

Gangware, C., W. Nemr (2019) 'Weapons of mass distraction: Foreign state-sponsored disinformation in the digital age', www.state.gov/weapons-of-mass-distraction-foreign-state-sponsored-disinformation-in-the-digital-age/.

Kleinberg, J.M. (1999) 'Authoritative sources in a hyperlinked environment', *Journal of the ACM* 46(5), doi:10.1145/324133.324140.

National Endowment for Democracy (2017) 'Issue brief: Distinguishing disinformation from propaganda, misinformation, and "fake news"', https://bit.ly/39E04xb.

Schmidt, A.L., F. Zollo, A. Scala, C. Betsch, W. Quattrociocchi (2018) 'Polarization of the vaccination debate on Facebook', *Vaccine* 36(25): 3606–12.

Shao, C., G.L. Ciampaglia, O. Varol, K.-C. Yang, A. Flammini, F. Menczer (2018) 'The spread of low-credibility content by social bots', *Nat Commun.* 9(1): 4787.

Starr, D. (2020) 'Fighting words', *Science*, 367: 16–19.

van Lidth de Jeude, J., R. Di Clemente, G. Caldarelli, F. Saracco, T. Squartini (2019) 'Reconstructing mesoscale network structures', *Complexity* 2019: 5120581:1–5120581:13.

Varol, O., E. Ferrara, C.A. Davis, F. Menczer, A. Flammini (2017) 'Online human-bot interactions: Detection, estimation, and characterization', *11th International Conference on Web and Social Media*, ICWSM 2017, Montréal, Québec, Canada, May 15–18, pp. 280–89.

Yang, K.-C., O. Varol, C.A. Davis, E. Ferrara, A. Flammini, F. Menczer (2019) 'Arming the public with AI to counter social bots' *Human Behaviour and Emerging Technologies* 1: 48–61.

Acknowledgements

This work has been supported by the Project TOFFEe (TOol for Fighting FakEs) funded by IMT School for Advanced Studies Lucca. The authors would like to thank Serena Giusti and Elisa Piras for the invitation to contribute to the volume and most of all for the feedback that helped us in polishing the paper.

13

RADICAL-RIGHT POLITICAL ACTIVISM ON THE WEB AND THE CHALLENGE FOR EUROPEAN DEMOCRACY

A perspective from Eastern and Central Europe

Manuela Caiani and Pál Susánszky

Introduction

The radical right[1] is on the rise both in the real world and online, not only in Western European democracies (Caiani, Della Porta, and Wagemann 2012; Hutter 2014) but also in Central and Eastern Europe (Buštíková 2018; Greskovits 2020). Overall, compared with the 1970s ('radical right first wave') and early 1990s ('second wave'), the turn of the century was marked by an increasing activity of radical-right organisations in institutional politics ('third wave') (Mudde 2017), especially after the 2008 economic crisis (Kriesi and Pappas 2015). Yet scholars started to talk about the beginning of a fourth wave (of normalisation) of these political forces. The radical right is mainstreamed (Mudde 2019). Also, new forms of radical-right social movements and protest mobilisations emerged (e.g. Pegida in Germany) (Bernhard and Kriesi 2019; Hutter 2014), which often work as 'incubators' of new political ideas and radical-right voters (Minkenberg 2013). In parallel, the success of radical right-wing online mobilisation has become quite obvious (Ekman 2018; Klein and Muis 2019; Kluknavská and Hruška 2019). As the Europol IOCTA 2019 report stressed: "the interplay of online [right-wing extremist] communities who share the same Internet slang and memes contributed to the widespread dissemination of the content and its digital endurance" (49). In fact, the issues around which radical-right groups mobilise their followers – such as Islamisation, globalisation, immigration, etc. – are highly debated on their websites (for an overview on Western Europe, see Caiani and Parenti 2013).

If the "mobilization of the losers" (Kriesi 2014) or "the new cleavage" in search of political entrepreneurs theses (Kriesi 2018) are often quoted to account for this recent radical-right revitalisation in European democracies, the role played by the Internet as a new tool of political mobilisation and communication is also gaining serious consideration among scholars (e.g. Bartlett, Birdwell, and Littler 2011), as the book within which this chapter is located testifies. In particular the radical-right use of the web is linked to hate speech and fake news (Klein 2019; Monti 2018). A recent study on the visual propaganda of the British National Party on Facebook, for example, (Klein 2019) stressed that half of the shared pictures (50%) were "manipulative" and "framed with selective statistics", especially against immigrants and Muslim people, encouraging online activism against them among the followers of the party.

The topic (i.e. radical-right political activism on the web) appears particularly crucial in Eastern and Central Europe since, as underlined, post-communist countries face challenges regarding their membership in the European Union. Moreover, parallel with the rise of nationalist radical-right politics, the quality of democracy has decayed, (Minkenberg 2017: 1–9).

In this chapter we address this topic by focussing on four Central Eastern European countries (the Czech Republic, Hungary, Poland, and Slovakia) and analysing, through a systematic formalised content analysis (for a similar method and tools see Caiani and Parenti 2013) on all radical right websites identified, the degree and forms of the use of the web by these political actors (from political parties to cultural radical websites, to neo-Nazi groups). A particular attention will be devoted to the textual and visual forms of radical-right online propaganda, as well as differences and similarities across various type of groups and countries. A comparison between Eastern and Western radical-right organisations on the use of the web and propaganda will be presented.

Indeed, to date, empirical research on the radical right and their political mobilisation, identity promotion and propaganda online is quite fragmented and selective, focussing still mainly on political parties (although with some important exceptions, e.g. Castelli Gattinara and Pirro 2019) and almost exclusively on Western countries (for some exceptions, see: Fofiu, 2015; Andreescu 2015; Karl 2017). Moreover, although the current resurgence of the radical right in Central Eastern Europe (CEE) has received much scholarly attention in recent years, most of these studies focus on offline radical-right activities (e.g. Minkenberg 2015; Mudde 2017; Pytlas 2015; Císař and Štětka 2016; Císař 2017) or online radical-right activism concerning single case studies (e.g. the Jobbik movement in Hungary). Comparative researches on radical-right online political activities in these countries are still rare.

Who are the radical right organisations active online in CEE? How do they address and attempt to reach out their supporters through the web? What kind of content is spread by radical-right organisations online, and which goals do they pursue? This study, with the limit of focussing on solely four Central Eastern European countries (the Czech Republic, Hungary, Poland, and Slovakia), tries to shed light systematically on these questions and offer an empirical contribution to them.

The chapter is organised as follows. In the first section we summarise the academic state of the art concerning the role of the Internet in radical-right mobilisation. After having illustrated our method and the sources of this study (section two), section three shows the comparative (cross-country and cross-organisational type) empirical analysis of radical-right political activism online, and section four concludes by critically discussing these findings in light of the challenge to European democracies (in particular as far as CEE is concerned).

The role of the Internet in radical-right organisations

Social movement scholars have argued that the Internet offers several advantages for the mobilisation of civil society collective actors, including low costs, fast and efficient communications for connecting isolated individuals and groups, along with tools for coordination and socialisation which are especially helpful to overcome problems of leadership (see, among others, Bennett and Segerberg 2013; Bennett, Breunig, and Givens 2008; Van Laer and Van Aelst 2010). It is said to allow new forms of political participation (Van Laer and Van Aelst 2010) as well as to organise collective actions more easily (Dolata and Schrape 2016). This is even more true for radical actors for whom the web provides a virtual arena in which they can have their views and lower the risk of being banned or persecuted (Caiani, Della Porta, and Wagemann 2012; Klein and Muis 2019). Online platforms help such movements to disseminate messages, organise and mobilise for protests, make symbolic actions, and "provide an opportunity to express oneself in 'online communities'" (Krämer 2017: 12). In fact, it has been stressed that the Internet may reduce the cost of radical-right mobilisations, also transnational ones, such as those organised by Pegida (Caiani and Kroel 2014; Enikolopov, Makarin, and Petrova 2016; Berntzen and Weisskircher 2016) and it can allow these actors to build an active and potent self-image with little effort (Arzheimer 2015; Berntzen and Weisskircher 2016). Finally, studies on social movements argue that the Internet can help in generating collective identities by facilitating the exchange of resources and information, as well as creating solidarity and shared objectives (Della Porta and Mosca 2006) and this is a crucial function for those radical-right political actors, who often feel marginalised from society. As it has been illustrated by recent research, "social media" works "as a second home" for radicals, and a form of "virtual shelter" for these groups (De Koster and Houtman 2008).

All these developments may open new opportunities for the mobilisation of radical-right organisations (as well as challenges for European democracies), which, in the shadow of the great recession, can capitalise on the discontent of the losers of globalisation (Kriesi et al. 2008) via the web (Caiani 2019). In this study, among the various functions the Internet can play for radical-right actors (i.e. mobilisation, identity formation, propaganda, communication, and recruitment, etc; see Caiani and Parenti 2013 for an overview), we will investigate the actual degree and forms of radical-right online activism in our selected countries.

Radical-right organisations are, in general, identified according to a common definition that includes, as core ideological elements: nationalism – i.e., the strong preference for a homogeneous nation (Minkenberg 2015), law and order, racism, conservative values, and anti-system or anti-establishment critiques (Mudde 2007). In this study, we have adopted this definition too, however, it should be considered that these political actors in the CEE have some specificities: a main focus on 'internal enemies', such as Roma groups or Jews instead of 'immigrants' as in Western Europe (Pirro 2015b); the communist legacy (Pytlas 2013), which made the radical right a more acceptable political actor in the public sphere; as well as a peculiar form of national identity[2] (Minkenberg 2017), made of strong nationalism (since most of CEE countries gained their independence relatively recently) and xenophobic sentiments more against aforementioned internal enemies rather than external immigrants. In this study the identification and classification of various radical-right organisations has been based on the self-definition of the groups and the content of the message transmitted through their websites.

Methods and data

In order to identify all radical right organisations with an online presence in our four countries we used a snowball technique, starting from the most important and well-known groups in each country and following explicit web links (e.g. 'our partners', 'our friends') to other radical right groups.[3] This allowed us to identify a total of 188 organisations, around 40–50 in each country. We then conducted a web content analysis on these radical-right organisational websites, using a formalised codebook consisting of more than 70 variables (open and closed questions) trying to capture several different functions of the political use of the web by these groups such as: propaganda, mobilisation, internationalisation, communication, and the creation of a collective identity/ideology. For each of these broader aspects we elaborated lower level indicators.[4]

Our research design includes two comparative dimensions: cross-national and cross-right-wing organisational type. As for the case selection, our four Central Eastern European countries have been chosen because, despite some common historical legacies (e.g. the communist past before 1989, the democratic transition in the early 1990s, and the accession to the European Union in 2004), they provide sufficient variation on the factor we consider relevant for understanding radical-right mobilisation (also online). They are: in terms of political opportunities for radical-right mobilisation, a different role of the so called 'allies in power' (i.e. different strength and duration of the radical-right electoral success) (Krekó, Juhász and Molnár 2011; for details on different countries, see Caiani and Císař 2018); different organisational milieu and associational life of the radical right, which offers a different 'market of consumers' for their online activism (Caiani and Parenti 2013); laws against the Nazi-fascist past; as well as variation in radical-right ideology along the history and activity of the radical-right actors (Minkenberg 2017) – which can influence the forms and content of their use of the web to do politics.

Moreover, this study focusses on both political parties and non-party organisations, including violent groups. They are:

(1) radical-right political parties[5] such as the Slovak Nationalist Party (Slovenská Národná Strana) in Slovakia, the Jobbik in Hungary; the Freedom and Direct

Democracy (Svoboda a Přímá Demokracie) in the Czech Republic, the National Movement (Ruch Narodowy) in Poland;

(2) radical-right movements[6] such as, for instance, the Sixty-four Counties Youth Movement (Hatvannégy vármegye ifjúsági mozgalom) in Hungary, the Endecja Club movement of young intellectuals in Poland;

(3) neo-Nazi groups[7] such as paramilitary groups – e.g. Troop of Social Bandits (Betyársereg) in Hungary, or the Aryan Rebel white supremacy group in the Czech Republic);

(4) revisionist/negationist and nostalgic[8] groups such as, for instance, the Trianon Association in Hungary or the National Institute for Education (Národně Vzdělávací Institute) in the Czech Republic;

(5) cultural and commercial organisations[9] such as for instance the Brotherhood e-shop in Slovakia or the Hungarian warrior clothes shop (Magyar Harcos);

(6) subcultural youth organisations, skinheads, music and sports groups[10] – e.g. the Sztorm 68 Polish skinhead band, Czech Hooligans group, Hungarian football Ultras;

(7) right-wing nationalists, present especially in Poland,[11] such as the National Rzeszow- National Leczna.

As we will show below, in the CEE countries under examination the radical-right area is not a monolithic actor (Minkenberg 2017), and this is also the case online: they use a broad repertoire of (visual and textual) online propaganda with different intensity and for different purposes.

Visual and textual propaganda via the web

As we can see from Figure 13.1, our analysis focusses on several broad aspects that we consider relevant to Internet used by right-wing groups, such as communication, ideology, internationalisation, mobilisation, with a particular view to *propaganda*. With regard to propaganda, the lower level indicators were variables capturing the presence of content concerning radical-right online propaganda towards both insiders and outsiders, such as: slogans, hate symbols, logos, narratives about operations of the groups, the names of the leader, news section, internal search engine, documentation material, and hit counter.

The dissemination of propaganda accounts for, in general, the most extensive use of the web by these organisations, across countries and types of groups (data not showed). In particular, our data suggests that the Polish radical-right groups are very active on their websites and also in their communication (e.g. they are reachable to the public, indicating on their websites their offices, information about the meeting point of the group, phone and mail, etc); Czech radical-right organisations have relatively extended international contacts with actors who operate in foreign countries, with a clear goal to use the web to build transnational contacts with similar organisations; Slovak groups show an average activity in all dimensions; and, finally, the Hungarian radical right seems to be in general less active

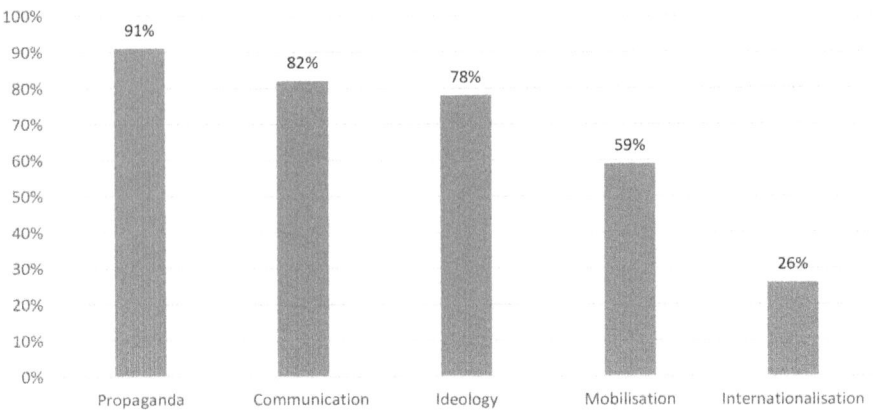

FIGURE 13.1 The political functions of radical-right websites in Central Eastern Europe
N= 188; mean values are showed.

online, something suggesting that the inverse relation hypothesis is at least partly confirmed (Hutter 2014). According to the inverse relation hypothesis between institutional and protest radical-right politics, it is not surprising to find a moderate level of online activism in the country (Hungary) where the radical right possess a super majority in government and in parliament since several mandates. In regards to propaganda, as we can see from Table 13.1, we have distinguished two forms of online propaganda: (1) textual and (2) visual. Textual forms of propaganda includes textual elements like: slogans, bibliography, conference materials, or articles. While pictures, hate symbols, maps, banners or video footage are coded as elements of the visual radical-right propaganda. Indeed, if one important function of these materials is rank and file mobilisation, recent studies have particularly emphasised the important role played by political pictures in online mobilisation (Kharroub and Bas 2016; Powell et al. 2015). According to a recent study by Casas and Webb Williams (2017), visual materials (e.g. pictures, symbols, banners) are particularly

TABLE 13.1 Textual and visual online radical-right propaganda, by country

Countries	Propaganda (%)	Textual propaganda (%)	Visual propaganda (%)
HU	76.4	61.8	67.3
PL	92.9	81.0	73.8
CZ	98.0	94.1	92.2
SK	100.0	95.0	87.5
Total	91.0	81.9	79.8

N= 188; mean values are showed. Abbreviations: HU (Hungary); PL (Poland); SK (Slovakia); CZ (Czech Republic)

effective for political mobilisation, since they 'work' through mechanisms that trigger emotions (e.g. enthusiasm, fear) addressing the passionate side of politics, and spark self-efficacy (Casas and Webb Williams 2017).

Our data shows that in the CEE countries, online propaganda (both visual and textual, 82% and 80% respectively) is widely used on the homepages of radical-right organisations and that, beyond the instrumental uses of the Internet (e.g. for mobilisation, recruitment, or fundraising), the majority of CEE right-wing groups are strongly oriented to propaganda (and therefore the use of the Internet for collective identity formation) towards members or sympathisers,[12] offering a rich repository of documents, photos, and propaganda material explicitly recalling nationalist, xenophobic, fascist, and Nazi iconography and rhetoric.

However, there are significant differences across the four countries. Slovak and Czech right-wing websites are the most active both in textual and visual forms of online propaganda (100% and 98% respectively). On the other hand, we found less propaganda material on the Hungarian and Polish homepages (76% and 93% respectively).

Examining national differences in further details, about visual propaganda we can see that one-fifth of the websites (20.7%) in the countries analysed contain 'hate symbols' such as swastikas, tristikas, and historical fascist symbols such as the *arrow cross* (used by the Hungarian Nationalist Movement) or the short *gladio* sword;[13] photos of nationalist leaders such as Hitler, Ferenc Szálasi or Andrej Hlinka; images related to the Third Reich; and flags from the local fascist pasts (with local symbols such as the phalanx, arrow crosses etc.). Militarist symbols (guns, marching soldiers, historical armed forces' emblems, etc.) also frequently appear, as do Celtic crosses.[14]

Data shows that hate symbols are most likely to be present on the websites of Polish and Hungarian radical-right organisations (42.9% and 25.5%), whereas Slovak and Czech right-wing websites are the least likely to have them (7.5% and 7.8%). These results can be linked to the context of stricter laws against the Nazi-fascist past in certain countries.[15] Half of websites contain banners[16] depicting representative figures, and graphic symbols or seals intended to incite hatred against social and/or political adversaries, such as 'left-leaning clubs' that are targeted by the Polish group Aktyw Północy. Otherwise, banners are most frequent on the Slovak and Czech websites (72.4%, 80.5%) and least on Hungarian websites (7.3%).

As mentioned earlier with regard to propaganda aimed towards outsiders, the main objective is *recruitment*, and the web is becoming a crucial device for that (Street 2011: 263). Neo-Nazis use the Internet and music primarily to reach out to youth members as, for many young people online, communication has become the most important tool for exchanging news and views on the world, and it is their main source of information. According to our analysis, whose main results are synthesised in Table 13.2, 'multimedia materials' are present in half of right-wing sites (50%).

Turning to the textual materials, we find textual propaganda slightly more frequently on radical-right webpages than pictures and other visual information. The most frequent element of textual propaganda is the 'articles' (66%), a section in which the group provide papers, articles, or dossiers. Czech and Slovak websites contain more (86.3% and 77.5% respectively), while Hungarian and Polish sites cite less of these materials (40.0%, 64.3%).

One-third of the radical-right websites analysed contain slogans, 17% bibliographical sources, and finally only a minority of radical-right organisations (7.4%) have a section in which they cite conference materials.

Beyond country contexts, however, we noticed also differences in the political use of the web by radical-right organisations according to the 'type' of group at stake. In particular, movements, neo-Nazi and nationalistic organisations use frequent multimedia material (in 23.4%, 19.1%, and 19.1% of cases respectively). Political movements and nostalgic organisations most commonly offer 'bibliographical references' (present in 21.2% in both instances). On the contrary, commercial groups and political parties seem the least oriented towards using 'bibliography' (in 6.1% and 3%).

On the other hand, cultural and commercial organisations are the least, but political movements are the most likely to have 'articles and/or papers and/or dossiers' on their pages.

Some right-wing organisations (often political parties) also provide more advanced multimedia materials. Also very common are videos of demonstrations and captions of direct actions (clashes with the police, confrontations of the police/'ordinary citizens' with refugees, immigrants, Roma people and other groups that are targets of hate).[17] The latter seem to play an important role, not only in transmitting a message concerning the group's ideology, but also in emphasising the existence of a numerically significant organisation behind the website.

Video and music downloads characterised by political content are especially common in political movements, as well as in Nazi and nationalistic organisations – not to mention, obviously, music groups. Moreover, among this content we find audio files of sermons and archival speeches (e.g. by leaders of fascist/Nazi regimes)[18] or podcasts accompanying radical right-wing journals.

When it comes to subcultural youth radical-right websites, traditional 'hate symbols', related to the national-socialist past, are less present; instead, symbols borrowed from the left are used (on this point, see also Di Tullio 2006; not only the symbols of the Schwarze Front of the Strasser brothers are in use, but also some symbols copied such as Good Night Left Side, etc.). The fact that, in this context, the structure of the Internet – and above all its small levels of surveillance – renders it legally less dangerous to diffuse extremist or even forbidden views through the web is also noteworthy. This is particularly visible in the case of websites of groups connected to the Blood and Honour network and subcultural skinhead groups that are registered as political parties or associations, where the visual evidence collected from the websites could become evidence to be used in court in a delegalisation case. In addition, in the case of social media (in particular Facebook), the occurrence of hate symbols is less visible and explicit, due probably to the synchronic nature of the networks and a number of anti-fascist activists who monitor radical-right fan pages or profiles and report them to the site admins who often block the profiles in question and delete content.[19]

Unsurprisingly, hate symbols are particularly present on neo-Nazi and subcultural right-wing groups' websites (in 35.9% and 25.6% of cases respectively). These latter groups are also the most likely to have banners and seals with hate symbols (68.4%). This is the case, for example, with a nationalist Czech site[20] where, on entering one of the site's subpages, the viewer is presented with a picture including a slogan against the Islamisation of Europe and, in the background, there is a crescent symbol and a minaret and a woman in a niqab in front. On the website of Hungarian Arrabona Crew, there is a picture representing Israel as an oppressor in Palestine, calling for "Protest against Zionist world domination". Similarly, on the site of the Polish nationalistic organisation Zadruga we find a banner showing two men and a woman as 'the Germanic ideal' calling for 'fight, resistance and action' and a call directed at women to defend their blood and motherland, with a drawing of a naked woman wearing the group's armband, an ammunition belt, and military boots.

Finally, regarding the regional West vs. East comparison we can see (Table 13.2) that both visual and textual propaganda elements are, in general, as highly diffused among radical-right groups in the CEE region as among the Western European countries. However, hate symbols, bibliography, and news sections are more prevalent in the Western European radical-right websites. On the other hand, radical-right organisations in the CEE countries place banners more frequently on their webpages. According to these results, we can conclude that the radical-right groups both in Western and in Central and Eastern Europe use the same forms of online propaganda, since we did not find regional patterns in their online communication. Notwithstanding there are differences between the regions regarding the intensity/frequency of some propaganda elements, suggesting that CEE countries are in the middle of the catching up process with the Western European radical right.

TABLE 13.2 Radical-right propaganda through the web in Western vs. Eastern Europe

	Central Eastern Europe	Western Europe*
Hate symbols	20.7%	40.0%
Multimedia	50.0%	50.2%
Banner	50.0%	30%
Article	66.0%	62.4%
Bibliography	17.6%	37.3%
Slogan	34.6%	28%
Conference material	7.4%	11.8%
News section	29.3%	49.8%

*Data based on Caiani and Parenti (2013: 84–91).

Conclusion

In this chapter, building on similar studies focussed on radical-right groups in Western Europe (Caiani and Parenti 2013), we have investigated the degree and forms of right-wing online propaganda in Central and Eastern Europe, a topic far from being developed in (social movement, media and communication) research.

By focussing on different kinds of radical-right organisations and conducting a formalised content analysis of the websites of almost 200 organisations based in four countries, our study showed radical-right CEE groups deploy a rich repertoire of action and variegated forms of political activism. The organisations under scrutiny emerged as fully aware of the new potentialities offered by the web; moreover, they appear able to effectively use these tools for their propaganda and mobilisation. Radical-right groups in the CEE region are practising online propaganda as actively as the Western European radical-right organisations.

First, radical-right organisations in our selected CEE countries use the Internet to reach their followers, to propagate their ideology and mission, and to build and re-affirm radical-right identity. Secondly, our study has also highlighted that Czech and Slovak radical-right organisations use visual and textual propaganda more actively than Hungarian and Polish ones. However, we found country differences in the usage of some particular elements of propaganda. Banners, hate symbols, and articles seem to be less frequent in Slovakia and the Czech Republic than in Hungary and Poland. Beyond country differences, our study also emphasised patterns of Internet political use related to the type of group at stake: focussing on the group differences we found that less 'institutionalised' groups (such as political movements and neo-Nazi organisations) use more visual propaganda elements with respect to more institutionalised groups, such as parties. Nevertheless, political parties are also actively using textual and visual propaganda on their webpages.

From a normative perspective, we must notice that through the Internet, people can access limitless news and information options. Where radical-right propaganda (e.g. anti-minority, pro-nationalism, advocating law and order, 'culture of obedience', etc.) and fake news emerge as a significant political force, the relationship between democracy and the Internet may become critical. Various 'watchdog' think tanks in Central and Eastern Europe (Globsec Report 2019) analysed fake news propaganda before the 2019 elections for the European Parliament in various CEE countries and found that the online media which spreads fake news content often used radical-right rhetoric, e.g. 'migration as a threat for the Christian Europe', Euroscepticism, 'nationalism as the only solution'. Moreover, these sources also often supported by radical-right parties, like Kotleba-ĽSNS in Slovakia, SPD in the Czech Republic, or the ruling party Fidesz in Hungary. As also our study has shown, hate speech and radical-right (fake) news can be helped in their diffusion within society by the increasing Internet use of radical-right organisations (Klein 2019). This, although still rarely investigated – especially in the East – can work as an additional factor explaining the electoral success of the institutional radical right (Greskovits 2020).

Notes

1 In the media and social sciences, actors on the political right of the spectrum are referred to by multiple interrelated concepts, with the term 'extreme right' often used interchangeably with labels like 'fascist', 'Nazi', 'rightist', 'right-wing', '(ultra)conservative', '(ultra)nationalist', 'populist right', and 'radical right', as well as 'extreme right' (Carter 2017).

2 In addition, national identity is shaped by the political and economic transformation process in the late 80s, and early 90s, which in the CEE countries has been regarded as 'modernisation'. This is significantly different than Western European societies' change from industrialism to post-industrialism (Minkenberg 2017, ch 2.).

3 The web content analysis was conducted between January and March 2017 by coders (proficient in the language of the specific country) trained in the sampling selection and coding procedure.

4 For a similar method and tool of analysis, see Caiani and Parenti 2013, but also more generally: Gerstenfeld, Grant, and Chiang 2003; Zhou et al. 2005; Qin et al. 2007.

5 In this class we inserted those groups defining themselves as political parties. In the case of these radical right parties, scale of importance and popularity is very wide. There are small and marginal parties containing just a few members and activists, other parties are active at the local level only. However, there are nationwide vivid parties that openly partake in elections, and sometimes enter the national assembly (especially in Slovakia and Hungary) (see Minkenberg 2017: 69–72 for a detailed list on radical right-wing parties in the CEE region).

6 Political movements are less institutionalised actors that do not run for public offices, but rather "try to mobilize public support" (Minkenberg 2017: 25). This category includes "party parallel organizations" (Veugelers and Menard 2018), referring to associations relating to political parties (for example, 64 county youth movement Hatvannégy vármegye ifjúsági mozgalom in Hungary, and Endecja Club, a movement of young intellectuals in Poland). In the category 'political movements', we have included also political journals and magazines that are often close to political parties (for example, *Dělnické listy* in the Czech Republic, and the monthly magazine *Právo národa* in Slovakia).

7 Neo-Nazi organisations refer to the German Nazis or their ideological cousins in the four examined countries (as the Hungarist movement in Hungary) (Mareš and Stojar 2012). Their sites often contain Nazi and neo-Nazi symbols (for example, the arrow cross) and references to events and nationalist leaders of the interwar period (Blood and Honour, Jozef Tiso, Ferenc Szálasi). Neo-Nazi groups also talk about purity of the Aryan race, white power, and racial hatred (for example, prisoners of war in the Czech Republic).

8 The nostalgic, revisionist, and negationist sites provide document collections on history (mostly on World War II). Revisionists often deny Nazi crimes, and bring vague, distorted interpretations of history. The main themes are the rewriting of history and documentation of the communists' crimes. According to Tucker "revisionist attempts to confuse knowledge with fiction, and founded on bad philosophy, invalid arguments and misunderstandings of contemporary epistemology and philosophy of science" (Tucker, 2008: 3, cited by Pető 2017). In the Hungarian context, there are a bunch of organisations referring to the Horthy Era, which spanned between the two World Wars. The main characteristics of these groups are the condemnation of the Trianon Treaty, and nostalgic feeling for Greater Hungary.

9 As Veugelers and Menard (2018) highlight, publishers play an important role in the radical-right's non-party sector. There are publishers and online shops who sell classical Nazi-fascist texts, memoirs, and also gadgets. The radical right has its own lifestyle which is characterised by specific clothing, clothing brands (Miller-Idriss 2017), and music styles. (Pollard 2016) That category is characterised by the commercial nature of the sites.

10 Subcultural organisations contains 'small groups' such as football fan clubs, skinhead music bands, (Veugelers and Menard 2018) or graffiti and hooligan groups. Some ER groups in Western Europe use the symbols of Celtic mythology or look at a sort of new

spiritualism challenging the official Christian religion. Pollard (2016) calls it Odinims, referring to the ancient German god. In the Central-East European region, there has also been a "tendency to appropriate elements of pre-Christian religious mythologies, including ancient Slavonic religions" (Pollard 2016: 410) In Hungary, pagan mythology and symbols are current in all social strata. This subcultural milieu is dominated by cultural elements of the early Hungarian history, like archery, horse riding, runic alphabet, traditional clothes.

11 Right-wing nationalist groups are close to the category of what Veugelers and Menard (2018) call political sects. "For sects, be they religious or political, the number of members matters less than their worthiness." (p.420) These groups highlight that morality is the most important (for example, the Czech Pro-Vlast). This category includes military groupuscules as well as the Polish Defence League.

12 In our analysis, we have distinguished between propaganda directed towards insiders, namely members and/or sympathisers, and propaganda directed toward a larger public (outsiders).

13 See, for example, the website for Droga Legionisty, http://drogalegionisty.pl/.

14 We relied here on the FIFA and UEFA catalogue of hate symbols, usually banned from stadiums and football games.

15 After rising popularity of radical right in Slovakia, restrictive legal measures have been introduced. (see Strážnická 2017).

16 Banners are images (GIF, flash) usually in a high-aspect ratio shape, often employing animation, sound, or video.

17 For example, see the website of the Slovak neo-Nazi group: https://vzdoruj.wordpress.com/.

18 For example, on https://aryanrebel.wordpress.com/.

19 Such anti-fascist and watch dog organisations are: in Czech Republic, e.g. Liga lidských práv or Nadace Tolerance. In Hungary, e.g. Tett és Védelem Alapítvány or TASZ. In Slovakia, e.g. European Roma Grassroots Organisations Network or Amnesty International, Human Rights Watch. In Poland e.g. HejtStop organisation focussing on hate speech, and the group Otwarta Rzeczpospolita working against discrimination.

20 www.nationalisti.wordpress.com.

References

Andreescu, G. (2015) 'The emergence of a new radical right power', in: M. Minkenberg (ed.), *Transforming the Transformation?: The East European Radical Right in the Political Process*, London – New York: Routledge, 251–77.

Arzheimer, K. (2015) 'The AfD: Finally a successful right-wing populist Eurosceptic party for Germany?', *West European Politics* 38(3): 535–56.

Bartlett, J., J. Birdwell, M. Littler (2011) *The New Face of Digital Populism*, New York: Demos.

Bennett, W. L., C. Breunig, T. Givens (2008) 'Communication and political mobilization: Digital media and the organization of anti-Iraq war demonstrations in the US', *Political communication* 25(3): 269–89.

Bennett, W. L., A. Segerberg (2013) *The Logic of Connective Action: Digital Media and the Personalization of Contentious Politics*, Cambridge: Cambridge University Press.

Bernhard, L., H. Kriesi, (2019) 'Populism in election times: A comparative analysis of 11 countries in Western Europe', *West European Politics* 42(6): 1188–208.

Berntzen, L. E., M. Weisskircher (2016) 'Anti-Islamic PEGIDA beyond Germany: Explaining differences in mobilisation', *Journal of Intercultural Studies* 37(6): 556–73.

Buštíková, L. (2018) 'The radical right in Eastern Europe', in: J. Rydgren (ed.), *The Oxford Handbook of the Far Right*, Oxford: Oxford University Press.

Caiani, M. (2019) 'Radical right wing movements: The rise and endurance', *Current Sociology* 1–18, doi: 10. 1177/00 11392 119868000 (early view).

Caiani, M., O. Císař, (eds) (2018) *Radical right movement parties in Europe*, London – New York: Routledge.

Caiani, M., D. Della Porta, C. Wagemann (eds) (2012) *Mobilizing on the Far Right: Germany, Italy, and the United States*, Oxford: Oxford University Press.

Caiani, M., P. Kroel, (2014) 'A transnational extreme right? New right-wing tactics and the use of the Internet', *International Journal of Comparative and Applied Criminal Justice* 39(3): 1–21.

Caiani, M., L. Parenti (2013) *The Dark Side of the Web: European and American Right-Wing Extremist Groups and the Internet*, London: Ashgate

Carter, E. (2017) 'Party ideology', in: C. Mudde (ed.), *The Populist Radical Right. A Reader*, New York: Routledge, 28–67.

Casas, A., N. Webb Williams (2017) 'Images that matter: Online protests and the mobilizing role of pictures', *Political Research Quarterly* 72(2): 360–75.

Castelli Gattinara, P., A.L. Pirro (2019) 'The far right as social movement', *European Societies* 21(4): 447–62.

Císař, O. (2017) 'Social movements after communism', in: A. Fagan, P. Kopecký (eds), *The Routledge Handbook of East European Politics*, London: Routledge, 184–96.

Císař, O., V. Štětka (2016) 'Czech Republic: The rise of populism from the fringes to the mainstream', in: T. Aalberg, F. Esser, C. Reinemann, J. Stromback, C. De Vreese (eds), *Populist Political Communication in Europe*, New York: Routledge, 285–98.

De Koster, W., D. Houtman (2008) 'Stormfront is like a second home to me. On virtual community formation by right-wing extremists', *Information, Communication & Society* 11(8): 1155–76.

Della Porta, D., L. Mosca (2006) 'Democrazia in rete: stili di comunicazione e movimenti sociali in Europa', *Rassegna Italiana di Sociologia* 47(4): 529–56.

Di Tullio, D. (2006) *Centri sociali di destra: occupazioni e culture non conformi*, Rome: Castelvecchi.

Dolata, U., J.F. Schrape (2016) 'Masses, crowds, communities, movements: Collective action in the internet age', *Social Movement Studies* 15(1): 1–18.

Ekman, M. (2018) 'Anti-refugee mobilization in social media: The case of Soldiers of Odin', *Social Media+ Society* 4(1): 1–11.

Enikolopov, R., A. Makarin, M. Petrova (2016) *Social Media and Protest Participation: Evidence from Russia* (No. 11254), CEPR Discussion Papers.

Europol (2019) 'Internet facilitated organized crime threat assessment' (IOCTA).

Fofiu, A. (2015) 'Stories of a white apocalypse on the Romanian Internet', in: V. Watson, D. Howard-Wagner, L. Spanierman (eds), *Unveiling Whiteness in the Twenty-First Century: Global Manifestations, Transdisciplinary Interventions*, Lanham – Boulder – New York – London: Lexington Books, 29–47.

Gerstenfeld, P.B., D.R. Grant, C. Chiang (2003) 'Hate online: A content analysis of extremist Internet sites', *Analysis of Social Issues and Public Policy* 3(1): 29–44.

Globsec Report (2019) 'European elections in Central Europe: Information operations and disinformation campaigns', www.globsec.org/wp-content/uploads/2019/05/EP-Elec tions_Information-Operations-Disinformation-Campaigns-1.pdf.

Greskovits, B. (2020) 'Rebuilding the Hungarian right through conquering civil society: the Civic Circles Movement', *East European Politics* 36(2): 247–66.

Hutter, S. (2014) *Protesting Culture and Economics in Western Europe: New Cleavages in Left and Right Politics*, Minneapolis: University of Minnesota Press.

Karl, P. (2017) 'Hungary's radical right 2.0', *Nationalities Papers* 45(3): 345–55.

Kharroub, T., O. Bas (2016) 'Social media and protests: An examination of Twitter images of the 2011 Egyptian revolution', *New Media & Society* 18(9): 1973–92.

Klein, O. (2019) 'Misleading memes. The effects of deceptive visuals of the British National Party', paper peresented at the annual SISP conference, University of Lecce 11–14 Sept. 2019.

Klein, O., J. Muis (2019) 'Online discontent: Comparing Western European far-right groups on Facebook', *European Societies* 21(4): 540–62.

Kluknavská, A., M. Hruška (2019) 'We talk about the "others" and you listen closely: The extreme right communication on social media', *Problems of Post-Communism* 66(1): 59–70.

Krämer, B. (2017) 'Populist online practices: The function of the Internet in right-wing populism', *Information, Communication & Society* 20(9): 1293–309.

Krekó, P., A. Juhász, Cs. Molnár (2011) 'A szélsőjobboldal iránti társadalmi kereslet növekedése Magyarországon', *Politikatudományi Szemle* 20(2): 53–79.

Kriesi, H. (2014) 'The populist challenge', *West European Politics* 37(2): 361–78.

Kriesi, H. (2018) 'Revisiting the populist challenge', *Politologický časopis-Czech Journal of Political Science* 25(1): 5–27.

Kriesi, H., E. Grande, R. Lachat, M. Dolezal, S. Bornschier, T. Frey (2008) *West European Politics in the Age of Globalization*, Cambridge: Cambridge University Press.

Kriesi, H., T.S. Pappas (eds) (2015) *European Populism in the Shadow of the Great Recession*, Colchester: ECPR Press, 1–22.

Mareš, M., R. Stojar, (2012) 'Extreme-right paramilitary units in Eastern Europe', in: A. Mammone, E. Godin, B. Jenkins (eds), *Mapping the Extreme Right in Contemporary Europe: From Local to Transnational*, Abingdon: Routledge, 159–72.

Miller-Idriss, C. (2017) 'Soldier, sailor, rebel, rule-breaker: Masculinity and the body in the German far right' *Gender and Education* 29(2): 199–215.

Minkenberg, M. (2013) 'From pariah to policy-maker? The radical right in Europe, West and East: Between margin and mainstream', *Journal of Contemporary European Studies* 21(1): 5–24.

Minkenberg, M. (2015) *Transforming the Transformation?: The East European Radical Right in the Political Process*, Abingdon: Routledge.

Minkenberg, M. (2017) *The Radical Right in Eastern Europe: Democracy Under Siege?*, Berlin: Springer.

Monti, M. (2018) 'The new populism and fake news on the internet: How populism along with Internet new media is transforming the fourth estate', *Stals Research paper* 4.

Mudde, C. (ed.) (2007) *Populist Radical Right Parties in Europe*, Belgium: University of Antwerp.

Mudde, C. (2017). 'Politics at the fringes? Eastern Europe's populists, racists, and extremists', in: A. Fagan, P. Kopecký (eds), *The Routledge Handbook of East European Politics*, London: Routledge, 254–64.

Mudde, C. (2019) *The Far Right Today*, Cambridge: Polity.

Pető, A. (2017) 'Revisionist histories, "future memories": Far-right memorialization practices in Hungary', *European Politics and Society* 18(1): 41–51.

Pirro, A.L.P. (2015a), *The Populist Far Right in Central and Eastern Europe: Ideology, Impact, and Electoral Performance*, London: Routledge.

Pirro, A.L.P. (2015b) 'The populist far right in the political process – Assessing party impact in Central and Eastern Europe', in: M. Minkenberg (ed.), *Transforming the Transformation?: The East European Far Right in the Political Process*, London: Routledge, 80–104.

Pollard, J. (2016) 'Skinhead culture: The ideologies, mythologies, religions and conspiracy theories of racist skinheads', *Patterns of Prejudice*, 50(4–5): 398–419.

Powell, T.E., H.G. Boomgaarden, K. De Swert, C.H. de Vreese (2015) 'A clearer picture: The contribution of visuals and text to framing effects', *Journal of Communication* 65(6): 997–1017.

Pytlas, B. (2013) 'Radical-right narratives in Slovakia and Hungary: Historical legacies, mythic overlaying and contemporary politics', *Patterns of Prejudice* 47(2): 162–83.

Pytlas, B. (2015) *Radical Right Parties in Central and Eastern Europe: Mainstream Party Competition and Electoral Fortune*, London: Routledge.

Qin, J., Y. Zhou, E. Reid, G. Lai, H. Chen (2007) 'Analyzing terror campaigns on the internet: Technical sophistication, content richness, and web interactivity', *International Journal of Human-Computer Studies* 65(1): 71–84.

Rydgren, J. (2007) 'The sociology of the radical right', *Annual Review of Sociology* 33: 241–62.

Strážnická, A. (2017) 'Extremism in Slovakia – throughout analysis', *European Journal of Transformation Studies* 5(2): 60–68.

Street, J. (2011) *Mass Media, Politics and Democracy*, Basingstoke: Palgrave Macmillan.

Tucker, A. (2008) 'Historiographic revision and revisionism', in: M. Kopecek (ed.), *Past in the Making. Historical Revisionism in Central Europe*, Budapest: CEU Press, 1–15.

Van Laer, J., P. Van Aelst (2010) 'Internet and social movement action repertoires: Opportunities and limitations', *Information, Communication & Society* 13(8): 1146–71.

Veugelers, J., G. Menard (2018) 'The non-party sector of the radical right', in: J. Rydgren (ed.), *The Oxford Handbook of the Radical Right*, Oxford: Oxford University Press, 285–304.

Zhou, Y., E. Reid, J. Qin, H. Chen, G. Lai (2005) 'U.S. domestic extremist groups on the web: Link and content analysis', *IEEE Intelligent Systems* 20(5): 44–51.

14

WHEN A CREDIBLE SOURCE TURNS 'FAKE'

The Relotius affair and the German system for combating fake news

Mihail Stojanoski

Introduction

The term 'fake news' has been omnipresent in society, particularly in political discourse for several years. In spite of its popularity among political figureheads, journalists, and researchers (or, maybe exactly because of that), a unified definition of the term proves somewhat elusive. It is, of course, quite natural that a term as recent[1] and controversial as 'fake news' should be used in a variety of (sometimes conflicting) ways, which is partly why academia cannot agree on a single definition. The Cambridge Dictionary defines 'fake news' as false stories that appear to be news, spread on the Internet or using other media, usually created to influence political views or as a joke.[2] Another definition which takes different factors into account defines fake news as the deliberate presentation of (typically) false or misleading claims as news, where the claims are misleading by design (Gelfert 2018). There appear to be many definitions around, all of which take various aspects of the phenomenon into account, whether it is the presence of intent, the results, the environment where it emerges, or something else.

In any event, there appears to be common ground between the sources that measures need to be taken to impede, block, punish, or (better) prevent the spread of fake news. Although the risks and dangers which follow fake news are not a topic of central interest of this chapter, we would stress that one of the primary concerns of legislators seems to be elections, or rather information available to voters during election periods. This narrative follows the premise that decisions in times of elections are made on a personal level, on the basis of available information. Therefore, if the flow of information cannot be trusted, the whole democratic process, including the result, would be compromised.[3]

In this article, we will examine the recent German anti-fake-news law ('Gesetz zur Verbesserung der Rechtsdurchsetzung in sozialen Netzwerken, Netzdurchsetzunggesetz', or just 'NetzDG') in a very practical context. The whole idea surrounding the law, which takes a novel and unique approach, was built on the premise that the greatest risk for the flow of information comes from the spread of fake news on social media. These platforms have largely replaced traditional media to a large extent as the primary source of news.[4] Meanwhile, operating under the assumption that they can generally be trusted, nobody thought to look at traditional media. And why would we? The occasional left or right leaning journalist is nothing that old democracies are not used to. The fearful finger was pointed at social media, and oh my, were we surprised.

However, in the defence of the lawmakers, given that the Relotius affair (the details of which will be presented below) may not even be considered as fake news at its most fundamental understanding, the affair presented somewhat of a *sui generis* challenge for the system, one which was difficult to anticipate. In these circumstances, the chapter touches on issues such as the limits of truth and fact checking, responsibility of the State *vis-à-vis* the individual in the field of free speech and the (practical and legal) limitations, which exist as to what can be achieved by legislating.

The chapter follows a two-pronged analysis, with an attempt at a synthesis of those two topics in a third, final section. At the outset, factual background is provided in order to explain the Relotius affair, its significance, and its consequences. Then, we will briefly analyse the new legal system aimed at combating hate speech and fake news in place in Germany as a starting point for any contextual analysis of the Relotius affair. Finally, the chapter attempts to reconcile the two ideas and develop some observations in that regard.

The Relotius affair

Claas Relotius is a German freelance reporter wrote for a number of German-language publications, including *Cicero*, *Frankfurter Allgemeine Sonntagszeitung*, *Neue Zürcher Zeitung*, *Financial Times Deutschland*, *Die Tageszeitung*, and *Die Welt*. Since 2017 he had been working as an editor for *Der Spiegel* (Der Spiegel 2018c). During his career he managed to collect an impressive number of awards, including CNN's journalist of the year (2014), the European Press Prize (2017), and the Deutscher Reporterpreis (four times, including 2018).

There is little need to introduce *Der Spiegel*. It is a Hamburg-based weekly news magazine with a circulation of around 740,000 copies, which in the past exceeded one million (European Publishing Monitor 2007). In addition, it has an estimated base of 6.5 million online readers (Connolly 2018). It is widely considered as one of the most influential news magazines in Germany and Europe, responsible for uncovering several scandals and affairs thanks to its pronounced and thorough investigative journalism (Strawn and Hogan 1984/1985). What became known as the Relotius affair can be described in the following way.

Since 2011, when his cooperation with the reputed magazine began, almost 60 articles written by Relotius were published by *Der Spiegel* magazine or *Spiegel Online*, its Internet counterpart. The articles reached a high audience, were widely regarded as top-notch journalism and can be directly linked to some of the awards listed above. Being an already successful journalist of a relatively young age, he was a rising star.

The first suspicions regarding the veracity of his articles emerged in November 2018 following the publication of the article entitled 'Jaeger's border' ('Jaegers grenze')[5] about an American vigilante group that patrolled the border between Mexico and the United States. Juan Moreno, who reported the story together with Relotius, was one of the first to grow distrustful of his colleague. He had raised suspicions about the work carried out by Relotius before the magazine's editors by late 2018, but his concerns were largely ignored.

> Some at *Der Spiegel* even believed that Moreno was the real phony and that Relotius was the victim of slander. Relotius skilfully parried all allegations and all of Moreno's well-researched evidence, constantly coming up with new ways of sowing doubt, plausibly refuting accusations and twisting the truth in his favour (Fichtner 2018).

"At the start it was the small mistakes, things that seemed too hard to believe that made me suspicious." Moreno went on to describe how it had been strange that some of the protagonists in Relotius's articles had not wanted to be photographed, in spite of being already prominent in the US media. "At some point I just thought something is monumentally wrong here . . . I started to do my own research only to discover that that [the same] protagonist [who had allegedly refused to be photographed] had already appeared in *The New York Times*," said Moreno.[6]

Relotius was eventually confronted by the magazine's management. By the beginning of December, facing a growing pile of evidence and distrust, he made a full confession. News of the affair was broken to the public on December 19th by *Der Spiegel* itself. According to the confession, at least 14 articles written by him were at least partly fabricated.[7]

Among the articles in question are major features that were nominated for or won journalism awards. For example, an article entitled 'The last witness', about an American who allegedly travels to witness an execution, is among the 14 articles. Another two, entitled 'The lion children', about two Iraqi children who have been kidnapped and re-educated by the Islamic State, and 'Number 440', a story about prisoners at Guantanamo, also fall within those which, according to the confession, contain falsities. In the stories, he included individuals who he had never met or spoken to, but he told their stories and quoted them. Instead of actually meeting them, he revealed that he had based the depictions on other media or video recordings.[8] By doing so, sometimes he created composite characters based on several actual people, but whose stories he fabricated. He also made up entire lines of dialogue and quotes.[9]

As to Relotius's reasons for fabricating the articles, before handing in his resignation, he said: "It wasn't about the next big thing. It was the fear of failure. The pressure not to fail grew as I became more successful" (Fichtner 2018).

Following the revelation, *Der Spiegel* publicly apologised to its readers and undertook to conduct a thorough investigation. They called it "the lowest point in the 70-year history of *Der Spiegel*" (ibid.). They created a three-member expert commission that was tasked to evaluate the damage and to find ways to prevent similar incidents from happening in the future.[10]

The outcry in the wake of these events was enormous. The German Federation of Journalists called the case "the biggest fraud scandal in journalism since the Hitler diaries," referring to a story that Germany's *Stern* magazine published in 1983, which was later proven to be fake.[11]

For the moment, all the articles written by Relotius remain publicly available on the website of the magazine, with a notification about the scandal added for clarity. As argued, they did it to provide the possibility for transparent research on the issue (Der Spiegel 2018c).

As a final touch, *Der Spiegel* announced that they would file criminal charges against Relotius for fraud with regard to donations collected in the name of Syrian orphans, featured in one of his articles (Klusmann 2019). As alleged, he collected donations from concerned readers claiming that the money would be used with the aim of helping these children, but the money eventually ended up in his own bank account.

Relotius remained silent following the outbreak of the affair, avoiding public appearances. However, on 27 December 2018 in response to the claims made regarding the alleged fraud, he admitted through his attorneys that the donations were made to his bank account, but he claimed that he had never intended to keep the money. He had collected 7000 euros from readers, to which he added 2000 euros of his own and made a donation to a relief agency. The agency in question, when contacted by *Der Spiegel*, confirmed that a donation of the above amount had been made by Relotius in October 2016 (ibid.). The proceedings are ongoing.

At the moment of writing and according to the available information, apart from breaking his relationship with *Der Spiegel*, there is no indication of any sanctions or proceedings against Relotius specifically regarding the falsities contained in his articles.

The regulation of disinformation in Germany

A recently conducted census representative survey by Dalia Research found that 34% of Germans using social media have read articles or news that were intentionally misleading or not truthful (fake news), 16% have received offensive messages or comments from someone they do not know, 14% have received sexually offensive messages, and 3% have received threats. 16% of Germans have also reported a user for abuse on social media (Dalia Research 2018). Although the survey is based on self-reporting, the results are worrisome.

Before the introduction of the NetzDG, disinformation was dealt with under the existing legislation. Although spreading disinformation was not a crime *per se*, hate speech was prohibited and regulated in Section 130 of the German Criminal Code (listed as 'Incitement to hatred'), and provided for imprisonment up to five years.

In this regard, the provisions of the EU e-commerce Directive adopted in 2000[12] should be mentioned. The directive prescribes liability for social media that would host illegal content, unless they can prove that they have no actual knowledge of, or act promptly to remove or disable access to the content in question.

Recognising a threat in the effect that fake news may have on elections, on 30 June 2017, three months before the federal elections, the German parliament adopted a law targeting specifically hate speech and fake news, which some consider the most extreme reaction to disinformation among Western countries (Cerulus 2017). The danger of fake news affecting election results, following the 2016 election campaign in the United States, was explicitly referred to in the government's reasoning justifying the need for the new law (NetzDG draft bill 2017: 1). As earlier efforts to curb hate speech had been considered ineffective by the German Minister Heiko Maas (ibid.), the primary objective of the new law was to improve the otherwise insufficient regulation of the spread of hate speech online. Then Justice Minister (and current Foreign Minister) Heiko Maas presented it as a means to tackle online hate speech and viral deception: "The freedom of expression also protects offensive and hateful statements. But it is not an excuse to commit crimes" (Der Spiegel 2018a).

Under the so-called Network Enforcement Act (NetzDG), which came into effect on 1 January 2018, Germany introduced new obligations for social networks aimed at combating hate speech and fake news.

Among these, social networks with at least two million registered users in Germany are obliged to create and maintain a procedure for complaints with regard to "unlawful content"[13] which is defined as content meeting the elements of certain provisions of the German Criminal Code. Among other provisions the NetzDG here makes reference to sections § 166 (Defamation of religions, religious and ideological associations), § 185 (Insult), § 186 (Defamation), and § 187 (Intentional defamation). The Act further makes a distinction between "unlawful" and "manifestly unlawful" content,[14] which remains somewhat unclear. In any event, social networks are required to remove or block access to the impugned content within either seven days or 24 hours of the user's complaint.

Social media are required to decide on the compliance of content with the above Criminal Code sections themselves, or externalise the decision to an independent third party, essentially granting them a quasi-judicial role. It should be noted that fines for social media are only envisaged for systemic non-compliance with the requirements, and not on a case-by-case basis.

Critics of the new law attacked it for surrendering the control over important social issues to private companies. The key concern revolved around the argument that in order to avoid being fined, social media would apply a 'take down first, examine later' policy, which would in turn have a chilling effect on free speech.

TABLE 14.1 Number of reports of fake news and removal rate

Social network	Total no. of reports	Removal rate
Facebook	1704	362 (21.2%)
Google (YouTube)	241,827	58,297 (27.1%)
Twitter	264,818	28,645 (10.8%)
Change.org	1257	332 (26.4%)

The most relevant feature of the NetzDG for this chapter is that journalistic and editorial content were explicitly removed from its scope.[15] This means that online news portals, online magazines, journalistic platforms, and the like are not to be treated identically with social media. These fall outside the scope of the NetzDG and remain regulated under the existing legislative framework.

The effects of the NetzDG were immediate. On 1 January 2018, the day that the NetzDG came into effect, Twitter and Facebook removed a post from a German far-right politician who accused the Cologne police (who had tweeted a new year message in Arabic) of appeasing "barbaric, gang-raping Muslim hordes of men" (Oltermann and Collins 2018).

When it comes to EU monitoring of unlawful online content and its removal in Germany, in January 2018 the Commission reported that "companies have strengthened their reporting systems, making it easier to report hate speech, and have improved their transparency vis-à-vis [. . .] users in general". Subsequent rounds of EU monitoring demonstrated steady improvements in content removal rates across the EU. In Germany, the average rate of removals for Facebook, Twitter, and YouTube combined went from 52% in December 2016 to 100% in the third monitoring exercise the following year (Echikson and Knodt 2018). It should be noted, however, that this 100% figure, although somewhat concerning, in practice refers to a little over 200 pieces of content taken down pursuant to requests made by two accredited German flaggers, who are at the origin of this data (ibid.).

Since the above events, blocks and removals under the NetzDG have failed to draw significant media attention. As far as it could be established, there have been no reports of controversial false positives, and no fines for the social media providers have been imposed under the law. The total reports and removals for the first six months from the four social networks currently affected under the NetzDG are shown in Table 14.1 (ibid.).

Conclusion

For more than a year, the selfie of a Syrian refugee with Angela Merkel has been coursing through the social networks, combined with the lie that the refugee in question was an Islamic State assassin. The person in question has sued Facebook and the original photo montages have been eventually deleted. In spite of this, a number of people will nevertheless remember an image of Angela Merkel posing with a terrorist (Beuth et al. 2017). Similar reports can be found everywhere and they cause great harm, with the reputation of public persons and politicians being at the front line of fire.

Initial results of the implementation of the NetzDG testify that there is very little evidence of mass take-downs of content (see Table 14.1). The German courts have already had time to produce case-law on the application of the NetzDG, which, although not entirely coherent at the moment, underlines the complexity of the issue.[16] It should also be said that the removals concerning defamation and insult make for around 19% of the total removals done by Google for the first six months of the application of the NetzDG. Furthermore, 75% of these were removed under Google's community guidelines, which means that they would have been removed in spite of NetzDG.[17]

Getting back to the Relotius affair, it would seem that, given the explicit exclusion of journalistic content from the scope of the NetzDG, the Act would simply not apply in this case. The criminal charges for fraud (which are not a direct consequence of his false reporting) cannot lead to a different conclusion.

On a side note (and with some irony), it would appear that the NetzDG's scope would extend to the articles in question, had any of them (or conclusions based on them) been shared on social media.

Given the above, questions arise as to the effectiveness and level of protection against falsities under the current German legislation. If we take a look at comparable legislation in neighbouring France,[18] it should be noted that the French legislative reform brought online platforms (including journalistic platforms and social media) under the already existing obligation of the Consumers Code to make any financial links, sponsorship, or contractual obligations with regard to content public.[19] Further to this, new interlocutory proceedings were introduced where a judge can order any proportionate and necessary measure against Internet service providers and hosts to stop the spread of fake news.[20]

Observing the above measures one cannot but note that much like its German counterpart, the French legislation also addresses fake news in a responsive manner. Neither Germany nor France have enacted legislation which aims at preventing the appearance of fake news or strengthening media literacy.[21]

Could the French model have suppressed the fraudulent articles published by Relotius? Doubtful. Analysis of further models, such as the one proposed in the United States, or the one in force in Russia, do not reveal an alternative approach that could have prevented an event such as the Relotius affair.

It is beyond doubt that the harm caused by Relotius's articles is serious and significant, to the point that it may have shaped the opinion of readers and individuals in ways that we cannot begin to comprehend. How did the articles shape long-term societal values, political views, and by extension, election results? At this point we can only speculate that the damage is at least comparable to the one caused by articles such as the ones which fit the *prima facie* definition of fake news, presented at the beginning of this chapter.[22]

If the damage is significant and the existing legislation does not cover the example at hand, is this something which can be solved by further regulation? Most likely, not. What is the solution, then?

Der Spiegel has one of the most advanced and dedicated fact-checking systems in Europe (Southern 2017), which can only serve to testify as to the dedication of the magazine to truthful reporting, but that did not help them in preventing the Relotius incident. This is primarily due to the nature of the articles that the reporter wrote, the fact that he intentionally covered his tracks, but also the nature of investigative journalism in general. To put it simply, what a Syrian child said to a foreign reporter in a dusty alley in a small town in eastern Turkey is simply beyond the scope of fact-checking as such. However, some facts that were clear fabrications and could be fact-checked (for example, some of the facts surrounding the article 'Jaeger's border' described above), were the ones that led to Relotius's downfall. So, the obvious, inherent limitations to fact-checking as a process should not discourage society's pursuit for responsible journalism, and by extension, truth. Should we simply come to terms with the fact that embellishing, misrepresenting, and even straight out fabrications are inherent to journalism? Can *Der Spiegel* be blamed for their failure? Not unless we put our finger on where they failed. And it seems that they did an excellent job at dotting all of their i's and still let a big one slip through.

Responsible journalism cannot be regulated any more than it already is without infringing on the freedom of expression. This is why the ultimate responsibility lies with the news consumers themselves. They (or, rather, 'we') need to be aware that the system of news reporting and journalism is essentially dependent on a human element, and is therefore bound to inherit human imperfections as such. The alternative would be a completely regulated flow of information and filtered truth, and although that did not happen in 1984 as some had anticipated, the risks are very much present today.

Notes

1 The term is somewhat recent. The concept, some would argue, is hundreds of years old. To this end see: Sol (2016).
2 https://dictionary.cambridge.org/dictionary/english/fake-news.
3 Some examples capable of influencing the outcome of elections include the allegations that German soldiers had raped a young girl during a NATO operation in Lithuania, that NATO had put 3600 tanks into position against Russia, that 700,000 Germans had left their homes because of Angela Merkel's refugee policies, or that 1000 immigrants had lit a church in Dortmund on fire. Needless to say, none of these are true. For these and other examples, see Beuth et al. (2017).
4 For example, around 20% of adults in the United States stated that they "get news often" through social media. See Perez (2018).
5 The article was, of course, published in German. Some argue that this, along with his reluctance to have his work translated into other languages was deliberate, as the language gap between his readers and his interviewees, who were mostly foreign, made it easier for him to maintain the deception. See: Slyomovics (2018).
6 Statements from a video released by Juan Moreno, cited by *the Guardian* in Connolly (2018). For more, see: Carbajosa (2019).

7 *Der Spiegel* has since provided ample information on the development of the case (Der Spiegel 2018c). As the affair develops, further information is made available by the magazine itself, which is now attempting to rebuild its former reputation by taking responsibility and dealing with the affair head on.

8 For example, in one of his earlier articles Relotius wrote about an American town called Fergus Falls. In his article he wrote that the movie *American Sniper* had been running in the local cinema for two years consecutively, at the entrance to the town there had been a sign saying 'Mexicans Keep Out', a school was protected with a metal detector and three armoured glass doors, and much more. All of this was eventually established to be false.

9 Sources are various articles published by *Der Spiegel* following the affair, all of which are cited in the References.

10 For more information on the commission and its composition, see: Der Spiegel (2018b).

11 The diaries were later found to be forgeries (Sharman 2018).

12 It is the Directive 2000/31/EC, Directive on electronic commerce, available at: https://eur-lex.europa.eu/legal-content/EN/ALL/?uri=CELEX%3A32000L0031.

13 See Section 3, paragraph 1 of the Act. An official English version of the NetzDG – 'Act to Improve Enforcement of the Law in Social Networks (Network Enforcement Act) – is available on the German Ministry of Justice website, at: https://www.bmjv.de/SharedDocs/Gesetzgebungsverfahren/Dokumente/NetzDG_engl.pdf?__blob=publicationFile&v=2

14 The wording used in German is "offensichtlich rechtswidrigen Inhalt". The distinction between the two appears to be of crucial importance and, up to the point of writing, nothing to clarify this issue has been made available by the government. The NGO Article 19 has been particularly critical of this (Article 19 2017: 19).

15 This is clear from the outstart of the approved text: see Article 1, paragraph 1 (1).

16 A few examples are provided in Echikson and Knodt (2018), p.11.

17 Not all social media platforms submitted detailed reports on their activities under the NetzDG specifically as to the heading under which the content was removed. That is why the analysis is limited to Google (which includes Google+ and YouTube), which was a rare example of providing pondered data by sections of the Criminal Code. It should be noted that although the obligation to submit such reports stems from the NetzDG, the level of detail of the data in those reports is not specifically prescribed. Therefore, it could be said that Google exceeded the requirements of the law in this regard.

18 '*Loi relative à la lutte contre les fausses informations*', No. 799, Article 1, inserting Article L. 163–2 in the French Electoral Code, from 2018.

19 Code de la consommation - Article L111–7, paragraph 2, subparagraph 2

20 The list of measures presented here is not exhaustive.

21 This conclusion is, of course, notwithstanding any ongoing campaigns for media literacy which are not strictly the consequence of the laws in question. Such campaigns were promoted by several journalistic associations and NGOs, which is a topic better left for another time.

22 See note 4 above. At this point it appears important whether the current definitions of 'fake news' may or may not cover the articles written by Relotius. There are several elements that need to be taken into account before a final decision is reached on this issue, such as the existence of intent, the effect, the medium where the news was published, to name just a few. Every country, in line with its margin of appreciation, will decide on a definition. In any event, reaching a decision on this point is not the aim of this chapter.

References

Article 19 (2017) 'Germany: The act to improve enforcement of the law in social networks', August 2017, www.article19.org/wp-content/uploads/2017/09/170901-Legal-Analysis-German-NetzDG-Act.pdf (last consulted 1 August 2019).

Bekämpfung von Hasskriminalität und strafbaren Falschnachrichten (2017) 'Bessere Rechts-durchsetzung in sozialen Netzwerken', www.fair-im-netz.de/SharedDocs/Artikel/DE/2017/03142017_GE_Rechtsdurchsetzung_Soziale_Netzwerke.html;jsessionid=74F939 C38342BBB7AAC3333C69FB82CF.1_cid289 (last consulted on 20 April 2019).

Beuth, P., M. Brost, P. Dausend, S. Dobbert, G. Hamann, (2017) 'War without blood', *Zeit*, 26 February 2017, www.zeit.de/digital/internet/2017-02/bundestag-elections-fake-news-manipulation-russia-hacker-cyberwar (last consulted on 22 August 2019).

Carbajosa, A. (2019) 'How a Spanish journalist unmasked the "Der Spiegel" forgery scandal', *El País*, 1 March 2019, https://english.elpais.com/elpais/2019/02/26/inenglish/1551176169_246969.html (last consulted on 25 August 2020).

Connolly, K. (2018) 'Der Spiegel reporter who faked stories returns awards', *The Guardian*, 21 December 2018, www.theguardian.com/world/2018/dec/21/sacked-der-spiegel-reporter-claas-relotius-returns-awards (last consulted on 25 August 2019).

Cerulus, L. (2017) 'Germany's anti-fake news lab yields mixed results', *Politico* [interactive], www.politico.eu/article/fake-news-germany-elections-facebook-mark-zuckerberg-correctiv (last consulted on 17 April 2019).

Dalia Research (2018) '87% of Germans approve of social media regulation law', 17 April 2018, https://daliaresearch.com/blog-germans-approve-of-social-media-regulation-law/ (last consulted 19 April 2019).

Der Spiegel (2018a) 'Maas verteidigt Gesetz gegen Hass im Internet', 4 January 2018, www.spiegel.de/netzwelt/netzpolitik/netzdg-heiko-maas-verteidigt-netzwerkdurch setzungsgesetz-gegen-kritik-a-1186118.html (last consulted on 9 September 2019).

Der Spiegel (2018b) 'Kommission aus erfahrenen Journalisten soll Routinen beim SPIEGEL hinterfragen', 19 December 2018, www.spiegel.de/kultur/gesellschaft/der-fall-claas-relotius-wie-der-spiegel-auf-die-faelschungen-reagiert-a-1244569.html (last consulted on 15 April 2019).

Der Spiegel (2018c) 'The Relotius case – Answers to the most important questions', 19 December 2018, www.spiegel.de/international/the-relotius-case-answers-to-the-most-important-questions-a-1244653.html (last consulted on 1 August 2019).

DW (2018) 'Der Spiegel files suit against ex-star reporter Claas Relotius', 23 December 2018, www.dw.com/en/der-spiegel-files-suit-against-ex-star-reporter-claas-relotius/a-46849218(last consulted on 16 August 2019).

Echikson, W., O. Knodt (2018) 'Germany's NetzDG: A key test for combating online hate', CEPS Research Report No. 2018/09, www.ceps.eu/publications/germany%E2%80%99s-netzdg-key-test-combatting-online-hate (last consulted 19 April 2019).

European Publishing Monitor (2007) *Germany*, Media Group Turku School of Economics, March 2007, http://edz.bib.uni-mannheim.de/daten/edz-du/gda/07/med-ind-germany_en.pdf (last consulted on 1 April 2019).

Fichtner, U. (2018) 'Der Spiegel reveals internal fraud', *Der Spiegel,* 20 December 2018, www.spiegel.de/international/zeitgeist/claas-relotius-reporter-forgery-scandal-a-1244755.html (last consulted on 13 August 2019).

Gelfert, A. (2018) 'Fake news: A definition', *Informal Logic* 38(1): 84–117, https://informallogic.ca/index.php/informal_logic/article/view/5068/4350 (last consulted on 22 April 2019).

German Ministry of Justice (2017) 'NetzDG draft bill prepared by the Federal Ministry of Justice and Consumer Protection', draft version of 27 March 2017, www.gesetze-im-internet.de/englisch_stgb/englisch_stgb.html (last consulted on 25 August 2020).

Human Rights Watch (2018) 'Germany: Flawed social media law', 14 February 2018, www.hrw.org/news/2018/02/14/germany-flawed-social-media-law (last consulted on 17 April 2019).

Klusmann, S. (2019) 'The lessons we are drawing', *Der Spiegel*, 7 January 2019, www.spiegel. de/international/claas-relotius-affair-the-lessons-we-are-drawing-a-1246823.html (last consulted on 17 August 2019).

NetzDG Draft Bill (2017) 'Entwurf eines Gesetzes zur Änderung des Netzwerkdurchsetzungsgesetzes', German Government, text in Germany available at: www.bmjv.de/SharedDocs/ Gesetzgebungsverfahren/Dokumente/RegE_Aenderung_NetzDG.pdf;jsessionid=D89 52A9C53BA2715E7C504D2C0BE7A44.2_cid297?__blob=publicationFile&v=2.

Oltermann, P., P. Collins (2018) 'Two members of Germany's far-right party investigated by state prosecutor', *The Guardian*, 2 January 2018, www.theguardian.com/world/2018/ jan/02/german-far-right-mp-investigated-anti-muslim-social-media-posts (last consulted on 12 April 2019).

Perez, S. (2018) 'PEW: Social media for the first time tops newspapers as a news source for US adults, *Tech Crunch*, https://techcrunch.com/2018/12/10/pew-social-media-for-the-first-time-tops-newspapers-as-a-news-source-for-u-s-adults (last consulted on 19 July 2019).

Sharman, J. (2018) 'Award-winning journalist at *Der Spiegel* admits making up stories including interview with Colin Kaepernick's parents', *The Independent*, 20 December 2018, www.independent.co.uk/news/world/europe/der-spiegel-reporter-fake-stories-claas-relotius-journalist-made-up-interviews-fabricated-a8692006.html (last consulted on 16 August 2019).

Slyomovics, N. (2018) 'Der Spiegel reporter who faked his stories isn't the real problem', *Haaretz*, 27 December 2018, www.haaretz.com/us-news/.premium-der-spiegel-reporter-who-faked-his-stories-isn-t-the-real-problem-1.6787453 (last consulted on 22 April 2019).

Sol, J. (2016) 'The long and brutal history of fake news', *POLITICO Magazine*, 18 December 2016, http://politi.co/2FaV5W9 (last consulted on 2 August 2019).

Southern, L. (2017) 'Inside Spiegel's 70-person fact-checking team', *Digiday UK*, 15 August 2017, https://digiday.com/media/inside-spiegels-70-person-fact-checking-team/ (last consulted on 22 August 2019).

Strawn, J., C. G. Hogan (1984/1985) 'Democracy on the take, Flick scandal shakes West German politics', *The Multinational Monitor* 12(6), awww.multinationalmonitor.org/ hyper/issues/1984/12/strawn.html (last consulted on 19 April 2019).

Sullivan, M. (2013) 'Repairing the credibility cracks', *The New York Times*, 4 May 2013, www.nytimes.com/2013/05/05/public-editor/repairing-the-credibility-cracks-after-jayson-blair.html (last consulted on 3 April 2019).

The Cambridge Dictionary Online, 'Fake news', https://dictionary.cambridge.org/dictionary/ english/fake-news (last consulted on 25 August 2019).

15

"BUT VERIFYING FACTS IS WHAT WE DO!"

Fact-checking and journalistic professional autonomy

Urban Larssen

Introduction

This chapter presents ethnographic material on journalists' experiences, routines, and views regarding fact-checking and fake news, based on field studies conducted at three Swedish media organisations on a local, regional and national level. The studies are part of a Swedish project aimed at developing a digital tool that can assist journalists in their everyday news work. Through interviews and participant observation, the field studies considered the need for and interest in this kind of tool. The findings were then used as a pre-study to inform the development of the broader fact-checking project.

The project was organised as a collaboration between researchers and representatives from competing sectors of the Swedish media industry. It thus resonates with the kind of open boundary work that has come to characterise the recent rise of a global fact-checking movement (Graves 2018). Although this project did not seek to create a specific fact-checking institution, but instead attempted to supply journalists with better resources for verification in the digital communication landscape, the project can nonetheless be related to academic discussions about fake news, verification as key to journalistic professionalism, and, more generally, on journalistic authority in a so called post-truth news ecosystem (McNair 2018).

In terms of the findings of the field studies, the journalists expressed both the need for and interest in a digital fact-checking tool, but also a fear that institutionalised forms of fact-checking could infringe on professional autonomy, involving an increased control over employees from their employer's perspective. This indicates that the context in which the field studies were pursued is contingent with social and cultural aspects and dimensions that goes beyond a straightforward technical solution to a pressing problem.

In this chapter, I take the opportunity to present the project and set out the ethnographic material that formed part of the basis on which the project was developed. I start out by describing the project and particularly the objectives and specific features of the main product: *The Fact Assistant* – a web app meant to help journalists verify the legitimacy and validity of claims, media, and sources that appear in their everyday newsroom work. I present the background to the project, how it developed during its process, and some of the problems it has encountered. I proceed by situating the project within academic debate regarding fake news and fact-checking, and then turn to the ethnographic material gathered during the field studies.

The Fact Assistant project – collaborating towards enhanced verification routines

The research and development project named "Faktaassistenten" (The Fact Assistant) ran between March 2018 and April 2020 at the Department of Journalism at Södertörn University in Stockholm. It was carried out as a collaboration between the university and different Swedish news organisations who are all participants in a media industry partnership, "Framtidens Journalistik" (Journalism of the Future). This partnership is led by a consortium coordinated by the public service Swedish Television. Both private and public service media operations are included in the cooperation, and the Fact Assistant project was partly funded by the state-run innovation agency Vinnova, as part of the agency's programme "From analogue to digital."

The main goal of the project was to improve procedures by journalists regarding the verification of digital content and to develop a web app that can be used by journalists for fact-checking in their newsroom work. Once its prototype was fully developed and tested, the app would be available to utilise by consortium members to help their journalists verify news content on the web as well as in routine verification processes needed for day-to-day journalistic tasks.[1] The app was designed in such a way that it could be integrated into the news-making process. In addition to providing journalists with methodological steps to verify online content, including pictures, videos, and text, the app enables journalists to store and share their fact-checks and allows them to evaluate the credibility of media and sources. The individual fact-checks contribute to the construction of a knowledge bank, designed to become a resource for journalists in the future. When they subsequently encounter a particular text, picture, or video in their work they can look up whether it has already been fact-checked or not. If it has not, then they would have the opportunity to add and review it. The project aimed at making online content verification a solid and well-established part of journalistic work by facilitating access to tools and data when the need for quick verification arises.

The Fact Assistant app is based on a systematisation of verification in three stages, focussing on three different objects: (1) media content (pictures, videos, statements, etc.); (2) the media in which the statements are published (the website, institutional social media account, etc.); and 3) the sources behind the claim (basically the person or entity that posted the claim). In the app, journalists go through a step-by-step process connected to each of the three objects. The steps basically consist of series of questions posed in relation to the object under investigation. Within each step, the app has a section titled "resources" that points to various relevant tools that can be used for assessment and analysis (such as Google Reverse Images to establish whether an image has been used previously). The process can be made more or less extensive depending on how much time the journalist has and depending on the claim that is being fact-checked. The investigations can also be saved before completion and then picked up at a later stage. At the end of the process, the user has a basis for assessing the validity of the claim he or she wants to fact-check. The final assessment is something that every journalist can do – the app is just a help along the way. The result of each fact-check is stored in the system. The individual user can choose whether to keep the fact-check private or share with other app users in the same media organisation or with the public at large by publishing the results in an article that embeds machine-readable hyper data in the ClaimReview.[2]

As for the procedure of the project, a first preparatory step finished in November 2018. This included the field studies of journalists' interests and needs generating the material to which this chapter refers. In December 2018, development work began with meetings with editorial managers drawn from three media organisations: SVT (Swedish public service television), SR (Swedish public service radio), and *Dagens Nyheter* (the largest national daily newspaper in Sweden, commercial with a liberal editorial standpoint). At these meetings, the idea of The Fact Assistant app was presented and discussed, and suggestions on the component parts were made by the participant media, regarding matters such as usability and the degree of sharing that would be appropriate for the accumulated results of the fact-checks.

Step two involved developing the prototype for the web-based app. Responsible for this technical part was Walid Al-Saqaf, a lecturer in journalism and researcher at Södertörn University who specialises in the use of Internet and media technology for journalism. In April 2019, there was a first version of the prototype and the testing could start in workshops organised by the university for a small number of journalists. The prototype was placed under Södertörn University's domain on a server that belongs to the University's shared network. Initially, students in the journalism programmes were included in the testing. Approaches were made to further involve individual journalists in the development work as their comments were seen as instrumental to the project, and they were asked to test the prototype in their day-to-day news work. However, this proved impossible, as outside the confines of the workshops, the journalists who had been introduced to the app were fully occupied with their daily work and could not contribute further. There was, however, a positive attitude to the project and the idea of a digital assistant in the work environment, but despite this encouraging reception, the plan to further involve journalists was postponed. An improved version of The Fact Assistant app was launched shortly after and journalists were again invited to test it in real news work. However, after the initial enthusiasm from journalists, this new version did not spark any further interest or involvement from individual journalists.

The third and final step took into account the results from the surveys after the workshops, along with input and feedback from the steering board. The main focus was to further develop the prototype to make a more attractive and user-friendly app to accomplish testing in real editorial environments. Yet another version of The Fact Assistant app was launched in April 2020 and journalists were invited to test it in their day-to-day news work. However, due mainly to changing work routines as a consequence of the Covid-19 pandemic, there was no opportunity to carry out these real newsroom tests, and instead a number of usability tests via Zoom were carried out. The results confirmed earlier conclusions that journalists were positive about the functioning of the app and deemed it a relevant tool for verification work.

To sum up, The Fact Assistant project addressed the need for improvement in the fact-checking procedures of practicing journalists by specifically targeting everyday news work and routines. Journalists were thus viewed as the professional group under whose authority the fact-checking institution ought to be placed and strengthened. The project was based on the development of a technical solution, and its organisational form was interdisciplinary with academia and media businesses working collaboratively, and with academia furthermore integrating its own development and research activities with teaching. One surprising result arising from the project was the reluctance of journalists to engage fully in the app development process. Lack of time was pointed out by journalists in the follow-up surveys as the main reason, but also a degree of technique fatigue – statements were made that there are simply too many newsroom tools available right now. Whether the latest and more user-friendly version of The Fact Assistant will attract journalists to start using it remains to be evaluated.

Post-truth fact-checking and the crisis of journalism in academic debate

The lack of time and technique fatigue referred to by journalists participating in the workshops can be seen against the background of profound changes affecting the conditions for journalistic production, well-known and thoroughly researched by scholars of media and journalism across the world during the last decades (see e.g. Croteau and Hoynes 2019). A decline in journalistic authority and debate about journalism in crisis has followed, but there is little consensus among scholars, media professionals, and commentators on what this means for the future of journalism and for democracy more broadly (see e.g. Curran 2011; McChesney 2012; Waisbord 2016). Fake news appears as a central and symptom-like but certainly not exhaustive concept in this context. Rather, studies on fake news and fact-checking are merely part of a larger research area on journalism's credibility, position, ideals, and routines in a digitised and 'post-truth' era (McNair 2018).

The changes which have been debated include topics such as: technology developments, competing forms of information provision, convergence of media outlets, and tougher economic conditions. Moving from analogue to digital, the speed of news production has increased substantially. "Liquid journalism" (Deuze 2008) has replaced linear news models, and journalists need to produce more material on more platforms in the multimodal environment that characterises today's journalism, resulting in "softer attitudes towards verification" (Nygren and Widholm 2018: 39). Current values of immediacy, interactivity, and participation are altering what it means to do journalism today, with key players such as web designers and computer programmers entering the newsroom side-by-side with journalists (Usher 2014), contributing to a de-professionalisation of journalism (see e.g. Witschge and Nygren 2009).

The Internet and social media have caused the evolution of an "inflationary public sphere" (McNair 2018: 42), resulting in a proliferation of journalistic forms and the possibility for basically anyone to produce news and share information on a massive scale. The gatekeeping role previously confined within the borders of the journalistic profession has thus decreased (Bruns 2005), opening up for the possibility of fruitful cooperation and engagement with audiences, e.g. through citizen journalism (see Reich 2008), as well as antagonistic media criticism from populist and far-right alternative media where especially the credibility of legacy media is severely questioned (Figenshou and Ihlebael 2019).

Responses to the changes by the media industry have contributed to the general decline in trust for journalistic authority: managerialism, audience metrics, commercialisation through native advertising, downsizing of work force, and a reduction of fact-checking prior to publishing – not necessarily damaging in themselves, but potentially compromising established journalistic norms and ideals. Thus, to a degree the decline in journalistic authority is partly self-inflicted (Reese 2018). Added to these can be repeated incidents of ethical misconduct (Allan 2005; Otto and Köhler 2018; Allern and Pollack 2019), exemplified by the phone-hacking scandal involving UK newspapers which lead to the Leveson inquiry in 2011–2012; a public, judicial review into the general culture and ethics of the British press (Elstein 2013).

Furthermore, the changes and responses have not only resulted in ambiguity within journalistic ranks regarding their role-conception and authority (Vos and Thomas 2018), but also in a "culture of insecurity" regarding their positions (Ekdale et al. 2015: 383). Layoffs and closings are common phenomena, and convergences and technology development have resulted in different forms of employment based on principles of flexibility, multitasking, and cost efficiency, leading to what Deuze (2013) calls "precarious labor". Bunce (2019) points to a flip side of audience metrics – while (on the positive side) aggregating news consumption habits, providing advertisers with more exact information, and making journalism more responsive to its audiences, it also allows managers to more efficiently monitor and discipline their journalists. Reinardy (2011) documents an increase in burnouts and Ekdale et al. (2015) suggest that journalists who believe their jobs are at risk are resistant to change.

There is thus ample ground for talking about a 'crisis of journalism', but the way scholars depict and analyse this crisis varies. On the one hand, there is a kind of relief that a crisis has finally arrived, so that journalism can be reinvented in a better form (see Curran 2011; Wasserman 2019). On the other hand, there is confidence in the ability of professional journalism to solve the crisis and endure as the authority for the provision of truthful, reliable, and sustainable news (e.g. Schudson 2018). Zelizer (2015) cautions against the use of the notion of "crisis" in the first place, arguing that "it misses an opportunity to recognize how contingent and differentiated the futures of journalism might be" (ibid.: 888). Tong (2018) suggests that many news organisations are successfully adopting and possessing digital and technological skills and can defend their journalism, not least by regrouping around certain norms such as fact-checking. Others point out that even if mainstream media have problems, there is much to indicate that the crisis has also meant a strengthening of journalism, at least regarding its ideological frame (Wiik 2009; Waisbord 2018).

A more holistic and cultural perspective has gained ground. Scholars following this direction make use of theories that pitch journalism within a larger societal and cultural context. Carlsson (2018a; 2018b) takes a 'metacommunication' perspective and reflects on the future of journalism in terms of boundary-making processes and increased self-reflexivity among journalists; Vos and Thomas (2018) talk about internal and external contingencies of the discursive construction of journalistic authority; Kreiss (2019) investigates the social identity of journalists, constructed both by themselves and for themselves by others in distinct socioeconomic contexts. In her study of media and participation (e.g. through citizen journalism), Ahva suggests "viewing journalism as a structure of public communication that is enacted through the practices of various actors at sites that *go beyond the newsroom*" (Ahva 2017: 242, my emphasis). In these approaches, journalism is conceptually brought out of its status as a single institution practiced by professional journalists and analysed in terms of the meaning-making processes of public communication more broadly, not least through new and hybrid forms of cooperation (Peters and Broersma 2013; Pickard 2019).

This brings me back to The Fact Assistant project. The project can be seen as resonating with a growing occupational reform movement on an international scale where journalists work together with non-journalists to stem the spread of fake news and disinformation (Graves 2018; Allern 2019). Graves (2018) documents and explores this movement in detail by attending the two first global summits of fact-checkers, in 2014 and 2015, gathered in the International Fact-Checking Network (IFCN). He suggests that the births of US institutions such as FactCheck.org, PolitiFact, and Poynter Institute mark important events that set the movement in motion from 2003 and onwards (cf. Amazeen 2020; Allern 2019). These quickly developed into dedicated fact-checking organisations, conducting their own research, participating in audits during election campaigns and, as a token of their relevance on a transnational level, assisting in the establishment of fact-checking institutes and routines in countries around the world (including Sweden). The movement has gained further momentum since the beginning of the Trump-era during which claims that legacy media are elite, corrupt, and the main provider of fake news became a worldwide phenomenon. Graves points to differences in the objectives, procedures, and organisations of particular fact-checking initiatives, at the same time identifying areas of convergence among them. Differences lie, for example, in the presentation of findings about fake news, be it misinformation or disinformation. This can be done either in public or privately with involved parties, it can employ rating systems such as PolitiFact's *Truth-O-Meter*, or by using descriptive and more nuanced terms like 'misleading', or instead lengthy explanatory articles.

There are also differences in the organisational form the fact-checkers take. Some are incorporated in traditional news organisations, some are based at an academic department or formed as an NGO, whilst others are combinations of these. Regarding convergence, Graves finds that a broadly shared concern among fact-checkers is the promotion of democratic discourse and accountable government. Furthermore, while professional discourse generally centres on the assertion of difference and the drawing of boundaries between professional fields, he concludes that "international gatherings of fact-checkers are most notable for the boundaries *not* drawn – for the willingness of professional journalists to share jurisdictional authority with non-journalists in ways they typically do not" (Graves: 627, emphasis in original). Graves argues that the ideal of objectivity gains relevance here, and that strengthening the fact-checking procedures is about maintaining the relevance and central position of journalism in the first place. He also points out that different organisational structures for fact-checking makes different sense in different journalistic cultures and calls for ethnographic studies to explore how the construction of autonomy and authority depend on particular ties between actors.

Fact-checking institutions in the Scandinavian countries are part of this global movement, such as the Swedish *Viralgranskaren* (The Viral Reviewer), established in 2014, and the Norwegian *faktiskt.no,* which started its fact-checking work in 2017, both affiliated with the IFCJ. *Faktiskt.no* subsequently inspired the launching of *faktiskt.se* in Sweden with a similar design involving journalists from different well-established media outlets teaming up to pursue fact-checking work (The Facts Assistant project can be seen as stemming from the *faktiskt.se* collaboration). Although there are differences between Swedish and Norwegian fact-checking initiatives, they have much in common and a study of the first 99 fact-checks of *faktiskt.no* (Allern 2019) supplies relevant insights for the Swedish context and for the material presented in this chapter. Allern points out that the organisational form of the Swedish and Norwegian fact-checking initiatives – a collaboration of private media organisations, private and public foundations, and state-run public service media – resonates with Hallin and Mancini's (2004) democratic-corporative media model they saw as typical for Nordic countries. He notes that the fact-checking activity of *faktiskt.no* remains situated within traditional journalism and that the fact-checking endeavour is regarded by the industry as an instrument to strengthen the position and legitimacy of the news media involved.

Allern (2019) clearly sees the value of stimulating and developing media literacy among readerships and members of the political class in the face of a complex and sometimes bewildering informational landscape. Yet Allern is predominantly critical in his detailed evaluation of the actual work that has been pursued by *faktiskt.no*. He sees little relevance in fact-checking pieces of information that can be regarded as fake news, judging these verifications as having little effect on political debate and opinion-making. He argues that there is a risk that many investigations come out as an accountant-like preoccupation with unimportant details, missing the opportunity to focus on central facts with a more profound meaning for political choices, priorities, and values. He also notes that investigations of news and information with an international scope have been left out intentionally and suggests this is unfortunate given that the mainstream Norwegian media has a well-known weakness of staying loyal to national security and foreign relations interests (see Nohrstedt and Ottosen 2014). Allern also questions the organisational format. "It is puzzling", he writes, "that fact-checking as an own genre in a Norwegian context is represented by one organization, and thus depends on the priorities that are made in a limited editorial environment. For political democracy, there is no advantage that media who freely and actively should be able to critically evaluate each other's journalism, outwardly appear as one block in relation to both politicians and the media organizations that are outside the fact-checking community" (ibid.: 185, my translation from Norwegian).

This last point of Allern, corresponding with Graves' note on ties between actors, is particularly valid for the Swedish context where the launching of *faktiskt.se* in 2018 stirred up considerable public debate. Editorial writers from a broad range of political standpoints (e.g. Linderborg 2018; Boström 2018), and from outside of the *faktiskt.se* group, pointed to difficulties of the fact-checking method. They argued that the first fact-checks done by *faktiskt.se* concerned issues so multifaceted and charged with ideology that it was difficult if not impossible to deliver a true or false verdict, and that *faktiskt.se* had landed wrong in most of their conclusions. They also questioned the teaming up of several of the leading media houses in Sweden and argued that the collaboration hindered them from investigating each other, contrary to the idea of journalism's role in a democratic and pluralistic public sphere. Moreover, the financial support by the state-run innovation agency Vinnova was seen as problematic since it made the project vulnerable to critique not only from established political camps favouring a downgrading of public service media but also from more antagonistic groups linked to alternative media and the far right. Despite consensus on the need to stem the spread of mis- and disinformation, and contrary to the intentions of the project, the ties between actors involved in *faktiskt.se*, according to its critics, thus put the credibility and autonomy of journalism and the media industry in Sweden at risk.

Fact-checking in the news field: Needs and ambiguities

Having thus situated The Fact Assistant within a broader context and academic debate, let me now turn to the field studies conducted prior to the launching of the project. A central objective of the project was to adopt a bottom-up perspective rather than top-down. For this reason, a series of field studies among journalists was pursued at a preparatory stage, to involve them in the development of the project. The field studies were carried out in three newsrooms in local, regional, and national media – two public service operations (radio) and one privately owned newspaper, all of whom were members of the partnership Journalism of the Future. Taking responsibility for these studies, I organised a program of 1–2 days with interviews and in-situ observations. I had two general questions in mind when entering the newsrooms: (1) what is the interest for some type of digital tool or assistant and 2) what are the fact-checking needs? The method used to consider these questions was ethnographic and can be roughly divided into three parts. First, semi-structured interviews lasting approximately 30 minutes conducted face to face with individual journalists. The interviews began with the two questions (in connection to which I introduced the basic idea of The Fact Assistant) and then pursued a more open-ended approach. These interviews were mostly carried out in environments separated from the newsroom. Second, ethnographic interviews conducted as conversations with journalists while they were carrying out their day-to-day work. A total of approximately 20 interviews were carried out. Third, observations in the newsrooms during which little or no conversation took place.

In general terms, the answers to my questions were that there is both an interest in a digital fact-checking tool and a need for such a tool. Against this background two associated themes unfolded. One is in relation to the range of programmes or digital tools that are available today or currently in development. The second theme relates to a more general need for control and continuity in the current work situation.

First theme: The interviewed journalists told me they are quite aware of the multitude of technical and software solutions related to fact-checking. The awareness generates different feelings. Some described it as a constant and overwhelming stream of innovation and product development. Others expressed curiosity and joy in trying out new products. Most said they have enough knowledge of a few of them while expressing a concern to acquire more skills, and to get more used to the programmes they consider relevant. Examination of the authenticity of images, for example, is something the respondents experience as challenging, but they do not feel they have problems with fact-checking in this area. Google's Reverse Image Search, for example, is familiar to most and regularly used. At the same time however, there is a need for more advanced fact-checking and to establish routines in relation to aspects such as finding website owners, their histories, origins, and respective positions within networks more quickly. Journalists frequently use Twitter postings in regular news work but getting beyond anonymous or fake profiles and mapping networks is rarely done. In such cases, journalists regarded specific programmes that may facilitate more advanced procedures as a good idea if they contain a clear work schedule. Tools should be easy to use with easy instructions about how the programmes work. If they also contain updates, short news snippets about programmes and recent reviews, then one can easily keep abreast of developments.

Second theme: When it comes to relationships between journalists – the team-work, the discussions, the handovers, the news process as a collective act – and the fact-checking procedures within these relations, there was a general consensus on the idea that an assistant could function as a support mechanism. It would help systematise processes and make formal the knowledge that is kept in the heads and minds of individual journalists, ensuring that knowledge is available to all. In turn, all journalists would thus gain more control. Furthermore, it was considered as an advantage if specific individual fact-checks could contribute to an easily accessible and searchable database, with a system of alerts or red flags on people, organisations, and websites. Journalists felt such a fact-check assistant might then be valuable since you would save time in your day-to-day work, not having to 'reinvent the wheel' every time you wanted to check something.

Moving beyond the general questions about interest for and need of a digital tool such as The Fact Assistant, lack of time and stress constantly popped up during the conversations as features of everyday news work. The journalists explained that this is predominantly caused by the fast continuous news cycle, with demands on immediacy not only in delivering the latest news but in keeping an eye on and responding to reactions from audiences through social media and elsewhere. Several of the journalists I spoke to explained that this means less time for fact-checking and research, and that the warning bell for incorrect or doubtful information is less and less heard before publication. As a result, they are relying more on established sources than before, although in cases where misinformation has been spread it is not seldom the trusted sources that fail to deliver correct information. A feeling of stress is further enhanced by frequent reorganisation and turnover of staff, as well as a continuous introduction of new policies from management levels and superiors; policies that several of the journalists I spoke to feel are developed over their heads. Yet another source of stress is technology development connected to so-called deep fakes, i.e. in the sense of manipulating moving images and voices. One local reporter commented: "frankly speaking, when this becomes available for anyone out there, I don't know how we can keep up with our work."

In more abstract terms, stress was also expressed as a result of recent public debates over the credibility of established media, paired with uncertainty about how to relate to social media that so easily generates hate storms or triggers debates that are difficult to control. This has less to do with fake news in its more concrete form, as fabricated occasional news. In the local and regional newsrooms I visited, journalists regarded fake news as not particularly present in daily work, or not present at all. They associated this kind of fake news more with superpower and politics on an international level and saw it as a matter for the national media to deal with (still, as one local journalist stated, "if it would happen here, then we are not really prepared, there is no plan for how it would be handled"). Instead, local journalists described a situation where fake news is merely one part of a more complex informational climate. Many attested to a clear switch having occurred over the course of just a few years regarding social media. Whilst earlier social media was seen and frequently used as a source of information and news, it is now being handled with more care. The journalists said they experience a kind of high-profile climate on social media nowadays where local and traditional media are targeted, particularly by local representatives of the Sweden Democrats party (populist, national conservative) and their populist and far-right supporters. Obviously, mistakes occur every now and then, and this sometimes leads to heated commentary on social media. But it doesn't have to be outright mistakes; heated commentary frequently occurs in relation to regular reporting as well, especially on sensitive and politicised issues such as migration, honour violence, and climate change. As one local reporter commented, "it doesn't matter how well you have checked the facts and how clearly you have sourced it, things just go out of hand anyway". The dynamics of situations when things go wrong, several journalists tried to explain, tend to spiral towards an eschewed reality description where values such as truth and facts have secondary meanings. Journalists and their organisations are accused of not being truthful and in the end pictured as disseminating fake news themselves. A few occasions had occurred among the journalists I spoke to where the result had struck them personally, where hateful campaigns had been directed at them as individuals. A couple of journalists also told me that they had refrained from accepting assignments concerning topics they reckoned would trigger this kind of 'storm'. This decision of theirs had subsequently been brought up during yearly negotiations with their superiors regarding their salaries as failures to fulfil their duties. During conversations about this complex issue, some journalists raised the question of whether a fact-checking app, developed as it would be partly by support from a state agency, would not become just another argument that could be used against them by their critics in a similar manner as with *faktiskt.se*.

Many journalists told me they had been regularly following the viral reviewer *Viralgranskaren* and *faktiskt.se* when they were active, and they saw both of them as good initiatives. However, all of those that commented on *faktiskt.se* felt that the connection to the state-run innovation agency Vinnova was unnecessary as it affected the credibility, not only of *faktiskt.se*, but of the public service media as a whole. "It was very easy for our critics to point their conspiratorial fingers at us and accuse us of being instruments of the government". one public service radio reporter commented. Some also had reservations on the idea of forming a separate fact-checking institution. One of them said, "I was a little provoked by the idea of a particular fact-checking site since it might give the impression that regular journalism does not do fact-checking. But that is exactly what we do, it's what we are good at and what journalism is all about." Many pointed out that fact-checking is about traditional journalistic work. The conversations centered among other things on the importance of local knowledge. In a local context, journalists are situated in a network of decision makers, public officials, and other kinds of authorities on local matters, most of whom the journalists know personally after a few years on the local beat. A digital tool, a few of the journalists argued, could in this situation be regarded as a kind of overkill when the traditional method to just pick up the phone and call people works in most cases. Yet this was problematised with regards to convergence and increased collaboration across municipal and regional boundaries as local newspapers were bought up and integrated into larger conglomerates where journalists were expected to cover news in several municipalities. Fact-checking thus becomes more important because local knowledge is not enough in such cases. A post-it note on one of the reporters' pinboards next to the phone indicated this, with a list of names of local politicians in neighbouring cities and their political affiliations added in bold style, ready to be glanced at during work beyond the familiar beat.

Several journalists also argued that knowledge and competence regarding advanced fact-checking is unevenly distributed. A few become very knowledgeable through their own efforts. At the same time, they regarded news work as increasingly dependent on people with expert knowledge on digital information and communication. Reporters or managers sometimes travel to pursue further education but turning their newborn skills into concrete application upon their return to the newsroom is rare. On some occasions, experts come to visit and give workshops. These workshops are highly appreciated, but poorly followed up and thus they turn into isolated events. Unless user-friendly, several journalists reckoned, a digital tool might play into the hands of those more skilled members of staff – it will be they who use it and their fact-checking work that appears in the records. In connection to this, some expressed skepticism or concern that a fact-checking tool or assistant would further increase the pressure on the individual journalist, and that an introduction of the tool would mean increased control over the employees from an employer's perspective. One local reporter commented: "Won't there be just more statistics and measurement of our work, just like the measuring of how many clicks my texts generate?"

Conclusion

The field studies presented in this chapter were conducted with a limited group of journalists and during a short period of time and further studies are necessary to produce more solid documentation of enduring patterns and varieties on different levels of analysis. However, the material speaks to several of the issues I pointed at in the literature review. A recurrent theme during my conversations was ambiguity regarding organised forms of fact-checking. Lack of time and technique fatigue can explain a good deal of the reluctance of journalists to take part in the development of The Fact Assistant prototype. But there is also a broader set of aspects of the journalists' work environment which contribute to their hesitation and ambiguity toward the specific form of fact-checking envisaged by the project. To some, the mere suggestion that they need to strengthen their verification competencies provoked their sense of professional integrity. To others, the idea of collecting data on the fact-checks was seen as potentially contributing to enhanced control and surveillance on a managerial level. Another envisioned risk was that the tool itself, financed partly by state funds, would make journalists increasingly vulnerable to critique posed by antagonistic actors outside of the newsroom, a risk which had previously materialised through earlier fact-checking projects and the public debate that followed. The technical solution in the form of a digital tool, and the potential appropriation of it, is thus considered to be ambigous and its reception is ambivalent, since it could have applications in several domains: social, professional, and political. In the current complex informational and communicational landscape that journalists are part of, and expected to report on, sustaining journalists' autonomy and authority is a delicate task with remarkable implications for democracy. Taking measures at improving procedures for verification of digital content answers to the ideal of delivering accurate and thoughtful information and analysis, and thus helping to create an enlightened citizenry. Most journalists subscribed to this objective. But just how this should be organised is a more open question and responses to The Fact Assistant model show that journalists are prone to take into consideration the particular ties involved when such measures are taken. If interpreted by their audiences as compromising their autonomy, they would lose their authority to critically scrutinise the powerful.

Notes

1 The app is available as open source: https://github.com/wsaqaf/faktaassistenten.
2 See www.claimreviewproject.com/the-facts-about-claimreivew.

References

Ahva, L. (2017) 'How is participation practiced by "in-betweeners" of journalism?', *Journalism Practice* 11(2–3): 142–59.

Allan, S. (2005) 'Introduction: Hidden in plain sight – journalism's critical issues', in: S. Allan (ed.), *Journalism: Critical Issues*, Maidenhead: Open University Press.

Allern, S. (2019) 'Journalistikk som faktasjekking', in: P. Bjerke, B. Kjos Fonn, B. Röe Mathisen (eds), *Journalistikk, profesjon og endring*, Stamsund: Orkana Akademisk.

Allern, S., E. Pollack (2019) *Källkritik! Journalistik i lögnens tid*, Lund: Studentlitteratur.

Amazeen, M. A. (2020) 'Journalistic interventions: The structural factors affecting the global emergence of fact-checking', *Journalism* 21(1): 95–111.

Boström, H. (2018) 'Faktiskt.se mestadels ett fiasko', *Göteborgsposten*, 4 June 2018, www.gp.se/ledare/bostr%C3%B6m-faktiskt-se-mestadels-ett-fiasko-1.6326097 (last consulted 2 March 2020).

Bruns, A. (2005) *Gatewatching: Collaborative Online News Production*, New York: Peter Lang.

Bunce, M. (2019) 'Management and resistance in the digital newsroom', *Journalism* 20(7): 890–905.

Carlsson, M. (2018a) 'Confronting measurable journalism', *Digital Journalism* 6(4): 406–17.

Carlsson, M. (2018b) 'The information politics of journalism in a post-truth age', *Journalism Studies* 19(13): 1879–88.

Croteau, D. R., W. D. Hoynes (2019) *Media/society. Technology, Industries, Content, and Users*, Thousand Oaks: SAGE Publications.

Curran, J. (2011) *Media and Democracy*, New York: Routledge.

Deuze, M. (2008) 'The changing context of news work: Liquid journalism for a monitorial citizenry', *International Journal of Communication* 2: 848–65.

Deuze, M. (2013) *Media Work*, Cambridge: Polity Press.

Ekdale, B., M. Tully, S. Harmsen, J.B. Singer (2015) 'Newswork within a culture of job insecurity: Producing news amidst organizational and industry uncertainty', *Journalism Practice* 9(3): 383–98.

Elstein, D. (2013) 'Press freedom in The United Kingdom and the Leveson debate', *Journal of Applied Journalism & Media Studies* 2(1): 19–31.

Figenshou, T.U., K.A. Ihlebael, (2019) 'Challenging journalistic authority: Media criticism in far-right alternative media', *Journalism Studies* 20(9): 1221–37.

Graves, L. (2018) 'Boundaries not drawn: Mapping the institutional roots of the fact-checking movement', *Journalism Studies* 19(5): 613–31.

Hallin, D., P. Mancini (2004) 'Comparing media systems: Three models of media and politics', New York: Cambridge University Press.

Kreiss, D. (2019) 'The social identity of journalists', *Journalism* 20(1): 27–31.25 April 2019.

Linderborg, Å. (2018) 'Lägg ner faktakollen', *Aftonbladet*, 25 April 2018, www.aftonbladet.se/kultur/a/jP7yM9/asa-linderborg-lagg-ner-faktakollen (last consulted on 2 March 2020).

McChesney, R.W. (2012) 'Farewell to journalism? Time for a rethinking', *Journalism Practice* 6(5–6): 614–26.

McNair, B. (2018) *Fake News: Falsehood, Fabrication and Fantasy in Journalism*, London: Routledge.

Nohrstedt, S.A., R. Ottosen (2014) *New Wars, New Media, and New War Journalism: Professional and Legal Challenges in Conflict Reporting*, Göteborg: Nordicom.

Nygren, G., A. Widholm (2018) 'Changing norms concerning verification', in: K. Otto, A. Köhler (eds), *Trust in Media and Journalism*, Wiesbaden: Springer.

Otto, K., A. Köhler (eds) (2018) *Trust in Media and Journalism: Empirical Perspectives on Ethics, Norms, Impacts and Populism in Europe*, Wiesbaden: Springer.

Peters, C., M.J. Broersma (2013) *Rethinking Journalism: Trust and Participation in a Transformed News Landscape*, London: Routledge.

Pickard, V. (2019) *Democracy Without Journalism? Confronting the Misinformation Society*, New York: Oxford University Press.

Reese, S.D. (2018) 'The threat to the journalistic institution', *Journalism* 20(1): 202–05.

Reich, Z. (2008) 'How citizens create news stories: The "news access" problem reversed', *Journalism Studies* 9(5): 739–58.

Reinardy, S. (2011) 'Newspaper journalism in crisis: Burnout on the rise, eroding young journalists' career commitment', *Journalism* 12(1): 33–50.

Schudson, M. (2018) *Why Journalism Still Matters*, Cambridge: Polity Press.

Tong, J. (2018) 'Journalistic legitimacy revisited: Collapse or revival in the digital age', *Digital Journalism* 6(2): 256–73.

Usher, N. (2014) *Making News at the New York Times*, Ann Arbor: The University of Michigan Press.

Vos, T.P., R.J. Thomas (2018) 'The discursive construction of journalistic authority in a post-truth age', *Journalism Studies* 19(13): 2001–10.

Waisbord, S. (2016) 'Afterword: Crisis? What crisis?', in: C. Peters, M. J, Broersma, *Rethinking Journalism Again: Societal Role and Public Relevance in a Digital Age*, London: Routledge.

Waisbord, S. (2018) 'Truth is what happens to news', *Journalism Studies* 19(13): 1866–78.

Wasserman, H. (2019) 'Relevance, resistance, resilience: Journalism's challenges in a global world', *Journalism* 20(1): 229–32.

Wiik, J. (2009) 'Identities under construction: Professional journalism in a phase of destabilization', *International Review of Sociology* 19(2): 351–65.

Witschge, T., G. Nygren (2009) 'Journalistic work: A profession under pressure?', *Journal of Media Business Studies* 6(1): 37–59.

Zelizer, B. (2015) 'Terms of choice. Uncertainty, journalism, and crisis', *Journal of Communication* 65: 888–908.

16

THE EU CODE OF PRACTICE ON DISINFORMATION AND THE RISK OF THE PRIVATISATION OF CENSORSHIP

Matteo Monti

Introduction

The Internet ecosystem has completely transformed the way in which we consume information, and the role of social networks and search engines in spreading news – the so-called "platformisation of news distribution" (Martens et al. 2018: 15) – is increasing rapidly. The transformation of the media environment brought about by the Internet platforms has weakened the role of journalists as gatekeepers of news – as highlighted in the report of the Committee on Culture, Science, Education and Media (2017: 3); Levi (2012: 1555–72) talked about "deinstitutionalization of the press" – passing this role "to engineers, coders, and designers" (Carroll 2017: 71), and has created a commingling of different phenomena that has been called 'information disorder' (Wardle 2019; cf. Bayer 2019). The main problem with this disorder is that the mix of political propaganda, foreign influences, disinformation, satire, and other phenomena has undermined the classic legal categories regarding the media and the limits on the freedom of expression and information (Koltay 2019: 45). Given the ambiguity of the term 'freedom of information' – which can mean the right of access to public data or the freedom to inform and receive information and news in a broader sense – it is necessary to specify that this expression is given the second of these meanings in this chapter.[1] In this framework, the lack of regulation of Internet platforms,[2] and the fact that the rules of journalism do not cover them,[3] has led to the spread of fake news (*rectius* disinformation).[4]

The aim of this chapter is to analyse the action of the European Union (EU) – in particular the Code of Practice on Disinformation (the Code) – and its limits. To do this, the first section will analyse the legal framework of the EU action, while the second will study it in comparison with the initiatives developed by the Member States. Particular attention is paid here to the issue of the privatisation of censorship, which is taken to mean the delegation of powers to private actors in a field as important as that of fundamental rights. In the Conclusion, some general considerations are developed, by summarising the limits of the EU action and by looking forward to the development of some forms of control over the actions of the Internet platforms.

The genesis and the limits of the EU action in the struggle against fake news

The effort to contain online disinformation started as a reaction against the possibility that there were external influences in the European democratic system.[5] The first step was a resolution of the European Parliament (EP) "to analyse in depth the current situation and legal framework with regard to fake news and to verify the possibility of legislative intervention to limit the dissemination and spreading of fake content."[6] In January 2018, a High Level Group was established by the European Commission to develop strategies to counter the spread of fake news and finally, in September 2018, the Code of Practice on Disinformation was 'enacted'. The Code is a soft law tool that suggests to its signatories – among whom are the most important Internet platforms such as Google, Facebook, and Twitter – some possible strategies and practices to avoid the spread of fake news.

The most important of these actions are: (1) to avoid giving financial support to fake news factories through advertisements; (2) to dilute the visibility of fake news and to improve the 'findability' of trustworthy content; (3) to prioritise relevant, authentic, and authoritative information and to invest in technology to reinforce this prioritisation; (4) to ensure there is transparency in advertisements and sponsored content; and (5) to remove false accounts and regulate the activity of bots on platforms. This summary shows how this soft law instrument is having a great impact on the freedom of information (or press freedom), that is, the right to impart and receive news and information.

In this paragraph, the legitimacy of the actions undertaken by the EU will be analysed. Given the limited scope of application of Article 11 of the EU Charter of Fundamental Rights and the absence of specific case law of the Court of Justice of the European Union (CJEU) (Pollicino 2020: 9), the analysis will look at the European Convention on Human Rights (ECHR), particularly Article 10. In relation to this, one can recall the fact that Article 52.3 of the Nice Charter establishes that if there are rights corresponding to ECHR rights, the meaning and the scope of those rights shall be the same. Article 52.3 allows us to speculate on whether fake news can be considered as a protected expression under the European freedom of expression and information paradigm – as is the case in the United States – by looking at the European Court of Human Rights (ECtHR) case law.

Before analysing the issue of the protection of fake news as free speech, it is important to stress another aspect of the EU initiative: it is forged in a way that does not touch sectors that are not harmonised, and it does not affect the Member States' fundamental rights.

It is necessary to focus now on the case law of the ECtHR. The ECtHR has recognised a right to be informed and to receive news,[7] the urgency of protecting pluralism in the media environment,[8] the necessity for journalists to act in good faith and to respect the 'duties and responsibilities' of journalism if they are to obtain the protection of Article 10 of the ECHR,[9] and the need to check information and news sources.[10] The Court has specified that even in the exercise of free speech based on value judgments, which is slightly different from the right to spread news and information, there are some circumstances in which events and facts cannot be invented:

> a distinction needs to be made between statements of fact and value judgments in that, while the existence of facts can be demonstrated, the truth of value judgments is not susceptible of proof. (. . .) However, where a statement amounts to a value judgment, the proportionality of an interference may depend on whether there existed a sufficient 'factual basis' for the impugned statement: if there was not, that value judgment may prove excessive.[11]

In this sense, it can be concluded that fake news certainly cannot be considered as protected speech in the field of the press, that is, if the news is diffused as a piece of journalism. More controversial is the application of the concept of fake news to political propaganda, which can use lies – within the limits of defamation – in its development (Monti 2018). In this sense, it is evident that freedom of information faces more particular limits than does the general freedom of expression, being linked to the role played by the press in a democratic society, which is the role of the watchdog of democracy, informing citizens, making governments accountable, and furnishing the basis for public debate. It is important to stress that "[u]nlike in the US practice, European constitutions and the individual legal systems actively try to separate the freedom of speech from the freedom of the press" (Koltay 2019: 45).

As specified in the Introduction, in the digital world the situation is a bit more complex since it is not easy to identify whether we are in the presence of a piece of news, a political message, or something else. However, extrapolating some principles from the case law of the ECtHR, it is possible to explore and use the 'traditional' legal categories to frame some of the new phenomena on Internet platforms. The Court, indeed, has, on the one hand, widened the definition of the media[12] that are constrained by the rules of journalism[13] and has, on the other hand, applied the limits of the freedom of information to journalists engaging in activities that are different from traditional news reporting (as in the case of comments posted on a forum).[14] Thus, taking into consideration the fact that the rules of objective [15] journalism can be adapted for different types of media, as stressed in the *Delfi v. Estonia* case,[16] the case law of the ECtHR makes it possible to imagine a widening of the scope of application of the rules on freedom of information to new media such as websites, blogs, and social network pages (which could be classified as types of newspaper because of their aim) or to journalists' activities on the Internet and on social networks (e.g. Facebook posts or tweets).

In this context, however, it is necessary to underline that the types of self-produced media content (Croteau 2006; Cram 2015) are changing, and that more and more often it is possible to see disinformation circulating in memes or social network posts without any mention of a website or the work of a journalist (Wardle 2019; this aspect may be linked to the collective credulity that seems to operate on the web: cf. Mocanu et al. 2015). Regardless of this, the ECtHR seems to have held that even an individual who cannot be defined as a journalist is bound by the rules applicable to journalists when he or she is engaged in spreading news and information in a public debate:

> [t]he Court reiterates that the protection of the right of journalists to impart information on issues of general interest requires that they should act in good faith and on an accurate factual basis and provide 'reliable and precise' information in accordance with the ethics of journalism (. . .). The same principles must apply to others who engage in public debate.[17]

Additionally, the ECtHR has affirmed that even a self-regulatory body of internet service providers has to respect the principles developed for the press in some circumstances.[18] A broad application of these principles in the world of Internet platforms would lead to a revolution in the regulation of the giants of the web.

Moreover, in the case of *Brzeziński v Pologne* – the first case in which the term 'fake news' was used in a European decision – the Court "*admet qu'il est nécessaire de lutter contre la dissémination d'informations fallacieuses à propos des candidats aux élections afin de préserver la qualité du débat public en période préélectorale.*"[19] Even while censoring the way in which the Polish courts managed the issue – an imprecise piece of news diffused by a mayoral candidate – the Court seems to have considered the censorship of fake news to be consistent with Article 10 of the Convention, despite the fake news having been diffused by a political actor in a public political debate. In this sense, it seems that the use of the term fake news is a little dangerous in the context of political debate, because if we reconnect the term 'fake news' with the term 'disinformation' we are looking at the specific topic of the press, and then by applying these terms to political and value judgments we risk misunderstanding the categories. It is true that false statements made by politicians could be censored (e.g. as defamation), but it is important not to apply the strict press rules to actors engaged in spreading political propaganda and not in diffusing news and information as journalists.[20] In this sense, the EU's action in drafting the Code seems to contain a careful separation of the two categories, on the one hand ensuring that sponsored political content is clearly understood as such, and on the other favouring authentic news.[21]

Therefore, seconding Katsirea's argument (Katsirea 2018: 173) and focussing on the case law of the ECtHR, it is possible to defend that the paradigm of the press is susceptible to be legitimately applied to the digital world as well. As a consequence, fake news cannot be considered as a protected expression under Article 10 ECHR. Accordingly, using the words of Pollicino, "[t]he real challenge in Europe is not then – as in the US – *if* the issue of fake news can be tackled legally, but rather *how* this can be done in order to avoid a disproportionate restriction on the fundamental rights at stake, above all the freedom of speech" (Pollicino 2019a).

To conclude, it is possible to state that, so long as the EU does not invade fields that are not harmonised, the actions it has taken to force Internet platforms to self-regulate and avoid the spread of fake news seem to be consistent with its nature. Indeed, on the one hand, the EU's action does not prevent Member States from taking further initiatives and does not infringe on national fundamental rights; on the other hand, the EU's action is consistent with Article 10 ECHR.

The double challenge of fighting fake news and avoiding the privatisation of censorship

The Code can be framed as part of a broader general trend that delegates to Internet platforms the process of balancing fundamental rights online, the so-called "privatisation of censorship" (Tambini, Leonardi, and Marsden 2008). For instance, the German NetzDG[22] establishes that, after notification to a social network by any user, hate speech and illegal false content (Claussen 2018: 118) must be removed by the social network itself within 24 hours (or seven days as required by Art. 3(2)), without any check by the public authorities (courts or independent authorities). This procedure has been criticised by those who believe that users' fundamental rights to free speech on Internet platforms should be protected.[23] A very similar delegation of power to private actors would have been granted by the two proposed laws developed in the Italian legal order to fight fake news. The first one, the so-called Gambaro project, provided (among other articles) for the need for Internet platforms to undertake a general monitoring obligation for removing fake news and to allow the possibility of complaints by users against fake news.[24] The second one, the Zanda–Filippin project, was inspired by the German law and required social networks to remove illegal content after a complaint.[25] Both procedures were devoid of public authority control (by judges or independent authorities). Italian scholars have also underlined the 'constitutional' role that Internet platforms would have played in this case.[26] In this scenario, the only law embracing a paradigm not involving the privatisation of censorship is the French one,[27] which requires a judge to check the nature of online fake news before its removal. However, it is important to stress that the French law only concerns electoral periods and candidates in an election,[28] thus appearing to be more a law regulating political communication in electoral periods than a law on the freedom of information.

Moreover, the Code of Practice also can be framed – partially – within the European approach to fundamental rights online, which is highlighted by the Code of Conduct on Countering Illegal Hate Speech (referred to here as the Code of Conduct) and the CJEU case law on the right to be forgotten. This approach, too, involves the privatisation of censorship. From the first point of view, the Code of Conduct requires Internet platforms to remove content that includes illegal hate speech after a report by a user.[29] The EU Commission has claimed that

> [t]he balance between freedom of speech and what is prohibited illegal hate speech is set out in European case law, starting with the Jurisprudence of the European Court of Human Rights (. . .). It is neither a privatisation of justice nor is it excessive to ask all companies to do the same when they are notified about the existence of illegal content on their services.[30]

However, despite the claims of the Commission, it is clear that the balance is drawn by the Internet platforms, which can decide how to act and can proceed to censor content (Zhen Gan 2017: 118; Article 19 2016: 16). In a very similar way, the CJEU has legitimised, after the Google Spain decision[31], the possibility of Internet platforms developing an autonomous balance between Internet users' right to be informed and the right to be forgotten (Pollicino and Romeo 2016: 249). As a consequence, in the European scenario, both at the EU level and the level of the Member States, there seems to be a trend that encourages and favours the privatisation of censorship. Indeed, most policies of the Member States and the European Union appear to be directed away from guaranteeing the freedom of expression and information on Internet platforms by not subjecting the actions taken by private actors against online content to checks by judges or independent authorities (and granting no effective right of appeal against the decisions of the Internet platforms).

Against this background, the Code of Practice on Disinformation is partially aligned with this trend by delegating to Internet platforms the obligation to remove fake accounts, and by favouring 'authentic' news.

Taking into account the practices developed by Google and Facebook, the two main actors in the search engine and social networks markets, respectively, it has to be stressed that the Code has delegated important content-based choices to the Internet platforms.

Indeed, both Google and Facebook remove 'profiles' that engage in the spread of fake news, the first one by giving a negative ranking to untrustworthy websites,[32] and the second by removing from social networks those pages and personal accounts that participate in campaigns characterised by 'Coordinated Inauthentic Behavior' (CIB)[33] or that simulate different identities (Lyons 2018). These actions have an effect on content, because giving a negative rank to a website makes it difficult for users to reach it, and removing a page or a personal account from Facebook affects all the content diffused on that page or account. These actions involve the actual risk of the removal of political speech or media content that are not approved of by the Internet platform or the private actors behind it, or simply the removal of content because of pressure by the majority of users and/or for economic reasons. Imagine what a campaign of notices against some information and pages or websites by users coordinated by political actors could generate. In addition, the risk of the general removal of all reported content to avoid any future fines or 'reactions' by the EU is an equally dangerous perspective.[34]

From the second point of view, privileging some content over other content on the basis that it is the 'most authentic' news has a strong impact on pluralism. In the US, for instance, Internet platforms have been accused of setting their algorithms to favour progressive news over conservative news (Koltay 2019: 196). The European system is very sensitive to this matter, and independent authorities usually watch over pluralism on the media ecosystem.

It is, thus, important to underline how the Code of Practice – even if it does not encourage the removal of content – ends up increasing private censorship in the Internet ecosystem. Regarding the topic of private censorship, it is necessary to underline that in the EU framework a specific guarantee against private censorship seems to be absent,[35] while in the ECHR system (Koltay 2019: 94), the Declaration of the Committee of Ministers on Human Rights and the Rule of Law in the Information Society[36] and Recommendation CM/Rec(2011)7[37] on intermediaries committed the Member States to preventing private censorship. Focussing on the recent case law of the two European Courts, it is possible to see two different approaches. The European Court of Justice, in the recent case of *Glawischnig Piesczek v. Facebook*,[38] has taken an ambiguous stance. On the one hand it has not taken into consideration – contrary to what was proposed by the Advocate General[39] – the need for a check on the removal of content by Internet platforms (a right of appeal against their decisions) in order to guarantee the freedom of expression of users of Facebook, but, on the other hand, it seems to exclude the possibility of removal without an automated process.[40] However, what is clear is that the Court has not set out a strong defence of the right to freedom of expression online. By contrast, the ECtHR has started to explore the issue of the privatisation of online censorship, excluding its presence in the activities of news portals,[41] because "there are ample opportunities for anyone to make his or her voice heard on the Internet."[42] It seems that the Court could consider the presence of a private censorship if there were no alternatives available: in this sense, it is interesting to consider whether the reasoning of the Court would change if it was contemplating the censorship activities of Facebook or Google, given the *de facto* monopoly under which they operate in the European market and their importance for public discourse (Koltay 2019: 185; cf. Hindman 2018).

This position would be very similar to the proposal by certain US scholars (Klonick 2018; *contra*: Peters 2017) to extend the so-called state action doctrine [43] to Internet platforms to force them to respect users' rights of freedom of speech in the same way that governments must.[44]

Conclusion

The Code of Practice on Disinformation is a good attempt to give Internet platforms responsibility, to force them to attempt to counter the spread of fake news, and to rebuild the role of journalism on the Internet, with the intention of preserving the role of the press – in a broad sense – in European democracies.

However, the vital task of fighting disinformation online cannot be delegated entirely to Internet platforms in the way that the Code provides: the risks that dwell in the privatisation of censorship (in this case, the removal of politically oriented content instead of fake news, or the prioritisation of conservative news over progressive news or vice versa) are too big to be ignored. Indeed, Internet platforms have become too important as public forums to remain outside every type of legal regulation. In the specific field of fake news and the Code, granting a right of appeal to independent authorities against decisions made by platforms and establishing a general monitoring system for the operations of Internet platforms in the matter of pluralism, with both tasks being assigned, for instance, to the Body of European Regulators of Electronic Communications in coordination with the independent national authorities, could be sufficient to ensure that Internet platforms do not distort democracy.

Notes

1 "The European Convention on Human Rights and the constitutions of the European states recognize, for example, freedom of information as a qualified part of freedom of speech; and they present that freedom in three different modes: active (freedom to inform, or to spread information), passive (freedom to receive information), and medium (freedom to search for information)" (Pollicino 2020: 16).
2 For a study of the Italian legal system, as a prototype case for investigating the topic of freedom of information – to be interpreted as the freedom to inform and the right to be informed and receive news – see Monti (2017). On the power given to Internet platforms because of the lack of regulation: Tutt (2014: 241).
3 On the form of the 'production' and distribution of news and the media logic of Internet platforms, see Klinger and Svensson (2015: 1246 ff.).
4 For the purposes of this chapter, fake news is news (sold as an output of journalism) that is invented and false (that is, it is based on invented or non-existent facts or events). Fake news is thus used as a synonym for disinformation. From this point of view the definition given by the EU 'Code of Practice on Disinformation' (2018) is quite interesting: disinformation is "'verifiably false or misleading information" which, cumulatively, (a) "Is created, presented and disseminated for economic gain or to intentionally deceive the public;" and (b) "May cause public harm," intended as "threats to democratic political and policymaking processes as well as public goods such as the protection of EU citizens' health, the environment or security'" (Code, *Preamble*). The Code excludes from this notion "misleading advertising, reporting errors, satire and parody, or clearly identified partisan news and commentary." For a broader analysis of how fake news circulates on Internet platforms, see Monti (2018).
5 European Council conclusions, 19–20 March 2015 (EUCO 11/15).
6 European Parliament resolution of 15 June 2017 on online platforms and the digital single market (2016/2276(INI)).
7 *Ex pluribus: Observer and Guardian v. the UK* App no. 13585/88 (ECtHR, 26 November 1991), § 59; *Guerra and Others v. Italy* 116/1996/735/932 (ECtHR, 19 February 1998), § 53.

8 *Ex pluribus: Centro Europa 7 srl and Di Stefano v. Italy* App no. 38433/09 (ECtHR, 7 June 2012), § 129–134.
9 *Ex pluribus: Fressoz and Roire v. Francia* App no. 29183/95 (ECtHR, 21 January 1991), § 54; *Mcvicar v. The UK* App no. 46311/99 (ECtHR, 7 May 2002), § 73.
10 *Fuchsmann v. Germany* App no. 71233/13 (ECtHR, 19 October 2017), § 43. On proportionality see: *Prager and Oberschlick v. Austria* App no. 15974/90 (ECtHR, 26 April 1995), § 37. However it has to be remembered that also the press could exaggerate the terms of an issue: *Ibid.*, § 38. The duty of checking sources is weaker in the political speech field as in the case of trustfulness in journalists' works: *Salov v. Ukraine* App no. 65518/01 (ECtHR, 6 December 2005), § 113.
11 *GRA Stiftung gegen Rassismus und Antisemitismus v Switzerland* App no. 18597/13 (ECtHR, 9 January 2018), § 68.
12 § 7 of Recommendation CM/Rec(2011)7. Cf. Koltay (2019: 46 and ff.).
13 "The broad definition of the 'media' adopted by the Court suggests that new media engaged in the spread of 'fake news' would be held to account for failing to act in good faith and to verify untruthful allegations" (Katsirea, 2018: 173).
14 "Nevertheless, it is clear that, by posting under the username 'Eynulla Fatullayev', the applicant, being a popular journalist, did not hide his identity and that he publicly disseminated his statements by posting them on a freely accessible popular Internet forum, a medium which in modern times has no less powerful an effect than the print media." *Fatullayev v. Azerbaijan* A no. 40984/07 (ECtHR, 4 October 2010), § 95.
15 'Objective' does not mean impartial or with an absence of bias (Cf. American Press Institute, 'The lost meaning of "objectivity"', available at: www.americanpressinstitute.org/journalism-essentials/bias-objectivity/lost-meaning-objectivity.
16 *Delfi v. Estonia* App no. 64569/09 (ECtHR, 16 June 2015), § 134.
17 *Braun v. Poland* App no. 30162/10 (ECtHR, 4 February 2015), § 40.
18 "The Court notes that both the first applicant, as a self-regulatory body of internet service providers, and the second applicant, as a large news portal, provided forum for the exercise of expression rights, enabling the public to impart information and ideas. Thus, the Court shares the Constitutional Court's view according to which the applicants' conduct must be assessed in the light of the principles applicable to the press." *Magyar Tartalomszolgáltatók Egyesülete and Index.Hu Zrt v. Hungary* App no. 22947/13 (ECtHR, 2 May 2016), § 61.
19 *Brzeziński c. Pologne* App no. 47542/07 (ECtHR, 25 July 2019), § 55.
20 The ECtHR recognised that point but did not give it sufficient attention: Idem, § 53. The only problem with this decision is probably the naive use of the term 'fake news' to describe a fact that is not connected with the activities of the press and cannot be completely described as online disinformation, in which some actors want to assume the role and authoritative power of the press to spread fake news that is described and sold as authentic news.
21 It is important to note that in the definition of disinformation the Code excludes the possibility that political information falls within the concept of disinformation. See note 4.
22 Netzwerkdurchsetzungsgesetz– NetzDG, 2017, § 2 and 3.
23 "*Durch die Löschungen von Meinungen seitens der Betreiber sozialer Netzwerke wird auch die Informationsfreiheit (Art. 5 Abs. 1 Satz 1 GG) aller Nutzer beeinträchtigt*", Liesching (2018: 28). And about the risk of a general removal of contents to avoid fines see ibid.: 27.
24 Art. 7, co. 2, Senate of the Italian Republic, proposal Gambaro, S. 2688–17ᵃ Legislature.
25 Art. 2, Senate of the Italian Republic, proposal Zanda-Filippin, S. 3001–17ᵃ Legislature.
26 Bassini and Vigevani (2017: 20) talked of "*un fortissimo spazio di discrezionalità, tale da poter insinuare la trasfigurazione della funzione di selezione in un'attività censoria o comunque svolta secondo un'impostazione 'di tendenza' e 'orientata'.*"
27 Loi no. 1202/2018.

28 As stressed: "*[l]e champ d'application de la loi ne regarde donc que les périodes électorales et laisse donc en suspens la question des fake news qui surgissent hors des périodes d'élections ou qui ne concernent pas les candidats*." Ponthoreau (2019 : 30).
29 EU Code of Conduct on countering illegal hate speech online (2016). Cf. Coche (2018).
30 Code of Conduct – Illegal online hate speech, Questions and answers, 2016, https://ec.europa.eu/info/sites/info/files/code_of_conduct_hate_speech_en.pdf.
31 CJEU, Case C-131/12. The case concerns the balance between privacy and freedom of expression and information online, and it specifically relates to the right to be forgotten in the information and news diffused by search engines.
32 Last intermediate results of the EU Code of Practice against disinformation: Google May 2019 Report, 2.
33 Annual self-assessment reports of signatories to the Code of Practice on Disinformation: Facebook, 29 October 2019, 13.
34 It should be considered that "the European institutions themselves have promised to verify the effects of this initial form of cooperation, without excluding the possibility of 'raising the bar' with different types of interventions." Pollicino (2020: 13).
35 EU Human Rights Guidelines on Freedom of Expression Online and Offline, 19 May 2014; although the European Parliament recommendation of 26 March 2009 noted the fact the freedoms should "be protected adequately and effectively from intrusions by both *private* and public actors" (*emphasis* mine).
36 CM(2005)56-final 13 May 2005.
37 Recommendation CM/Rec (2011) 7 of the Committee of Ministers to Member States on a new notion of media, § 63.
38 CJEU, Case C-18/18.
39 *Conclusions AG,* case *C 18–18*, § 65.
40 According to Pollicino (2019b: 8), the Court would have tried to avoid delegating too many powers to the Internet platforms, as happened on the contrary in the right to be forgotten regime.
41 See *Delfi v. Estonia*, § 157.
42 See ibid., § 137.
43 According to the US Supreme Court, when a private actor – for instance, a so-called company town – is functionally equivalent to a state actor, the private actor has to guarantee First Amendment rights in the same way as a government by, for instance, avoiding censorship. The leading case in this field is *Marsh v. Alabama*, 326 U.S. 501 (1946). For an analysis of the US Supreme Court case law and its scrutiny see Klonick (2018: 1609 and ff.).
44 For now this theory was rejected by federal circuits (*Johnson v. Twitter, Inc.*, n. 18ECG00078 (Cal. Superiore Ct. 6 giugno 2018); *Williby v. Zuckerberg*, 3:18-cv-06295-JD (N.D. Cal. June 18, 2019)) and according to some scholars, the US Supreme Court has decided to not take a position about the issue in the decision *Manhattan Community Access Corp. v. Halleck*, No. 17-1702, 587 U.S. (2019).

References

Article 19 (2016) 'EU: European Commission's Code Of Conduct for Countering Illegal Hate Speech Online and the Framework Decision', 14 June 2016, www.article19.org/data/files/medialibrary/38430/EU-Code-of-conduct-analysis-FINAL.pdf (last consulted 20 March 2020).

Bassini, M., G. E. Vigevani (2017) 'Primi appunti su fake news e dintorni', *Medialaws* 1: 11.

Bayer, J. (ed.) (2019) 'Disinformation and propaganda – impact on the functioning of the rule of law in the EU and its Member States' (PE 608.864 – February 2019).

Carroll, C.E. (2017) 'Making news: Balancing newsworthiness and privacy in the age of algorithms', *Georgetown Law Journal* 106: 69.

Claussen, V. (2018) 'Fighting hate speech and fake news. The Network Enforcement Act (NetzDG) in Germany in the context of European legislation', *MediaLaws* 3: 110.

Coche, E. (2018) 'Privatised enforcement and the right to freedom of expression in a world confronted with terrorism propaganda online', *Internet Policy Review* 7: 1.

Cram, I. (2015) *Citizens Journalists: Newer Media, Republican Moments and the Constitution*, Cheltenham: Edward Elgar.

Croteau, D. (2006) 'The growth of self-produced media content and the challenge to media studies', *Critical Studies Media Communication* 23: 340.

Hindman, M. (2018) *The Internet Trap. How the Digital Economy Builds Monopolies and Undermines Democracy*, Princeton: Princeton University Press.

Katsirea, I. (2018) '"Fake news": Reconsidering the value of untruthful expression in the face of regulatory uncertainty', *Journal of Media Law* 10: 159.

Klinger, U., J. Svensson (2015) 'The emergence of network media logic in political communication: A theoretical approach', *New Media & Society* 17: 1241.

Klonick, K. (2018) 'The new governors: The people, rules, and processes governing online speech', *Harvard Law Review* 131: 1598.

Koltay, A. (2019) *New Media and Freedom of Expression*, Oxford: Hart.

Levi, L. (2012) 'Social media and the press', *North Carolina Law Review* 90: 1531.

Liesching, M. (2018) 'Die durchsetzung von verfassungs – und europarecht gegen das NetzDG – überblick über die wesentlichen kritikpunkte', *MultiMedia und Recht* 1: 26.

Lyons, T. (2018) 'Hard Questions: What's Facebook's strategy for stopping false news?', *Facebook*, 23 May 2018, https://about.fb.com/news/2018/05/hard-questions-false-news (last consulted 20 March 2020).

Martens B., L. Aguiar, E. Gomez-Herrera, F. Mueller-Langer (2018) 'The digital transformation of news media and the rise of disinformation and fake news', JRC Tecnhical Reports 2018.

Mocanu, D., L. Rossi, Q. Zhang, M. Karsai, W. Quattrociocchi (2015) 'Collective attention in the age of (mis)information', *Computers in Human Behavior* 51: 1198.

Monti, M. (2017) 'Perspectives on the regulation of search engine algorithms and social networks', *Opinio Iuris in Comparatione* 1: 71.

Monti, M. (2018) 'The new populism and fake news on the Internet', *Stals Research Papers* 4: 1.

Peters, J. (2017) 'The "sovereigns of cyberspace" and state action: The First Amendment's application (or lack thereof) to third-party platforms', *Berkeley Technology Law Journal* 32: 989.

Pollicino, O. (2020) 'Freedom of expression and the European approach to disinformation and hate speech: The implication of the technological factor', *Liber Amicorum per Pasquale Costanzo*, www.giurcost.org/LIBERAMICORUM/INDICEliber.html (last consulted 20 March 2020).

Pollicino, O. (2019a) 'Fundamental rights as bycatch – Russia's anti-fake news legislation', *Verfassungsblog*.

Pollicino, O. (2019b) 'L'"autunno caldo" della Corte di giustizia in tema di tutela dei diritti fondamentali in rete e le sfide del costituzionalismo alle prese con i nuovi poteri privati in ambito digitale', *Federalismi* 19: 1.

Pollicino, O., G. Romeo (2016) 'Concluding remarks: Internet law, protection of fundamental rights and the role of constitutional adjudication', in: O. Pollicino, G. Romeo (eds.), *The Internet and Constitutional Law. The Protection of Fundamental Rights and Constitutional Adjudication in Europe*, Abingdon: Routledge.

Ponthoreau, M.-C. (2019) 'Liberté d'expression, une perspective de droit comparé: France', EPRS.

Report of the Committee on Culture, Science, Education and Media (2017), 'Online media and journalism: Challenges and accountability', Council of Europe 2017, Doc. 14228.

Tambini, D., D. Leonardi, C. Marsden (2008) 'The privatisation of censorship: Self regulation and freedom of expression' in: D. Tambini, D. Leonardi, C. Marsden (eds), *Codifying cyberspace: Communications Self-Regulation in the Age of Internet Convergence*, Abingdon: Routledge – UCL Press.

Tutt, A. (2014) 'The new speech', *Hastings Constitutional Law Quarterly* 41: 235.

Wardle, C. (2019) 'Understanding information disorder', (First Draft).

Zhen Gan, H. (2017) 'Corporations: The regulated or the regulators?', *Columbia Journal of European Law* 24: 111.

INDEX

ableism 32
accountability 53, 57, 132, 147, 205, 216
ad targeting 46
advertising revenue 78
Advertising Standards Agency 57
ageism 32
AI ethics 40–1, 45–9
algorithmic bias 46
algorithms 8–9, 41, 46–7, 66, 78, 82, 85, 96, 157, 165, 220
Allcott, H. 86
Allern, S. 205–6
Al-Saqaf, W. 201
Amazon 47
Andropov, Y. 110
anti-globalisation 133
anti-Gypsyism 32
anti-Semitism 32
Anti-Vax movement 113
Arab Spring 6, 145
Aral, S. 83
Arendt, H. 10, 19–24, 26–7
authoritarianism 1, 4, 9, 121
automated accounts 9, 48, 109, 126–8, 132, 157–71

Bacon, F. 99
Baila, C.A. 84
Banksy 4
Barr, W. 126
Beaumont, R. 122
Becatti, C. 163
Bechis, F. 11
Bellucci, P. 79

Berelson, B. 78
Berlusconi, S. 107, 150
Besussi, A. 19–20
Bobbio, N. 21
Boeing air disaster 109, 137
Boldin, V. 110
Bolsonaro, J. 6
Borrell, J. 3
bots. See automated accounts
Boykoff, J. 100
Boykoff, M. 100
Breaking Point poster 59–61
Brennen, J. 97–8
Brexit 3–4, 8, 66, 68, 70, 87, 133; effect of post-truth politics on 53–61
Briand, S. 93
British Museum 4
Broockman, D.E. 82–3
bubble democracy 33–4
Bufacchi, V. 5
Bunce, M. 203
Burioni, R. 163
Butler, D.H.E. 64

Caiani, M. 12
Caldarelli, G. 12, 163
Cambridge Analytica 46, 147
Cameron, D. 55
Campbell, A. 64
Cantarella, M. 86
Cardenal, J.P. 121
Carlsson, M. 204
Casas, A. 178–9
Cassidy, J. 11

censorship 60, 151; privatisation of 13, 214–15, 218–21; in Russia 111–12, 127
Centers for Disease Control and Prevention 97
Change.org 193
Chernobyl disaster 109
citizen journalism 203–4
citizenship 5
classism 41–2, 44
click-bait 115, 127
climate change 23–4, 98, 100, 209
Clinton, H. 3, 8, 125, 146–8, 157. *See also* US presidential election (2016)
Code of Conduct on Countering Illegal Hate Speech 219
Code of Practice on Disinformation 214–21
code-switching 45
Cold War 114, 123
Comai, G. 12
Communism 111, 114, 174, 176
confirmation bias 66, 82
conspiracy theories 2, 66, 68–9, 94, 127–8, 145
Converse, P.E. 64
Coordinated Inauthentic Behaviour 219
coronavirus. *See* Covid-19 pandemic
corruption 112–13
Court of Justice of the European Union 215, 219–20
Covid-19 pandemic 1, 5, 7, 19, 24, 92–101, 128–9, 158–65, 169–71, 202
credibility 30, 35–7, 54, 61, 200, 202–3, 206, 208–9
Crenshaw, K. 41–3
Cresci, S. 158
crisis actors 54
crisis of journalism 203–4
Cummings, D. 58
Curini, L. 11
cyberattacks 8, 122, 137–8, 143, 145–6, 149. *See also* hybrid warfare
cyber-security 147–9
cyberwarfare. *See* hybrid warfare

D'Agostini, F. 24
Danks, D. 46
dark money 150
De Nicola, R. 12
debunking 7–9, 109, 112, 115
Declaration of Independence 24–5
deep learning 48
deepfakes 2, 48, 208
democracy 1, 4, 6–7, 23–4, 26, 31, 33, 65–70, 113–14, 202, 220; radical right's

challenge to 173–82; vulnerabilities of 143–51. *See also* elections
Der Spiegel 12–13, 144, 189–91, 195
Désir, H. 127
Deuze, M. 203
Dewey, J. 33
dialogic injustice 36–7
digital natives 113
digital revolution 119, 121
digitalisation 125, 147
diResta, R. 98
discrimination 31–2, 34–6, 41–2, 47, 60
disease narratives 93–5
disinformation 4; and AI ethics 40, 46, 48; and Brexit referendum 56–61; and Covid-19 92–101; definition of 2–3; EU Code of Practice on Disinformation 214–21; information operations in Russia 119–29; and Russian meddling 146–7. *See also* fake news
Donovan, J. 97
Drieschova, A. 56
Dubrovaskaya, T. 135
Durant, J. 100

echo chambers 34, 66, 68, 83–4, 88, 171
economic crisis (2008) 173
education 33, 64–5, 100, 114
Ekdale, B. 203
elections 100, 113, 192; 2016 US presidential 8, 66, 70, 84–8, 143–51, 157, 192; 2018 Italian parliamentary 77, 86–7, 148; alleged Russian interference in 143–51; fake news and electoral behaviour 77–88
empirical evidence 11, 83–5
ENISA 148–9
epistemic bubbles 34
epistemic injustice 35–6
epistemic obstacles 58, 61
epistemic solidarity 34
ethics 40–9
European Commission 147
European Convention on Human Rights 215–16, 218, 220
European Court of Human Rights 215–20
European External Action Service 3, 9
European Parliament 9, 147, 215
European Union 2–3, 70–2, 124, 127–8, 133, 140, 145, 159, 174, 176, 192–3; Code of Practice on Disinformation 214–21. *See also* Brexit
European Union Agency for Cybersecurity 148–9

Euroscepticism 55, 182. *See also* Brexit
experimental psychology 123

Facebook 6, 9, 19, 47–8, 83–4, 95, 97,
 128, 134, 147, 174, 180–1, 193–4, 206,
 215, 217, 219–20
facial recognition 47
Fact Assistant 200–2, 204, 208, 210–11
fact-checking 8, 48, 86, 189, 194, 199–211,
 216; journalistic 86, 100, 115, 199–211,
 216
fact-checking organisations 9, 96–7, 108–9,
 204–5
FactCheck.org 204
factual truths 22–3, 25, 27
fake accounts. *See* automated accounts;
 trolls
fake bot accounts. *See* automated accounts
fake news 2, 5–8, 19, 54, 132–3; and
 AI ethics 40, 46, 48; and Arendt's
 philosophy 22–7; automated accounts
 see automated accounts; constructing
 8–9; definition of 3–5, 77–8, 188;
 and disruption of democracy 65–70;
 and electoral behaviour 77–88; as an
 emotional weapon 64–72; and empirical
 evidence 83–7; EU Code of Practice on
 Disinformation 214–21; fact-checking
 see fact-checking, fact-checking
 organisations; German system for
 combating 188–95; and the radical right
 174; in Russia 107–15, 133–6, 140;
 spreading and consumption of 83–5.
 See also disinformation
Faktaassistenten. *See* Fact Assistant
faktiskt.no 205–6
faktiskt.se 205–6, 209
far left 127
far right 127, 193, 203, 206, 209. *See also*
 radical-right political activism
Farage, N. 55, 59
fascism 165, 176, 179–81
Fellows, M.L. 42
feminism 41–4, 115
filter bubbles 66, 82, 85–6
financial crisis (2008) 6
foreign direct investment 121
foreign policy 11, 125, 136–7
fourth generation warfare. *See* hybrid
 warfare
Fraccaroli, N. 86
freedom of expression 32, 109, 113, 189,
 192, 215–16, 218, 220
freedom of information 214, 216–17
Fricker, M. 35–7

Fried, D. 126
full spectrum warfare. *See* hybrid warfare

Galeotti, M. 120, 122
Gambaro project 218
gatekeeping 7, 203
Gaudet, H. 78
gender 41–2, 44, 46, 139
gender bias 46–7. *See also* sexism
Gentzkow, M. 86
Gerasimov doctrine 120–1, 139, 145
Ghebreyesus, T.A. 93
Giles, K. 120, 122, 124
Global Cybersecurity Index 139
Global Inventory of Organised Social
 Media Manipulation 158
globalisation 114, 121, 129, 133, 150, 173,
 175
Google 46, 97, 193–4, 215, 219–20
Google Reverse Images 201, 207
Gorbachev, M. 110
Graves, L. 204–6
Grinberg, N. 84
group defamation 60. *See also* hate speech
group libel 32, 60. *See also* hate speech
Guess, A. 84–5

H1N1 94
Habermas, J. 32
hacking 133
hacking-and-dumping 146–9
Hagerty, A. 47
Hallin, D. 205
hallucinations 69
Hashmi, A. 47
hashtags 134, 159
hate speech 2, 32, 60, 174, 191–3
hate symbols 177–82
Hazelton, A. 11
hermeneutic injustice 35–6
hidden virality 97
historical bias 46
hoaxes 66, 87, 157
Hockenhull, T. 4
Holston, J. 47
Holzscheiter, A. 139
homophobia 32, 41–2
honour violence 209
Hopf, H. 99
hybrid warfare 119–20, 124, 136–9. *See
 also* cyberattacks; Gerasimov doctrine

Ibrahim, A. 100
illicit funding 149–50
independent media 97, 109, 126

individualisation 80–1
inequality in the public sphere 30–7, 47
infodemic 7, 93, 96–7
information manipulation. *See*
    disinformation; fake news;
    misinformation; propaganda
information operations 119–29, 146–7
information silo-ification 66, 68–9
information warfare 133
informational bubbles 66, 87
Informational Network for Epidemics
    96
infotainment 115
injustice 34–6
Instagram 9, 53, 95
instant messaging 3–4, 6–7
interaction effect 44
International Conference on Cyber
    Conflict 137
International Fact-Checking Information
    Network 97, 204–5
International Relations 2, 135
Internet Research Agency 84, 126
intersectionality 40–9
Ireni-Saban, L. 10–11
Islamisation 173–4, 181
Italian parliamentary elections (2018) 77,
    86–7, 148

Jefferson, T. 24–5, 64–5
Jennan, G. 121
Johnson, B. 59
journalism 5, 24, 100, 108–9, 114–15,
    133–5, 148, 188–9, 214, 216–17; crisis
    of 203–4; journalistic fact-checking 86,
    100, 115, 199–211, 216; Relotius affair
    12–13, 189–91, 194–5

Kalla, J.L. 82–3
Kant, I. 20, 31–2
Kaspersky Labs 137, 139
Katsirea, I. 218
Kavanagh, J. 67–8
Kenez, P. 133
Key, V.O. Jr. 64
Kleinberg, J.M. 165
Kreiss, D. 204
Kriuchkov, V. 110
Kurlantzick, J. 121

Larssen, U. 13
Lavrov, S. 112
Lazarsfeld, P. 78
Le Pen, M. 149
Lee, J.D. 94–5, 98

Leveson inquiry 203
Lippmann, W. 1
liquid journalism 203
Lisa case 128
living standards 58–9
Locke, J. 34
London, A.J. 46
Loveless, M. 11

Maas, H. 192
machine learning 8–9, 47–8
mainstream media. *See* traditional media
Maksimov, S. 127–8
Malaysia Airlines Flight 17 109, 137
malware 137
Mancini, P. 205
Marshall, H. 56
mass media 32, 80, 134, 139
Matthews, M. 122
May, T. 134
McCain, J. 147–8
McCall, L. 44
McGeever, B. 59–60
measures short of war 121
media; definition of 216, 222; independent
    97, 109, 126; new 216–20, 222, *see also*
    social media; official 11, 112, 114, 122–3,
    160–1, 206; Russian 112–15, 122–3,
    125–8, 133–40; traditional/mainstream
    7–8, 11, 32, 65, 67, 80, 84, 115, 143–5,
    148–50, 188–9, 204
media literacy 8–9, 71, 133, 194, 205–6
Mehrabi, N. 47
Mejias, U.A. 135
Meloni, G. 165, 169–70
Merenda, F. 10
Merkel, A. 107–8, 193–4
Messa, P. 125
Messenger 6
Microsoft 139
micro-targeting 68, 147
migration 3, 42, 56, 68, 70, 114, 140,
    158–60, 162–8, 170–1, 173–4, 180, 182,
    209; Breaking Point poster 59–61
Miller, W.E. 64
misinformation 5, 69, 81, 132, 157; and
    Covid-19 92–101; definition of 2–3
Miskimmon, A. 133
Monti, M. 13
Moore, M. 56
Moore, M.R. 45
Moreno, J. 190
Morini, M. 11–12
Mueller report 125–6, 144, 146–7, 149
multilateralism 129

Muscat, J. 160
MySpace 95

Nagler, J. 84–5
National Health Service 56–9, 61, 97
nationalism 59–60, 111, 133, 139, 174–7,
    179–82
NATO 124, 127, 140
Navalny, A. 112
neo-Nazi groups 174, 177, 179–81
Network Enforcement Act. *See* NetzDG
NetzDG 12–13, 188, 192–4
new-generation warfare. *See* hybrid warfare
new media 216–20, 222. *See also* social
    media
non-governmental organisations 114,
    158–61, 163, 205
Nye, J. 121
Nyhan, B. 85

Oates, S. 135
Obama, B. 108, 147–8
Ochigame, R. 47
official media 11, 112, 114, 122–3, 160–1,
    206
oligarchs 110, 112, 126, 149
O'Loughlin, B. 133
opinion pieces 2
oppression 10, 34, 37, 41–5
Oreskes, N. 99
Ostrovsky, A. 133

pandemics. *See* Covid-19 pandemic; disease
    narratives
patriarchy 43
Paul, C. 122
personalisation 6, 46
Petrocchi, M. 12
philosophy 19–28, 40–9
phone-hacking scandal 203
Piras, E. 10
Pizzimenti, E. 11
Plato 20
pluralism 31
political advertising 4, 6, 70, 77, 82, 87, 179
Political Science 10, 64–5, 70, 78
PolitiFact 204–5
Pollicino, O. 218
Polyakova, A. 126
Ponomariov, B. 107
populism 6, 23, 26, 77, 87, 114, 132, 139,
    203, 209
positional objectivity 54
poststructuralism 45

post-truth politics 19, 23, 26–7, 98;
    analytical compass for exploring 9–10;
    definition of 5–8, 132; effect on Brexit
    referendum 53–61; Putinism in 132–40
poverty 113
Poynter Institute 204
pre-bunking 9
prevention of harm 32
Prigozhin, E. (Y.V.) 109, 126
privacy 32, 46–7, 147
privatisation of censorship 13, 214–15,
    218–21
privilege 41–3
propaganda 2–3, 27, 58, 77, 157, 216;
    and the radical right 174–5, 177–82; in
    Russia 107–9, 111–15, 119, 123, 127,
    133–6; Soviet 107–8, 114, 122–3, 133,
    139
pseudo-satire 2
psychology 64, 70, 87, 123
public health emergencies. *See* Covid-19
    pandemic
public opinion 2, 30–4, 37, 85, 114, 121
Putin, V. 107–11, 113, 115, 124–5, 127,
    129, 134, 139–40, 144–5, 150
Putinism 132–40

racism 32, 41–3, 94, 98, 140
radical-right political activism 173–82
Ramsay, G. 56
rational truths 22–3
Rawls, J. 21–2
Razack, S. 42
Reid, A. 58–60
Reinardy, S. 203
religious values 22–3
Relotius, C. 12–13, 189–91, 194–5
Remian, D. 48
Reporters Without Borders 134
retweeting 83–4, 158–9, 163, 165, 167–9
Reyes, P. 45
Rich, M.D. 67–8
Rokkan, S. 79
Roselle, L. 133
Ross-Sheriff, F. 42–3
Roudakova, N. 134
Roy, D. 83
RT 125–6, 128, 134
Rubinov, I. 47
rule of law 113
Russia Today. *See* RT
Russiagate investigation. *See* Mueller
    report
Russian meddling 143–51

Russian Public Opinion Research Center 135
Russophobia 134

Saakashvili, M. 124, 137
Salvini, M. 159, 163, 165, 169–70
Samuels, G.M. 42–3
sanctions 60, 110, 135, 191
Saracco, F. 12
Sarkozy, N. 124
scaremongering 56, 61
Schopenhauer, A. 20
Schröder, G. 150
scientific evidence 98–101, 132
Seaboyer, A. 124
search engines 66, 214
second-wave feminism 41–2
secret deals 149–50
secularisation 114
securitisation 6, 133, 136
Security Studies 2
selective exposure 66, 81–2, 85
self-selection 66, 86–7
Sen, A. 54
sensor networks 47
severe acute respiratory syndrome 94–5
sexism 32, 43. *See also* gender bias
sexuality 44, 114, 139. *See also* homophobia
Shao, C. 157
sharp power 11, 120–1, 129
Sherman, M. 10–11
Shipman, T. 58
Shoigu, S. 109
Signal 6
silo-ification of information 66, 68–9
Skripal, S. 134
Skripal, Y. 134
smartphones 2, 95
Snegovaya, M. 123
Snopes 9
social bots. *See* automated accounts
social justice 7, 30, 41–2
social media 2–4, 7, 9, 48, 68, 77–8, 81, 83–5, 87, 208–9; and Covid-19 93, 95–100; fake accounts *see* automated accounts; and German legislation 192–4; and the radical right 175, 180–1; in Russia 122–6, 128, 133; and Russian meddling 146–7; tracking 47. *See also individual companies*
soft fakes 5
soft power 120–1
Solzgenitsyn, A. 111
sovereignty 6, 114, 145

Soviet Union; government 110–11; history 107–12, 114, 120–3, 136; propaganda 107–8, 114, 122–3, 133, 139
spear-phishing 127–8
spiral of silence theory 34
Sputnik News 126, 128, 134
standard of living 6
Stanley, J. 58, 61
stereotypes 35–7, 61
stigmatisation 47
Stojanoski, M. 12–13
Stokes, D.E. 64
Stone, O. 109
Strache, H.-C. 149
strategic narratives 133, 135
structural injustice 35–6
Sun Tzu 157
Surkov, V. 113, 145
surveillance 9, 47, 211
Susánszky, P. 12

Telegram 6
Tencent 97
terrorism 48, 59, 68, 193–4
think tanks 121, 150, 182
Thomas, R.J. 204
Thomas, T. 123
TikTok 95
Tong, J. 204
Törnberg, P. 83–4
totalitarianism 23–4, 26
traditional media 7–8, 11, 32, 65, 67, 80, 84, 115, 143–5, 148–50, 188–9, 204
transparency 147, 150, 190, 193
trolls 127–8
Trump, D. 3, 6, 8, 24, 85, 87, 93, 95, 133, 144, 149, 204. *See also* US presidential election (2016)
trustworthiness 9, 36, 135
truth decay 67–8
Tucker, J. 84–5
Tufekci, Z. 146
Tumblr 95
Twitter 9, 53, 83, 97, 99–100, 128, 134, 193, 215; fake accounts on 157–71, *see also* automated accounts; retweeting 83–4, 158–9, 163, 165, 167–9

undermining propaganda 58
universalism 42
US presidential election (2016) 8, 66, 70, 84–8, 157, 192; alleged Russian interference in 143–51
user-generated content 95

vaccine hesitancy 98. *See also* Anti-Vax
  movement
van Lidth de Jeude, J. 163
verification. *See* fact-checking
violence 31–2, 176
viral stories 3, 9, 78, 96, 157
Viralgranskaren 205, 209
Virdee, S. 59–60
Vokeuv, N.E. 135
Volpe, R. 86
Vos, T.P. 204
Vosoughi, S. 83
voting behaviour 77–88
vulnerabilities of Western democracies
  143–51

Waldron, J. 32, 60
Waltzman, R. 119
Wang Y. 6
weapons of mass destruction 5

Webb Williams, N. 178–9
Weber, M. 28
WeChat 95
WhatsApp 6
Whiteley, P. 79
word of mouth 3, 88
World Economic Forum 47
World Health Organization 7, 92, 96–7
World Press Freedom Index 134

xenophobia 32, 94, 133, 179

Yablokov, I. 145
YouTube 9, 95, 97, 112, 126, 193

Zafesova, A. 11
Zaller, J. 65
Zanda-Filippin project 218
Zelizer, B. 204
Zoom 202